IAA Reports, No. 32

TEL MOR

THE MOSHE DOTHAN EXCAVATIONS, 1959–1960

TRISTAN J. BARAKO

With contributions by
Donald T. Ariel, Baruch Brandl, Jennie R. Ebeling, Nicolle Hirschfeld, Robert Maddin,
Edward F. Maher, Mario A.S. Martin, James D. Muhly, David S. Reese, Steven A. Rosen,
Tamara Stech and Jacob Vardi

ISRAEL ANTIQUITIES AUTHORITY
JERUSALEM 2007

IAA Reports
Publications of the Israel Antiquities Authority

Editor-in-Chief: Zvi Gal

Series Editor: Ann Roshwalb Hurowitz

Volume Editor: Ben Gordon

Front Cover: Composite aerial view of tell and Egyptian vessels (top right, Fig. 4.9:10; bottom left, Fig. 4.11:8)
(IAA Archives).
Back Cover: Cypriot Bichrome krater and goblet (photographer: T.J. Barako).

Typesetting and Layout: Ann Abuhav, Margalit Hayosh
Cover Design and Production: Ann Abuhav
Illustrations: Natalia Zak
Printing: Keterpress Enterprises, Jerusalem

CONTENTS

ABBREVIATIONS

ADAJ	*Annual of the Department of Antiquities of Jordan*
ÄDS	Ägyptische Denkmäler in der Schweiz
AASOR	Annual of the American Schools of Oriental Research
'Atiqot (ES)	*English Series*
'Atiqot (HS)	*Hebrew Series*
AJA	*American Journal of Archaeology*
BA	*Biblical Archaeologist*
BaghF	Deutches Archäologisches Institut, Abteilung Baghdad, Baghdader Forschungen
BAH	Haut-commissariat de la république française en Syrie et au Liban. Service des antiquités, bibliothèque archéologique et historique
BAR	*Biblical Archaeology Review*
Bar Int. S.	British Archaeological Reports (International Series)
BASOR	*Bulletin of the American Schools of Oriental Research*
BIES	*Bulletin of the Israel Exploration Society* (Hebrew)
BSA	*Annual of the British School at Athens*
BSAE	Bulletin of Publications of the Egyptian Research Account and British School of Archaeology in Egypt
CAARI	Cyprus American Archaeological Research Institute
CNI	*Christian News from Israel*
EA	*Tell el-Amarna Tablets.* W.L. Moran transl. Baltimore 1992
HA	*Hadashot Arkheologiyot* (Archaeological News)
IAA Reports	Israel Antiquities Authority Reports
IEJ	*Israel Exploration Journal*
JAOS	*Journal of the American Oriental Soceity*
JEA	*Journal of Egyptian Archaeology*
JNES	*Journal of Near Eastern Studies*
JPOS	*Journal of the Palestine Oriental Society*
KRI	K.A. Kitchen. Ramesside Inscriptions I–VI. Oxford 1975–
KTU	*Die Keilalphabetischen Texte aus Ugarit* I (AOAT 24). M. Dietrich, O. Loretz and J. Sanmartín eds. Kevelear and Neukirchen-Vluyn 1976
LÄ	W. Helck and E. Otto eds. *Lexikon der Ägyptologie.* Wiesbaden 1975–
MSIATAU	Monograph Series of the Institute of Archaeology, Tel Aviv University
NEAEHL	E. Stern and A. Lewinson-Gilboa. *New Encyclopedia of Archaeological Excavations in the Holy Land.* Jerusalem 1993
OBO	Orbis Biblicus et Orientalis

OBOSA	Orbis Biblicus et Orientalis, Series Archaeologica
OIP	Oriental Institute Publications
OJA	*Oxford Journal of Archaeology*
OLA	Orientalia Lovaniensia Analecta
PEFQSt	*Palestine Exploration Fund Quarterly Statement*
PEQ	*Palestine Exploration Quarterly*
PMJB	*Palestine Museum Jerusalem, Bulletin*
QD	Quaestiones Disputatae, Editiones Herder
QDAP	*Quarterly of the Department of Antiquities of Palestine*
RB	*Revue Biblique*
RDAC	*Report of the Department of Antiquities, Cyprus*
RS	*Ras Shamra*
SAOC	Studies in Ancient Oriental Civilization
SBA	Saarbrücker Beiträge zur Altertumskunde
SIMA	Studies in Mediterranean Archaeology
UT	C.H. Gordon. *Ugaritic Textbook* (Analecta Orientalia 38). Rome 1965

The excavation team. Standing (from left to right): Shlomo Moskowitz, unknown, Moshe Dothan, Gideon Foerster,
Nehama Foerster, Menashe Busiri, Jan Voskuil, Mia Hershkowitz, Tamar Licht, unknown, Dodo Shenhav.
Seated (from left to right): Aharon Keminski, Nissim Mevorach, Ya'akov Meshorer.

ACKNOWLEDGEMENTS

Excavations at Tel Mor commenced in the fall of 1959
and continued for three months that year and for three
additional months in the spring of 1960 (License Nos.
A-10/1959, A-27/1960-1). They were carried out on
behalf of the Israel Department of Antiquities and
Museums (IDAM; now the Israel Antiquities Authority
[IAA]) and with financial support from the Ashdod
Development Company. The chief archaeologist and
director of the excavations was Professor Moshe
Dothan. He was assisted by Immanuel Dunayevsky
and Shlomo Moskowitz. The following individuals
also participated in the excavations: Pirhiya Beck,
Mia Hershkovitz, Gideon Foerster and Ephraim Stern
(field supervisors); Y. Katzenstein, Aharon Kempinski,
Ya'akov Meshorer and Jan Voskuil; R. Sopher and
Nehama Forester (registrars); Tamar Licht; Nissim
Mevorach (draftsperson); A. Broner (photographer);
Menashe Busiri (driver); and local Arab workmen.

This volume, the final report on the Tel Mor
excavations, was made possible first and foremost
through generous funding from the Shelby White–
Leon Levy Program for Archaeological Publications.
I am grateful especially to Philip King, Lawrence
Stager and Kimberley Connors for their support and
patience. Trude Dothan gave me permission to publish
the excavations directed by her late husband and
provided me with the preliminary pottery plates and
text. Her expertise and encouragement were of no less
importance in seeing the project through to completion.
The Israel Antiquities Authority (IAA) helped locate
all the artifacts and documentation from Tel Mor and
granted me full access to them. In these respects, I
am indebted to Michal Dayagi-Mendels and Osnat
Misch-Brandl (Israel Museum), Yael Barschak (IAA,
photographic archives), and especially Baruch Brandl

(IAA) and Galit Litani (Israel National Antiquities
Collection). I am grateful to Ehud Netzer, who located
and made available to me all of Dunayevsky's plans
from Tel Mor, which are currently contained in the
archives of the Institute of Archaeology of the Hebrew
University of Jerusalem. The W.F. Albright Institute for
Archaeological Research hospitably provided lodging
and a work space during the time I was in Jerusalem.
Penina Arad and, particularly, Julia Rudmann produced
most of the object drawings.

I benefited enormously from the input of various
specialists. The contributions of the authors of various
studies included in the book are self-evident. Mario
Martin's knowledge of all things Egyptianized was
indispensable. The following excavators kindly made
available to me unpublished pottery plates from
Egypto-Canaanite and neighboring sites: Trude Dothan
and Bonnie Gould (Deir el-Balaḥ); Amihai Mazar and
Nava Panitz-Cohen (Tel Baṭash-Timna); and Yuval
Gadot (Tel Afeq). Numerous other people gave of
their expertise on a more informal basis. Notable in
this regard are David Aston, David Ben-Shlomo, Celia
Bergoffen, Seymour Gitin, John Huehnergard, Robert
Mullins, Beno Rothenberg, Benjamin Saidel, Sariel
Shalev and Naama Yahalom-Mack. I wish to thank also
the external reader, Ann Killebrew, and editors Ann
Hurowitz and Ben Gordon, whose combined efforts
greatly improved the volume's content, consistency and
style. Finally, my wife Doreen went above and beyond
the spousal call of duty. In addition to providing moral
support, she designed the database and endured long
days in dusty warehouses.

Tristan J. Barako

CHAPTER 1

INTRODUCTION

The Moshe Dothan excavations (1959–1960) at Tel Mor uncovered a series of large buildings that dominated the summit of this small tell throughout the Late Bronze Age. Two of these buildings (Strata VIII–VII and VI–V) have the appearance of forts and were accompanied by significant quantities of Egyptianized pottery. It is argued here that they functioned as Egyptian garrisons in Canaan. This excavation report presents the stratigraphy and building remains of the site, as well as the Late Bronze and Iron Age pottery and other smaller studies on various categories of finds. The Hellenistic stratigraphy, but not the associated pottery, is also presented. Despite its small size and limited publication, Tel Mor has figured prominently for decades in the scholarship of Late Bronze and early Iron Age Canaan (e.g., Bietak 1993; Stager 1995). The publication of Tel Mor will help illuminate how Egyptian hegemony gradually gave way to newly emergent peoples, such as the Philistines, at a time when the entire Levant experienced major upheavals.

SITE ENVIRONMENT

Tel Mor is a small mound located in the southern coastal plain of modern-day Israel (map ref. OIG 117070/13680; NIG 167070/63680), approximately 1 km from the present-day shoreline of the Mediterranean Sea and 200 m north of Naḥal Lakhish (Wadi/Nahr Sukreir; Figs. 1.1–1.4).[1] It is situated on a sandstone outcrop in the midst of a belt of sand dunes that once

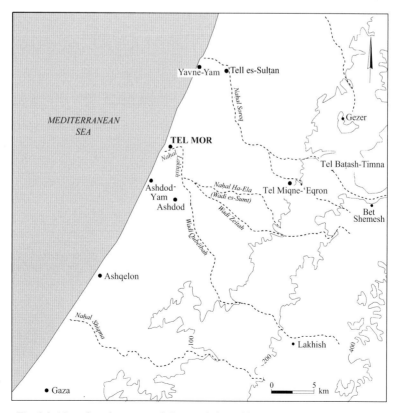

Fig. 1.1. Map of southern coastal Canaan (adapted from T. Dothan 2000: Fig. 7.1).

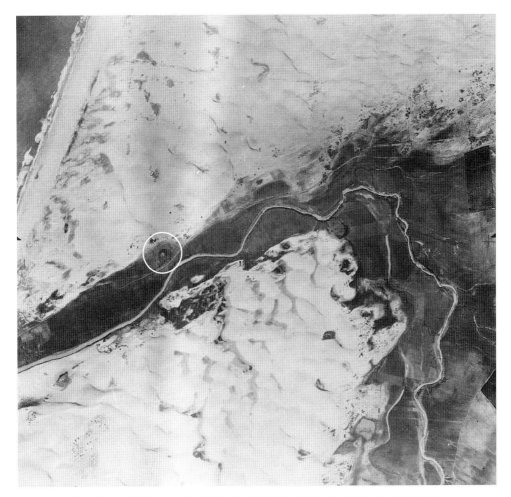

Fig. 1.2. Aerial photograph of Naḥal Lakhish (Wadi Sukreir). Tel Mor is highlighted.

Fig. 1.3. The tell (c. 1959).

Fig. 1.4. Aerial view of Tel Mor.

covered much of the southern Levantine coast. The tell rises 25 m above sea level and is 17 m from base to summit. The base of the mound covers an area of six dunams, whereas the summit, which has been reduced considerably by erosion, encompasses only one dunam (Plan 1.1). Because of Tel Mor's proximity both to Tel Ashdod (6 km southeast) and Naḥal Lakhish, a perennial stream that flows into the sea, it is likely that it served as a place of anchorage for the much larger, and harbor-less, site of Ashdod.

Runoff from winter rains flows from the Judean Hills into streams that seek the path of least resistance to the Mediterranean Sea (Orni and Efrat 1971:41). Approximately 7 km southeast of Tel Mor, the water from three such streams (Naḥal Ha-Ela [Wadi es-Sumt], Wadi Zeitah and Wadi Qubeibah) combine to form Naḥal Lakhish (Fig. 1.1; Baly 1974:141). Naḥal Lakhish then flows north to a breach in the sandstone ridge, at which point it carves a path westward toward the sea. These ridges are lithified dunes of calcareous sandstone (locally known as *kurkar*) that formed

during the Pleistocene era (Issar 1961) and stretch longitudinally across the coastal plain; Tel Mor is situated on one of them. Naḥal Lakhish created a small valley in the dunes approximately 2.5 km long and 450 m wide. As the mouth of the stream was choked by sand, especially during the late medieval and Ottoman periods (Bakler 1982:68), the water slowed, and eventually a swamp formed (Orni and Efrat 1971:41). The sand was a combination of alluvium from the wadi as well as the distant Nile River. Although swamps are rare south of the Yarqon River, the British survey of 1867 reports the existence of lagoons in the vicinity of where Naḥal Lakhish emptied into the sea (Warren and Conder 1998:442).

Of crucial importance for the interpretation of Tel Mor as an anchorage site is the navigability of this stream. Because there are no protected waters along the coast close to Ashdod, it has been assumed that the city relied upon the nearby Naḥal Lakhish (M. Dothan 1973:1–2). It is likely that the wadi was able to accommodate skiffs, certainly as far inland as Tel Mor, if not farther. To wit,

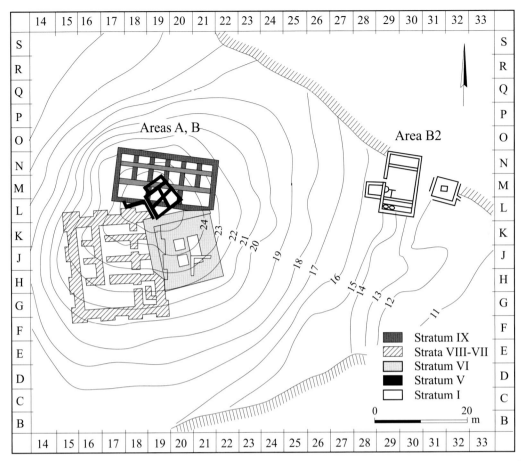

Plan 1.1. Topographic map of Tel Mor.

a local inhabitant reported to Dothan that members of the nearby Kibbutz Yavne navigated small boats along this stream from the kibbutz to the sea, a distance of approximately 10 km, as recently as the 1930s (Dothan and Dothan 1992:121).[2] When the First Australian Light Horse Brigade camped in the area in the winter of 1917, the wadi was reportedly *c.* 27 m wide and 3 m deep as far inland as Tel Mor (Gullett 1923:466). During the Late Bronze Age, prior to the intervening three millennia of silting, it is likely that the stream's bed was even deeper.[3]

Apparently, when Tel Mor was abandoned in Iron II (Stratum II), Ashdod-Yam (Minat Isdūd) became the point of maritime entry for the city-state of Ashdod (M. Dothan 1993:1074). Also situated along Naḥal Lakhish, but on the southern bank and closer to the sea, is Nebi Yunis (Miẓpe Yona). A 1960 probe at that site revealed Persian-period remains, including an Aramaic ostracon (Busiri 1964; Cross 1964; see also Stern 2001:407–408).

SITE IDENTIFICATION AND DISCOVERY

Both Egyptian *Mḥś/d/z* and Ugaritic *Mḥd* have been suggested as the ancient place name of Tel Mor (M. Dothan 1981:151, n. 3). In the earliest textual attestation, a topographical list of cities reportedly conquered by Tuthmosis III, *M<i>ḥś* (No. 61) is mentioned after Yurza (Tell Jemmeh) and before Jaffa (Simons 1937:117). According to EA 298:25, the younger brother of the ruler of Gezer "entered *Muḥḥazu* (= *alMu-u[ḥ]-ḫa-zi*) and pledged hi⟨m⟩self to the 'Apiru" (Moran 1992:340).[4] The site appears next as *M'wḥ3d3* (No. 69) between Sharuhen (Tell el-ʿAjjul) and Socoh (Khirbet Shuweiket er-Ras) in another topographical list at ʿAmara West, this one dating to the reign of Ramesses II (B. Mazar 1975; Kitchen 1996:75).

Perhaps the same town appears also in administrative texts from Ugarit in alphabetic form as *Mḥd* (UT 2014 = KTU 4.635) and in cuneiform as *alMa-ḫa-du* (RS 19:42:10; Stieglitz 1974), as opposed to the similar toponym *Maḫd/Miḫd/[al]Ma-a-ḫa-du*, which refers to the ancient port associated with Ugarit (Astour 1970; see also Huehnergard 1987:83; Del Olmo Lete and Sanmartín 2003:513–514). In this case, the association of the gentilic *mḫdy* with *aḍddy* ('Ashdodite') in KTU 4.635.16–17 strengthens the identification of *Mḫd* with Tel Mor.

Other suggested locations for Egyptian *Mḫś/ḍ/z* are not as convincing. To begin with, it is important to note that between Tell el-'Ajjul and Jaffa there are very few coastal sites which were inhabited throughout the Late Bronze Age *and* whose ancient name is not known. Furthermore, it may be possible to narrow this geographical range to the vicinity of Gezer (EA 298) and, possibly, Ashdod (KTU 4.635). Various scholars have proposed that *Mḫś/ḍ/z* should be equated with Yavne-Yam (Kutscher 1937:138; Stieglitz 1974) or the nearby inland site of Tell es-Sulṭan (Alt 1925:15–17; Aharoni 1979:45; Aḥituv 1984:144). Excavations at Yavne-Yam, however, do not support this identification. They revealed a square enclosure surrounded by a rampart that was constructed in Middle Bronze IIA (Layer 9), but fell out of use in Late Bronze I (Layer 1; Kaplan 1993). As for Tell es-Sulṭan, only Middle Bronze Age sherds were found at the site during a survey of the lower Rubin River (Naḥal Soreq; M. Dothan 1952:109–111). In point of contrast, Tel Mor was inhabited throughout the Late Bronze Age (Strata XI–V; see Chapter 2). Moreover, the site functioned primarily as an Egyptian outpost for much of this time (Strata VIII–V); thus the presence of Tel Mor in Egyptian topographical lists should be anticipated.

The semantic value of the root *mḫd/z*, as conveyed by the Ugaritic *ma-á'-ḫa-(du)*, the Hurrian *ma-ḫa-(zi)* (Sum. KAR, Akk. *ka-a-ru*; see RS 137:II:21 in Nougayrol et al. 1968:242, 243), and the Hebrew מחוז (Ps 107:30; Kutscher 1937; 1969–1970), is 'harbor' or, by extension, 'marketplace'. In light of this more general meaning, it is wise to exercise caution when attempting to identify the toponym *Mḫś/ḍ/z* with a specific coastal site. It is possible that more than one location went by this name or that the name shifted from one place to another. For example, Yavne-Yam was known as *māḫūz Yibnā* and Ashdod-Yam as *māḫūz Izdūd* in later times (Kutscher 1937:139). Until another harbor site that was clearly inhabited throughout the Late Bronze Age is excavated in southern Canaan, Tel Mor is the strongest candidate for ancient *Mḫś/ḍ/z*.

Tell el-Kheidar (Tell el-Akhdar, Tell Ukheidir) and Tell Murra (Tell el-Murreh) are the modern Arabic names for Tel Mor. Both names appear in the *Survey of Western Palestine* conducted by the British in the 1870s (Conder and Kitchener 1998: Sheet XVI); however, no reference is made to the site in the survey report of the area north of the village of Esdud (Ashdod), which included Wadi Sukreir (Warren and Conder 1998:442). Apparently, Tell el-Akhdar means 'the green mound', and Tell el-Murreh, according to E.H. Palmer, may refer to "the mound of the brackish water, near the mouth of the river" or to the local Beni Murreh Arabs (1998:274–275). That the water near Tel Mor (note the British survey report above) should contain salt is to be expected in light of its proximity to the sea.

During World War I, retreating Turkish forces established a defensive line along the northern bank of Wadi Sukreir, including the critical high ground of Tel Mor (Preston 1921:69–70; Gullett 1923:466–467). The Second Australian Light Horse Regiment forded the wadi at Nebi Yunis, where the stream was reported to be *c.* 45 m wide and 10 m deep, surprised the Turks in a nighttime attack and drove them from the hill. Once a beachhead was secured, British ships began landing much needed supplies at the mouth of the wadi. Equally important was the wadi's fresh water, available in abundance for the first time since the men and their mounts had left Egypt. No traces of this military activity, including the Turkish emplacement on Tel Mor, are mentioned by the excavators.

Mandate-period files document a number of visits to Tel Mor and record certain features about the site's usage. Jacob Ory, who visited in 1926, 1929 and 1933, reported that the site was used partially as a children's burial ground (see Chapter 2, Later Periods; Figs. 2.41–2.45), was partially cultivated, and that a railroad track stretched past the base of the mound (File 143; Map 2: Reprint of Mandate-period map or earlier). He mentions also that the land was owned by an Arab named 'Arab Abu Suweirih, and that the area was part of the subdistrict of Gaza. In 1934 R.W. Hamilton also visited Tel Mor, but recorded no specific information about the site.[5]

In 1954 Ory, now a regional inspector for IDAM, discovered four vessels at the site, among which were a Late Bronze Age dipper and a Base Ring I juglet (IAA 1955-81 and 1955-15, respectively; for the latter, see Fig. 5.3:15). It is likely that these vessels belonged to a Late Bronze Age tomb at the base of the tell, similar to L152 (see Chapter 2, Stratum IX; Figs. 2.9–2.12). Indeed, additional IDAM files from the 1950s report destroyed burials at the site, as well as a Late Roman winepress and a scarab.[6] In 1957 representatives from the Israel Nature Preserve noted, on the summit of the tell, the presence of a well that they tentatively assigned to the Roman period. Dothan cleared the top *c.* 14 m of this well (L55) and dated it to the Hellenistic period, whereas the Geological Survey of Israel fully excavated its contents in order to determine ancient ground water levels along the central coast of Israel, and (*pace* the Israel Nature Preserve) dated its construction tentatively to the Roman period (Nir and Eldar 1986:14–16; see also Chapter 2).

The construction of a modern harbor north of the current city of Ashdod in the late 1950s precipitated the excavation of Tel Mor. In order to pave the access road that would connect the coastal highway with the proposed port facilities, *kurkar* sandstone was quarried from the eastern slope of the tell (Fig. 1.5; see also M. Dothan 1960a: Fig. 1.3B, Pl. I:1). David Yair, a local kibbutznik and volunteer inspector for IDAM, recognized the archaeological significance of the site and reported the ongoing destruction. Subsequently, in the fall of 1959, Moshe Dothan began excavations at Tel Mor on behalf of IDAM with financial support from the Ashdod Development Company. For three months that year and three the following spring,[7] Dothan, assisted by Immanuel Dunayevsky and Shlomo Moskowitz,[8] excavated most of the tell's summit and cut a trench down the eastern slope (Plan 1.1).[9]

EXCAVATION AND RECORDING METHODOLOGIES

An unpublished manuscript on the excavations at Tel Mor, presumably composed by Dothan, reads:

> The tell was laid according to a grid of 5 sq m. The grids were numbered in sequence, beginning in the south with the letter 'A' to 'V' in the north; in the west with the number '10' to '37' in the east. The excavation was started at the highest point of the mound and a trench 5 m wide was laid out from the top to the eastern slope. The trench was subsequently enlarged to a square of at least 20 sq m on the tell proper.

After the first season of excavation in 1959, an area of approximately 200 sq m on the summit (Areas A and B) and 100 sq m on the eastern slope (Area B2) had been opened up for excavation (M. Dothan 1960c: 121–122, Fig. 2). By the end of the second and last season in 1960, the entire summit was excavated (900 sq m or about one dunam), in some places 7 m deep down to bedrock (M. Dothan 1973:3). The step trench near the base of the mound was also expanded in order to expose a purple dye (murex) installation of the Hellenistic period (Stratum I). This excavation methodology, whereby large areas of a site are exposed, is typical of the 'architectural' approach favored by most early Israeli archaeologists (A. Mazar 1988:120–122).

In the intervening 40 years, primarily during the 1960s and 1970s, significant progress was made toward the publication of the excavations at Tel Mor prior to

Fig. 1.5. View of Tel Mor showing the results of modern quarrying, looking southwest.

my taking up the project. It is clear that all the artifacts had been roughly sorted, much had been marked, and some registered.[10] Hundreds of pottery registration cards and a complete basket registry accompany the pottery, which was registered according to area and basket number. For example, A268/2 indicates that the sherd in question came from Area A, Basket 268, and was the second sherd from that basket registered. Hundreds of sherds and whole vessels were drawn and, to a lesser extent, photographed.[11] Most importantly, the excavators arranged 40 preliminary pottery plates for Strata XII–II (Bronze and Iron Ages); these plates include descriptions and brief discussions of parallels.[12] The pottery, as well as other small finds such as bone, shell, flint, groundstone and metal, is currently housed at the IAA storage facility in Bet Shemesh.

It is possible to assign most of the pottery and small finds to a 5 × 5 m square and, under the best circumstances, to a specific locus. The excavators kept a list of 172 loci (see Appendix 2); however, no locus cards have been found. Certain loci spanned two and even three strata. This counterintuitive practice results primarily from the assignment of a single locus to an area or room that was in use through multiple phases. For example, two floors separated by almost a meter of debris were excavated in Room (Locus) 63, yet the entire sequence, which corresponds to Strata VIII and VII, was assigned to a single locus (see Plan 2.4). It seems that in this case the excavators opened L63 when the tops of walls (W66, W73, W88, W143) appeared, and retained this locus until the earliest floor of the room was reached. Therefore, all the following depositional events, in reverse chronological order, belong to L63: the fill, destruction and occupational debris above the Stratum VII floor; the Stratum VII floor and subfloor; the destruction and occupational debris above the Stratum VIII floor; and the Stratum VIII floor and subfloor. Fortunately, top and bottom levels were recorded for many pottery baskets, which can serve as a stratigraphic check, especially when dealing with pottery from a multi-strata locus.

The primary criterion for the inclusion of pottery in this report is certainty of context. In descending order, the hierarchy of stratigraphic context is as follows: (1) subfloor fills, floors and debris in rooms within a well-defined building; (2) the same contexts but within a poorly defined building; (3) pits; (4) areas assigned to a locus outside buildings; and (5) areas assigned only to a square. If, however, a poorly stratified context

produced a whole vessel or an unusual form, then this pottery was included in the plates and its questionable find-spot noted.

The excavators of Tel Mor collected and registered approximately 11,000 artifacts, of which more than 90% are sherds or whole vessels (Table 1.1).[13] As the most plentiful and best processed data from the site, the corpus of Middle Bronze, Late Bronze and Iron Age pottery forms the core of this report. Unfortunately, because the criteria used either to retain or discard sherds are not known, it is difficult to determine the degree to which this corpus is representative of the pottery made (or imported) and used at the site. Based on a thorough inspection of the processed Tel Mor pottery, however, it appears that the excavators followed the general practice of saving only diagnostic sherds such as rims, handles, bases and decorated or slipped body sherds.

In light of the above uncertainties, statistical analyses of the ceramic corpus are suspect. Notwithstanding, an attempt was made to gauge the relative abundance of Egyptianized pottery through time (see Chapter 4). To this end, every sherd of Egyptianized and imported Egyptian pottery was counted and, when possible, assigned to a stratum. It was encouraging to discover that the percentages of Egyptianized pottery over time at Tel Mor (see Table 4.12) corresponded roughly to those reported from the recent excavations at the Egyptian garrison site of Bet She'an (see Chapter 4, Comparative Analysis, pp. 151–152).

As noted above, the excavators arranged preliminary pottery plates for all twelve strata. These plates were rearranged here because numerous vessel types, both drawn and undrawn, were not represented in the old system. Moreover, the decision to present separately the Egyptianized pottery further necessitated that the old plate arrangement be abandoned.

To be sure, the stratigraphic context of pottery from a locus is more secure than pottery derived from a square. In every stratum, the excavators did not always identify, describe or assign certain layers of soil to discrete loci. It seems that such layers were attributed to strata by reference to elevation and ceramic typology, and assigned only to the 5 × 5 m square in which they were excavated. For obvious reasons, pottery derived from secure loci was given precedence when establishing a ceramic typology and relative chronology at Tel Mor. Indeed, pottery derived only from squares ranks fifth and last in the stratigraphic hierarchy outlined

Table 1.1. Distribution of Sherds by Stratum

Stratum or Strata*	N of Pottery Baskets	N of Registered Sherds	% of Registered Sherds
I	175	654	8.7
II	8	117	1.6
III	69	509	6.8
IV–III	4	50	0.7
IV	13	138	1.8
V–IV	7	58	0.8
V	57	688	9.2
VI	111	945	12.6
VI–V	25	117	1.6
VII–VI	7	113	1.5
VII	82	1046	14.0
VIII	28	245	3.3
VIII–VII	26	232	3.1
IX–VII	7	41	0.5
IX	107	1161	15.5
X	5	52	0.7
XI–IX	8	98	1.3
XI–X	3	31	0.4
XI	28	427	5.7
XII–X	1	22	0.3
XII–IX	14	92	1.2
XII–XI	5	109	1.5
XII	46	535	7.2
Total	836	7480	100.0

* The excavators assigned numerous loci (and, therefore, pottery baskets) to more than one strata, which explains the large number of baskets belonging to more than one stratum (e.g., VI–V).

above. Because some of the figures contain pottery from various strata, the stratum number appears in parentheses after the locus or square number. Due to the apparent importance given to elevation in the attribution of pottery to strata, the absolute levels of the relevant pottery baskets, when available, are also provided.

The stratigraphy, unfortunately, is not as well documented as the pottery. The best sources of data are the stratum plans drawn by Dunayevsky, the locus list, some daily top plans from field notebooks and a number of section drawings (e.g., M. Dothan 1960c:123, Fig. 3). The excavators also composed a draft summary of Strata XII–VI, which forms the core of the stratigraphic description below. In addition, numerous excavation photographs were taken and labeled.[14] In order to emphasize the overall cultural continuity of settlement at Tel Mor, the stratigraphy and pottery are presented diachronically, and therefore separately, in the succeeding chapters.

Notes

[1] Unless indicated otherwise, photographs in this chapter are from the archives of the Israel Antiquities Authority. Figure 1.2 was taken by the British Royal Air Force in 1944 and appears courtesy of the Historical Aerial Photograph Collection of Israel, Department of Geography, the Hebrew University of Jerusalem.

[2] Elsewhere the distance is reported as only 3 km (Dothan and Freedman 1967:5, n. 3). According to Freedman, the wadi, which once flowed close to Tel Ashdod, was drained shortly before excavations at Tel Mor began (1963:135). In any event, it seems clear that the wadi was navigable as far as Tel Mor and probably farther inland.

[3] The author visited the site in the spring of 1998 and on August 25, 2000, September 20, 2000 and September 24, 2001, and observed that, even at the height or end of the summer, the stream was flowing. It was approximately 10 m wide at least as far inland as the tell, and broadened as it approached the sea.

[4] Note also that Na'aman reads *[m]a-[ah]-ḫ[a-zi]* in EA 272:3 and identifies this site with *Muḫḫazu* of the present letter (1975:68).

[5] I am indebted to Benjamin Saidel, who compiled the British Mandate-period information pertaining to Tel Mor.

[6] In 1967 Menashe Busiri similarly observed that Late Bronze Age cist burials on the eastern slope of the tell had become exposed after a heavy rain. The following burial goods that he collected had been washed out: a scarab bearing the name of Tuthmosis III (IAA No. 1967-167); a cylinder seal; an Egyptian-style amber bead in the shape of some kind of fruit (IAA No. 1967-168); a faience bead (IAA No. 1967-169); a bead bracelet (IAA No. 1967-170); broken Base Ring Ware juglets; a bowl; and various Cypriot sherds (Busiri 1967:26).

[7] It is reported that excavations in 1959 lasted from September 1 to October 31 (M. Dothan 1960c:121, n. 2); however, the pottery basket registry shows that the last basket of pottery was filled, or at least registered, on November 26 of that year.

[8] Dunayevsky reportedly took great interest in the stratigraphy of Tel Mor (M. Dothan 1973:2–3, n. 4), a fact demonstrated by the excellent plans he made of the site that appear in this report. For a list of these plans, see Netzer 1973:19, Table 8.

[9] Preliminary reports of these excavations appear in M. Dothan 1959; 1960a–e; 1965; 1972; 1973; 1977; 1981; 1993; and Dothan and Dothan 1992:120–126. The staff that participated in the excavations, mentioned in the Acknowledgements, is listed in M. Dothan 1960c:121, n. 2.

[10] Baruch Brandl, former curator of the State Collection, generously gave of his time and expertise in making the Tel Mor material available to me. I am indebted also to Galit Litani, assistant curator of the Bronze and Iron Age collections at Bet Shemesh.

[11] It was necessary to (re-)draw and (re-)photograph many artifacts (mostly pottery) for a variety of reasons. Furthermore, it was not possible to locate many artifacts that had once been drawn and/or photographed; therefore, the quality and conventions of the figures vary. I wish to thank Penina Arad, and especially Julia Rudmann, for drawing much of the pottery that appears in this volume.

[12] I was unable to find the Hellenistic pottery plates; however, Howard C. Kee's text on that pottery, which I did locate, clearly indicates that these plates also were arranged. The Hellenistic architecture, but not the pottery, is published in this volume.

[13] The total of 7480 registered sherds in this table does not reflect the numerous registered sherds from contexts that could not be assigned to a specific stratum.

[14] I am grateful to Yael Barschak, photograph archivist at the Har Ḥozvim branch of the IAA, who generously compiled lists of all photographic negatives pertaining to Tel Mor.

Chapter 2

Stratigraphy and Building Remains

Twelve strata dating from the Middle Bronze Age to the Hellenistic period were excavated at Tel Mor (Table 2.1); Roman-period and later finds were found as well. The principal remains date to the Late Bronze Age and early Iron Age (Stratum IX–V), during which time a single building dominated the tell. Scant architectural remains from earlier (XII–X) and later (IV–I) periods were found on the summit. Well-preserved installations for the processing of purple dye dating to the Hellenistic period (Stratum I) were uncovered at the base of the eastern slope. After a thorough analysis of the stratified pottery, it was determined that the dates assigned by Moshe Dothan to most of the strata are essentially accurate (e.g., M. Dothan 1993).

Table 2.1. Stratigraphic Table

Stratum	Period	Summary of Remains and Findings
XII	MB IIC	Courtyard 118
XI	LB IA	*Bāmāh*
X	LB IA	Ephemeral
IX	LB IIA	Building A
VIII	LB IIB	Building B
VII	LB IIB	Building B
VI	LB IIB/Iron IA transitional	Building F
V	Iron IA	Buildings F and H
IV	Iron IB	Building I
III	Iron IB	Pits
II	Iron IIA?	
I	Hellenistic period	Purple-dye installations

STRATUM XII (Plan 2.1)

The initial settlement at Tel Mor was excavated in only a small 20 sq m area located in Sqs M22 and N22 of Area B, which corresponds to the northeastern quadrant of the summit. There the excavators found a thick (c. 2.5 m) courtyard accumulation (L118; Figs. 2.1, 2.2), which they divided into four strata (XII–IX; M.

Dothan 1973:3–5). The earliest stratum (XII) overlaid a 0.4 m thick layer of coarse brown clay, which, in turn, rested on bedrock at an elevation of c. 17.9 m (Plan 2.2). A small amount of pottery was first found at the level of c. 18.3 m; whereas, at c. 18.6 m, the quantity of pottery is described as 'dense'.

Pit 166, which is located at the northern end of L118, accompanied this initial phase of the courtyard (XIIA). It is oval in shape, has dimensions of 1.6 × 2.3 m, and its elevations are 19.0/17.9 m. This pit, which is the best-stratified locus in Stratum XII, appears to have contained a small assemblage of MB IIC pottery (see, e.g., Fig. 3.1:17), including early Cypriot imports (see Figs. 5.1:1, 3; 5.3:3, 5).[1] The presence of cultic vessels, especially an unusual Bichrome Ware goblet (see Fig. 5.7:9) in Pit 166, suggests that it functioned as a *bothros*.

At c. 19.1 m there was a new courtyard accumulation layer (XIIB), approximately 0.3 m thick. According to Dothan, Pit 166 "was raised, its sides covered with clay, and three small clay installations were constructed" at the level of this new layer (M. Dothan 1973:4). These installations, of which two were elliptical and one round, contained gray (probably organic) residue, and in one was a scarab (see Chapter 7, No. 7). A limited probe (L167) along the western edge of this courtyard revealed a mass of mudbricks, 1.2 m in width and 1.0 m high, probably belonging to a poorly preserved mudbrick wall. Because of the small size of the probe it was not possible to determine the wall's dimensions; however, the excavators did conclude that it was oriented north–south (Plans 2.1, 2.2). Based on the discovery of cultic finds in this, as well as the succeeding stratum (XI), the excavators hypothesized that this open area (L118) functioned as a courtyard outside a sanctuary, which was presumably located on the other side of the wall. At the very least, there must have been some kind of architecture somewhere on the rest of the summit to accompany the rich assemblage of pottery excavated in Courtyard 118.

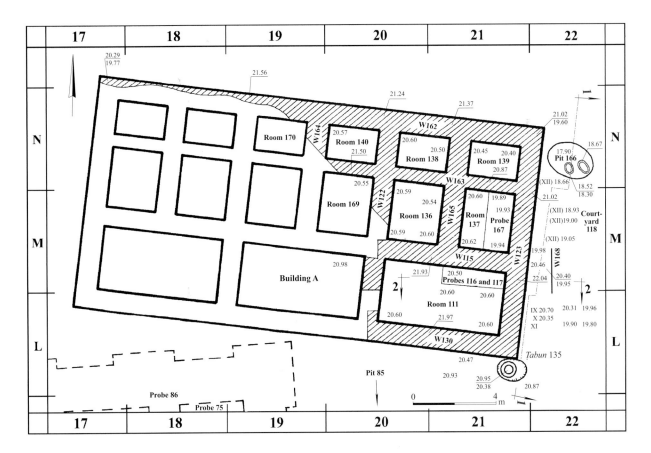

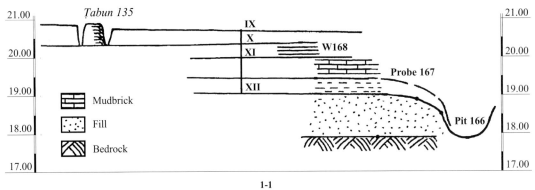

1-1

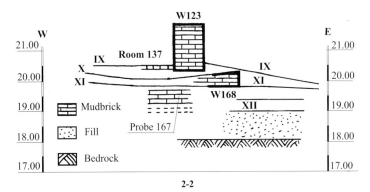

2-2

Plan 2.1. Strata XII–IX. Plan and sections.

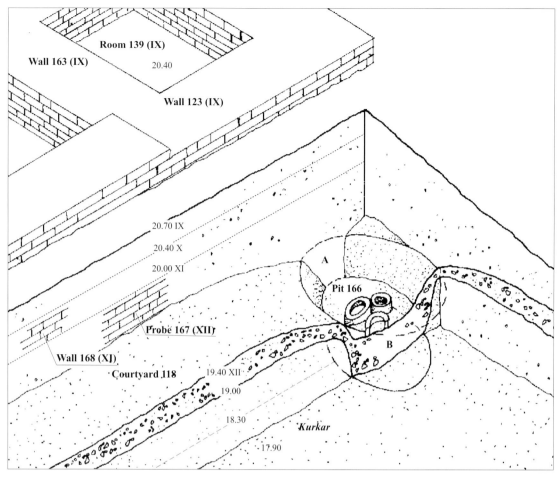

Plan 2.2. Isometric plan of Strata XII–IX, looking northwest (adapted from M. Dothan 1973: Fig. 2).

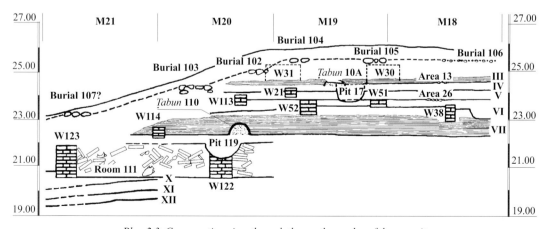

Plan 2.3. Cross section view through the northern edge of the summit.

Fig. 2.1. Courtyard 118, looking north.

Fig. 2.2. Courtyard 118 and W123(?), looking southwest.

STRATUM XI (Plan 2.1)

Before proceeding to a description of Stratum XI, it is important to acknowledge, as did the excavators, that it is difficult to differentiate the early strata (XII–X) at Tel Mor. Because there is no accompanying coherent architecture, stratigraphic separation was based primarily on an analysis of the pottery and on elevation. Pottery baskets from Stratum XI generally fall within the elevation range of *c.* 20.4 to 19.1 m. Perhaps it is better, then, to regard these strata instead as phases; however, in order to maintain consistency with the preliminary reports, the original stratification is retained here.

For topographical reasons, little of Strata XI and X remains. The area of L118 was prone to erosion due to its location on the northeastern edge of the tell. Indeed, erosion carried away even more of the upper strata and is responsible for the mound's conical shape (M. Dothan 1960c:121). To compensate for the slope, the walls of Building A in the succeeding Stratum IX were founded at a lower elevation, in the process of which the stratigraphy of Strata XI and X might have been further destroyed.

The main feature of the Stratum XI courtyard (still assigned to L118) was a scatter of cultic paraphernalia (Fig. 2.3), which collectively gave rise to the designation of this area as a 'high place' or *bāmāh* (M. Dothan 1959:271; 1960a:17; 1960c:123; 1960d:397). It should be noted, again, that there is no architecture associated with this *bāmāh*.[2] Perhaps most unusual among the

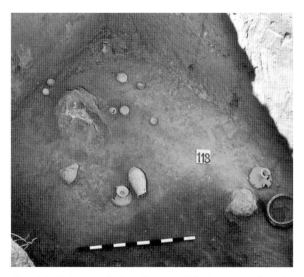

Fig. 2.3. Cultic vessels from the area of the Stratum XI bāmāh.

finds are the antlers of a fallow deer belonging to the species *Dama mesopotamica* (see Fig. 11.2). Surrounding these antlers were the following intact vessels, all of which rested at approximately 20 m asl: several miniature bowls (see Fig. 3.5:3–8; also, M. Dothan 1960a: Pl. I:3); chalices (see Fig. 3.12:6, 9; also, M. Dothan 1960a: Pl. I:2; 1960c: Fig. 4.2); a seven-spouted oil lamp (see Fig. 3.30:1; also, M. Dothan 1960a: Pl. I:2, 3); and an Egyptian slender ovoid jar (see Fig. 4.10:1; also, M. Dothan 1960c: Pl. 9:1). Also in this stratum, a better preserved, north–south mudbrick wall (W168) was built over and slightly to the east of the mass of mudbricks found in Probe 167. Finally, the excavation of Probe 116 revealed part of a floor on the western side of W168.

STRATUM X (Plan 2.1)

Insofar as there is no associated architecture, Stratum X is defined strictly by reference to elevation and ceramic typology. In general, Stratum X surfaces were identified at a level between 0.3 and 0.5 m above those of Stratum XI. The division of these two strata was reportedly clearest in the Stratum X Probe 117, located above Probe 116 of Stratum XI (see Fig. 2.4). As noted by the excavators, it is likely that Stratum X is simply a continuation of Stratum XI. It is to be recalled that these early strata (XII–X) were reached only in the northeastern quadrant of the tell, primarily in Sqs M22 and N22. Future excavations in the remainder of the summit would likely reveal architectural remains from MB IIC and LB I, as suggested by the poorly preserved mudbrick wall, W168.

STRATUM IX (Plan 2.1)

Stratum IX is the earliest stratum at Tel Mor that was excavated across a wide area (200 sq m) and contained coherent architecture, Building A. This building was a large, rectangular structure, approximately 11 × 22 m in dimension, located on the northern side of the tell's summit. Only the eastern half of the building (Rooms 111, 136–140, 169, 170) and the full length of the northern wall (W162) remained (Figs. 2.4, 2.5); however, based on the consistency of room sizes, it was possible to reconstruct the entire building (see below). The exterior and most of the interior walls were at least a meter thick, and some walls, including their foundation courses, were preserved to a height of *c.* 1.5 m.[3] The thickness of these walls suggests the previous existence of upper stories. The absence of gaps in any of the walls indicates that ladders lowered from openings in the ceiling provided access to the lowest floor, perhaps a basement.

It seems that this story of Building A was comprised of three blocks of rooms. Each block consisted of a large, 3.0 × 6.0 m, rectangular room (e.g., Room 111), a pair of small, 2.4 × 2.8 m, rooms (e.g., Rooms 136 and

Fig. 2.4. Southeastern corner of Building A, including Probes 116 and 117, looking north.

Fig. 2.5. Eastern half of Building A, looking north.

137), and a pair of even smaller, 1.6 × 2.4 m, rooms (e.g., Rooms 138 and 139). The fact that the eastern block of rooms, which was almost completely preserved, was one third the length of the entire building supports the excavators' reconstruction of the central and western blocks. One complete room (Room 140) and part of two others (Rooms 169 and 170) of the central block were excavated also.

The floors of this building, which sloped downward slightly from west to east, were excavated at an elevation between 20.6 and 20.4 m.[4] Similarly, the walls in the northeastern corner of the building (W123 and W162) were founded as deep as 0.8 m below floor level, as opposed to the walls in the rest of the building, which were founded only *c.* 0.1 m below the level of the floors. A deliberate fill was laid down first in this corner of the building to compensate for the natural slope of the tell. According to the excavators, the floor of Room 111 was made of mudbricks, over which an organic white material seems to have been compacted.

The destruction layer that covered the floors of Building A contained much pottery, particularly storage-jar fragments (Fig. 2.6) and fallen mudbricks (see Plan 2.3). Based on the large quantity of storage-jar fragments found within this building, especially in Room 111 (see Fig. 3.22:1–17, 19–23), Dothan hypothesized that Building A had served as the port's central storeroom (e.g., 1960c:125, Fig. 4:7, 8, Pl. 10:5; 1993:1073).

Immediately outside the southeastern corner of the building was a *ṭabun* (L135), built of sherds and set into a pit (Fig. 2.7). Its preserved dimensions were as follows: height, 0.6 m; diameter at base, 0.7 m; and diameter at top, 0.4 m. Directly to the east of the building, L118 continued to be excavated. Pit 85, *c.* 0.90 m in diameter and 0.55 m deep, was located approximately 15 m south of Building A. In light of the fact that there was no real stratigraphic connection between the building and the pit, it is probable that the pit was assigned to Stratum IX based primarily on its top level (20.7 m). Also south of the building was L86, a probe beneath a floor of the Stratum VIII–VII Building B, where a number of beer-jar bases were found (Fig. 2.8 and see Fig. 4.11:1, 2). Similarly, L75 in Stratum IX was probably a probe into the subfloor fill of the Stratum VIII Room 75 (see Plan 2.4).

At the base of the eastern slope, in the area of the Hellenistic purple-dye (*Murex brandaris*) production installations (Sq M30), the excavators uncovered a small Late Bronze Age burial (L152; Figs. 2.9–2.12; see Plan 2.7).[5] Based on the funerary assemblage (see below), especially the imported Cypriot pottery, the burial was assigned to LB IIA and associated with Stratum IX. Two large flat stones were positioned so as to form a gable, under which the body was laid in a pit, creating a type of cist grave. The orientation of the burial was north–south with most of the grave goods located at the southern end of the gable. These included a carinated bowl, pilgrim

Fig. 2.6. Destruction layer in Room 139 of Building A.

Fig. 2.7. Ṭabun 135.

flask, bronze dagger, two(?) White Shaved dipper juglets and two Base Ring II jugs and a juglet (Fig. 2.12; see also Figs. 3.6:4, 10, 3.22:18, 3.29:1, 5.3:16, 18, 5.6, 8.1:1). Mixed among them were disarticulated skeletal remains, perhaps including part of a human cranium and limb bone (E. Maher, pers. comm.). Against the northern side of the gable stood a storage jar with an upside-down bowl covering the mouth (Fig. 2.10).

All aspects of this burial are to be expected given the coastal location of Tel Mor and the LB IIA date of Stratum IX (Gonen 1992:15–20, Fig. 2, Table 3). Pit and cist graves were especially common at sites along the coastal plain and interior valleys during LB II. As with most pit burial cemeteries, Burial 152 was

Fig. 2.8. Beer-jar bases found in L86.

Fig. 2.9. Burial 152, looking south.

Fig. 2.10. Burial 152, looking southwest.

Fig. 2.11. Part of the funerary assemblage from Burial 152.

located outside the settlement proper, on the slope of the tell. In addition, the funerary assemblage contains the anticipated range of types: a storage jar (perhaps to serve as a grave marker), a covering bowl, an additional bowl, dipper juglets, small containers and a dagger. Even the frequency of Cypriot imports (50%) is consistent with LB II pit burials from other sites, as is the placement of the storage jar with a covering bowl. Typically one or two storage jars would have been placed near the head or foot of the deceased. A dipper juglet was left inside the jar, and a bowl, either locally made or a Cypriot import, covered the jar's mouth. This arrangement of burial goods has been found, for example, in Tomb 114 at Deir el-Balaḥ (T. Dothan 1979: Figs. 4–8) and Tomb 1 of Site XI at Tell Abu Hawam (Anati 1959: Fig. 4).

It is possible that Egyptian burial practices and conceptions of death—that is to say, a concern for the integrity of the deceased's body and, thereby, safe passage of its soul to the afterlife—contributed to the popularity of pit and cist burials (and the single interments that they contained) during the Late Bronze Age (Gonen 1992:37–38). The common Middle Bronze Age funerary practice, whereby old burials were unceremoniously pushed aside to make room for new bodies, stands in point of contrast. Those living at or near Tel Mor, if not Egyptians themselves, would have been especially susceptible to such an influence, if the material culture of the next few strata is any indication.

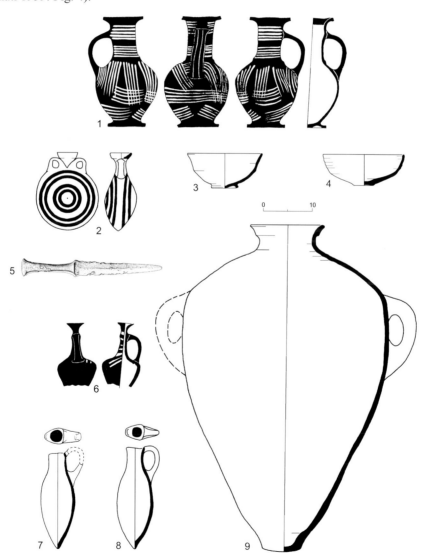

Fig. 2.12. The funerary assemblage from Burial 152.

Stratum VIII (Plan 2.4)

After the destruction of Building A in Stratum IX, a larger building (B) was constructed immediately to its southwest in Stratum VIII.[6] The orientation of Building B differed from that of Building A. The former was oriented 5° to the west of the north–south axis, whereas the latter was 7° to the east of this axis. Building B covered an area of *c.* 500 sq m, was roughly square in shape, and had 22.5 m long external walls.

Although the southwestern portion had been lost to erosion, it was possible to reconstruct the full extent of the building based primarily on the presence of a foundation layer of sand discovered beneath the walls (or former walls) at three of the four corners (i.e.,

northeast, northwest and southeast). It is important to note that when specific dimensions of the external walls are known with some precision, they correspond closely to the Egyptian royal cubit (of 0.5236 m). Four salients and three recesses per side buttressed the exterior walls (W66, W77, W145 and W144). Each salient and recess combined was approximately 3.2 m in length (*c.* 6 cubits). The walls at the point of a salient were *c.* 2.6 m thick (*c.* 5 cubits), and, at the point of a recess, *c.* 2.1 m thick (*c.* 4 cubits);[7] therefore, the recesses were approximately 0.5 m deep. As mentioned above, the walls of this building were founded on a layer of sand, which remained in certain places where the walls did not (i.e., northwestern and southeastern corners). The lengths of the external walls, as reconstructed by their sand foundations, are corroborated by calculating the

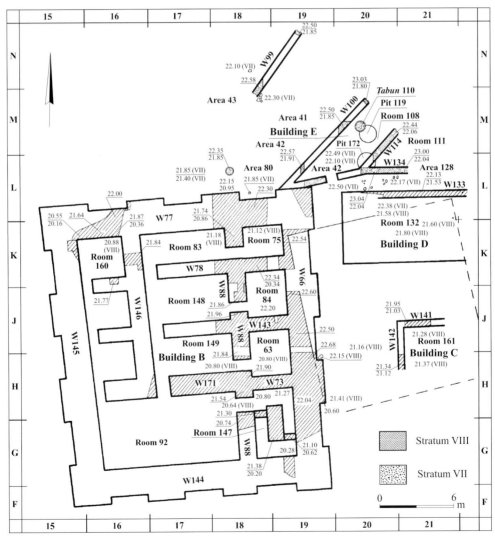

Plan 2.4. Strata VIII–VII. Plan.

cumulative length of a uniform number of salients (4) and recesses (3) per side (i.e., 3.2 m × 7 = 22.4 m).

In the unpublished preliminary stratigraphic summary, the excavators report that the walls at the northeastern corner of Building B were preserved to the extraordinary height of 2.8 m above the level of the floor.[8] In general, as the distance south and west from this corner increased, the walls' height of preservation decreased. The thickness of the walls, again, suggests at least a second story, which is clearly evidenced by the presence of a stairway in the southeastern corner of the building (Room 147). Three clay steps, 0.38 m wide and 0.17 m high, were excavated between W73 and a rectangular (1.30 × 2.70 m) mudbrick support or 'pillar' in the middle of the room. The excavators estimated that around the pillar there was space for 20 steps, which allows for a distance of 3.4 m between the floors of the first and second stories. If one assumes that the space between floors taken up by joists and compacted brush probably did not exceed 0.5 m, then the ceilings of the ground floor of Building B were approximately three meters high. Given the building's monumental nature, this unusual height is possible.

Two north–south thick walls, W88 and W146, divided the interior of the building into three zones of interconnected space. Wall 88 was a series of screen walls on the same alignment that separated the eastern from the central zone (Fig. 2.13). The rooms in the eastern zone, which were excavated in their entirety, were relatively small: Room 75 measured 2.5 × 3.0 m; Rooms 84 and 63, 3.0 × 3.5 m; and the previously discussed Room 147 was 3.0 × 5.0 m. The rooms of the central zone (L83, L148 and L149), of which only the eastern side was excavated, were approximately twice the size of the rooms in the eastern zone that adjoined them. The walls in the western zone (W145 and W146) were largely destroyed by erosion. Based on the dimensions (3.12 × 3.50 m) of the room in that zone with the best preserved walls (Room 160), the excavators

Fig. 2.13. Composite photograph of Building B, looking east.

reconstructed two additional rooms (not assigned locus numbers) of similar size to the south of it.

The fact that W146 ends at the same latitude as W171 demonstrates that there was probably a large, *c.* 5.5 × 11.0 m hall (Room 92) in the southwestern portion of this building, spanning the central and western zones. Assuming that the reconstruction of the southwestern corner of Building B is correct, Room 92 was by far the largest enclosed space on the ground floor. Perhaps W171 was made wider (1.5 m) than the other east–west dividing walls—W78, W143 and W73 (each 1.0 m)—in order to bear the broader and heavier ceiling necessitated by the great dimensions of Room 92. It is also possible that this large area was only partially roofed.

No entranceway to Building B was found; however, much of the exterior walls, particularly on the western (W145) and southern (W144) sides, had been destroyed by erosion. From a geographic perspective, it is likely that one would have approached the summit of the tell from the direction of the wadi to the south, where the slope was less steep. Thus, one would have entered Building B through the capacious Room 92, as shown in the isometric reconstruction (Fig. 2.14). The elevations of the Stratum VIII floors within the building were fairly consistent, ranging in general between 20.8 and 21.1 m asl. The walls were founded no deeper than 0.2 m below the level of these floors; thus shallow foundation trenches were used.

Building B possesses the following characteristics associated with Egyptian-style 'Administrative Buildings', sometimes called 'Governors' Residencies', that appear in Canaan during the Late Bronze and early Iron Ages (Weinstein 1981:18; Higginbotham 2000:284–290): (1) mudbrick walls set in shallow trenches lined with sand; (2) exterior walls *c.* 2.5 m thick; (3) a generally square shape with walls between 15 and 25 m in length; (4) building measurements according to the Egyptian royal cubit; (5) symmetrically arranged rooms that are small and often narrow; (6) a staircase, sometimes connected to a large entrance hall; and (7) buttresses or corner towers.

Buttressing on an Egyptian-style building in Canaan is unique to Tel Mor.[9] This architectural feature brings to mind the forts along the 'Ways of Horus' as depicted in a relief of Seti I on the northern exterior wall of the hypostyle hall in the Temple to Amun at Karnak (Gardiner 1920: Pls. 11, 12; more recently, Epigraphic Survey 1986: Pls. 2–6). Here are shown eleven fortified outposts along the military road that stretched across the northern coast of Sinai. Despite the rigid two-dimensionality of the scene, one can easily discern the buttressed facades of these fortresses (Fig. 2.15). Most of them appear with four salients, three recesses, and an entrance in the center, as has been reconstructed for Building B at Tel Mor.

Fortresses are shown in the relief with either one or two tiers of battlements. For those with two (Gardiner's

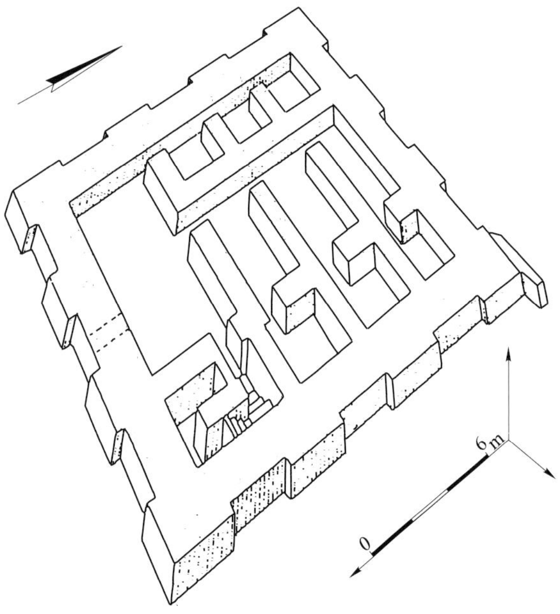

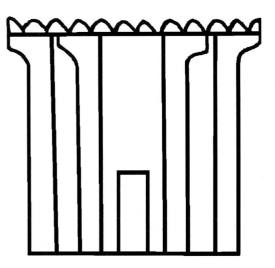

Fig. 2.14. Isometric reconstruction of Strata VIII–VII (adapted from M. Dothan 1993:1073).

Fig. 2.15. A fortress along the 'Ways of Horus' as depicted on the northern exterior wall of the Karnak temple's great hypostyle hall (Fort K; adapted from Gardiner 1920: Pl. XI). The fortress' buttressed facade, like that of Building B at Tel Mor, is apparent.

Forts M, P and U), the lower tier must belong to the enclosure wall, similar to those found at New Kingdom sites in the northern Sinai. At Ḥaruvit the excavators uncovered a single buttress in the middle of the northern enclosure wall (Oren 1980:27), and reconstructed a similar buttress in the poorly preserved western and southern walls (Oren and Shershevsky 1989: Fig. 4). At Tell Hebwa long sections of a fully buttressed, double enclosure wall were cleared along the western and northern perimeter of the site (el-Maksoud 1987). The upper tier probably corresponds to a fortified citadel. Given that Tel Mor was not encircled by a wall during the Late Bronze Age or any other period, Building B is closer to the single-tiered variety.

Despite the fact that buttressed walls are a common feature of fortifications, Building B's primary function was likely not military in nature. Its salients did not protrude enough (only 0.5 m) to allow defenders positioned on the battlements to direct effective flanking fire against attackers (Yadin 1963:20). In point of contrast, salients on Middle Kingdom fortresses in Nubia project between two and three meters beyond the face of massive enclosure walls (Badawy 1966: Figs. 95 [Mi'm], 96 [Buhen], 100 [Mirgissa] and 102 [Askut]).

Rather, Building B and similar structures in Canaan probably mainly functioned as centers of administrative activity (Weinstein 1981:18, 19; Oren and Shershevsky 1989:18; Higginbotham 2000:284–286). In terms of the interior arrangement of space, the closest parallel in Egypt derives from Block VII of the Middle Kingdom fortress at Uronarti (Wheeler 1967: Map III). The main building in this block (Fig. 2.16) has the following characteristics in common with Building B: a stairway with a central pillar and attached to a large hall near the entrance (Room 12; dimensions 5.3 × 8.8 m); three long narrow rooms (Rooms 32–34; dimensions c. 2.0 × 6.5 m); and four small rooms (Rooms 8, 9, 30 and 31; dimensions c. 2.5 × 3.0 m). Assuming a gradient of 1.00 in 1.65 for the stairway, the excavators reconstructed a height of 3.40 m for the ceiling (Wheeler 1967:9), similar to the height projected for the ceiling of Room 147 of Building B (see above). More than 2000 mud sealings found in Blocks IV–VI at Uronarti bear the impression 'granary of the fortress of Khesef-Yuwnuw (= Uronarti)' (Seal Nos. 5a, b), thus confirming the site's administrative function (Reisner 1955:37–40).[10]

The 'Governor's Residence' (Building 1104) in Stratum X-12 at Tel Afeq (Fig. 2.17), which is closest to Building B at Tel Mor in terms of architectural plan (Higginbotham 2000:290), also produced administrative texts (Rainey in Kochavi 1990:XVI). One fragmentary Akkadian tablet enumerates large quantities of various commodities, the names of which, unfortunately, do not survive (Rainey 1975).

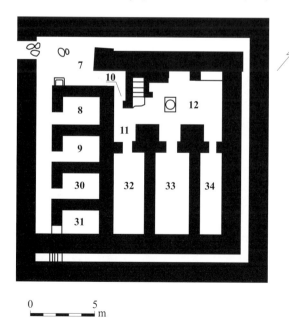

0   5
m

Fig. 2.16. The main building in Block VII of the Middle Kingdom fortress at Uronarti (adapted from Wheeler 1967: Map III).

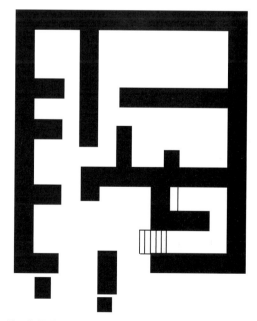

Fig. 2.17. Reconstruction of the 'Governor's Residence' at Tel Afeq (adapted from Kochavi 1990:12).

More famous is the Akkadian letter sent by Takuḫlina, prefect of Ugarit, to the Egyptian vizier Ḫaya in regard to a transaction involving wheat (Owen 1981). Attesting to the building's use as a storage facility was the discovery of storage jars and collared-rim pithoi in the destruction level of two of the ground floor 'halls' (Kochavi 1990:XII). Aside from a largely intact storage jar excavated in Room 75 (Fig. 2.18), there was nothing unusual about the preservation or quantity of storage jars in Building B at Tel Mor.

To the east of Building B were two poorly preserved, smaller buildings. Wall 141 and W142 belonged to Building C. Both walls were approximately 0.5 m thick, and W141 was preserved to a height of almost 1.0 m. The floor was paved with mudbricks *c*. 0.5 m thick. To the north of Building C was Building D, of which only the northern wall (W133) remained (Fig. 2.19). The floor of this building was also paved with mudbricks. It is not clear why either of these smaller buildings was assigned to Stratum VIII as opposed to Stratum VII. In terms of elevation, their floors are within the range of either stratum. In terms of pottery, there is little difference between the strata; moreover, the rooms in question (L132 and L161) produced few sherds. To the north of Building D were Pits 119 and 172. Each was *c*. 1.3 m in diameter and *c*. 0.5 m deep. Apparently, Pit 119 cut a Stratum IX wall (W122) of Building A (see Plan 2.3; Fig. 2.20). The areas above Room 111 of Stratum IX (Sq L21) and beneath Room 108 of Stratum VII (Sq M20) were also excavated as part of Stratum VIII.

Fig. 2.19. Building D, looking west.

Fig. 2.18. Partially intact storage jar found in Room 75.

Fig. 2.20. The stratigraphic relationship between Pit 119 (Stratum VIII) and W122 (Stratum IX).

STRATUM VII (Plan 2.4)

In terms of architecture, little changed between Strata VIII and VII. The layout of the main building, Building B, remained the same; however, Buildings C and D went out of use, and a new building, Building E, was constructed. A layer of debris as thick as 0.9 m separated the floors of Stratum VIII from Stratum VI in Building B (see Plan 2.5). A significant portion of this debris was comprised of mudbrick fall, yet there was no evidence of burning, which led the excavators to suspect that an earthquake caused the partial collapse of Building B in Stratum VIII.

At the northeastern corner of Building B, a few poorly preserved walls (W100, W114 and W134) of the smaller Building E were found (see Plan 2.4). Inside the two exterior(?) walls (W100 and W134) was an oddly shaped room (L108). On the floor of this room was *Tabun* 110, which was built over the northwestern portion of the Stratum VIII Pit 119 (Fig. 2.21). Parallel to W100 was interior W114, which formed a slightly less acute angle with W134, and created another irregular room (L111).[11] The existence of Building E (and especially Room 108) is questionable in that its fragmentary walls form unusually acute angles. What is more, its orientation is completely different from that of Building B.

Directly south of Building E was L128, described as a 'passage' in Stratum VIII and as an 'area' in Stratum VII. It is more likely to have been the latter for two reasons: first, Buildings D and E were not contemporaneous, and, therefore, the space between them technically did not constitute an alleyway; and, second, the large quantity of stones found in L128 (Fig. 2.22) is atypical of alleyways. To the northwest of Building E, another poorly preserved wall (W99),

Fig. 2.21. Ṭabun 110 (Stratum VII) built into Pit 119 (Stratum VIII) in Room 108 (Stratum VII).

Fig. 2.22. Area 128 and W134, looking north.

roughly parallel to W100, was found. The area between W99 and Building B was excavated as a few different loci, all of which probably corresponded to fill. Locus 41 was excavated in Sq M19, L42 in Sq L19, L43 in Sq M18 and L80 in Sq L18. It appears that a *ṭabun* was found in Sq L18, but it was not assigned a locus number. A scarab that was also recovered from this square was assigned to L62, but the nature of this locus is not clear; it is also not possible to identify the scarab.

A heavy destruction layer, in places as thick as 1.5 m, covered the buildings of Stratum VII. Although thickest north of Building B, this layer was exposed in every room excavated. Unlike the collapse that separated Strata VIII and VII, it contained a large amount of ash

and burnt mudbrick. Apparently, the site was abandoned for a time after this fiery destruction, as evidenced by a thin, superimposed layer of windblown sand.

STRATUM VI (Plan 2.5)

In Stratum VI, a new building (F), at least 13.0×13.0 m in area, was built in the southeastern portion of the tell's summit. The western edge of Building F was founded directly on top of the destroyed remains of the eastern edge of Building B from Stratum VII (Plan 2.5). Unfortunately, only the northwestern half of Building F was preserved, the southeastern half having been lost to erosion.[12] At 4.0 m thick, the external walls (W39

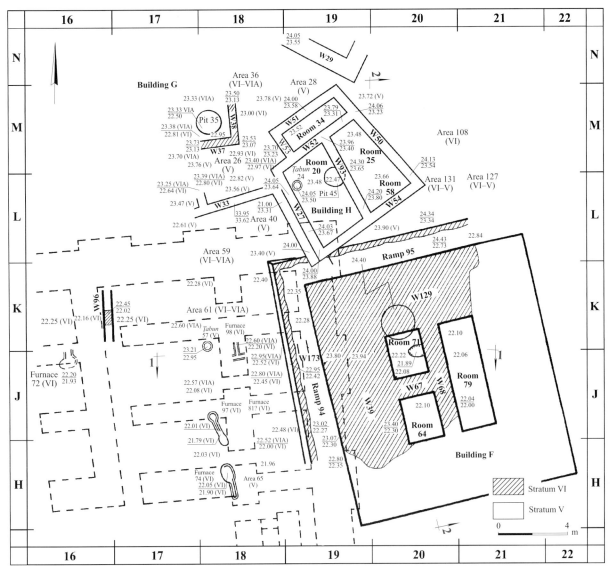

Plan 2.5. Strata VI–V. Plan and sections.

and W129) of this building were massive. The internal walls (W67 and W68) were considerably narrower, not exceeding 1.5 m in thickness. Segments of the northern external wall (W129) were preserved to a height of 2.2 m above the level of the floor, perhaps as high as the ceiling. The walls of Building F farther downslope were less well preserved because of erosion.

Most of the walls were set in foundation trenches that were between 0.2 and 0.3 m deeper than the level of the room floors (Plan 2.5: Sections 1-1, 2-2). Part of the western external wall (W39) was not founded in a trench, but, instead, rested atop a destroyed Stratum VII wall (W66). These trenches, especially those for the external walls, were wider than the walls they contained, and were packed with sand. As with Stratum VIII, it was possible to reconstruct parts of Building F based on this foundation layer of sand. By such means the excavators were able to determine the extent of the southern wall of Room 64 and, by extension, Room 79.

The ground floor of Building F contained two small, 1.9 × 2.4 m rooms (L71 and L64) and one large, 1.9 × 6.3 m room (L79). Room 71 was completely preserved except for the intrusion of a Roman-period well (L55)

in its northernmost section. Apparently, a shallow pit was also dug into the floor of this room (see Plan 2.5: Sections 1-1, 2-2). More restorable pottery was found in Room 71 than any other well-defined stratigraphic context on the summit of the tell (see Chapter 3). Erosion destroyed portions of both Rooms 64 and 79.

A ramp (L94 and L95) ran along the western and northern sides of the building. It was faced with mudbrick; the space between this facing and the external walls of Building B was filled, presumably with soil and stones. The ramp, which was preserved in places to a height of between 1.5 and 1.7 m, clearly indicates the existence of an upper story. Indeed, the extraordinarily thick external walls could have supported multiple stories. The absence of entrances, similar to Building A of Stratum IX, and the presence of an exterior ramp, suggest that access to the ground floor of Building F was through openings in the ceiling from which ladders could be lowered.

Dothan described Building F as a *migdol* and connected it with the type of Canaanite fort that appears in New Kingdom Egyptian texts and reliefs (e.g., 1960e; see also Weinstein 1981:18; James and McGovern 1993:57).[13] Indeed, the unusually thick

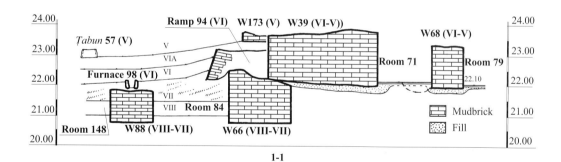

1-1

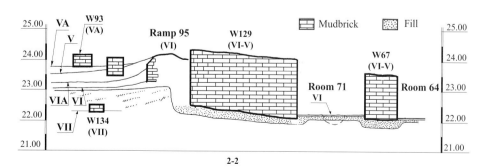

2-2

Plan 2.5 (cont.). Sections.

walls strongly suggest that Building F was constructed with defense in mind. The closest architectural parallel for Building F in Canaan or Egypt is a rectangular building, also termed a *migdol*, found at Bet She'an in Level VII (Rowe 1929:53–56; 1930:21, Fig. 2). As reconstructed by the excavators, its dimensions were 15.5 × 23.5 m with outer walls *c.* 2.5 m thick. Subsequent analysis of the building has shown that its western side lacked the tower rooms originally postulated (L1383 and L1384; Oren and Shershevsky 1989:14; James and McGovern 1993:56–58). With this updated reconstruction, the similarities between the Bet She'an Level VII *migdol* and Building F at Tel Mor are more compelling. The two buildings are closer in size given the reduced dimensions of the Bet She'an *migdol* (i.e., *c.* 13.5 × 16.3 m). The division of interior space is also roughly the same. Rather than five or six, there are only four rooms in the Bet She'an *migdol*, two of which are oriented east–west (L1382 and L1380) and two north–south (L1363 and L1353). In Building F at Tel Mor all three rooms are rectangular and oriented north–south; the largest room (L79) is approximately equal to the size of the two smaller rooms combined (L64 and L71).

To the west of Building F were at least five furnace installations identified as foundries (L72, L74, L81, L97, L98).[14] Insofar as practically no walls were found in the area, it is likely that this industry took place in the open air. The only exception was a wall fragment (W96) excavated in Sq K16. The discovery of ash, a small quantity of slag, bronze casting spatter, hundreds of tuyère fragments (including nozzles; see Fig. 8.1:2–4) and a crucible (see Fig. 8.1:5) in and around the installations clearly illustrate their involvement in metalworking (see Waldbaum 1978:60; Stech-Wheeler et al. 1981:259, 260; Ilan 1999:222–223).

The best preserved installations are Furnaces 81 and 97, which each consist of one, possibly two, roughly circular pits connected by a channel lined with a clay mortar (Figs. 2.23–2.25).[15] The diameter of the larger pit of Furnace 81, which was not drawn on any plan, ranges between 0.8 and 1.1 m. Tuyère fragments were found either in or near the smaller pit. The connecting channel of Furnace 81 is approximately 0.3 m wide, 0.7 m long and has thick clay walls. Such walls are better preserved on Furnaces 72 and 74 (Figs. 2.26–2.28), where they are almost 0.1 m thick. The height of the walls of the furnaces, as preserved, ranged from 0.15 m (Furnace 74) to 0.30 m (Furnaces 72 and 98). It is clear from Plan 2.5 that a clay wall did not line the bottom of these channels (at least for Furnace 98). It appears that some of the above-ground superstructure of Furnace 74's pit (diameter *c.* 0.9 m) also survived (Fig. 2.27). Furnace 97's southern pit (diameter *c.* 0.45 m) is visible immediately to the north of it. Emission spectroscopic and atomic absorption analyses of two pieces of spatter revealed a varying tin content (1.19% and 11.42%), which suggests that bronze recycling, rather than smelting, took place at Tel Mor (see Tables 8.1, 8.2).

Fig. 2.23. Furnace 81 before excavation, looking west.

Fig. 2.24. Furnace 81, looking west.

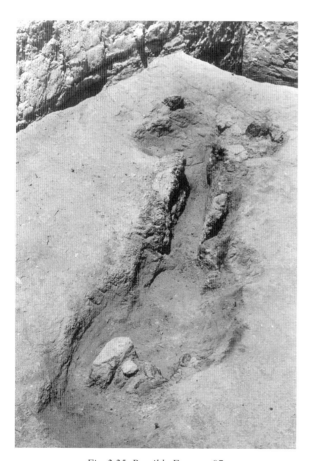

Fig. 2.25. Possibly Furnace 97.

Fig. 2.26. Furnace 72, looking north.

Fig. 2.27. Furnace 74 and 97(?), looking east.

In a later phase of this statum (VIA), the industrial area fell out of use, as evidenced by the installations having been buried beneath surfaces that ran up to the ramp (L94 and L95), which continued to function (Plan 2.5). The corner of a poorly preserved building (G) accompanied these surfaces, which were otherwise defined by elevation (between 0.25 and 0.60 m above those of Stratum VI). Inside Building G, formed by W37 and W38, was an ash-filled pit (L35), 0.5 m deep and 1.4 m in diameter.

Most of the open area outside Building F was excavated as loci divided into earlier (Stratum VI) and later phases (Stratum VIA) according to elevation. These loci include Area 36 in Sq M18, Area 59 in Sq L18, Area 61 in Sq K18 and Area 131 in Sq L20. Locus 108 corresponded to the area above a room of the same number in Stratum VII (see above), and L127 was assigned to the area of Sq L21 in both Strata VI and V. Locus 32 seems simply to have been a large flat stone surrounded by smaller stones in Sq L19.

Stratum VI also ended in destruction. Numerous whole or almost whole vessels lay smashed on the floors of Building F, particularly in Room 71 (Figs. 2.29, 2.30). On top of these vessels were fallen mudbricks and then more broken pots, which, taken altogether, indicates a second story collapse. After this destruction, Ramps 94 and 95 fell out of use, as did Building G.

Fig. 2.28. Close-up view of Furnace 74, looking east.

Fig. 2.29. The Stratum VI destruction level in Room 71.   *Fig. 2.30. Balk section showing mudbrick debris in Room 71.*

STRATUM V (Plan 2.5)

In Stratum V, a rebuilt Building F (without the ramp) continued to dominate the tell's summit.[16] To the north of Building F, a new building (H) was constructed, the southwestern corner of which overlapped Ramp 95. Similarly, a fragmentary Stratum V wall (W173) in Sq K19 rested above Ramp 94 with approximately 0.35 m of fill or occupational debris in between them (see Plan 2.5). It seems that Building H was initially comprised of only two rooms, L34 and another room made up of L20, L25 and L58 (for a discussion of the problematic L25 and L58, see below). This observation is based on the fact that interior W93 was founded at a higher level than the other narrow Building H walls (thus W93 is assigned to Stratum VA). Moreover, W93 stretched across and above Pit 45, which appears to have been cut from the earliest floor level of Building H.

In general, the total preserved height of the Building H walls was between 0.4 and 0.6 m, of which perhaps 0.1 to 0.2 m was taken up by a foundation course(s). On the floor of Room 20 was a *ṭabun* (L24), preserved to a height of *c.* 0.50 m with a 0.75 m diameter. The thickness of Building H's western external wall (W27) appears to have been doubled by the addition of another row of bricks. Wall 33 extended westward from W27, and another wall might have extended northward from W33. Therefore, it appears that there was another room, or at

least a semi-enclosed space, attached to Building H. The corner of another separate building was found north of Building H. The only wall from this building assigned a locus number (W29) was a meter thick and preserved to a total height of half a meter.

Once W93 was constructed, naturally, Building H contained three rooms. For some reason, both L25 and L58 were assigned to the easternmost room of this building. The two loci differ slightly in terms of elevation and location: Locus 25 was located in the northwestern half of the room in Sq M19, and was excavated at an elevation of between 23.50 and 23.60 m, and L58 was located in the southeastern half of the room in Sq L20 and was excavated at an elevation of 23.65 m. It seems that L20 and L25 were first assigned to the western and eastern rooms of Stratum IV Building I, which followed roughly the outline of Building H, but was oriented slightly differently (see Plan 2.6).

The area around Building H was excavated according to the following loci: to the east of the building, Areas 127 and 131 in Sq L21 and Sq L20, respectively, both of which were continued from Stratum VI; to the north, Area 28 in Sq M19; to the west, Area 26 in Sq M18; and also to the west, Area 40 in Sq L18. To the west of Building F, Area 65 was excavated in Sq H18. A *ṭabun* (L57), preserved to a height of *c.* 0.25 m and 0.60 m in diameter, was found in Sq K18.

Because there is no mention of a destruction level having ended Stratum V, it is best to assume that its buildings, particularly Building F, simply fell out of use. In the succeeding strata (IV–I), the character of the site changed considerably. A single massive building no longer dominated the tell as in the preceding five strata (IX–V). Instead, the settlement became more open with relatively little architecture. Indeed, by the Hellenistic period (Stratum I), the summit was largely abandoned in favor of the base of the eastern slope.

STRATUM IV (Plan 2.6)

Stratum IV consisted only of a poorly preserved building (I), which, as mentioned above, followed the outline of Building H from Stratum V. Three walls from Building I were excavated; however, only two (W21 and W22) were assigned identification numbers. Both W21 and W22 were preserved to a height of approximately 0.30 m. Similarly, only two of the three partially preserved rooms (L20 and L25) received locus

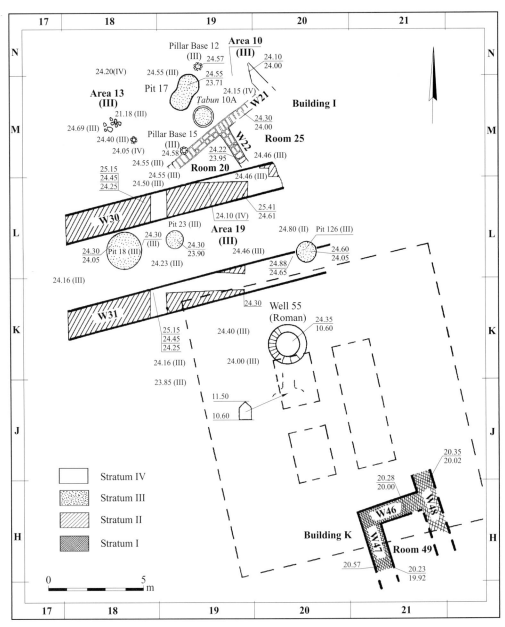

Plan 2.6. Strata IV–I. Plan.

numbers. It appears that the surfaces associated with this building were identified at an elevation between 24.25 and 24.05 m. In light of the fact that Stratum IV contained so little architecture, and, moreover, that the few extant walls conformed to the layout of a building (H) from the previous stratum,[17] it is probably better to regard Stratum IV instead as a reuse phase of Stratum V. Notwithstanding, the established stratigraphic sequence is retained here for the sake of consistency with the published preliminary reports. Like the previous stratum, the absence of a destruction layer suggests that, rather than having met a violent end, the sole building (I) of Stratum IV simply fell out of use.

STRATUM III (Plan 2.6)

A partially covered courtyard with pits and installations stood atop the tell in Stratum III. At least three pillar bases (L12, L15 and a third not assigned a locus number) stood in proximity to each other. In between them (and beneath a roof long since vanished) a *ṭabun* (L10A) was built and a large peanut-shaped pit, or possibly a silo, was dug (L17). The diameter of Pit 17 ranged from 0.9 to 1.9 m; it was approximately 0.5 m deep and contained a large amount of pottery (see, e.g., Fig. 3.29:4–12; also, M. Dothan 1960a: Pl. III.4; 1960c:125, Fig. 5:6, 7, Pl. 11:1, 3). *Ṭabun* 10A, located next to the pit, was 1.10 m in diameter and preserved to a height of only 0.14 m. To the southwest in Sq L18 another relatively large pit (L18) was found; it was 1.80 m in diameter, but only 0.25 m deep. To the east of this pit was a smaller pit (L23), 0.9 m in diameter and 0.4 m deep.

Farther east in Sq L20 the excavators found the upper half of an enormous storage vessel, about a meter in diameter and half a meter tall, turned upside down and partially sunken into the ground (L126; Figs. 2.31, 2.32; and see Fig. 3.16:9). Although in secondary use, it seems that this jar-krater was still used for storage purposes. The upper half of the vessel apparently served to line the inside of a pit. It is important to note that, except for a slight downward slope from north to south, all the pits were dug and the pillar bases and *ṭabun* built in Stratum III at approximately the same elevation.

Because there were no walls to define rooms, the only other loci were assigned to areas. Area 10 in Sq M19 and Area 13 in Sq M18 corresponded to the area of the courtyard proper as defined by the pillar bases,

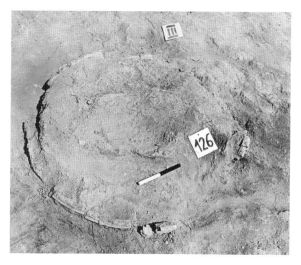

Fig. 2.31. Locus 126 before excavation.

Fig. 2.32. Locus 126 after excavation.

and Area 19 was excavated farther south in Sq L19. A thick, ashy layer covered Stratum III, above which was a deposit of sand indicating that the summit was destroyed and then abandoned.

STRATUM II (Plan 2.6)

Stratum II consisted only of two large walls (W30 and W31) that were oriented roughly from east to west across the summit of the tell. They were 1.5 m thick, preserved to a maximum height of 0.8 m, to an average length of 12.5 m, and there was a *c*. 3 m space between them (see also Plan 2.3). The walls were set into foundation trenches dug into the ash layer that covered Stratum III. As with the walls of Buildings B and F, W30 and W31 were founded on a layer of sand that allowed the excavators to reconstruct the outline of the walls in certain places where the mudbricks had not survived. Unfortunately, the surfaces associated with these walls could not be traced.

Dothan described W30 and W31 as casemate walls (1993:1074); however, it is hard to believe that they functioned defensively. Rather than encircling the tell's summit, as would be expected for a fortification wall, they apparently stretched straight across its middle. In the absence of any associated architecture in Stratum II, it is difficult to determine how these walls were used. Whatever the case might have been, a destruction layer covered the Stratum II settlement and Tel Mor lay abandoned until the Hellenistic period.

STRATUM I (Plans 2.6, 2.7)

During the Hellenistic period, the focus of the site shifted from the summit of the tell (Areas A and B) to the base of its eastern slope (Area B2). In Area B2 the excavators discovered a well (L153), the remains of a building (J) and several installations (Loci 150, 151, 154, 155, 179, 180), most of which appear to have been part of a single complex for the production of purple dye (Plan 2.7). Attached to the western side of Building J were a plastered basin (L150) and an interconnected semicircular basin (L151).[18] Apparently one of them contained *Murex brandaris* shells (Horn 1968:21). The larger, rectangular basin (L150) was partly hewn from bedrock, partly built of stone, and lined with plaster (Figs. 2.33, 2.34). Although its eastern side was poorly preserved, it was possible to reconstruct the lateral dimensions of Basin 150 at *c.* 3.0 × 3.5 m; its depth was between 0.5 and 0.6 m. The smaller, semicircular basin (L151) was at a lower elevation than Basin 150; therefore, liquids flowed from the larger to the smaller pool. Basin 151 may have been added in a later phase of the complex. A similar combination of installations was found in a Hellenistic stratum at Tel Dor in Area D1 (for descriptions and references, see Chapter 12, Evidence for Purple-Dye Production at Coastal Levantine Sites).

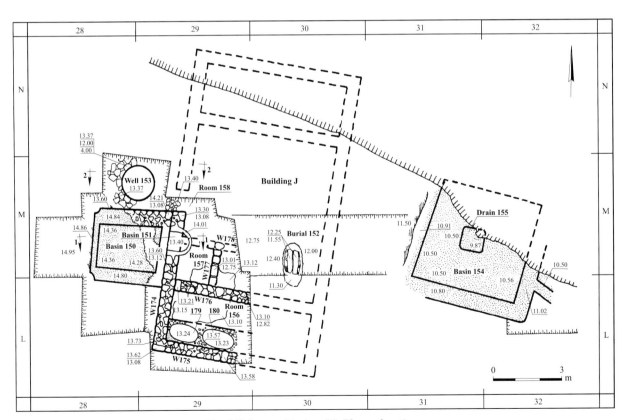

Plan 2.7. Stratum I in Area B2. Plan and sections.

Fig. 2.33. Basin 150, looking east.

Fig. 2.34. Basins 150 and 151, looking west.

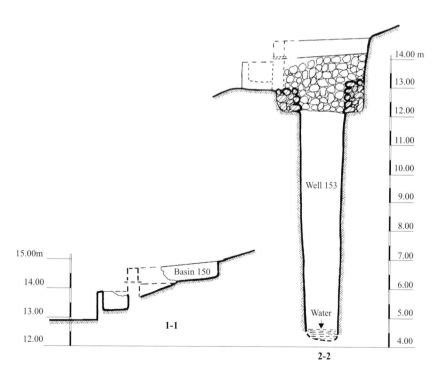

Plan 2.7 (cont.). Sections.

The walls (W174–W178) of the building (J) associated with these installations were poorly preserved and composed of rough *kurkar* stones (Fig. 2.35). Only one room (L157) in Building J was excavated in its entirety, the other two (L156 and L158) only partially. The basis for the excavators' reconstruction of the full extent of Building J is not clear. Patches of the floor, presumably compacted earth, were identified in all three rooms at approximately the same level. In Room 156 along the southern wall (W175) were excavated Basins 179 and 180, 0.49 and 0.34 m deep respectively. If the excavators' reconstruction of Building J is correct, then it originally covered at least one Late Bronze Age burial (L152; see above, Stratum IX), and its northern end was destroyed by the modern quarrying that led to the discovery of the site (see Chapter 1, Site Identification and Discovery; Plan 1.1).

Directly north of Basin 150 was a well (L153), which was cut approximately 10 m deep through bedrock. The diameter of the top of the well shaft (over 3.0 m) was wider than the average diameter of the rest of the shaft (*c.* 1.5 m). At a depth of approximately 2.5 m (on the western, higher side), the diameter of the well shaft abruptly narrowed; thus creating a ledge. The sides of the shaft above this ledge were packed with stones, some of which were dressed and had fallen into the well shaft (Fig. 2.36). Originally the stones probably extended above ground level to form a ring wall around the well's opening. In antiquity the well was backfilled with debris, which included numerous restorable vessels (Fig. 2.37). There were also thousands of *Murex brandaris* shells, both crushed and intact, located approximately halfway down the shaft (see Chapter 12). The excavators cleared the well down to the level of the water table below 5 m asl.

To the east of Building J was a large basin (L154), much of which, unfortunately, has been destroyed by modern quarrying. Basin 154, which probably covered an area of *c.* 5 sq m, was cut from bedrock, plastered and varied in depth from 0.3 to 0.5 m. In the center of the basin was a *c.* 0.6 m deep, square-shaped depression that might have served as a drain or sump (L155). It is possible that there was also a channel that branched off to the southeast from the basin.

Many of the features required for the processing of purple dye are present in Area B2. To begin with, Tel Mor is situated along the Levantine coast, where various species of muricid snails may be found in abundance. The location of Area B2 at the base of the tell's eastern slope is significant also: The prevailing westerly winds would have carried the foul odor created by the purple dye industry away from the settlement (Karmon and Spanier 1987:149). In order to extract the flesh, which contains the hypobranchial gland and its precious purple dye, murex shells were pierced or crushed (Pliny, *NH*, IX.60, 126), most likely in a stone vessel of some sort. Basin 150 probably served in this capacity; its large dimensions could have accommodated the enormous

Fig. 2.35. Room 157, looking southeast.

Fig. 2.36. The top of Well 153.

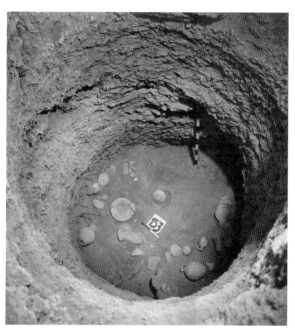

Fig. 2.37. Whole vessels in the fill of Well 153.

quantity of shells necessary for the production of only a small amount of dye. As mentioned above, thousands of intact and broken murex, the primary byproduct of the dyeing process, were found in the fill of nearby Well 153 (see Fig. 12.1). In addition, it is likely that shell middens, not yet excavated, are located in the vicinity of Area B2.

The next step involved salting the flesh, primarily to prevent decomposition, and exposing it to the sun and air for a few days (Pliny, *NH*, IX.62, 133; see also Forbes 1964:118; Reese 1980:83). To this end, the flesh might have been laid out in the spacious Basin 154 with the salt water, readily available from the nearby sea, collecting in Drain 155. Afterwards the mass of flesh was collected, combined in vats with five to six times the amount of water, and slowly heated for several days. Fresh water for this purpose could easily have been carried from Well 153 or the nearby wadi. At the end of this stage, once the dye had been extracted from the gland, the inspissated liquid was strained out of the vats. Unfortunately, neither the vats nor the means to heat them were found in Area B2. Finally, the textile was dipped in basins filled with the dye solution. Basins 179 and 180, which were set into a bench along the southern wall of Room 156, probably served in this capacity. Petrie excavated numerous similar basins stained dark blue that were part of a late Hellenistic-period 'dyers' workshop' at Athribis in northern Upper Egypt (1908:11, Pl. 35).

The end result was a highly prized textile dyed some shade of purple (Heb. אַרְגָּמָן [red-purple], תְּכֵלֶת [blue-purple]; Gk. πορφύρα). In the case of Tel Mor, where the overwhelming majority of the shells were *M. brandaris*, the shade was probably closer to violet-pink. Perhaps dyed cloth from Tel Mor was among Judas Maccabeus' plunder following his victory over the Seleucid general Gorgias at Emmaus (Horn 1968:21). Soon after pursuing their enemies as far as Azotus (Ashdod) and Jamnia (Yavné), Judas' men "seized much gold and silver and (cloth dyed) dark blue and sea purple (πορφύραν θαλασσίαν) and great riches" (1 Macc 4:15, 23). The date of this battle (i.e., 165 BCE) falls well within the chronological range of Stratum I and its purple dye industry, which, according to the excavators, existed from *c.* 300 BCE until the latter half of the second century BCE (M. Dothan 1993:1074).

Only a few dressed stone walls (W46–W48) from a small building (K) were found on the southeastern corner of the tell's summit (Fig. 2.38; see Plan 2.6). These walls were preserved to an approximate height of 0.3 m, and, as excavated, partially enclosed a room (L49). It is likely that much of Building K had been lost to erosion. It was not reported whether Stratum I, either on the summit of the tell or at the base of its eastern slope, was destroyed or simply fell out of use.

Fig. 2.38. Building K, looking northwest.

ROMAN PERIOD

The main surviving feature from the Roman period at Tel Mor was a well (L55), located on the tell's summit (see Plan 2.6). As mentioned in Chapter 1, the excavators, who cleared the top *c.* 14 m of the shaft, dated the well to the Hellenistic period. Nir and Eldar, as part of the Geological Survey of Israel, cleared the entire shaft and tentatively assigned the well to the Late Roman period (1986:14–16). The later dating is favored here for three reasons: (1) the complete clearing of the well shaft produced mostly Roman, some Iron Age and Persian, but no Hellenistic pottery; (2) the majority of the 15 coins retrieved were dated by Meshorer to the fourth century CE; and (3) the top level of the well (24.35 m) was approximately 2 m higher (even after taking into account the 2 m difference in elevation created by the slope of the tell) than the top levels of Building K's walls (*c.* 20.3 m), which were the only Hellenistic features on the summit.

The sides of Well 55 were revetted to a depth of 12.8 m with roughly hewn stones, set in alternating, horizontally and vertically laid courses; after this point the shaft was simply cut from bedrock.[19] Between 9 and 8 m asl, a tunnel was cut into the western side of the well shaft. The tunnel was at least 10 m long and only 1 m high. Across from the opening into the tunnel, which was *c.* 0.6 m in diameter, a niche was carved into the eastern side of the shaft. Most of the pottery came from this level (9–8 m asl) within the well. From this point down to 2.5 m asl, the well fill was primarily comprised of stone rubble. Other than this well, a Late Roman winepress is mentioned in an IDAM file from the 1950s (see Chapter 1, Site Identification and Discovery), and Dothan refers vaguely to a 'poor agricultural settlement' during the Roman–Byzantine period (1993:1074).

None of the finds associated with this architecture were present in the IAA's collection. Donald T. Ariel, however, recently located an intrusive Herodian coin found in a poorly stratified, early Iron Age context (see Appendix 1).

LATER PERIODS

For many centuries after the Roman–Byzantine period, Tel Mor was abandoned, perhaps until the early modern period.[20] Prior to excavations it appears that there was a small, dilapidated, domed structure on the summit (Figs. 2.39, 2.40). It was built of stone, plastered, and stood approximately 3 m high. Its general appearance and prominent location atop a low mound suggest that it was a sheikh's tomb or *welî*, probably from the Ottoman period (A. Petersen, pers. comm.).[21] Of the various architectural features common to these structures (Canaan 1924:10–18), only the dome (*qubbeh*) and, perhaps, a single door, are discernible from the photograph.

Fig. 2.39. General view of the welî, probably of the Ottoman period, on the summit of the tell.

Awliâ (pl. of *welî*) are commonly associated with Muslim cemeteries, as at Tel Nagila, Tell el-Hesi, Tel 'Erani and Gezer (for references, see Toombs 1985:16–17, 30–32). As noted in the introduction, Ory reported that local Arabs buried their children on the tell as recently as the Mandate period (see Chapter 1, Site Identification and Discovery). Dothan's excavations brought to light at least 17 burials from this cemetery (Loci 1–9, 101–107, 112, 125[?]), many of which, indeed, appear to have belonged to children.

Most of the burials were simple cists dug no deeper than half a meter below the surface and covered by flat stone slabs (Loci 4, 5, 102–105, 107, 125; Figs. 2.41–2.43; see Plan 2.3). More than a third of the classifiable Ottoman-period burials at Tell el-Hesi (n = 108), where the largest Muslim cemetery in Palestine has thus far been excavated, were of the same construction (Type II; Toombs 1985:38). It is likely that the sides of Burial 103 at Tel Mor were also lined with stones (Fig. 2.42). The short length (approximately one meter) of most of these cist burials (e.g., Loci 103–105) indicates that they contained children, thus bearing out Ory's report. Locus 125, which is well over a meter long, however, must have held an adult (Fig. 2.43).

The excavators uncovered at least one jar burial, which probably once contained an infant (L112; Fig.

Fig. 2.40. Close-up of the welî.

2.44). Only one such burial was excavated at Tell el-Hesi (Type V; Toombs 1985:39–40, 107, Pls. 26, 27, 84), whereas four were found in the Muslim cemetery at Tel Mevorakh (Type D; Stern 1978:4–5, Fig. 1:1–1:4, Pls. 6:4, 5, 21). Either the base (Tel Mevorakh) or the mouth (Tell el-Hesi) of the jar was removed

Fig. 2.41. Arab Burials 104 and 105.

Fig. 2.42. Arab Burial 103.

Fig. 2.43. Arab Burial 125.

Fig. 2.44. Arab Burial 112.

in order to admit the body. The latter seems to have been the case with Burial 112 at Tel Mor. An unlabeled field photograph from the Tel Mor excavations shows what appears to be a second jar burial containing the skeletal remains of an infant (Fig. 2.45). The intact rim and handles look similar to those belonging to one of the amphorae at Tel Mevorakh, which the excavators dated to the mid-nineteenth century CE or later (Stern 1978:5, Fig. 1:2, Pl. 21:1).

Bodies in Muslim graves are laid out, almost invariably, along a general east–west axis (e.g., Toombs 1985:35–36, 110, 114). Thus, the body or the head could be positioned in such a way that the eyes faced southward in the direction of Mecca (i.e., *qibleh*; see Ashkenazi 1938:110). The rendering of the Arab burials (especially L103) in the main west-to-east section drawing (see Plan 2.3) suggests that they, too, were oriented along this axis. No accompanying grave goods are reported. Common funerary offerings (when present) at other sites include bronze and iron jewelry

Fig. 2.45. Unidentified infant jar burial.

and beads from a variety of materials (e.g., Toombs 1985:91–109). Funerary practices in rural Palestine during the Muslim period were very conservative and, consequently, changed little over time. Thus, it is difficult to date with much precision the cemeteries at Tel Mor and other sites in the region.

NOTES

[1] According to the basket registry, Pit 166 produced no pottery; however, because no pottery was collected from L118 below *c.* 18.3 m, whereas pottery was presumably taken from Pit 166 from as low as *c.* 17.9 m, it is reasonable to assume that L118 pottery collected between 18.3 and 17.9 m belongs, in fact, to Pit 166. Most of this pottery corresponds to Basket B365.

[2] A few years prior to his work at Tel Mor, Moshe Dothan directed excavations at Nahariya, where he uncovered a cultic area that included a small square temple and a *bāmāh* (M. Dothan 1956). Scattered amongst the stones of the *bāmāh* were cultic vessels similar to those found at Tel Mor (see below). It is likely that his discovery of abundant evidence for cultic activity at Nahariya, some of which mirrored the finds at Tel Mor, prompted Dothan to interpret the relatively meager evidence from Tel Mor Stratum XI as belonging to another *bāmāh*.

[3] All walls that belonged to Bronze and Iron Age strata at Tel Mor were made of sun-dried mudbricks; therefore, when encountering the simple description 'wall' in the following discussion, the reader should assume that it was made of this material.

[4] It is assumed that the floor elevations correspond to those shown in the architect's plan of Building A (see Plan 2.1).

[5] For preliminary reports concerning this burial, see M. Dothan 1960a:17, Pl. 2:3 and 1960c:125, Pl. 9:3–5. For Late Bronze Age surface finds on the eastern slope, probably washed out from similar tombs, see Chapter 1. The available evidence strongly suggests that the inhabitants of Tel Mor used this area as a cemetery during the Late Bronze Age. Given the likelihood that Egyptians were among them—certainly in the succeeding strata—it is reasonable to suppose that future excavations might produce anthropoid coffins (cf., for example, Bet She'an [Oren 1973] and Deir el-Balaḥ [T. Dothan 1979]).

[6] According to a preliminary report published after the first season of excavation, Stratum VIII was comprised of only a pit, which might have been used as a granary, and its associated floor (M. Dothan 1960c:125). However, subsequent reports (e.g., M. Dothan 1993:1073), including this one, assign the first occupational phase of Building B to Stratum VIII.

[7] Recent excavations at Ashqelon revealed a substantial segment of a large mudbrick wall that dates to the end of the Late Bronze Age (Phase 21). The wall is *c.* 2.1 m thick (4 cubits) and a significant amount of the associated pottery is Egyptianized (Cross and Stager 2006:130, Plan 1).

[8] After the first season of excavation, Dothan reported a preserved height of 2 m for these walls (1959:272). According to the elevations on the final Strata VIII–VII plan, the tallest height of a preserved wall in Building B is 1.65 m. Because the mudbrick ramp (L94) of the Stratum VI Building F rested directly on top of W66 (see Plan 2.5), it is possible that courses of the Stratum VI ramp were, in this instance, erroneously attributed to the Strata VIII–VII wall.

[9] The Stratum VII fortified structure at Deir el-Balaḥ has towers at the corners, but not true wall buttresses (T. Dothan 1993:343; and more recently Killebrew, Goldberg and Rosen 2006: Figs. 3, 17).

[10] Note, however, the tentative suggestion that the main building in Block VII may have functioned as a temple (Wheeler 1967:9). The excavators provide no data, either in terms of the architecture or associated finds, to support this proposal.

[11] This locus number was in use from Stratum VII through IX. It seems that L111 was assigned first to a room in Building E of Stratum VII, then to a fill that corresponded in elevation to Stratum VIII and, finally, to a room in Building A of Stratum IX.

[12] The erosion must have occurred sometime after Stratum V (mid-twelfth century BCE)—most likely following the site's abandonment in the tenth century BCE (Stratum II)—and before the Hellenistic period (Stratum I). Otherwise it is difficult to explain the construction of Building K in Stratum I over part of the southeastern half of Building F (see Plan 2.6). Moreover, the top levels of Building K's walls (*c.* 20.3 m) are lower in elevation than Building F's floors (*c.* 22.1 m).

[13] Building B, which has a significantly different architectural plan, is also referred to sometimes as a *migdol* (e.g., Yadin 1963:95; James and McGovern 1993:57). Used so broadly, the term has little typological value.

[14] It is surprising that Building F was located downwind from the foundries. The inhabitants of the Hellenistic period, on the other hand, seem to have taken into account the westerly winds that predominate along the Levantine coast for most of the year (*Mediterranean Pilot* 1988:19): installations for the production of purple dye were situated at the base of the eastern slope (see below, Stratum I).

[15] According to the stratum plan, L81 is an area; however, according to the locus list, it is either an installation or an area. In the photographs published here, it is clearly an installation.

[16] Unfortunately, as mentioned above (see Chapter 1), the draft stratigraphic summary covered only Strata XII–VI. For Strata V–II the primary sources of stratigraphic data were architectural plans, section drawings and the locus list. For Stratum I there were also the daily notebooks for Area B2, where the majority of Hellenistic architecture and pottery was found.

[17] Note, however, that W22 of Stratum IV is located farther west than the corresponding W93 of Stratum V.

[18] Ephraim Stern, who supervised excavations in the area, reports that there was a "plastered basin with three small pools cut into the slope of the mound, one below the other" (1994:198). On the same point, Dothan refers to "several plastered pools connected by pipes" (e.g., 1993:1074). Aside from Basins 179 and 180 (see below), which do not seem to be connected, these other pools are absent from photographs and plans of Area B2.

[19] This description of Well 55 is based on the report by Nir and Eldar (1986:15). For photographs of the well, see Fig. 8 on p. 12 and Fig. 10 on p. 17 therein.

[20] There is, however, an Early Islamic pilgrim flask, reportedly from Tel Mor, on display at the Ashdod Museum. A cursory analysis suggests that it may date to the late Umayyad or early Abbasid period (A. de Vincenz, pers. comm.).

[21] There was also a Muslim *maqām* dedicated to the prophet Jonah less than 1 km away at Nebi Yunis (Petersen 2001:159).

CHAPTER 3

CANAANITE AND PHILISTINE POTTERY

The locally produced Canaanite pottery is divided into the following morphological types: bowls; chalices and tripods; kraters; cooking pots; storage jars, amphoriskoi and pithoi; jugs and juglets; flasks; lamps; and miscellaneous. Subtypes, which pertain especially to bowls, are described, broadly speaking, in order of frequency. In order to demonstrate the general continuity in ceramic style and production at Tel Mor, each vessel type is presented individually as it developed over time. The Philistine pottery is treated as a separate assemblage at the end of the chapter.

Because of the relatively small size of the corpus and the questionable stratigraphic context of some of the pottery, a typology specific to Tel Mor was generally not employed. Furthermore, the ceramic assemblage for most of the strata is represented mainly by sherds, whole vessels having rarely survived. Reference is made to well-established types from other sites whenever possible (Table 3.1). From south to north, these sites include: Tel Seraʿ (Oren 1984); Deir el-Balaḥ (Gould, forthcoming); Lakhish (Tufnell, Inge and Harding 1940; Tufnell 1953, 1958; Ussishkin 1983; Yannai 1996, 2004; Clamer 2004a, 2004b, Singer-Avitz 2004a); Bet Shemesh (Grant and Wright 1938); Tel Miqne-ʿEqron (T. Dothan 1998; Killebrew 1998a; Ortiz 2000; Dothan, Gitin and Zukerman 2006); Ashdod (Dothan and Freedman 1967; M. Dothan 1971; Dothan and Porath 1982, 1993; Ben-Shlomo 2005); Tel Baṭash-Timna (Mazar and Panitz-Cohen 2001; Panitz-Cohen and Mazar 2006); Gezer (Dever, Lance and Wright 1970; Dever et al. 1974; Dever 1986; Seger 1988); Tel Afeq (Beck and Kochavi 1985; Kochavi, Gadot and Yannai, forthcoming); Tell Qasile (A. Mazar 1985); Shechem (Seger 1974; Dever 1974); Bet Sheʾan (Fitzgerald 1930; Oren 1973; James 1966; Yadin and Geva 1986; James and McGovern 1993); Megiddo

Table 3.1. Sites with Comparative Ceramic Material (listed south to north)

Site	Parallel Strata				
	Tel Mor XII–X	Tel Mor IX	Tel Mor VIII–VII	Tel Mor VI–V	Tel Mor IV–III
Tel Seraʿ				IX	
Deir el-Balaḥ				6–4	
Lakhish	VIII, P-4–3	VII, S-3–1, P-2	VII, P-1	VI	VI–V
Bet Shemesh	V	IV	IV	IV–III	
Tel Miqne-ʿEqron		IX	VIII	VII	VI–IV
Ashdod	XXIII–XVIII	XVII–XVI	XV–XIV	XIV–XIII	XII–X
Tel Baṭash-Timna	XI–VIII	VII	VI	VI	V–IV
Gezer	XIX–XVII	XVI	XIV	XIII	XIII–XI
Tel Afeq	X-15–14	X-13	X-12	X-12	
Tell Qasile				XII	XI–X
Shechem	XVI–XIV				
Bet Sheʾan	XA–IXB			VIIA–VIB	
Megiddo	X–IX, F-11–10	VIII		VII	
Tel Dor				Ir1a	Ir1a (late), Ir1b
Tel Yoqneʿam	XXI–XX				
Ḥazor	XVI–XV	XIV–XIII			

(Guy 1938; Loud 1948; Ilan, Hallote and Cline 2000; Gadot, Yasur-Landau and Ilan 2006); Tel Dor (Gilboa 2001b; Gilboa and Sharon 2003); Tel Yoqne'am (Ben-Ami 2005; Ben-Ami and Livneh 2005); and Ḥazor (Yadin et al. 1958; 1960; 1961; 1989). In terms of these typological parallels, proximity dictates priority. For this reason, special reference is made to the nearby regional center of Ashdod. Note that the provision of parallels is by no means exhaustive.

A few comments about the fabric typical of the locally produced pottery at Tel Mor can be offered. Four types of sediment are present in the Ashdod area: kurkar, ḥamra, alluvial loess and dune sand (Bakler 1982). The main outcrop at Tel Ashdod is ḥamra, which was probably the primary raw material used to make pottery at the site. It is likely that any pottery produced at Tel Mor, which is located directly within the alluvial basin of Naḥal Lakhish, on the other hand, was made principally from loessial soils, more specifically, coastal loess that contains quartz with abundant heavy minerals (Mazar and Panitz-Cohen 2001:18; Master 2003:55). A Stratum XII jar base, for example, was found to contain mostly quartz, along with hornblende, minerals of the mica group and feldspar (A. Cohen-Weinberger, pers. comm.; see also Chapter 7, No. 6, n. 21).

The locally produced pottery at Tel Mor, with the exception of cooking pots, is made of clays that fire to a light red (2.5YR 6/6), red (10R 5/6) or reddish yellow (5YR 6/6). The colors of the surface (including slip and paint) and fabric were assigned according to the revised edition of the *Munsell Soil Color Charts* (2000). In order to view the true color of the fabric, most sherds were freshly broken with a 'nail-puller'. By so doing, it was also possible to see more clearly the type, size and quantity of inclusions. Approximately half of the sherds have a gray core, an indication of uneven firing conditions. White (carbonate), sparkling (micaceous) and dark inclusions are common.

Various other methods were employed to inspect the fabric visible in these fresh breaks. First, a magnifying glass with a ×150 magnification was used. Second, some freshly broken sherds were placed on a flatbed scanner and scanned at a high resolution (650 dpi). Finally, and most successfully, sherds were photographed with a stereomicroscope. For pottery containing straw temper, a hallmark of the Egyptianized and some Canaanite pottery, it was important to clip the sherds parallel to the wheel marks. Because straw is orientated horizontally during the vessel formation process, it would appear as a single point of organic temper (or a void if burnt out) in a cross section perpendicular to the wheel marks.

The surface is almost always left untreated; however, a self-slip frequently causes the surface color to assume a lighter shade than the fabric. A self-slip is created by the application of an emulsion of the same clay in water, either by dipping or wiping the vessel. Under the heading of 'Description' in the tables accompanying the figures, the first entry describes all treatments carried out by the potter that affected the exterior of the vessel. These include wheel marks created during the formation process (i.e., 'rilling'), as well as the deliberate treatments of painting, slipping, burnishing, scraping, combing and incising.

Missing information about stratigraphic context and pottery description appears as N/A ('not available') in the figure tables.

CANAANITE POTTERY

CONTEXTS AND PARALLEL MATERIAL

Strata XII–X

As noted in the preceding chapter, the separation of early strata (i.e., XII–X) at Tel Mor is not based on clear stratigraphic evidence. Indeed, no real architecture accompanies these strata. Instead it is based on elevation and ceramic typology, the latter of which is susceptible to circular reasoning. This stratigraphic conundrum is compounded by a typological difficulty—namely, that MB IIC and LB I pottery assemblages have much in common. For these reasons, the Strata XII–X Canaanite pottery is presented here together. Notwithstanding, clear examples of MB IIC or LB I pottery are duly noted, as is the stratum to which every vessel and sherd was originally assigned. For example, the majority of the finer, thin-walled vessels are derived from Stratum XII, whereas the pottery from Strata XI–X tends to have thicker walls and less well-levigated clay.

Strata XII–X, which correspond to MB IIC and LB I, are roughly coeval with Strata XXIII–XVIII at Ashdod. Other well-stratified and published sites in southern Canaan from these periods include Lakhish Stratum VIII and Levels P-4–3, Bet Shemesh Stratum V, Tel Baṭash-Timna Strata XI–VIII, Gezer Strata XIX–XVII and Tel Afeq Strata X-15–14.[1] Important sites in the north are Shechem Strata XVI–XIV, Bet She'an Strata XA–IXB, Megiddo Strata X–IX and F-11–10, Tel Yoqne'am Strata XXI–XX and Ḥazor Strata XVI–XV. Because the majority of the Canaanite vessel types found at Tel Mor in Strata XII–X are fairly common, reference is made only to the above sites in most cases.

Courtyard 118 produced virtually all the pottery from Strata XII–X. In the northern half of this locus is Pit 166 (see Plans 2.1, 2.2), which yielded 100 registered sherds and whole vessels. Pit 166 is the most secure context of the first three strata at Tel Mor and contained the earliest pottery at the site.

Stratum IX

There are no significant differences between the fabric of the locally produced pottery of Strata XII–X as opposed to Stratum IX or the rest of the Late Bronze Age (Strata VIII–V). The color and types of inclusions are roughly the same and the manufacturing techniques appear to have been similar. The tendency during the Late Bronze Age for clay to be less well levigated and fabric to be unevenly fired as compared to the Middle Bronze Age, however, is occasionally evident at Tel Mor.

The most important sites for comparative purposes are largely the same as for the previous strata. The relevant strata for Tel Mor IX, which corresponds approximately to LB IIA, are as follows: Ashdod XVII–XVI; Lakhish VII and Levels S-3–1 and P-2; Bet Shemesh IV; Tel Miqne-'Eqron IX, Tel Baṭash-Timna VII; Gezer XVI and the Upper Tomb phase of Cave I.10A; Tel Afeq X-13; Megiddo VIII; and Ḥazor XIV–XIII. The presence of coherent architecture (Building A) for the first time at Tel Mor in Stratum IX allows for the examination of room assemblages, particularly Room 111, from which 16 baskets of pottery were recovered and 162 sherds registered.

Strata VIII–VII

The main development of the two combined Strata VIII–VII, which correspond roughly to LB IIB, is the appearance of a significant amount of Egyptianized pottery. Because this pottery, which comprises almost 10% of the total Stratum VII assemblage, is presented separately (see Chapter 4), the quantity of Canaanite pottery described here will seem small relative to previous strata. Aside from the introduction of distinctive Egyptianized forms and fabric, the ceramic assemblage of Strata VIII–VII evolved gradually from previous periods. Notable in these and later strata is the increasing amount of hybridization—namely, the production of

typical Canaanite forms using an Egyptianized, straw-tempered fabric (e.g., Figs. 3.7:11, 12, 18; 3.9).

Building B, which dominated the summit during Strata VIII–VII, yielded the best stratified material during this period; however, only the largely intact Rooms 63 (8 baskets, 56 registered sherds) and 75 (10 baskets, 83 registered sherds) produced a significant amount of pottery. Otherwise, the greatest quantity of pottery, by far, from a reasonably secure Strata VIII–VII context was excavated in Area 128 (22 baskets, 242 registered sherds). The most relevant sites for comparative purposes, all of which are located in the coastal plain and Shephelah, are Ashdod Strata XV–XIV, Lakhish Stratum VII and Level P-1, Bet Shemesh Stratum IV, Tel Miqne-'Eqron Stratum VIII, Tel Baṭash-Timna Stratum VI, Gezer Stratum XIV and Tel Afeq Stratum X-12.

Strata VI–V

In general the pottery of Strata VI–V, which corresponds roughly to the first half of the twelfth century, is a continuation of the Canaanite tradition of preceding strata. There appears to have been no significant changes in terms of pottery fabric, forms or manufacturing techniques. From the perspective of pottery alone, it seems that, after a brief period of abandonment, the inhabitants of Tel Mor Stratum VII rebuilt and resettled the site in Stratum VI.

Room 71 of Building F was by far the most secure and productive context in Strata VI–V. All four walls were preserved to a considerable height and a thick destruction level was uncovered on its Stratum VI floor (see Fig. 2.29). Given that Stratum V ended in abandonment, it is reasonable to suppose that all or most of the intact vessels from Building F belong to the Stratum VI destruction level. A total of 35 baskets were retrieved and 112 items—sherds as well as intact vessels—were registered from Room 71. In the adjacent and smaller Building H from Stratum V, Room 34 produced 3 baskets and 54 registered sherds. Pit 35 yielded 9 baskets and 39 sherds.

Strata from the following sites have produced the best parallels for the pottery from Tel Mor VI–V: Ashdod XIV–XIII; Tel Sera' IX; Deir el-Balaḥ 6–4; Lakhish VI and Fosse Temple III; Bet Shemesh IV–III; Tel Miqne-'Eqron VII; Tel Baṭash-Timna VI; Gezer XIII; Tel Afeq X-12; Tell Qasile XII; Bet She'an VIIA–VIB; Megiddo VII; and Dor in the Ir1a horizon.

Strata IV–II

There were significant changes in the types of pottery present in Strata IV–II as compared to the previous strata. In terms of the vessel forms in the Canaanite tradition, however, continuity remains the rule. In Stratum IV, which corresponds to the second half of the twelfth and beginning of the eleventh centuries, Egyptianized pottery virtually disappears and Philistine pottery makes its first appearance (see below). In the following Stratum III, which may have lasted into the tenth century, Philistine pottery continues and is joined by Red Slip Burnished Ware (see Fig. 3.11). Very little pottery was excavated in Stratum II. Moreover, none of this pottery derives from secure stratigraphic contexts.

There were also major changes in terms of architecture after the abandonment of Stratum V. No longer did a single building dominate the site as had been the case for centuries at Tel Mor (i.e., Building A of Stratum IX, Building B of Strata VIII–VII, Building F of Strata VI–V). In its place on the summit was either a poorly preserved structure (Building I of Stratum IV) or a semi-enclosed space surrounded by pits (L17, L18, L23 and L126 of Stratum III). Unfortunately, very little pottery was retrieved from Building I, the only source of stratigraphically secure contexts in Stratum IV. Indeed, only about 150 sherds were registered for this stratum overall. As for Stratum III, Pit 17 is the single locus that produced a substantial amount of pottery (14 baskets, 73 registered sherds and whole vessels).

The Tel Mor Strata IV–III ceramic assemblage corresponds broadly to the pottery from the following regional sites: Ashdod Strata XII–X; Lakhish Strata VI–V; Tel Miqne-'Eqron Strata VI–IV; Tel Baṭash-Timna Strata V–IV; Gezer Strata XIII–XI; and Tell Qasile Strata XI–X. Farther north, the Iron 1a (late) and Iron 1b horizons at Tel Dor (Area B1, Phase 12 and Area G, Phases 9 and 8/7) also provide good parallels. Tel Mor Stratum II was so poorly stratified that the provision of parallel strata from neighboring sites would be misleading.

TYPOLOGY

Bowls

Strata XII–X (Figs 3.1–3.5)

The corpus of bowls from Strata XII–X can be divided into two main groups based on the absence or presence

of carination. The uncarinated bowls can be further subdivided on the basis of whether or not the rim has been thickened, inverted, everted or otherwise modified. As always there are intermediate types and vessels that fall outside this or any classificatory system.

Several shallow (or platter) bowls with a plain rim and rounded sides were excavated in Strata XII–XI (Fig. 3.1:1–7). This simple bowl type is common during both MB IIC and LB I. It has been found in MB IIC contexts at Ḥazor Area D in Stratum 1 (Yadin et al. 1958: Pl. 103:1) and Megiddo in Tomb 24 (Guy 1938: Pl. 23:5); and in LB I contexts at Bet She'an in Tomb 42 (Oren 1973: Fig. 27:4), Tel Yoqne'am in Stratum XXa (Ben-Ami 2005: Fig. III.6:7–11 [= CIIa]) and Tel Baṭash-Timna in Stratum IX (Panitz-Cohen and Mazar 2006: Pl. 16:1, 3). The same rim appears on a Strata XII–XI chalice from Tel Mor (see Fig. 3.12:1), thus raising the possibility that some of these bowls may, in fact, be chalices.

Figure 3.1:8 is a similar type of bowl except for the slightly thickened rim, a tendency evident also in Fig. 3.1:7. The former bowl was recovered at an elevation associated with Stratum XI (i.e., above 19.10 m asl) and, indeed, close parallels derive from LB I and later contexts as at Gezer in Cave I.10A (Seger 1988:80, Pl. 9:10) and Ḥazor in Stratum XV (Yadin et al. 1989: Pl. 157:15). Figure 3.1:9, on the other hand, has an unusually tapered rim that almost forms a gutter.

Some shallow bowls have a slightly inverted rim (Fig. 3.1:10–13). These platter bowls also are common in both MB IIC and LB I strata. For example, they are known from MB IIC contexts at Shechem in the Foundation Phase of the East Gate (Seger 1974: Figs. 3:20, 21, 23; 5:3–5; 6:39, 40); Megiddo in Strata XI–IX (Ilan, Hallote and Cline 2000:186, Fig. 9.1:2, 4); and Ḥazor in Area D, Stratum 4 (Yadin et al. 1958: Pl. 119:3, 5, 6) and in Area H, Stratum 3 (Yadin et al. 1989: Pl. 259:3–5); and from an LB I context at Bet She'an in Tomb 42 (Oren 1973: Fig. 27:15). Figure 3.1:10, which is completely intact, has an uneven rim and a high ring base.

The two deep bowls with plain rim, rounded sides and concave disk base (Fig. 3.1:14, 15), which were excavated at a relatively high elevation in Courtyard 118 (i.e., above 20 m asl), belong more to the Late Bronze Age tradition. Comparable bowls have been found at Lakhish in Tombs 501 and 532 (Tufnell 1958: Pl. 70:599, 610 [Curved Bowl, Class H]), Tel Baṭash-Timna in Stratum VII (Panitz-Cohen and Mazar 2006:

Pl. 38:1–3) and Tel Afeq in Stratum X-14 (Kochavi, Gadot and Yannai, forthcoming: Type BH2). Figure 3.1:16, which appears to be a smaller version of these bowls, may in fact belong to a chalice.

Figure 3.1:17 is a deep bowl that is slipped and burnished on both the exterior and interior. The tip of the rim is slightly everted and it has a double-coil handle with a 'button' or 'pellet', which is a typical feature of the late MB II (see M. Dothan 1973:5, Fig. 3:8). The double-coil handle, with or without the button, is a common feature of MB II pottery, but primarily on jugs and juglets, as at Ashdod in Stratum XXIIa (Dothan and Porath 1993:25, Fig. 3:11, Pl. 30:9). The presence of such a handle on a bowl is unusual. It comes from Pit 166, the earliest and best stratified Stratum XII context. Its contents, which correspond primarily to Basket 365, include Cypriot Monochrome (see Fig. 5.1:1, 3), Base Ring I bowls (see Fig. 5.3:3, 5) and Bichrome Ware (see Fig. 5.7:3, 5, 9).

Figure 3.1:18 is a deep bowl with a simple rim, loop handles, rounded sides and ring base. The second handle is reconstructed based on parallels. Rilling and wet-smooth marks are visible on the exterior. Similar bowls, but with an internally thickened rim, have been found in the following MB II contexts: Lakhish in Tombs 129 and 1552 (Tufnell 1958:180, Pl. 69:579, 580 [Carinate Bowl, Class F]), Tel Baṭash-Timna in Stratum XII (Panitz-Cohen and Mazar 2006: Pl. 5:4) and Ḥazor Area D in Stratum 2 (Yadin et al. 1958: Pl. 101:1).

Figure 3.2:1 and 2 have a simple rim and thick, straight side-walls with prominent rilling on the exterior. Manufacturing techniques evident with these bowls, such as the use of straw temper and the decision not to smooth out heavy rilling marks, may betray an early Egyptian influence on ceramic production at the site (see Chapter 4). No parallels for this bowl type have been found. Figure 3.2:3 is similar in terms of the overall shape of the vessel and the thickness of its side-walls, but lacks the prominent rilling and straw temper.

Figure 3.2:4–7 are shallow bowls with thickened, almost bulbous, rims and rilling visible on the exterior. Its smaller size and slightly everted rim set Fig. 3.2:6 apart somewhat from this group. The closest parallel for this bowl may be found in the Lower Tomb Phase of Cave I.10A at Gezer (Seger 1988: Pl. 33:11). Figure 3.2:8 and 9 are shallow bowls with slightly everted rims.

Only a few bowls with an internally thickened rim, a common trait throughout MB IIC and LB I, were discovered at Tel Mor (Fig. 3.2:10–12). Figure 3.2:11 is a much larger and heavier version of Fig. 3.2:10. Unusually thick side-walls, a flattened rim and coarse fabric distinguish Fig. 3.2:12. Similar bowls were excavated at Tel Yoqne‘am in Stratum XXIIIa (MB IIB; Ben-Ami and Livneh 2005: Fig. IV.4:6 [Type DVI]) and in Phase 2 of the Northwest Gate area at Shechem (MB IIC; Dever 1974: Fig. 13:20). Two bowls, which vary considerably in terms of size, have rims that were folded out and over so as to form a flange (Fig. 3.2:13, 14). Similar bowls have been found at Ashdod in Stratum XVII (M. Dothan 1971:81, Fig. 32:11, Pl. 30:6) and Gezer in Strata XIX–XVIII (Dever 1986: Pl. 5:23, 24), the latter of which are red slipped and burnished. Another bowl with a flange rim was retrieved at Tel Mor from a questionable Stratum IX context (see Fig. 3.6:17).

Figure 3.2:15 is a curlicue or spiral projection that originally was attached to the rim of a bowl (see also M. Dothan 1973:5, Fig. 3:4). Such decoration first appeared on bowls during MB IIA and continued through MB IIC (Amiran 1969:91). Typically two (e.g., Tel Baṭash-Timna Stratum X; Panitz-Cohen and Mazar 2006: Pl. 15:2) or four curlicues (e.g., Megiddo Tomb 3081 [Stratum XI]; Loud 1948: Pl. 38:10) were evenly spaced and attached horizontally around the rims of round-sided bowls. Wooden bowls with this type of decoration were recovered from Middle Bronze Age tombs at Jericho (H6 and H18; Kenyon 1960: Fig. 202).

Carinated bowls, a hallmark of MB IIC and LB I, are common in the early strata at Tel Mor. Equal numbers and a similar range of subtypes are found across Strata XII and XI. Apart from their bases, there is little to distinguish carinated bowls from chalices during this period (cf. Fig. 3.12:5, 6); therefore, given that only their rims survive in most cases, some of the bowls discussed here may in fact be chalices. The carinated bowls from Tel Mor roughly fall into two groups with the following morphological features: generally deeper, sharply carinated bowls possessing rims with greater eversion (Fig. 3.3:1–9); as opposed to shallower, softly carinated bowls with less everted rims (Fig. 3.3:10–21). Bowls in both groups have ring bases.

Middle Bronze Age IIC and LB I tombs provide the best comparisons for both subgroups. Parallels for the first subtype may be found at the following sites: Ashdod in Stratum XXIIa (Dothan and Porath 1993:24, Fig. 2:8, Pl. 30:5); Lakhish in Tombs 129 and 1502 (MB II–III; Tufnell 1958:178–179, Pls. 68:510 [Class A], 69:542, 543 [Class C]) and Levels P-4 (Singer-Avitz 2004a: Figs. 16.20:2, 3; 23:1; 24:1, 2) and P-3 (Figs. 16.30:6–8; 33:2); Gezer in Cave I.10A (MB IIC; Seger 1988:73, Pl. 32:1); Tel Batash-Timna in Stratum XI–X (Panitz-Cohen and Mazar 2006: Pls. 6:18–20; 10:3, 5, 10, 11); and Bet She'an in Tomb 42 (LB I; Oren 1973: Fig. 28:33). Parallels for the second subtype occur at Ashdod in Stratum XX (Dothan and Porath 1993:27, Fig. 4:5), Lakhish in Tomb 119 (MB III; Tufnell 1958:178, Pl. 68:501 [Class A]), Gezer in Cave I.10A (Seger 1988:73, Pl. 32:2, 4), Megiddo in Tomb 856 (LB I; Guy 1938: Pl. 44:9) and Bet She'an in Tomb 42; Fig. 3.3:10 has the sunken center on the inside of the bowl and trumpet-like base typical of the Class G carinated bowls found in the Northern Cemetery at Bet She'an (Oren 1973:71–73, Fig. 28:1– 21 [Class G]).

Conspicuously absent at Tel Mor is the type of bowl/ chalice characterized by an exaggerated carination at a lower point on the side-wall (e.g., Amiran 1969: Pl. 27:18–24). Such bowls and chalices are typical of the end of MB IIC, as at Shechem in the Foundation Phase of the East Gate (Seger 1974: Figs. 3:12, 16–18, 4:21, 6:29, 31, 32). A more rounded carination, at the point of the vessel's maximum diameter, characterizes Fig. 3.3:22, 23. Figure 3.3:24 is an unusually deep carinated bowl.

Both carinated and uncarinated bowls, as well as other vessel types from Strata XII–X, frequently have ring bases (e.g., Figs. 3.1:10, 18; 3.3:4, 5, 9–11, 15, 24; 3.4:2–10, 13, 14; cf. Amiran 1969:91). These ring bases are often high on carinated bowls (cf., however, Fig. 3.3:9), sometimes to the point of making the bowl a chalice (Fig. 3.3:10, 11). On the interior of one bowl with a ring base (Fig. 3.4:2) is an omphalos, a feature that first appears during the Middle Bronze Age and continues into the Late Bronze Age. Concave disk bases, which first appear in Canaan at the end of the Middle Bronze Age, are less common than ring bases on all types of vessels at Tel Mor, especially during the Late Bronze Age (e.g., Figs. 3.1:14, 15; 3.4:1). Concave disk bases may be found, for example, in MB IIC strata at Shechem in Phase 2 of the Northwest Gate Area (Dever 1974: Fig. 13:25) and in Strata XI–X at Megiddo (Ilan, Hallote and Cline 2000: Fig. 9.2:11).

Flat bases do not appear on bowls until Stratum IX at Tel Mor (e.g., Fig. 3.6:14).

Two miniature bowls were assigned to Stratum XII (Fig. 3.5:1, 2). Several miniature bowls were discovered together in an area of Stratum XI known as the *bāmāh* (Fig. 3.5:3–8; see also Fig. 2.3; M. Dothan 1960a: Pl. I:3). Some of the bowls (e.g., Fig. 3.5:4, 5, 7) look very much like smaller versions of the familiar MB IIC–LB I carinated bowls discussed above. The uneven and/or string-cut bases of others (Fig. 3.5:1, 6) betray careless manufacture. Elsewhere in Canaan, similar miniature bowls appear in Late Bronze Age funerary (e.g., Megiddo; Guy 1938: Pl. 40:17 [Tomb 38]; Loud 1948: Pl. 53:5) and settlement contexts (e.g., Hazor; Yadin et al. 1989: Pls. 269:1–20; 293:15). Numerous votive bowls were recovered also from the various strata of the MB IIB cultic area at Nahariya (M. Dothan 1956:19, Fig. 5:1, 2). Lamps with seven wicks were associated with *bāmôt* at both Nahariya (cf. M. Dothan 1956: Fig. 4) and Tel Mor (see Fig. 3.30:1). Also from the area of the Tel Mor *bāmāh* were chalices (see, e.g., Fig. 3.12:6), an Egyptian slender ovoid jar (see Fig. 4.10:1) and the antlers of a fallow deer belonging to the species *Dama mesopotamica* (see Fig. 11.2).

Stratum IX (Fig. 3.6)

There were far fewer carinated bowls in Stratum IX than in Strata XII–X. Of those that were recovered from Stratum IX, the majority (Fig. 3.6:1–3) resemble bowls from MB IIC and LB I strata at Tel Mor and other sites, such as Tel Batash-Timna Stratum X (Panitz-Cohen and Mazar 2006: Pl. 10:5), Lakhish Tomb 1552 (Tufnell 1958: Pls. 50:1, 68:510) and Gezer Strata XIX–XVIII (Dever 1986: Pl. 7:20, 21). Because the Tel Mor carinated bowls found on the summit of the tell either derive from questionable contexts (Fig. 3.6:1) or survive only as rim sherds (Fig. 3.6:2, 3), it is likely that they are residual from earlier strata.

Figure 3.6:4 is an intact carinated bowl that was part of the assemblage of Burial 152 excavated at the base of the eastern slope (see Figs. 2.11, 2.12). It has a slightly everted, simple rim and a ring base. An LB IIA tomb from Lakhish (Tomb 1003) contained bowls quite similar in shape to it (Tufnell 1958: Pl. 69:570, 573 [Class E]). The type was found also at Ashdod in Stratum 3/XVI (Dothan and Freedman 1967: Fig. 17:3) and at Tel Miqne-'Eqron in Stratum IX (Killebrew 1998a: Ill. II:6:1 [Form CA 4]).

There are also two carinated bowls, distinguished by a subtle carination at mid-body, that are clear Late Bronze Age types (Fig. 3.6:5, 6). Late Bronze Age I parallels may be found at Tel Afeq in Stratum X-14 (Kochavi, Gadot and Yannai, forthcoming: Type BC1) and Tel Baṭash-Timna in Stratum VIII (Panitz-Cohen and Mazar 2006: Pl. 21:6); similar bowls from LB II appear at Gezer in the Upper Tomb Phase of Cave I.10A (Seger 1988: Pls. 14:13, 16:2), Megiddo in Level F-9/Stratum VIII (Ilan, Hallote and Cline 2000: Fig. 9.10:10) and in great quantity at Ḥazor in Stratum 1 (e.g., Yadin et al. 1958: Pls. 91:14, 106:7, 10, 11, 17, 19, 126:26; 1989: Pl. 279:21). At Tel Mor a bowl with a similar carination was found also in Stratum IV, probably in a residual context (see Fig. 3.10:6). Figure 3.6:7 and 8 are shallow bowls with a very slight carination similar to Fig. 3.3:16–19 of the previous strata. Figure 3.6:9 has an internally thickened rim that is slightly everted at its tip. A close parallel occurs at Tel Baṭash-Timna in Stratum VIII (Panitz-Cohen and Mazar 2006: Pl. 27:9).

Figure 3.6:10 is the bowl that covered the mouth of the storage jar (see Fig. 3.22:18), which stood on the northern side of Burial 152's gable (see Figs. 2.10, 2.12). It has a simple rim, rounded sides and a low ring base, the diameter of which is small relative to the size of the body. Similar bowls, but with inturned rims, appear in Strata VI–V (see Fig. 3.8:3–5). A close parallel may be found at Ashdod in Stratum 3/XVI (Dothan and Freedman 1967: Fig. 17:2).

Stratum IX also yielded additional bowls with plain rims and rounded sides (Fig. 3.6:11–13). Flat bases appear on bowls for the first time at Tel Mor in this stratum. The closest parallels for Fig. 3.6:11 derive from LB IIB strata such as Ashdod XV–XIV (Dothan and Freedman 1967: Fig. 22:1–3; Dothan and Porath 1993: Fig. 11:8) and Tel Afeq X-12 (Kochavi, Gadot and Yannai, forthcoming: Type BH5a). The pronounced rilling on the exterior of Fig. 3.6:13 appears on similar bowls from Lakhish Level S-3 (Yannai 2004: Fig. 19.9:2 [Group B-4c]) and Gezer XVI (Dever 1986: Pl. 10:4), and in a great number of bowls from Ḥazor 1/XIV–XIII (e.g., Yadin et al. 1958: Pls. 96:2, 125:19; 1989: Pl. 160:2).

Figure 3.6:14 has straight sides, wet-smooth marks around the lower body and a string-cut disk base. It is made of the typical Egyptianized fabric characterized by a large amount of organic temper. Increasing amounts of Canaanite pottery (mostly bowls and kraters) were made from this fabric over time at Tel Mor. Because Canaanite potters occasionally used straw temper also, it is best to reserve the designation 'Egyptianized' for those vessels that were influenced by Egyptian styles not only in terms of fabric, but also other manufacturing techniques and form (see Chapter 4). Hybrid vessels that are Canaanite in form, but made of Egyptianized fabric, appear particularly in Strata VIII–V, where the percentage of truly Egyptianized pottery is higher (e.g., Fig. 3.9). Bowls similar to Fig. 3.6:14, but with different types of bases, come from Lakhish Level S-3 (ring; Yannai 2004: Fig. 19.9:3 [Group B-4c]), Megiddo Stratum VIII (ring; Loud 1948: Fig. 61:12) and Ḥazor Area E (concave disk; Yadin et al. 1958: Pl. 143:9).

Figure 3.6:15 is a shallow bowl with rounded sides and a slightly inturned rim that is similar to bowls from previous strata (cf. Fig. 3.1:12, 13). A comparable bowl from LB IIA for this common type may be found at Gezer in Stratum XVI (Dever 1986: Pl. 10:13). Figure 3.6:16, which has a bulbous rim, also resembles bowls from earlier strata (e.g., Fig. 3.2:3). Figure 3.6:17 has a flange below the rim similar to smaller bowls from Stratum XI (cf. Fig. 3.2:13, 14). The rims of some shallow bowls have been somewhat flattened (Fig. 3.6:18–20), a morphological development that also begins in earlier strata (cf. Fig. 3.1:11). An LB I parallel may be found at Ḥazor in Stratum 2 (Yadin et al. 1989: Pl. 261:27).

Flat bases (Fig. 3.6:11, 24) first appear alongside disk (Fig. 3.6:14) and ring bases (Fig. 3.6:21, 22) at Tel Mor in Stratum IX. Throughout Strata VIII to V flat bases remained popular, particularly on Egyptianized bowls (see Fig. 4.6:5–11). High ring bases disappear in Stratum IX and string-cut bases appear (Fig. 3.6:11), both of which are developments characteristic of the Late Bronze Age.

Strata VIII–VII (Fig. 3.7)
Figure 3.7:1–3 are carinated bowls very much in the tradition of LB I (e.g., Fig. 3.3:6). In light of this affinity and their poor stratigraphic contexts, it is safe to assume that these sherds are residual. Figure 3.7:4 and 5 have a very subtle carination and everted rims. Similar bowls have been published from both Ashdod (M. Dothan 1971: Fig. 81:6) and Gezer in Stratum XIV (Dever 1986: Pl. 16:10).

Figure 3.7:6 and 7 each have a slight carination and a rim that is almost vertical with a faintly defined lip.

This bowl type has early precedents at Tel Mor in Strata XII (see Fig. 3.3:14, 15) and IX (see Fig. 3.6:7). Thirteenth-century parallels, particularly for the deeper bowl (Fig. 3.7:6), may be found at Lakhish in Level VIIA (Yannai 2004: Fig. 19.27:9 [Group B-11]) and Tel Afeq in Stratum X-12 (Kochavi, Gadot and Yannai, forthcoming). Figure 3.7:8 and 9 have rounded sides and slightly inturned rims. The better preserved bowl (Fig. 3.7:8) is more hemispherical with a flat base, similar to larger bowls from later strata at Tel Mor (e.g., Fig. 3.8:5).

Figure 3.7:10–12 have rims that are occasionally bulbous, slightly rounded side-walls and disk bases. The latter two bowls were made with Egyptianized fabric. The form is well attested in such LB IIB and early Iron I strata as Ashdod XV–XIV (Dothan and Porath 1993: Figs. 10:1, 11:3), Gezer XIV (Dever 1986: Pl. 16:11) and Lakhish VI (Yannai 1996: Fig. 18:10; Clamer 2004b: Fig. 20.15:5 [Type I.B.b]). Similar bowls appear also in Stratum VI at Tel Mor (see Fig. 3.8:12). Figure 3.7:13 is a decorated bowl with a bulbous rim. There is a red band on the lip, and the head and part of the upper body of an ibex below the rim. A vertical line, perhaps the trunk of a tree, is barely visible to the right of the ibex.

The bowls depicted in Fig. 3.7:14–17 are characterized by thickened, inturned rims. In most cases the extra clay was folded outward and pinched so as to create a flange (Fig. 3.7:14, 16, 17). Bowls with flanged rims are present throughout the Late Bronze Age at Tel Mor, appearing also in Strata XI–X (see Fig. 3.2:13, 14) and IX (see Fig. 3.6:17). A deep bowl or krater with a flanged rim was found in Stratum VII (see Fig. 3.14:9), after which this type is no longer found at the site.

Figure 3.7:18, which was made with an Egyptianized fabric, has a flattened, inward-sloping rim and a slight carination in the upper part of the side-wall. Bowls with the same rim have been excavated at Tel Miqne-‘Eqron in Stratum VII (Killebrew 1998a: Ill. II:22:3), Tel Baṭash-Timna in Stratum VI (Panitz-Cohen and Mazar 2006: Pl. 55:3) and Bet Shemesh in Stratum IV (Grant and Wright 1938: Pl. 58:1, 8), where the ring base is preserved. Stratum V at Tel Mor produced a similar bowl (see Fig. 3.8:13). It seems, then, that this bowl type is a feature of terminal Late Bronze Age and early Iron Age strata.

Figure 3.7:19 is a deep bowl with a very bulbous rim and an exterior covered with a thick creamy slip. Its non-local fabric probably corresponds to Levantine

Fabric P-30 (D. Aston, pers. comm.), which is similar in appearance to Egyptian Marl F (see Chapter 4). The description of this fabric, as is known from imported vessels found in Egypt, matches very closely that of Fig. 3.7:19:

> . . . distinct zones in section comprising an outer band of red 2.5YR 5/8 and an inner zone of very pale brown 10YR 7/6, though in thicker parts of the pot the inner section fires gray 10YR 6/1. Inclusions within the paste are sand, mica, small translucent pebble and numerous fine limestone particles. The outer surface fires whitish but it is not certain whether this is the result of a slip or a bloom (Aston, Aston and Brock 1998:142, 143).

When found at Egyptian sites, however, Fabric P-30 was used to produce Canaanite storage jars (see also Nicholson and Rose 1985:138 [Fabric III.10]; Aston 1998:70 [Fabric IV.07.05]), whereas Fig. 3.7:19 is a bowl. The other two sherds from Tel Mor likely made from this fabric, on the other hand, belong to Stratum VII storage jars (Fig. 3.23:8 and Reg. No. A305/23 [not drawn]).

Strata VI–V (Figs. 3.8, 3.9)

Two types of bowls in Strata VI–V are typical of the LB IIB/Iron I transitional period: semi-hemispherical bowls with incurving rims and cyma bowls. The former bowls appear (albeit less frequently) in earlier and later strata (see Figs. 3.1:14, 15 [Strata XI–IX], 3.7:8 [Strata VIII–VII], 3.10:8, 9 [Stratum III]), thus demonstrating that they enjoyed a long life at Tel Mor. Various subtypes of this semi-hemispherical bowl were recovered from Strata VI–V. The first is almost perfectly semi-hemispherical with thin walls and a ring base (Fig. 3.8:1). Similar bowls were discovered at Tel Baṭash-Timna in Stratum VI (Panitz-Cohen and Mazar 2006: Pl. 55:1) and Megiddo in Tomb 3 (LB II; Guy 1938: Pl. 37:9). The general type corresponds to Killebrew's Form CA 2 (1998a: Ill. III:1:5–11). Like many bowls in Strata VIII–V, Fig. 3.8:1 is a typical Canaanite form made of the distinctive Egyptianized fabric with heavy straw temper.

The second subtype of the semi-hemispherical bowl is shallow with more of an incurving rim (Fig. 3.8:2), reminiscent of bowls from earlier strata at Tel Mor such as Strata X (see Fig. 3.1:12) and VIII (see Fig. 3.7:9). Elsewhere parallels have been excavated primarily at sites to the north, such as Tell Qasile in Stratum

XII (A. Mazar 1985: Fig. 11:1 [Family A, BL 1]), Tel Afeq in Stratum X-12 (Kochavi, Gadot and Yannai, forthcoming: Type BH5a) and Dor in the Ir1a(l) horizon (Gilboa and Sharon 2003: Fig. 2:3 [BL25]). The third subtype, which varies in size, has the following characteristics: a simple rim; short, approximately vertical, upper side-walls; slight carination near the mid-body; and a flat base (Fig. 3.8:3, 4). Similar bowls may be found at Dor in the Ir1b horizon (Gilboa and Sharon 2003: Fig. 7:10 [BL33]), Megiddo in Level F-5/VIA (Finkelstein, Zimhoni and Kafri 2000: Fig. 11.2:3) and Bet She'an in transitional LB II/Iron I tombs (Oren 1973: Figs. 42a:7 [Tomb 66], 50:1 [Tomb 241]). Figure 3.8:5 is similar except for the lack of gently carinated side-walls; thus it is transitional between the first and third subtypes. Parallels occur, for example, at Ashdod in Stratum XV (Dothan and Porath 1993: Fig. 10:2) and Bet She'an in Level VII (Killebrew 1998a: Ill. III:1:7 [Form CA 7] with further references).

Cyma bowls are first discovered at Tel Mor in Stratum VI; however, they are more common in Strata IV–III (see Fig. 3.10:1–5). They begin to appear at sites throughout Canaan at the end of the thirteenth century and become increasingly popular during Iron I (Killebrew 1998a: Ill. III:2:3–6 [Form CA 7). Like many cyma bowls, Fig. 3.8:6 has a painted red band on the interior of the rim. The majority of cyma bowls appear in the following strata of sites in the southern coastal plain and the Shephelah: Ashdod XII–XI, Lakhish VI, Tel Miqne-'Eqron VIII, Tel Batash-Timna V, Gezer XIII–XI and Tell Qasile XII–X (for references, see Killebrew 1998a:88).

Figure 3.8:7 and 8 are shallow, carinated bowls of varying depths. Similar rims have been found at Ashdod in Stratum XIV (Ben-Shlomo 2005: Fig. 3.1:3), Tel Miqne-'Eqron in Stratum VII (Killebrew 1998a: Fig. II:22.3, 4 [Form CA 1]) and later at Tel Mor in Stratum IV (see Fig. 3.10:7). The presence of these bowls at Tel Mor contradicts Killebrew's assertion that the type does not appear at sites 'with a strong Egyptian presence'. Figure 3.8:11 and 12 are semi-hemispherical bowls with bulbous, everted rims. The same type appears also in Stratum VII (see Fig. 3.7:10–12). Figure 3.8:11 is made from an Egyptianized fabric and is covered with a white wash on the interior.

Figure 3.8:9 and 10 are large bowls characterized by an everted rim, a rounded semi-hemispherical profile and a disk base, either concave or flat (see also M. Dothan 1960c: Fig. 5:3). This type of bowl is common at sites

throughout much of Canaan during LB IIB, for example, at Tell Beit Mirsim in Stratum B1 (Albright 1932: Pl. 26:3), Deir el-Balah in Stratum V (Gould, forthcoming: Type F2; Killebrew 1998a: Ill. III:1:11 [Form CA 3]), Bet Shemesh in Stratum IV (Grant and Wright 1938: Pl. 58:12), and Tel Harasim in Stratum IV (Givon 1995: Fig. 11:1; 1998: Fig. 10:12, 13; 1999: Fig. 10:2, 3).[2] The foregoing list belies the tentative suggestion that the type should be associated with sites exhibiting an Egyptian presence (Killebrew 1998a:84). Figure 3.8:13 and 14 are also large, roughly semi-hemispherical bowls. Rather than being everted, however, the rims are flattened and slope inward. A bowl quite similar to Fig. 3.8:13 was uncovered in Stratum VII (see Fig. 3.7:18). A good parallel for Fig. 3.8:14 comes from Tel Miqne-'Eqron Stratum VIIB (Construction Phase 9C; Dothan, Gitin and Zukerman 2006: Fig. 3.6:9).

The interior of Fig. 3.8:15 is elaborately decorated with concentric lines, stylized vegetal motifs and a bird's head. Although the bowl is poorly preserved, it is still possible to reconstruct the rest of the composition as follows: birds move among vegetation spaced evenly within the registers created by the concentric circles. Bowls with a decorated interior are common at sites in southern Canaan at the end of the Late Bronze Age and beginning of the Iron Age. Typically the decoration consists of radial parallel lines that enclose wavy lines, as with bowls from Lakhish (Tufnell, Inge and Harding 1940: Pl. 37B:27, 31; Aharoni 1975: Pl. 39:11), Gezer (Amiran 1969: Pl. 61:4) and Tel Afeq (Beck and Kochavi 1985: Fig. 3:1). Occasionally, there are also stylized palm trees. The types and arrangement of motifs found on Fig. 3.8:15, however, are not known from other bowls of this period.

Several large, deep bowls with a ring or concave disk base, rounded sides and out-turned rim were recovered from Strata VI–V (Fig. 3.9; see also M. Dothan 1960c: Fig. 5:3).[3] In one instance a handle is preserved (Fig. 3.9:1); it extends from rim to shoulder. Fabric heavily tempered with straw and thick vessel walls set them apart from other large bowls from this period (e.g., Fig. 3.8:9, 10). Also, around the mid- and upper body there are often rope impressions, apparently made while the vessel was in a leather-hard state. The ropes probably held these large bowls together before they were fired. Room 71 of Building F yielded at least six of these deep bowls probably from the Stratum VI destruction layer.

This bowl type, which is more common in southern Canaan, has been found at the following sites: Deir el-Balaḥ in Stratum V (Gould, forthcoming: Fig. 1:15 [Type F2]; see also Killebrew 1998a: Ill. III:1:11 [Form CA 3]), Tell Beit Mirsim in Stratum B1 (Albright 1932: Pl. 26:3), Lakhish in Fosse Temple III (Tufnell, Inge and Harding 1940: Pls. 39A–B:63, 42A–B:147, 149, 43A–B:163), Bet Shemesh in Stratum IV (Grant and Wright 1938: Pl. 58:12), Tel Afeq in Stratum X-13 (Kochavi, Gadot and Yannai, forthcoming), and Bet She'an in Level VI (James 1966: Fig. 55:5). Its presence at sites such as Tell Beit Mirsim, Bet Shemesh and Tel Baṭash-Timna casts doubt on Killebrew's tentative suggestion that there exists a correlation between this bowl type and sites exhibiting an Egyptian presence (1998a:84). A krater similar to these Stratum VI deep bowls, except for its thin walls and lack of straw temper, was excavated in Stratum VIII (see Fig. 3.14:10).

Strata IV–II (Figs. 3.10, 3.11)
The most common bowl type in Strata IV–III has a cyma or s-shaped profile (Fig. 3.10:1–5). Cyma bowls have everted rims and a carination in the upper body, and are roughly semi-hemispherical in shape. At Tel Mor their rim diameter ranges between 18 and 28 cm. All the cyma bowls from Strata IV–III bear some kind of decoration, usually a red band on the inside of the rim. Some also have concentric red bands on the interior and are covered inside and out with a white wash (Fig. 3.10:2), similar to that applied to the contemporaneous Philistine Bichrome pottery. At Tell Qasile a white wash was exhibited primarily on cyma bowls from Stratum XII (1150–1000 BCE; A. Mazar 1985:40).

As noted above, cyma bowls first appear at the end of the thirteenth century (see Fig. 3.8:6), but are more common in the twelfth and eleventh centuries, as is the case at Tel Mor. The type is well represented, for example, in Iron I strata from the following regional sites: Ashdod XIII (Ben-Shlomo 2005: Fig. 3.5:7, 8, 10) and XII–XI (e.g., Dothan and Freedman 1967: Fig. 27:1–8; Dothan and Porath 1993: Fig. 33:9, 11–14); Tel Miqne-'Eqron VII–VI (Dothan, Gitin and Zukerman 2006:77, Figs. 3.6:18–23, 7:1–16); Gezer XIII–XI (e.g., Dever 1986: Pls. 19:14; 22:1, 2; 24:5–7; 30:4–6; 32:4, 9, 10, 12); and Tell Qasile XII–X (A. Mazar 1985:39–41 [Type BL 8]; for further references, see Killebrew 1998a:88 [Form CA 7]).

Figure 3.10:6–9, notwithstanding differences in their overall form, all have simple rims. Figure 3.10:6 resembles carinated bowls of the Late Bronze

Age, particularly toward the end of that period (e.g., Fig. 3.6:5). Figure 3.10:7, which has a more subtle carination, is similar to bowls from the preceding Stratum V (see Fig. 3.8:7, 8). Figure 3.10:8 and 9 are small, semi-hemispherical bowls with simple, incurving rims. The former has a shallow ring base and a white wash that covers the exterior of the vessel as well as the rim's interior. As noted above (see above), this basic bowl type occurs, with slight variations, throughout the Late Bronze Age at Tel Mor. Iron I parallels elsewhere may be found at Ashdod in Stratum XI (Ben-Shlomo 2005: Fig. 3.57:1–3), Tel Miqne-'Eqron in Stratum V (T. Dothan 1998: Pl. 11:1 [IBL1]), Tel Baṭash-Timna in Stratum V (Panitz-Cohen and Mazar 2006: Pl. 61:1), Tell Qasile in Strata XII (A. Mazar 1985: Figs. 12:1, 16:1 [BL 1]) and XI (A. Mazar 1985: Figs. 24:1, 28:5) and at many other sites in southern Canaan (for references, see Killebrew 1998a:89 [Form CA 8]).

Figure 3.10:10–13, on the other hand, have rims that have been somewhat modified. Figure 3.10:10 is a semi-hemispherical bowl with a slight carination not far below a rounded, T-shaped rim. Comparable bowls have been found at Dor in Area G, Phase 8/7 (Gilboa 2001b: Fig. 5.21:9 [BL 24a]) and Tel Ḥarasim in Stratum IV (Givon 1997: Fig. 10:6). Figure 3.10:11 is a roughly semi-hemispherical bowl with an everted rim that nearly forms a horizontal ledge. A brown wash covers both the interior and exterior of the vessel. A smaller version of this bowl was excavated at Dor in Area G, Phase 9 (Gilboa 2001b: Pl. 5.5:9 [BL 23e]). Figure 3.10:12 has thick, rounded side-walls and a flattened rim. A similar bowl, but with thinner and straighter side-walls, was found at Dor in Area G, Phase 8/7 (Gilboa 2001b: Pl. 5.21:2 [BL 3b]). Figure 3.10:13 is a shallow bowl with an inwardly folded rim, a common feature of Late Bronze Age pottery (for references, see Killebrew 1998a:82 [Form CA 1]) generally absent at Tel Mor. Such rims are still evident in the Iron Age, but less frequently, as at Dor in Area B1, Phase 12 (Gilboa 2001b: Pl. 5.18:2, 3 [BL 4]).

As noted above, Red Slip Burnished (RSB) Ware first appears in Stratum III.[4] Approximately 30 sherds of this ware (mostly bowls) were excavated in Strata III and II and in unstratified contexts. Kraters (see Fig. 3.16:10–12) and an unstratified kernos fragment (Reg. No. A30/19) are the only other RSB vessel types attested at Tel Mor. Most of the Stratum III sherds derive from poor stratigraphic contexts (primarily L10). It is possible, therefore, that much of this RSB pottery has been incorrectly assigned to Stratum III. Indeed, tenth-century strata at neighboring sites provide, in many cases, the closest parallels for this pottery. Because they are so few in number, the RSB bowls from Stratum II (Fig. 3.11:4, 8), which are also poorly stratified, are presented together here with the Strata IV–III bowls.

The burnishing on the majority of the RSB is regular and tends to cover both the interior and exterior of the vessel. The slip is red (10R 4/6) and the fabric is yellowish red (5YR 5/6) with mostly a few fine to small white inclusions. All the RSB bowls are carinated to some degree. Figure 3.11:1 is a shallow bowl with a simple rounded rim, slight carination at mid-body and thick side-walls. Similar bowls, but with thinner side-walls, have been found in tenth-century contexts at Lakhish in Level V (Zimhoni 1997: Fig. 3.5:2), Megiddo in Level K-3 (= VB; Finkelstein, Zimhoni and Kafri 2000: Fig. 11.18:2, 3) and Dor in Area B1, Phase 9 (Gilboa 2001b: Pl. 5.67:26 [BL 32]).[5] Figure 3.11:2 also has a slight carination at mid-body; however, this bowl is deeper with grooves or ridges below the rim, a feature of the tenth and, perhaps, ninth centuries (see Fig. 3.11:9 below).

The carination on the bowls in Fig. 3.11:3 and 4 is more pronounced, to the point of forming a ridge, and the simple rim is slightly everted. Parallels appear at Ashdod as early as Stratum XI (Dothan and Porath 1982: Fig. 1:1, 2; Ben-Shlomo 2005: Fig. 3.82:17) and as late as Stratum VIII (M. Dothan 1971: Fig. 39:10–12). The type also appears at Tel Baṭash-Timna in Stratum IV (Mazar and Panitz-Cohen 2001: Pl. 7:6 [BL 27]) and Lakhish in Level V (Zimhoni 1997: Fig. 3.21:17, 20).

Figure 3.11:5 is a deep, carinated bowl with an everted, thickened rim that is typical of the tenth century. It appears, for example, at Ashdod in Stratum X (Dothan and Porath 1993: Fig. 47:7) and Lakhish in Level V (Zimhoni 1997: Fig. 3.21:21). Figure 3.11:6 is a smaller version of Fig. 3.11:5. Figure 3.11:7 has a sharp carination at mid-body, above which the vessel wall, including the rim, is straight and slants outward. Similar bowls from Ashdod appear in Strata IX (Ben-Shlomo 2005: Fig. 3.82:20) and VIII (M. Dothan 1971: Fig. 45:6, 7).

Figure 3.11:8 is a small bowl with a sharp carination in the lower body and a nearly vertical upper side-wall and rim. There is a groove or ridge below the rim and irregular burnishing only on the vessel's interior. A similar bowl from Tel Baṭash-Timna Stratum IV has a slightly everted rim (Mazar and Panitz-Cohen 2001: Pl. 8:15 [BL 24]). Figure 3.11:9 has a series of grooves on the exterior of an incurving rim. Such ridging appears on RSB bowls as early as the eleventh century, as at Tell Qasile in Stratum XI (A. Mazar 1985: Fig. 22:2 [BL 5]), but is more common during the tenth century. It may be found, for example, at Ashdod in Stratum IX (M. Dothan 1971: Fig. 76:10; Ben-Shlomo 2005: Fig. 3.82:10), Tel Miqne-'Eqron in Stratum IV (Ortiz 2000: Figs. 6:1 [BL 9], 9:1 [BL 19]), Tel Baṭash-Timna in Stratum IV (Kelm and Mazar 1995: Fig. 6:5) and Lakhish in Level V (Zimhoni 1997: Fig. 3.8:10). This bowl type continues to appear as late as the ninth century, as at Ashdod in Stratum VIII (M. Dothan 1971: Fig. 39:26). Figure 3.11:10 is a bowl with a slight carination at mid-body and an everted rim that is flattened and slopes inward so as to form an interior ledge. Only the inside of the vessel is burnished. A similar bowl was uncovered at Tel Baṭash-Timna in Stratum V (Kelm and Mazar 1995: Fig. 5:12).

As noted above, a very small amount of pottery was retrieved from Stratum II. For this reason—and despite the apparent settlement gap between Strata III and II (see Chapter 2)—the pottery from Stratum II is presented here together with the Strata IV–III assemblage. Figure 3.10:14 is a shallow carinated bowl with an everted rim. The interior of the rim is decorated with a thick red band that was sloppily applied, as evidenced by the drip marks. This bowl is derivative of the cyma type popular during Iron I (see above). Figure 3.10:15 is a deep bowl with a simple rim, relatively straight side-walls and a low point of carination. A bowl similar in shape, but with a red-slipped interior, was found at Tel Ḥarasim in Stratum IV (Givon 1997: Fig. 10:7). The poor stratigraphic context of all these bowl rims (along with the rest of the Stratum II pottery) undercuts any further speculation about their respective dates.

Chalices and Tripods (Fig. 3.12)

Of the dozen or so well-preserved chalices and tripods found at Tel Mor, the majority belong to MB IIC and LB I (Strata XII–X; for a Bichrome goblet, see Fig. 5.7:9). In terms of morphology, they closely resemble bowls from the same period. Most of the chalices belong to one of two general groups distinguished by the shape of the upper, or bowl, part of the vessel. Either they are shallow with rounded side-walls and a simple rim, or they are somewhat deeper and carinated. The height and profile of the pedestal bases in both groups vary.

Figure 3.12:1–3 belong to the first group. Figure 3.12:1, which derives from a transitional MB IIC/LB I context, has a relatively short, splayed base. The upper part of the vessel is virtually identical to bowl rims from the same strata at Tel Mor (Fig. 3.1:2, 4). Elsewhere a similar chalice was found at Gezer in an LB IB context in Cave I.10A (Seger 1988: Pl. 29:9). Figure 3.12:2 and 3 were both found in Room 137 of Building A; thus they belong to LB IIA. The base of each is tall and widely splayed. Figure 3.12:3 also has a ring at the juncture of the bowl and the base. A comparable chalice, but covered with white slip and decorated with concentric red bands, was excavated at Lakhish in Tomb 635 (LB II; Tufnell 1958: Pl. 72:635).

Of Fig. 3.12:4, only the bowl and the juncture with the base are preserved. It resembles the preceding chalices except for its greater depth and straighter side-walls. This chalice may have been excavated in the area of Courtyard 118 referred to as the *bāmāh* (see Fig. 2.3). The same Stratum XI context produced another chalice (Fig. 3.12:6), an Egyptianized ovoid jar (Fig. 4.10:1), a lamp with seven spouts (Fig. 3.30:1) and several miniature bowls (Fig. 3.5:3–8).

Figure 3.12:5–8 belong to the second group of chalices that are distinguished, above all, by a carination (see also M. Dothan 1960a: Pl. 1:2; 1960c: Fig. 4:2). In terms of morphology, again, the upper part is virtually the same as carinated bowls from the same strata (e.g., Fig. 3.3:9–11). A pedestal base that is profiled and spreads at its foot distinguishes Fig. 3.12:5, which was recovered from a questionable LB I context, from the rest of the chalices at Tel Mor. Bases with elaborate profiles are associated with chalices, either rounded or carinated, at Tel Baṭash-Timna in Stratum VIII (Panitz-Cohen and Mazar 2006: Pl. 21:9) and at Lakhish in various LB II tombs (e.g., Tufnell 1958: Pl. 72:636 [Tomb 1006]).

Figure 3.12:6 was also discovered in the vicinity of the Stratum XI *bāmāh* (see Fig. 2.3). It resembles Fig. 3.12:5 except for its base, which is shorter and simpler (see also Fig. 3.12:9). Only the upper part of Fig. 3.12:7, which derives from a Stratum XII context, is preserved. The curvature of the side-wall at the base of the bowl indicates that this vessel is a chalice. Carinated chalices are unusual for the end of Late Bronze Age; therefore, Fig. 3.12:8, which is the only pottery registered for Room 79 of Stratum VI, is probably residual.

With a height of nearly 20 cm, the pedestal base of Fig. 3.12:10, from a vague Strata XI–IX context, is unusually tall. The base of a chalice from Stratum 1B of Area H at Ḥazor is similarly high (Yadin et al. 1989: Pl. 273:6). Only the stem of Fig. 3.12:11, which was discovered in an unreliable Stratum III context, survives. Unlike that of all the previous chalices, it is cylindrical in shape and decorated with horizontal red bands on a light slip. The decoration is reminiscent of Philistine Bichrome pottery, most of which appears at Tel Mor also in Stratum III (see below). Intact Bichrome decorated chalices were found at Lakhish in Level P-1 (Clamer 2004a: Fig. 20.30:3) and Tel Ẓippor in Stratum II (Biran and Negbi 1966: Fig. 6:8).

Two tripods also came from Tel Mor, one from Stratum XII (Fig. 3.12:13) and the other from Stratum IX (Fig. 3.12:12). They are very similar in terms of the bowl portion, which is shallow with rounded side-walls and a bulbous rim; however, the placement of the tripod legs differs. On Fig. 3.12:13 the legs, which are broken off cleanly at the point of attachment, are located close to the rim (see also M. Dothan 1973: Fig. 3:3). A similar tripod (with legs intact) comes from Fosse Temple I at Lakhish (Tufnell, Inge and Harding 1940: Pl. 44:172). The leg stubs in Fig. 3.12:12, on the other hand, are situated closer to the center, similar to another tripod excavated in Fosse Temple I (Tufnell, Inge and Harding 1940: Pl. 44:171). Figure 3.12:13 is red slipped and Fig. 3.12:12 is burnished and perhaps also covered with a red slip.

Kraters

Strata XII–X

Aside from the Bichrome kraters (see Fig. 5.7:1–4), this vessel type is conspicuously absent from the early strata at Tel Mor. They are rare also at Ashdod in Strata XXIII–XVIII (cf. Dothan and Freedman 1967: Fig. 32:15; Dothan and Porath 1993: Fig. 2:14). Undecorated kraters are commonly found, however, in MB IIC and LB I strata at regional sites, such as Tel Baṭash-Timna X–IX (Panitz-Cohen and Mazar 2006: Pls. 10:1, 11:4–6), Gezer XIX–XVIII (e.g., Dever et al. 1970: Pl. 31:3) and Lakhish Tombs 1552 and 6002 (e.g., Tufnell 1958: Pls. 68:511, 69:578).

Stratum IX (Fig. 3.13)

A small number of undecorated kraters first appear at Tel Mor in Stratum IX. Figure 3.13:1 has a T-shaped rim, vertical neck, rounded shoulder and handles that extend from shoulder to rim. A very similar krater, but decorated, was recovered from Ashdod Stratum XV, where it is said to be a popular LB II type (Dothan and Porath 1993:43, Fig. 10:13). Further parallels, which tend to be larger in size, are known from Tel Baṭash-Timna in Stratum VIII (Kelm and Mazar 1995: Fig. 4:13) and Ḥazor in Stratum 1A (Yadin et al. 1989: Pl. 258:10, 12; see also Pl. 161:19).

Figure 3.13:2 has a thickened rim and vertical side-walls. A similar sherd from Ḥazor Stratum 2 was tentatively identified as belonging to a stand (Yadin et al. 1989: Pl. 267:15), which may be the case also with Fig. 3.13:2. Figure 3.13:3 has a well-everted rim, hemispherical body and especially thick side-walls. Whether it is classified as a deep bowl or krater, no close parallels have been found for this vessel.

Strata VIII–VII (Fig. 3.14)

Kraters first appear in significant quantity at Tel Mor in Strata VIII–VII. In most cases, only the rim and the upper body survive; however, two kraters are almost completely preserved (Fig. 3.14:9, 10). In spite of the small size and fragmentary nature of this corpus, two tendencies may be observed. First, the 'hammer' or 'T-shaped' rim is well represented (Fig. 3.14:2–5), as it is also in the following Strata VI–V (e.g., Fig. 3.15:6) and III (e.g., Fig. 3.16:1). Second, the kraters generally fall within two groups according to size: small (diameter 20–25 cm; Fig. 3.14:1–3, 5, 9) and large (diameter 35–40 cm; Fig. 3.14:4, 6–8, 10).

Figure 3.14:1 has a thickened rim and vertical side-walls. It resembles a rim from the preceding stratum (see Fig. 3.13:2), which may, in fact, have belonged to a stand. Figure 3.14:2–4, despite their varying sizes, all have T-shaped rims and side-walls that slant inward. There is a black and red checkerboard pattern on the upper body of Fig. 3.14:2 and a red band on its rim. It is likely that all three were carinated near mid-body, as are better preserved and similar kraters from later strata at Tel Mor (e.g., Fig. 3.15:6) and sites elsewhere. Parallels may be found at Gezer in Strata XIV–XIII (Dever 1986: Pl. 18:9) and Tel Baṭash-Timna in Stratum VI (Panitz-Cohen and Mazar 2006: Pl. 55:14).

The mid-body carination is preserved on Fig. 3.14:5, which also has a T-shaped rim; however, its upper side-wall is more vertical. The fabric, which is grayish in color and contains fine red inclusions, differs from that of the majority of pottery excavated at Tel Mor, which

was presumably made from local loessial soils. In terms of the shape, similar kraters have been found, again, at Gezer in Stratum XIV (Dever 1986: Pl. 15:10) and Tel Baṭash-Timna in Stratum VI (Panitz-Cohen and Mazar 2006: Pl. 55:13).

Figure 3.14:6 and 7 are similar in shape to Fig. 3.14:5, but differ in other respects. The diameter of Fig. 3.14:6 is nearly twice as large, and the rim of Fig. 3.14:7 is well everted and has been squared off. Vestiges of a T-shaped rim are barely discernible in Fig. 3.14:8. The slight internal thickening results from the crossbar of the 'T' having been pressed into the side-wall. A krater rim intermediate between Fig. 3.14:8 and the true T-shaped profile was excavated in Stratum V (see Fig. 3.15:7). The thickening has disappeared completely on a similar rim from Stratum III (see Fig. 3.16:5).

Figure 3.14:9 is a deep, semi-hemispherical bowl or krater with a thickened, inturned rim. The excess clay was folded outward and pinched so as to create a slight flange. The same type of rim appears on shallower bowls at Tel Mor, also from Strata VIII–VII (see Fig. 3.7:14, 16). Parallels for Fig. 3.14:9 may be found to the north, at Megiddo in Stratum VIIA (Loud 1948: Pl. 15:68) and Bet She'an in Level VII (James and McGovern 1993: Fig. 33:1).

Figure 3.14:10 is a fully restored krater that was discovered in Room 132 of Building D. The rim is short and everted and there is a ridge on its high, rounded shoulder. The body, most of which is covered with wet-smooth marks, is roughly piriform and rests on a ring base. In terms of the overall shape, Fig. 3.14:10 resembles a distinctive type of deep bowl known from Stratum VI (see Fig. 3.9). As for manufacturing techniques, however, there are significant differences: The walls of Fig. 3.14:10 are relatively thin and exhibit little in the way of temper, whereas the walls of the deep bowls from Stratum VI are thick and contain a large amount of straw, a characteristic of Egyptianized pottery.

Strata VI–V (Fig. 3.15)

More kraters were recovered from Strata VI–V than in any other strata at Tel Mor. Unfortunately, no complete vessels were found.[6] Certain morphological tendencies are even more evident here than in the preceding Strata VIII–VII. In terms of shape, the kraters may be divided into two general groups. The first is characterized by an everted rim, upper side-walls that are relatively vertical and a mid-body carination (Fig. 3.15:1–4). A

T-shaped rim, side-walls that slope inwards and, again, a carination at mid-body distinguish the second group (Fig. 3.15:5–8). Based on later and better preserved kraters (see, e.g., Fig. 3.16:1–3), it is possible to reconstruct two or more vertical loop handles that extend from the rim to the point of carination. Regarding size, most of the kraters fall within the large range (diameter 35–40 cm).

Parallels for the first group (Fig. 3.15:1–4) may be found at the following regional sites, mostly in twelfth-century contexts: Ashdod in Strata XIV (M. Dothan 1971: Fig. 82:6; Dothan and Porath 1993: Fig. 11:15) and XIII (M. Dothan 1971: Fig. 82:6; Dothan and Porath 1993: Fig. 19:4), Tel Miqne-‘Eqron in Stratum VIIB (Dothan, Gitin and Zukerman 2006: Figs. 3.3:20, 3.8:6), Lakhish in Level VI (Ussishkin 1983: Figs. 15:8, 16:11), Tel Baṭash-Timna in Stratum VI (Panitz-Cohen and Mazar 2006: Pl. 55:13), Gezer in Stratum XIII/6C (Dever 1986: Pls. 19:9, 22:4), and Tell Qasile in Stratum XII (A. Mazar 1985: Fig. 17:1). Similar rims are present at Tel Mor in an earlier stratum (see Fig. 3.14:5), thus attesting to the long life of this general type (see also Type KR 1 at Tell Qasile; A. Mazar 1985:45–47). Note that two of the Strata VI–V kraters (Fig. 3.15:3, 4) were made with an Egyptianized fabric.

Parallels for the second group (Fig. 3.15:5–8) may be observed at the following sites, once again, mostly in twelfth-century contexts: Ashdod in Stratum XIII (Ben-Shlomo 2005: Fig. 3.5:14), Lakhish in Level VI (Ussishkin 1983: Fig. 16:11), Tel Miqne-‘Eqron in Stratum VIIB (Dothan, Gitin and Zukerman 2006: Figs. 3.3:23–25; 3.8:4, 5), Tel Baṭash-Timna in Stratum V (Panitz-Cohen and Mazar 2006: Pl. 61:15, 17–19), Gezer in Strata XIV (Dever 1986: Pl. 15:9) and XIII (Pl. 21:6), Tell Qasile in Stratum XII (A. Mazar 1985: Fig. 13:27 [Type KR 2a]), and Tel Afeq in Stratum X-12 (Kochavi, Gadot and Yannai, forthcoming). As with the first group, this krater type is present both in earlier (see Fig. 3.14:2–4) and later strata (see Fig. 3.16:1–3) at Tel Mor.

Stratum III (Fig. 3.16)

Most of the kraters from Stratum III are clearly derived from types that appear at Tel Mor in earlier periods.[7] For example, there are a number of kraters with vertical handles that extend from a T-shaped rim to a carination at mid-body (Fig. 3.16:1–3; cf. Fig. 3.15:6). The sharpness of the carination varies, as does the number

of handles (either two or four). The more rounded form of Fig. 3.16:1 suggests a tenth-century date. Parallels from regional sites may be found, for example, at Ashdod in Stratum X (Dothan and Porath 1982: Fig. 2:9), Lakhish in Stratum V (Aharoni 1975: Pl. 41:9) and Tell Qasile in Stratum X (A. Mazar 1985: Figs. 53:6, 54:14 [KR 1]). The greater angularity of Fig. 3.16:2 and 3, on the other hand, is more indicative of Iron I. Similar kraters have been excavated at Ashdod in Stratum XII (Dothan and Porath 1993: Fig. 33:15), Lakhish in Stratum VI (Yannai 1996: Fig. 20:2, 4–6) and Tell Qasile in Strata XII (A. Mazar 1985: Fig. 15:26 [KR 1]) and XI (A. Mazar 1985: Fig. 24:15).

Figure 3.16:4 also has a T-shaped rim, but its rim diameter is much smaller (21 cm) and the side-walls are almost perfectly vertical. A Philistine Bichrome krater rim from Ashdod Stratum XII–XI is quite similar in terms of shape, size and stance (Dothan and Porath 1993: Fig. 39:3), thus raising the possibility that Fig. 3.16:4 also belongs to this type of ware. Figure 3.16:5 has a simple vertical rim that gives way to a gently rounded shoulder. An antecedent of this krater rim came from Tel Mor in Stratum VII (see Fig. 3.14:8). Parallels from the tenth century have been excavated at Bet She’an in Stratum 1 (Level V; Yadin and Geva 1986: Fig. 6:9 [Type 1: Steep Rim]) and Lakhish in Stratum V (Aharoni 1975: Pl. 41:16 [CP 20]). The latter vessel, however, is a cooking pot, as Fig. 3.16:5 might also be. The presence of numerous white inclusions, a feature common to cooking-pot ware throughout the Late Bronze and Iron Ages (see below), supports this identification. Figure 3.16:6 has an everted rim, short neck and rounded shoulder. Relative to its overall size, the vessel walls are unusually thick.

There are two kraters from Stratum III that are quite unlike anything from previous strata at Tel Mor. Figure 3.16:7 is a tall, well-preserved krater that bears a decorative scene in its shoulder and neck zones (see M. Dothan 1960a: Pl. III:3). It has an everted, T-shaped rim and a tall, constricted neck. Vertical loop handles extend from approximately mid-neck to a well-rounded shoulder, and there is a ridge above the lower handle attachment. The lower body, which is semi-hemispherical, gives way to a thick ring or, more likely, trumpet base.

The main frieze is located in the neck zone and consists of metopes and triglyphs. Pairs of vertical bands and a wavy line enclosed by more vertical bands comprise the triglyphs. Both the triglyphs and much larger metopes are framed by two horizontal bands above and groups of zigzags enclosed by horizontal bands below. The main motif of the only preserved metope is a bird feeding upon a 'tree of life'. The bird, with its long sinuous neck, may be an ostrich. Similarly decorated kraters (see below) suggest the existence of a second animal positioned antithetically on the opposite side of the tree.[8] The combination of live upward-slanting and dead downward-hanging branches indicates that the tree is a date palm. There are additional horizontal bands on the rim and mid- and lower body. Based on the photograph, it appears that the painted decoration was applied to a slipped and burnished surface.

Tall kraters bearing decoration, often a palm tree flanked by ibexes, first appear at Canaanite sites during the Late Bronze Age (Amiran 1969:161–165). A good parallel for Fig. 3.16:7, especially in terms of the main motif, is from Lakhish in Fosse Temple III (Tufnell, Inge and Harding 1940: Pls. 48:249, 60:2). Decorated kraters from Lakhish Level P-1 (Clamer 2004a: Fig. 20.14:1 [Type III.a]) and Tel Baṭash-Timna Stratum VII (Panitz-Cohen and Mazar 2006: Pl. 50:12) are closer in terms of overall shape, but lack the palm tree flanked by either ibexes or birds. Production of these kraters continued into the early Iron Age, as shown by the discovery of exemplars at Megiddo in Tomb 1101C (Guy 1938: Pl. 9:2) and Bet She'an in Stratum 4 (Level VI; Yadin and Geva 1986: Fig. 24 [Type 4, Painted Krater]). The base of the latter krater, though not completely preserved, is clearly of the trumpet variety. The same is most likely true also of Fig. 3.16:7. Indeed, the vessel wall near the base is probably too thick for a simple ring base (see also Loud 1948: Pl. 72:3). In light of the predominantly eleventh-century date of Stratum III, Fig. 3.16:7 is among the latest attestations of this krater type in the Canaanite tradition (see also Givon 1998: Fig. 13:4; 1999: Fig. 11:5).

Figure 3.16:8 is an amphoroid krater, a rare vessel type for Iron I (see M. Dothan 1960c: Fig. 5:6). It is characterized by the following morphological features: a slightly everted, bulbous rim; a tall, nearly vertical neck with a ridge below the rim; angular handles that extend from neck to shoulder; a biconical body with a distinct carination at mid-body; and a ring base. In terms of the decoration, there are red horizontal bands on the rim, neck, shoulder and lower body. There are also crisscrossing lines that run the length of each handle. Thus far Tell Qasile Stratum XI has produced the

closest parallel to the vessel, both in terms of form and decoration (A. Mazar 1985: Fig. 30:12 [Type AM 3]).

Figure 3.16:9 is a large jar-krater with multiple handles and a molded decoration; it was found in secondary use (see Fig. 2.32). It has a thickened rim and shoulder that both slope inward. The dozen or so handles, which are attached vertically on the shoulder, are each decorated with a knob. Two horizontal rows of knobs wrap around the mid-body, immediately below the handles, and are enclosed by molded ridges. There is also a single, horizontal, molded ridge at the point of the upper handle attachment. The vessel walls are very thick and the fabric is coarse with a great deal of straw temper, most of which has been burnt out or carbonized. There are no close parallels for this vessel type. Similar large kraters often have an incised rope instead of a molded knob decoration and/or handles that attach directly to the rim. Most of these kraters derive from northern sites, such as Megiddo in Stratum V (Lamon and Shipton 1939: Pl. 21:125),[9] Tel Yoqne'am in Strata XV–XIV (Zarzecki-Peleg, Cohen-Anidjar and Ben-Tor 2005: Fig. II.7:1 [Type K V]) and Bet She'an in Level VI (Fitzgerald 1930: Pl. 46:13) and Lower Level V (James 1966: Fig. 59:16). There is also a large krater with multiple handles and an incised rope decoration in the Dayan Collection, reportedly from Tell es-Safi (see Amiran 1969: Photo 231). The general type is apparently long-lived, as evidenced by its appearance at Tel Miqne-'Eqron in Stratum I (Gitin 1998: Fig. 6:3 [Jar Krater 3]).

Among the limited corpus of RSB Ware in Strata IV–II (see above) are three krater rim sherds (Fig. 3.16:10–12). All have thickened, T-shaped rims and inward sloping side-walls. On Fig. 3.16:11 only the exterior is red slipped and burnished. Better preserved specimens of this krater type usually have vertical loop handles that extend from the rim to the carination, which is located somewhere in the mid- to upper body region. Such is the case with unslipped kraters also from Stratum III at Tel Mor (see Fig. 3.16:3). The majority of close parallels for RSB kraters derive from tenth-century contexts such as Lakhish Level V (where they are described as bowls; Zimhoni 1997: Fig. 3.30:9–11, 16), Tel Miqne-'Eqron IV (Ortiz 2000: Fig. 11:7 [KR 9]), Tel Baṭash-Timna IV (Mazar and Panitz-Cohen 2001: Pls. 8:17, 82:16 [KR 14b]), Tell Qasile VIII (A. Mazar 1985: Fig. 54:9–11 [KR 4]) and Tel Mikhal XIV (Singer-Avitz 1989: Fig. 7.1:6). There are no well-stratified, unslipped kraters in the limited corpus of

Stratum II pottery. Figure 3.16:12 is a large rounded bowl or krater with an out-turned rim. The burnishing, which covers the vessel inside and out, is irregular on the lower body. The closest parallel, despite its rim ticks and lack of exterior slip, is a krater from Ashdod VII (M. Dothan 1971: Fig. 94:3).

Cooking Pots

Cooking-pot ware is distinct from that of the rest of the locally made Canaanite pottery. The clay typically fires to a brown (7.5YR 4/4) or red color (2.5YR 5/6) and the surface is often blackened on account of the pot's placement over a hearth. There is usually a thick dark gray core, and many small to medium calcite inclusions are frequently present in the fabric.

Strata XII–X (Fig. 3.17)
Stratum XII yielded a few cooking pots typical of MB IIC (Fig. 3.17:1–3; see also M. Dothan 1973:3, Fig. 3:6). The following characteristics distinguish them from cooking pots of the Late Bronze Age: an everted rim that has not yet acquired a triangular profile, a rounded shoulder that lacks a carination at the upper or mid-body, and a generally globular form. The rims of these cooking pots vary slightly: For example, Fig. 3.17:2 is rounded and simple, whereas Fig. 3.17:3 is folded inward.

Numerous parallels, some of which have handles that extend from rim to shoulder, have been retrieved at Ḥazor from strata that correspond to the end of the Middle Bronze Age (e.g., Yadin et al. 1958: Pls. 94:7, 98:21; 1989: Pls. 259:28, 30; 287:13–15). The type also appears in late MB II contexts at Ashdod in Stratum XXII (Dothan and Porath 1993: Fig. 2:19) and Gezer in Strata XX–XIX (Dever 1986: Pl. 5:12), and in LB I contexts at Gezer in Cave I.10A (Seger 1988: Fig. 31:25) and Tel Yoqne'am in Stratum XXa (Ben-Ami and Livneh 2005: Fig. IV.9:1 [Type CIa]). A cooking pot with a gutter rim (Fig. 3.18:8), another MB IIC type, was recovered from a poor Stratum IX context (see below). No cooking pots with folded rims, which are known from MB IIC contexts at sites to the north (e.g., Tel Mikhal; Negbi 1989: Fig. 5.3:1–4), were found at Tel Mor.

The majority of cooking pots from Stratum XI onwards have the familiar triangular-profile rim of the Late Bronze Age. The beginning of the development toward this type of rim is evident already in Stratum

XII (Fig. 3.17:4–6). By Strata XI–X the development is complete and triangular-profile rims predominate (Fig. 3.17:7–11, 13; see also M. Dothan 1960c: Fig. 4:1). Often a slightly pointed base (Fig. 3.17:7) and carination at mid-body (Fig. 3.17:9) also characterize these cooking pots. Parallels for this Late Bronze Age type are known from the following sites: Tel Baṭash-Timna in Stratum X (Panitz-Cohen and Mazar 2006: Pl. 15:6), Gezer in Cave I.10A (LB IB/IIA; Seger 1988: Pls. 7:4–6, 8:13–15, 9:3–6, 33:3), Tel Afeq in Stratum X-14 (Kochavi, Gadot and Yannai, forthcoming), Megiddo in Tomb 855 (LB I; Guy 1938: Pl. 43:12), Tel Yoqne'am in Stratum XXa (Ben-Ami and Livneh 2005: Fig. IV.9:11 [Type CIe3]) and Ḥazor Area H in Stratum 2 (Yadin et al. 1989: Pl. 265:10). This rim type appears in later strata at Tel Mor, perhaps as residual sherds (see Fig. 3.19:5, 6 [Stratum VIII]).

The entire profile of Fig. 3.17:14, which is a rare intact vessel assigned to Stratum X, is preserved. It has a triangular-profile rim that is everted and attenuated, a short neck and a high rounded shoulder. Unlike most cooking pots from this period, the maximum diameter is at the rim and not the shoulder. The body is less globular and the base less rounded than cooking pots from the earlier Stratum XII. A similarly shaped rim was discovered at Tel Afeq in Stratum X-14 (Kochavi, Gadot and Yannai, forthcoming: Pl. 8:10 [CP1b]).

Stratum IX (Fig. 3.18)
Most of the cooking pots from Stratum IX are either poorly preserved or derive from poor contexts;[10] therefore, it is possible that some rims belonged originally to earlier strata. The everted, triangular-profile rim still distinguishes the majority of Stratum IX cooking pots in LB II at Tel Mor. Figure 3.18:1, with its sharp carination at mid-body, is a classic exemplar. This type of cooking pot is common also in the preceding LB I strata (e.g., Fig. 3.17:9). The shoulder of Fig. 3.18:2 is more vertical and the flange has a greater overhang. Stratum X-14 at Tel Afeq produced a similar rim (Kochavi, Gadot and Yannai, forthcoming: Pl. 12:22). Figure 3.18:3 is another relatively tall cooking pot. The shoulder is nearly vertical, there is a faint ridge on the neck and the lip of the rim curves inward slightly.

The triangular profile is less distinct on other cooking-pot rims from Stratum IX at Tel Mor. The rim of Fig. 3.18:4, which has been squared off, is transitional between the rounded rims of MB IIC and the triangular profile of the Late Bronze Age. Similar rims were excavated at Ashdod in Stratum XVIII (M. Dothan 1971: Fig. 31:9, 10). Figure 3.18:5 is attenuated to such a degree that it appears to be a simple, everted rim (see also Fig. 3.17:12). The rims of Fig. 3.18:6 and 7, on the other hand, are squat and rounded. Similar rims on better preserved cooking pots may be found at Lakhish in Fosse Temple I (Tufnell, Inge and Harding 1940: Pl. 55:358) and Tel Afeq in Stratum X-14 (Kochavi, Gadot and Yannai, forthcoming: Pl. 6:2 [CP1a]).

Figure 3.18:8 has a gutter rim, no neck and a rounded shoulder. Cooking pots with this type of rim were especially popular during MB IIC, as for example at Tel Mikhal (Negbi 1989: Fig. 5.3:7) and Shechem (Seger 1974: Fig. 6:2). For this reason, and in light of the fact that it was recovered from a poor context, Fig. 3.18:8 is almost certainly a residual sherd.

Strata VIII–VII (Fig. 3.19)

The rim with a triangular profile still predominates among the cooking pots of Strata VIII–VII. The flange, however, tends to be more elongated and to point straight downward (e.g., Fig. 3.19:1, 3, 4). Figure 3.19:1 is the best-preserved cooking pot from these strata. It has a convex, triangular-profile rim (see also Fig. 3.20:4, 5) and a short neck and shoulder. The carination is located in the upper body and the lower body tapers to a slightly pointed base. A similar cooking pot, but with a somewhat flattened rim, was excavated at Tel Seraʿ in Stratum IX (Oren 1984: Fig. 5:5); thus the profile is transitional between Fig. 3.19:1 (Stratum VIII) and Fig. 3.20:10 (Stratum V). The rim of Fig. 3.19:2 is also convex, but the neck and shoulder are taller. The same type of cooking pot—bearing what the excavators describe as an 'adze-rim'—was found at Ashdod in Stratum XVII (M. Dothan 1971: Fig. 33:5).

Figure 3.19:3 is noteworthy for its unusually tall neck. Cooking pots with similar necks, some of which also have the elongated, triangular-profile rims described above, have been found at Tel Miqne-ʿEqron in Stratum IX (Killebrew 1998a: Ill. II:9:8), Lakhish in Level VI (Yannai 1996: Fig. 21:2) and, particularly, Tel Ḥarasim in Stratum IV (Givon 1995: Fig. 12:5, 7, 8; 1997: Fig. 11:3, 6). Enough of the elongated flange in Fig. 3.19:4 is preserved to determine that it is the same rim type.

The remainder of the cooking pots from Strata VIII–VII are either poorly preserved and/or resemble rims already described from previous strata. Figure 3.19:5 and 6, for example, are virtually the same as Fig.

3.17:11 (Stratum XI) and 13 (Stratum X). Indeed, it is likely that these two small rim fragments from Stratum VIII are residual. Except for its more developed triangular profile, Fig. 3.19:7 is similar to Fig. 3.18:4 from Stratum IX. A good parallel may be seen at Tel Baṭash-Timna in Stratum VIII (Panitz-Cohen and Mazar 2006: Pl. 28:3). With its more vertical stance, Fig. 3.19:8, on the other hand, is closer in appearance to cooking pots from the succeeding strata (see, e.g., Fig. 3.20:3–6).

Strata VI–V (Fig. 3.20:1–12)

The cooking pots from Strata VI–V, which correspond primarily to the twelfth century, continue in the Late Bronze Age Canaanite tradition. In general, they have the familiar triangular-profiled rim, no handles, soft carination in the upper body and rounded bottom. Figure 3.20:1 and 2 are the best exemplars of this type, similar to cooking pots discovered, for example, at Tel Baṭash-Timna in Stratum VI (Panitz-Cohen and Mazar 2006: Pl. 58:6) and Gezer in Stratum XIV/XIII (Dever 1986: Pl. 18:19). Note that the flange of Fig. 3.20:1 has been squared off.

Many of the rims, however, are less everted, giving the vessel a more vertical stance, which is characteristic of the Iron Age. The flange of the triangular-profiled rim is often convex, as with Fig. 3.20:3–6. Such rims occur at the following sites: Ashdod, Stratum XIV (Dothan and Freedman 1967: Fig. 22.10; M. Dothan 1971: Fig. 81:8); Tel Seraʿ, Stratum IX (Oren 1984: Fig. 5:4); Tel Baṭash-Timna, Stratum VII (Panitz-Cohen and Mazar 2006: Pl. 40:10); and Gezer, Stratum XIII (Dever 1986: Pl. 20:14, 15).

A slightly inverted rim and a carination that is high and more pronounced, both characteristics of Iron Age cooking pots, distinguish Fig. 3.20:7–9. All three of these vessels are well preserved and come from Room 71. Parallels are known from numerous sites, such as Ashdod, Stratum XII (M. Dothan 1971: Fig. 84:11), Bet Shemesh, Stratum III (Grant and Wright 1938: Pl. 62:26) and Tell Qasile, Stratum XII (A. Mazar 1985: Figs. 14:12–15, 16:12) and XI (Figs. 25:14, 27:20 [Type CP 1a]).

The folded-over rims on Fig. 3.20:10 and 11 have been flattened against the exterior wall of the vessel to the point that the triangular-profiled flange is hardly visible. Parallels have been excavated at Ashdod in Strata XV–XIV (Dothan and Porath 1993: Fig. 11:21), Tel Miqne-ʿEqron in Stratum VI (Killebrew 1998a: Ill.

III:7:6 [Form CA 18b]) and Bet Shemesh in Stratum III (Grant and Wright 1938: Pl. LXII:33). A cooking pot similar to Fig. 3.20:11, but smaller and with a more everted rim, was found in Stratum III (i.e., Fig. 3.20:13).

Figure 3.20:12 may be either a krater or a cooking pot. In either case it has a very large diameter (50 cm) and unusually thick walls. The rim, which has a flattened and elongated triangular profile, is somewhat reminiscent of Iron Age cooking pots (cf. Fig. 3.20:10). Large cooking pots similar to Fig. 3.20:12 have been found at Tel Baṭash-Timna in Strata VI and V (Panitz-Cohen and Mazar 2006: Pls. 59:5, 62:6). The presence of white inclusions in its fabric supports the identification of Fig. 3.20:12 as a cooking pot, a common feature of this type of ware at Tel Mor and sites elsewhere throughout the Late Bronze Age (see above). Finally, a globular cooking jar, probably made from Egyptian Nile silt clay, was found in Stratum V (see Fig. 4.9:10).

Strata IV–II (Fig. 3.20:13–15)
As with most other vessel types, there are very few cooking pots from the later strata at Tel Mor. Figure 3.20:13 resembles Fig. 3.20:11 from Stratum V except that its rim is more everted and profiled. Parallels, both smaller and larger in size, have been published from twelfth-century contexts at Tel Seraʻ in Stratum IX (Oren 1984: Fig. 5:3) and at Tel Zippor (Yannai 1996: Pl. 51:2). These cooking pots are unusual in that the maximum diameter is at the rim and not at the point of carination in the mid- or upper body. Aside from the more elongated flange, the rim depicted in Fig. 3.20:14 belongs to the same general type as Fig. 3.20:7–9 from Stratum VI. A good comparison for the later version may be found at Tell Qasile in Stratum IX (A. Mazar 1985: Fig. 53:22 [Type CP 1b]).

The stance of Fig. 3.20:15, by contrast, is more vertical. This cooking-pot type begins to appear, especially at southern sites, in the eleventh century and becomes increasingly popular during the tenth and ninth centuries (Gitin 1990:212–214; Mazar and Panitz-Cohen 2001:83). Most of these vessels, however, have rims that slant inward with an interior concavity. Cooking pots closer to Fig. 3.20:15, at least in terms of stance, have been excavated at Beʼer Shevaʻ in Stratum IX (Brandfon 1984: Fig. 18:5), Tel Baṭash-Timna in Stratum IVB (Mazar and Panitz-Cohen 2001: Pl. 4:11 [Type CP 15]) and Gezer in Field VI, Stratum 4 (Dever 1986: Pl. 43:7, 9).

Figure 3.20:16 is the well-rounded base of a cooking pot of indeterminate type. In addition, a simple, nearly vertical rim from a Stratum III vessel that was identified as a krater may, in fact, belong to a cooking pot (see Fig. 3.16:5). Finally, Stratum III produced a number of 'Aegean-style' cooking jugs (see below).

Storage Jars

Strata XII–X (Fig. 3.21)
No complete storage jars were recovered from Strata XII–X;[11] moreover, very few diagnostic sherds from storage jars were retrieved from Stratum XII (Fig. 3.21:3, 6, 13; for a residual MB IIC rim sherd in Stratum IX, see Fig. 3.22:17). All but two of the sherds from these strata are rims, which are generally characterized by eversion and/or thickening, often referred to as 'bulbous'. Bulbous rims first appear in Canaan at the end of the Middle Bronze Age and continue throughout the Late Bronze Age (as is the case at Tel Mor); therefore, rims of this type on their own are not very useful for the purposes of precise relative dating.

In the simplest version of the bulbous rim, the excess clay was rounded so as to create a convex, externally thickened profile (Fig. 3.21:1–5). The neck is short and roughly cylindrical, and the shoulder, when preserved (Fig. 3.21:4), is well rounded. Parallels, particularly from LB I, have been found in well-stratified contexts: Gezer in Cave I.10A (Seger 1988: Pl. 25:1); Tel Afeq in Stratum X-14 (Kochavi, Gadot and Yannai, forthcoming: Pl. 12:3, 4) and Ḥazor in Area H, Stratum 2 (Yadin et al. 1989: Pl. 266:10, 11).

There is bichrome decoration on the neck and shoulder of Fig. 3.21:5 that consists of a series of horizontal red bands, two of which enclose a dark wavy line. There is also a slight ridge at about the mid-neck point. Storage jars similar in terms of both form and decoration have been found at Ashdod in Stratum XVII (M. Dothan 1971: Fig. 33:13) and Tel Baṭash-Timna in Stratum VIII (Kelm and Mazar 1995: Fig. 4:14). The distinctive red color and numerous white inclusions of the fabric of Fig. 3.21:5, unlike that of the locally produced pottery, indicate that it is an imported storage jar.

Most bulbous rims have been modified to some degree. Some, for example, have been flattened (Fig. 3.21:6, 7) and everted (Fig. 3.21:8, 9). Parallels, mostly from MB IIC contexts, have been excavated at Gezer in Strata XX–XIX (Dever 1986: Pl. 6:18), Shechem in the East Gate (Seger 1974: Figs. 4:17, 5:31) and Ḥazor in Area H, Stratum 2 (Yadin et al. 1989: Pl. 266:8). The bulbous rim of Fig. 3.21:10 is even more everted, similar to storage jars from Tel Baṭash-Timna Stratum X (Panitz-Cohen and Mazar 2006: Pl. 13:8–10). The rims of Fig. 3.21:11 and 12 have been pinched, so as to give them a more complex profile (see also Fig. 3.22:12, 13 [Stratum IX]).

Figure 3.21:13–16 turn in slightly at the tip of the rim (see also Fig. 3.22:14 [Stratum IX]), a feature present on storage jars from Tel Baṭash-Timna in Stratum X (Panitz-Cohen and Mazar 2006: Pl. 13:7) and Tell Beit Mirsim in Stratum E (Albright 1933: Pl. 7:3). The unevenness of Fig. 3.21:3 and 13 is a sign of careless manufacture while the vessel was still on the wheel. The excess clay on Fig. 3.21:17 was folded over, creating a slight overhang, similar to rims found at Gezer in Stratum XVI (Dever 1986: Pl. 11:14) and Ḥazor in an LB I context (Yadin et al. 1958: Pl. 141:2). Parallels for the everted, almost flanged, rim of Fig. 3.21:18 appear at Gezer in Stratum XX–XIX (Dever 1986: Pl. 5:9) and Shechem in the Orthostat Phase of the East Gate (Seger 1974: Fig. 4:12). All the parallels provided above derive from MB IIC or LB I contexts.

The two storage-jar bases (Fig. 3.21:19, 20) are typical of LB I. Their bottoms retain the roundness of the Middle Bronze Age and have not yet developed the flattened stumps common to LB II (see, e.g., Fig. 3.23:16–19). Comparable bases occur at Tel Baṭash-Timna in Stratum X (Panitz-Cohen and Mazar 2006: Pls. 10:1, 13:4) and Gezer in Cave I.10A (LB IB; Seger 1988: Pls. 17:13, 25:1). Except for its thick gray core, the fabric of Fig. 3.21:19 is similar to that of the rim sherd with bichrome decoration (i.e., Fig. 3.21:5), both of which are probably imports. Note also that an incised storage-jar handle was observed in a Stratum XI level of Courtyard 118 (see Chapter 6, No. 5).

A small amphoriskos was recovered from a poor Stratum XII context (Fig. 3.21:21). Despite its diminutive size, the vessel was still formed on the wheel, as marks on the interior and exterior attest. Each handle consists of a tiny piece of clay attached to the shoulder. In terms of its overall form, the amphoriskos does not imitate any known amphorae of MB IIC or LB I.

Stratum IX (Fig. 3.22)

According to the excavators, a significant quantity of storage jars was found in the destruction layer of Building A, particularly in Room 111 (see Chapter 2, Stratum IX). Indeed, the rooms of this building produced, with only a few exceptions (i.e., Fig. 3.22:17, 18; and Chapter 6, No. 6), all the storage jars published from Stratum IX. Moreover, the only pithoi discovered at Tel Mor also derive from this stratum (Fig. 3.22:24–26). For these reasons, the excavators suggested that the building (at least the basement) functioned as a warehouse.

Figure 3.22:1 and 2 are the earliest restorable storage jars found at Tel Mor.[12] They have the following features in common: elongated ovoid body; bulbous rim; short vertical neck; well-rounded convex shoulder; vertically attached coil handles; and slightly flattened and thickened base. Figure 3.22:2 has a shallow rill at the base of the neck as well. Both jars have neither the carinated shoulder (cf. Fig. 3.24:1–3) nor stump base (cf. Fig. 3.23:14–19) characteristic of LB IIB. Similar well-preserved storage jars have been excavated at Tel Baṭash-Timna in Strata VIII (Panitz-Cohen and Mazar 2006: Pls. 22:9, 12; 35:3, 6) and VII (Panitz-Cohen and Mazar 2006: Pl. 41:1, 4).

The bulbous rim in its various forms continues to predominate in Stratum IX (Fig. 3.22:1–9). Figure 3.22:6 has a thin, dark red band on the interior and exterior of the rim, similar to a storage jar from Ashdod Stratum XVII (M. Dothan 1971: Fig. 33:13). In terms of the everted variety (Fig. 3.22:8–11; see also 3.21:8, 9 [Stratum XI]), comparable rims may be found, again, at Ashdod in Stratum XVII (M. Dothan 1971: Fig. 33:12; Dothan and Porath 1993: Fig. 8:15) and Gezer in Stratum XVI (Dever 1986: Pls. 10:7, 12:1). As in previous strata, some bulbous rims have been flattened or pinched (Fig. 3.22:12, 13; cf. Fig. 3.21:11, 12) and others have slightly incurving rims (Fig. 3.22:14–16; cf. Fig. 3.21:13–15). Rilling marks are prominent on the neck of Fig. 3.22:15 (see also M. Dothan 1960c: Fig. 4:7), similar to a later jar from Gezer Stratum XIV (Dever 1986: Pl. 16:4). Figure 3.22:16 has a triangular profile, like a rim from Megiddo Level F-9 (Stratum VIII; Ilan, Hallote and Cline 2000: Fig. 9.12:1).

The rim of Fig. 3.22:17 is T-shaped with an interior gutter. Such rims are characteristic of MB IIC and, at the very latest, LB I. Parallels may be found at Gezer in Stratum XIX–XVIII (Dever 1986: Pl. 7:6–8) and in the Lower Tomb Phase of Cave I.10A (Seger 1988: Pl. 31:20, 21). Given the poor context of Fig. 3.22:17 (i.e., Area 85), the residual nature of this rim sherd is not surprising.

Among the grave goods that accompanied the pit burial (L152) at the base of the eastern slope was a storage jar (Fig. 3.22:18; see also Chapter 2, Stratum IX, Figs. 2.10, 2.12:9). It differs from the other Stratum IX storage jars, especially the intact vessels, in that it has a more everted rim, shorter neck, broader shoulder and incipient stump base. A similar jar, particularly in terms of the overall piriform shape, was published from Tell el-'Ajjul (Petrie 1931: Pl. 46:43.22). Note also that an incised storage-jar handle was found in Area 85 on the summit of the tell (see Chapter 6, No. 6).

Storage-jar bases were also recovered from Building A (Fig. 3.22:19–23), again, mostly from Room 111. In general, they are similar to the two intact vessels described above (Fig. 3.22:1, 2): an elongated, tapered lower body, and a base that is flattened yet slightly convex. Similar bases have been found at Tel Baṭash-Timna in Strata VIII (Panitz-Cohen and Mazar 2006: Pls. 28:10, 11; 29:2, 4, 8) and VII (Panitz-Cohen and Mazar 2006: Pl. 41:1–5) and Tel Miqne-'Eqron in Stratum IX (Killebrew 1998a: Ills. II:6:14, 9:15). Figure 3.22:23 is rounded, yet slightly pointed, with a small 'button' of clay on the exterior (see also Fig. 3.21:19 [Stratum XI]). True stump bases, which are more characteristic of the latter part of LB II, first appear at Tel Mor in the next strata (Fig. 3.23:16–19).

A few rims of large storage jars or, more likely, pithoi were retrieved in Stratum IX (Fig. 3.22:24–26). The extraordinary wall thickness and large diameter of one rim (Fig. 3.22:24) clearly indicate that it belongs to a pithos. All the rims are simple and everted and rilling marks are visible on the exterior of the neck. During the Late Bronze Age, pithoi are found primarily at northern sites, particularly Ḥazor (Amiran 1969:143). Stratum IB, for example, produced a few rims similar to Fig. 3.22:24 (Yadin et al. 1958: Pls. 88:11; 97:10; 109:10, 13). It is possible that two large, flat bases found at Tel Mor in Strata XI (see Fig. 3.4:11) and IX (see Fig. 3.6:24) belong also to pithoi.

Strata VIII–VII (Figs. 3.23, 3.24)
Many storage-jar rims, shoulders and bases were excavated in Strata VIII–VII, but, in contrast to the previous stratum, no complete vessels were recovered. Also unlike Stratum IX is the fact that most of the storage-jar fragments from these strata were found outside the main structure, in this case Building B.

Bulbous rims continue to appear in Strata VIII–VII (Fig. 3.23:1–10), as they do at other LB IIB sites in the region such as Tel Baṭash-Timna in Stratum VI (Panitz-Cohen and Mazar 2006: Pl. 60:2) and Gezer in Stratum XIV (Dever 1986: Pl. 16:2, 3). Toward the end of the Late Bronze Age and into the Iron Age, however, these rims tend to be flattened, as is the case at Tel Mor (Fig. 3.23:3, 6, 8, 9). There is a clear demarcation between the rim and neck of Fig. 3.23:9, as is the case also with storage jars from Deir el-Balaḥ (Killebrew 1998a: Ill. III:15:13, 16 [Form CA 21?]). The fabric of Fig. 3.23:8, which is non-local, probably corresponds to Levantine Fabric P-30 (D. Aston, pers. comm.).

Two storage jars have ridges or 'collars' at the base of the neck (Fig. 3.23:7, 10). The ridge is more pronounced on Fig. 3.23:10 (see also M. Dothan 1960c: Fig. 4:11), parallels for which may be found at Gezer in Stratum XIV (Dever 1986: Pl. 16:1) and Megiddo in Tomb 8 (Guy 1938: Pl. 56:10). The larger rim (Fig. 3.23:7) may belong to a 'collared-rim store jar' or 'pithos'.[13] Although found predominantly in the hill country during Iron I, these vessels appear sporadically at coastal sites as early as the thirteenth century (Killebrew 1998a:118). Moreover, many of the earliest collared-rim pithoi have been excavated at sites possessing Egyptianized material culture, e.g., Tel Afeq (Beck and Kochavi 1985: Fig. 5:1), Bet She'an (James and McGovern 1993: Figs. 23:2, 4, 32:4) and Tell es-Sa'idiyeh (Tubb, Dorrell and Cobbing 1996: Fig. 20). To this list it may be possible now to add Tel Mor.

Figure 3.23:11 has an everted rim and a ridge at mid-neck. Although the type is found in the region during LB IIB, as at Ashdod in Stratum XIV (Dothan and Freedman 1967: Fig. 23:1) and Tel Baṭash-Timna in Stratum VI (Panitz-Cohen and Mazar 2006: Pl. 57:4, 5), it is more common at sites in the Jezreel Valley and northern Canaan during Iron I (for sites and further references, see Killebrew 1998a:116 [Form CA 24]).

Figure 3.23:12 has a rounded shoulder, four flattened coil handles and a number of potmarks around mid-body (for the latter, see Chapter 6, No. 10). Four-handled storage jars are commonly found at sites in the southern coastal plain and Shephelah at the end of the thirteenth and twelfth centuries (Killebrew 1998a:112–113). The majority of them are carinated, as is typical at the end of the Late Bronze Age (see below); however, some jars have rounded shoulders similar to Fig. 3.23:12. Late Bronze Age IIB tombs from the following sites have produced the best parallels: Lakhish (Tufnell 1958: Pl. 87:1020 [Tomb 532, Class D]); Deir el-Balaḥ (T. Dothan 1979: Ills. 22, 28 [Tomb 114], 81, 89 [Tomb 116], 124,

130 [Tomb 118]); and Tell el-Farʻah (S) (Petrie 1930: Pl. 19:43 P5 [Tomb 552]; Starkey and Harding 1932: Pl. 86:43 P6 [Tomb 905]).

Strata VIII–VII yielded three types of storage-jar bases. The first, which is similar to bases from Stratum IX (see Fig. 3.22:19, 21, 22), is flattened (yet still slightly convex) and thickened (Fig. 3.23:13–15). With this type there is no change in the curvature of the vessel wall from the tapered lower body to the base. There is a distinct change, however, with the second type—namely, the stump base (Fig. 3.23:16–19)—which is very common at the end of the Late Bronze Age. In some cases, the base is essentially hollow (Fig. 3.23:16, 18), whereas in others, it is solid (Fig. 3.23:17, 19). Parallels for the former, to give only a single site, are known from Ashdod in Stratum XIV (Dothan and Freedman 1967: Fig. 23:4; Dothan and Porath 1993: Fig. 13:11). Solid stump bases have been excavated at Tel Afeq in Stratum X-12 (Kochavi, Gadot and Yannai, forthcoming: Pl. 26:2) and Bet She'an in Level VII (Killebrew 1998a: Ill. II:73:2). The third type of base is rounded, yet slightly pointed, and hollow (Fig. 3.23:20; see also Figs. 3.22:23 [Stratum IX] and 3.25:9 [Stratum V]). A similarly shaped (but more solid) base was found at Tel Afeq in Stratum X-12 (Beck and Kochavi 1985: Fig. 2:4).

Storage jars with sharply carinated shoulders, often referred to as 'Canaanite jars' (Grace 1956), first appear at Tel Mor in Stratum VII (Fig. 3.24). This type is characterized by the following morphological features, some of which are not preserved on the vessel fragments in Fig. 3.24: a conical body; a plain, externally thickened rim and a mostly vertical neck that slopes into a straight, almost horizontal shoulder; a gently sloping, slightly convex shoulder with sharp carination; flattened vertical loop handles; and a thickened, flattened base. Canaanite jars first appear in LB IIA, particularly at sites on or near the coast, such as Lakhish in Tomb 501 (Tufnell 1958:224, Pl. 87:1019 [Class D]) and, famously, on board the Ulu Burun shipwreck (Pulak 1997: Fig. 9b; for further sites and references, see Killebrew 1998a:113 [Form CA 22]). They continue to appear in LB IIB strata, as at Bet She'an in Level VII (Killebrew 1998a: Ill. II:73:2) and, to a lesser degree, even into the Iron Age (see below, Strata VI–V).

Strata VIII–VII produced also a neck-less storage jar with a rolled rim made from the characteristic Egyptianized fabric (see Fig. 4.10:3) and an imported Egyptian 'amphora', which ironically imitates Canaanite jars, made of Marl F fabric (Fig. 4.9:4). Finally, an incised storage-jar handle appears to have come from Stratum VIII (see Chapter 6, No. 4).

Strata VI–V (Fig. 3.25)
The storage-jar rims and bases from Strata VI–V are, for the most part, the same as those known in Strata VIII–VII. There is, however, a tendency in this limited sample for the bulbous rims to be flattened (Fig. 3.25:1–3). Such rims have been found at Ashdod in Stratum XIII (Dothan and Porath 1993: Fig. 15:8), Tel Baṭash-Timna in Stratum V (Panitz-Cohen and Mazar 2006: Pl. 63:4) and Gezer in Stratum XIII (Dever et al. 1974: Pl. 29:1; Dever 1986: Pl. 23:2). The rounded shoulder of Fig. 3.25:2 is a common feature of storage jars throughout the Late Bronze Age (see Figs. 3.22:1 [Stratum IX] and 3.23:12 [Stratum VII]).

Some rims from Stratum V show little sign of the addition of a coil and, as such, are not bulbous (Fig. 3.25:4–6). Figure 3.25:4 is everted and slightly flattened at the tip. Storage jars with similar rims have been excavated at Tel Afeq in Stratum X-12 (Kochavi, Gadot and Yannai, forthcoming: Pl. 20:7) and Bet She'an in Level VI (James 1966: Fig. 54:16). The best parallels for Fig. 3.25:5 and 6, which have ridges below the rim, derive from sites in the north, such as Megiddo in Stratum VIA (Finkelstein, Zimhoni and Kafri 2000: Fig. 11.4:1), Bet She'an in Level VI (James 1966: Figs. 52:10, 54:6) and 'Afula in Stratum IIIB (M. Dothan 1955: Fig. 16:14). Figure 3.25:7 may, in fact, belong to a stand.

Stump bases continue to appear in Strata VI–V (Fig. 3.25:8; see also 3.23:15, 16 [Strata VIII–VII]). Similar bases have been found in early Iron I contexts elsewhere, such as Ashdod in Stratum XIII (M. Dothan 1971: Fig. 83:1, 2), Lakhish in Stratum VI (Ussishkin 1983: Fig. 16:17) and Gezer in Stratum XIII (Dever, Lance and Wright 1970: Pls. 27:2, 28:1, 2). Other storage-jar bases from this period at Tel Mor, all of which have precedents in earlier strata, are pointed (Fig. 3.25:9; see also Fig. 3.23:20 [Stratum VII]), more rounded and knob-like (Fig. 3.25:10; see also Fig. 3.23:18 [Stratum VII]) and flattened with a small 'button' (Fig. 3.25:11; see also Fig. 3.21:19 [Stratum XI]). Parallels may be found at Ḥaẓor in Stratum XII (Yadin et al. 1989: Pl. 167:9), 'Afula in Stratum IIIB (M. Dothan 1955: Fig. 16:23) and Gezer in Stratum XIII (Dever 1986: Pl. 20:18).

Strata VI–V also produced the majority of the Egyptian and Egyptianized storage jars excavated at Tel Mor, among which were the following vessel types: Egyptian 'amphorae' made either of Marl F (see Fig. 4.9:5) or D fabric (Fig. 4.9:8, 9); a large globular jar made of Marl D (Fig. 4.9:7); and neck-less storage jars with rolled rims made from Egyptianized fabric (Fig. 4.10:4–6), the lattermost of which may imitate a 'meat jar'.

Strata III–II (Figs. 3.26, 3.27)
Stratum III, particularly Pit 17, produced a number of intact and partially restorable storage jars.[14] The following morphological features characterize the best preserved vessel (Fig. 3.26:1): an elongated, ovoid body; a short, slightly everted rim; a convex, sloping shoulder, with the carination at the point of the upper handle attachment; coil handles attached at the upper body; a tapered lower body; and a thickened and flattened (yet convex) base. Figure 3.26:2 and 3 are similar except that the carination is poorly defined.[15] This type of storage jar appears primarily at sites along or near the Levantine coast during Iron I, particularly during the eleventh century. Nearby parallels may be found at Ashdod in Stratum X (M. Dothan 1971: Fig. 4:1), Gezer in Stratum XI (Dever 1986: Pl. 41:16) and Tell Qasile, especially in Stratum X (A. Mazar 1985:54–56 [with further bibliography], Figs. 43:19–21, 48:10 [Type SJ 1]). Figure 3.26:4 appears to be a bag-shaped version of this general type (cf. A. Mazar 1985: Fig. 48.3).

Stratum III also produced several storage-jar rims and bases. Figure 3.26:5 has a simple rim set off by a shallow rill and a tall neck that slants inward. The juncture between neck and shoulder is clearly demarcated. Storage jars with such tall necks are best known from eighth-century contexts, such as Ashdod Stratum VIII (Dothan and Porath 1982: Fig. 16:3) and Tel Batash-Timna Stratum III (Mazar and Panitz-Cohen 2001: Pl. 20:4, 6 [Type SJ 7c]); thus Fig. 3.26:5 is probably an intrusive sherd. Figure 3.26:6 is similar except that the rim is bulbous and the neck is narrower and more vertical. Figure 3.26:7, which is an entirely different type, has an everted rim, short neck and rounded shoulder. The rims of both Fig. 3.26:8 and 9 are incurving, similar to a storage jar discovered at Tel Afeq in Stratum X-10 (Kochavi, Gadot and Yannai, forthcoming: Pl. 34:3). The two bases (Fig. 3.26:12, 13)—in addition to those on the intact and partially

restored storage jars (Fig. 3.26:1, 3)—are typologically related to the stump bases familiar from previous strata (e.g., Figs. 3.23:16, 18 [Strata VIII–VII] and 3.25:8 [Stratum V]).

Very few storage jars were attributed to Stratum II. Figure 3.26:10 has a thickened, incurving rim and a short neck clearly set off from a rounded shoulder. Parallels have been found in tenth-century contexts such as Ashdod Stratum X (Dothan and Porath 1982: Fig. 9:2) and Tel Batash-Timna Stratum IV (Kelm and Mazar 1995: Fig. 6:5). Figure 3.26:11 has a thickened, everted rim and a tall neck that is slightly constricted. Note also that a storage-jar handle bearing an incised potmark was excavated in Stratum II (see Chapter 6, No. 3).

A number of storage-jar rims retrieved from unstratified contexts attest to a late Iron II presence at Tel Mor. Figure 3.26:14–16 are ridged rims belonging to cylindrical, holemouth jars that are found primarily at southern sites in eighth-century contexts. The rim in Fig. 3.26:14 slants upward toward the lip and extends beyond the vessel wall so as to form a ledge. The vessel wall curves in slightly beneath the rim. Similar jars have been excavated at Ashdod in Stratum VIII (M. Dothan 1971: Fig. 51:4–6), Be'er Sheva' in Stratum II (Aharoni 1973: Pl. 58:17–22), Lakhish in Level III (Zimhoni 1997: Fig. 5.20:4) and Tell Qasile in Stratum VII (A. Mazar 1985: Fig. 57:10–12). The rim in Fig. 3.26:15 is almost perfectly horizontal and the ledge protrudes farther beyond the vessel wall, which, in this case, curves outward beneath the rim. Parallels may be found, for example, at Ashdod in Stratum VII (M. Dothan 1971: Fig. 77:10; Dothan and Porath 1982: Figs. 23:4, 27:5) and Tel Batash-Timna in Stratum III, where it is tentatively identified as a krater (Mazar and Panitz-Cohen 2001: Pl. 21:4 [Type KR 35a?]). The rilled rim of Fig. 3.26:16, of which only a small fragment remains, appears to belong to a simple holemouth. A similar jar rim, but without the rilling, was found at Tel Batash-Timna in Stratum III (Mazar and Panitz-Cohen 2001: Pl. 21:5).

The discovery of Fig. 3.26:17 suggests even later activity at the site. The following morphological features characterize this distinctive storage jar: a short, simple rim that slants inward; a nearly horizontal shoulder, covered in places with excess clay that had been smeared on; a sharply carinated shoulder; and small, circular, crudely formed handles with much applied clay around the points of attachment. The handles would have been poorly suited for lifting, especially when these vessels were full with liquid. Instead, they were intended primarily as a means of securing cargoes, most likely of wine—namely, ropes were passed through the handles of these storage jars when they lay nested in the holds of ships (Zemer cited in Artzy 1980:69).

Figure 3.26:17 belongs to the Phoenician storage jar *par excellence* during the late Iron II and Persian periods.[16] This type appears throughout the eastern Mediterranean region, particularly at coastal Levantine sites. Toward the end of Iron II it may be found at such nearby sites as Ashdod in Stratum VI (M. Dothan 1971: Fig. 6:2), Tel Baṭash-Timna in Stratum II (Mazar and Panitz-Cohen 2001:103 [with further references] Pl. 47:1–3 [Type SJ 15a]) and Tell Qasile in Stratum VII (A. Mazar 1985: Fig. 58:11). The type appears in significant quantities during the Persian period as, for example, at Tel Mevorakh in Strata VI–IV (Stern 1978:33–34 [with further references], Fig. 6:1–3, 6, Pl. 24:1, 2), Gezer in Stratum IV (Gitin 1990: Pl. 28B:13–21) and Tell el-Hesi in Stratum V (Bennett and Blakely 1989: Fig. 170). Neutron Activation Analyses carried out on these storage jars from Tel Baṭash-Timna (Gunneweg and Yellin 1991:100) and Tell el-Hesi (Bennett and Blakely 1989:221) determined that they are of probable northern coastal/Lebanese origin.

Figure 3.26:18 is a decorated body sherd that belongs either to a jar or a krater. The fragmentary scene contains a popular motif of Canaanite pottery—a palm tree flanked by animals, probably ibexes.

Figure 3.26:19 is a type of amphoriskos especially popular during Iron I (see M. Dothan 1960c: Pl. 11:6).[17] It is characterized by the following morphological features: a simple rim and tall, narrow neck; a round shoulder and elongated, ovoid body; flattened coil handles attached to the upper body; and a tapered lower body and button base. The decoration consists of groups of vertical bands flanking the handles and horizontal bands on the lower body and near the base.

It is likely that these ceramic amphoriskoi imitate glass versions made in Egypt as early as the XVIIIth Dynasty (Amiran 1969:250; T. Dothan 1982:263). The type appears most commonly at southern sites, particularly in tombs. Similar amphoriskoi have been found, for example, in the following Iron I contexts: Tell el-Farʿah (S) in Tomb 935 (Starkey and Harding 1932: Pl. 87:W 6), Zakariya (Duncan 1930: Fig. 55 W 7), Tel ʿEṭon in Tomb C1 (Edelstein and Aurant 1992:

Fig. 10:4) and a tomb located between Ashdod and Ashqelon (Gophna and Meron 1970: Fig. 2:7). The type was produced also during the Late Bronze Age, as evidenced by its presence at Tel Miqne-ʿEqron in Stratum IX (Killebrew 1998a: Ill. III:18:1 [Form CA 31]).

Jugs and Juglets (Figs. 3.27, 3.28)

Strata XII–X

Two well-preserved jugs and several juglets were found in the early strata at Tel Mor. Figure 3.27:1 is a squat jug with a double-coil handle that extends from the shoulder to an everted rim (see also M. Dothan 1973: Fig. 3:9). Between the two coils and next to the rim is a button. Double-coil handles, with or without buttons, are well known throughout MB II on various types of jugs and juglets.[18] A close parallel for this jug comes from Lakhish Tomb 1552 (Tufnell 1958:187, Pl. 74:671 [Class A]). A triple-coil handle was found also at Tel Mor in Stratum XII (Fig. 3.27:2). The three coils are arranged side by side, whereas frequently they are grouped so as to create a triangular cross section, as on jugs from Megiddo in Tomb 911 (MB II; Guy 1938: Pls. 28:44 [911 A1], 31:20 [911 D]), Ḥazor in Stratum 2 of Area D (Yadin et al. 1958: Pl. 101:25) and Tel Mikhal (Negbi 1989:48, Fig. 5.3.20).

Figure 3.27:3 is an unusual vessel with basket handles and bichrome decoration on a burnished slip. The decoration consists of groups of pendant lines, either straight or a single wavy line enclosed by pairs of straight lines. It might be a local imitation of Bichrome Wheel-Made Ware; however, there are no known parallels for either the form or decoration at sites on Cyprus or in Canaan. Two true Bichrome jugs were found in Strata XII–X (see Fig. 5.7:7, 8).

Two jug or jar rims from Stratum XI also bear painted decoration. Figure 3.27:4 is covered with a weak white wash with painted dark 'ticks' applied to the rim and diagonal lines below it. Figure 3.27:5, on the other hand, is covered with a slip with groups of ticks on the rim. Both vessels have almost perfectly vertical necks. In terms of morphology, the rims resemble those occurring on storage jars from the same approximate period (cf. Fig. 3.21:2, 5).

Strata XII–X produced the most and best preserved dipper juglets at Tel Mor. Of all these juglets, the two with elongated bodies are most characteristic of MB IIC (Fig 3.28:1, 2; see also M. Dothan 1973: Fig. 3:11).

They also have an ovoid, slightly pinched mouth, a handle that extends from rim to shoulder and a pointed base. Parallels have been found, for example, at Lakhish in Tomb 1552 (Tufnell 1958: Pl. 78:779, 780 [Class A]), Gezer in Stratum XVIII (Dever et al. 1970: Pl. 30:16) and Cave I.10A (Seger 1988: Pl. 31:37), and Tel Yoqne'am, particularly in Strata XXI and XXb (Ben-Ami and Livneh 2005: Fig. IV.17:2 [Type JT Ia], 4 [Type JT Ib]).

Despite their Stratum XII context, the form of Fig. 3.28:3 and 4 is closer to that of LB I dipper juglets, which are distinguished by a squat truncated body and incipient button base (see also Fig. 3.28:8). Similar juglets have been excavated at Lakhish in Tomb 1555 (Tufnell 1958: Pl. 78:782) and Tel Baṭash-Timna in Stratum X (Panitz-Cohen and Mazar 2006: Pl. 14:9). Figure 3.28:5 and 6 are similar except for the more piriform shape of the body. The body of Fig. 3.28:7 is almost cylindrical, which is more a feature of LB II (cf. 3.28:8). Strata XI–X also produced a number of Base Ring I jug rims (see, e.g., Fig. 5.3:11, 12).

Strata IX–VII

Very few locally produced jugs and juglets were recovered from strata corresponding to LB II. Apparently the demand for these vessel types was largely met by the importation of Cypriot (see Figs. 5.3:13–19; 5.6) and, to a lesser extent, Mycenaean pottery (see Fig. 5.8:1–6).

Figure 3.27:6 is a small globular jar or jug with a handle that extends from the shoulder to an unpreserved rim. The painted decoration consists of horizontal bands at mid-body, a horizontal and diagonal line on the handle and pendant strokes that descend from another band around the neck. With the exception of a single red band at mid-body, the rest of the decoration is dark on a light self-slip. Figure 3.27:7 has a trefoil mouth, wide neck, strap handle that extends from shoulder to rim and a flat base (see also M. Dothan 1960c: Fig. 4:14). A similar jug was found at Megiddo in Tomb 25 (Guy 1938: Pl. 57:1). Strata IX–VII yielded no complete juglets. Only the cylindrical lower body and small button base of Fig. 3.28:8 are preserved. Many imported Base Ring (see, e.g., Fig. 5.3:10, 13, 14, 16–19), White Shaved (see Fig. 5.6) and imported Mycenaean (see Fig. 5.8:1, 4, 6) jugs and juglets also came from Strata IX–VII.

Strata VI–V

More locally produced jugs were found in Strata VI–V than in the immediately preceding strata. This increase is probably attributable to the decline (Stratum VI) and cessation (Stratum V) of Cypriot imports, particularly Base Ring II Ware (see Chapter 5). As for juglets, whether locally made or Cypriot, very few were excavated in Strata VI–V.

Figure 3.27:8 is the largest and best preserved of the Strata VI–V jugs (see also M. Dothan 1960c: Fig. 5:1). It is characterized by the following morphological features: a wide trefoil mouth; a flaring neck; a thick handle that extends from the mid-neck to a well-rounded shoulder; a pointed base; and an overall piriform body. Most comparable jugs from this period are smaller, less piriform, and have a handle that extends instead from the rim to the shoulder. These parallels may be found, for example, at Deir el-Balaḥ (Killebrew 1998a: Ill. III:6:3 [Form CA 16a]), Lakhish in Stratum VI (Yannai 2004: Fig. 19.48:2), Tel Baṭash-Timna in Stratum VII (Panitz-Cohen and Mazar 2006: Pls. 43:1, 54:1), Gezer in Tomb I (Panitz-Cohen and Maier 2004: Pls. 5:3, 12:5) and Tel Afeq in Stratum X-12 (Kochavi, Gadot and Yannai, forthcoming: Pl. 19:11 [Type J3]). Figure 3.27:9, of which only the upper body remains, resembles more closely this better attested type of jug, at least in terms of the handle attachment.

Figure 3.27:10 is a biconical jug, sometimes referred to also as a 'mug' or 'tankard'. It has a small handle that extends from an everted rim to the upper part of a low, sloping shoulder. The poorly defined carination is in the lower half of the body, and the base is not preserved. The main painted decoration consists of wavy vertical lines framed by vertical and horizontal bands. There are also transverse strokes on the rim and some faint decoration on the handle. Similar jugs have been discovered at Ashdod in Stratum XV (M. Dothan 1971: Fig. 20:5), Deir el-Balaḥ (Killebrew 1998a: Ill. III:6.7 [Form CA 17]) and Lakhish in Tomb 501 (Tufnell 1958: Pl. 84:961). Biconical jugs with a poorly defined carination, like Fig. 3.27:10, are particularly common at northern sites during LB IIB and early Iron I (for references, see Killebrew 1998a:102).

Figure 3.27:11 is a small jug with the following physical attributes: a simple, slightly everted rim; a tall narrow neck; a handle that extends from rim to shoulder; a flat base; and a squat, globular body. Close parallels are known from Tel Afeq, in Stratum X-12

(Kochavi, Gadot and Yannai, forthcoming: Pl. 21:16 [Type J5]) and Megiddo, in Tomb 989 A1 (Guy 1938: Pl. 16:15). A similar jug, but with a significantly more everted rim, was found at Tel Mor in Stratum III (Fig. 3.28:12).

Figure 3.28:9 is the upper half of a dipper juglet. A coil handle extends from its everted rim to a sloping shoulder. The lower point of attachment, where the clay from the handle was spread against the vessel wall, is clearly visible in section. The fabric and surface treatment (i.e., vertical paring marks) are imitative of White Shaved Ware in similar fashion to a juglet found at Tel Afeq in Stratum X-12 (Kochavi, Gadot and Yannai, forthcoming: Pl. 24:9). An imitation Base Ring II jug was also found in Stratum VI at Tel Mor (see Fig. 5.3:20).

Stratum III
Very few jugs and juglets in the Canaanite tradition were found in Stratum III (Figs. 3.27:12, 3.28:10). The Philistine ceramic assemblage, on the other hand, includes numerous Bichrome-decorated, Ashdod Ware and 'Aegean-style' cooking jugs (see Fig. 3.32:11–20). As with the importation of Cypriot pottery during most of the Late Bronze Age (Strata IX–VII), Philistine pottery seems to have met the demand for certain vessel types at Tel Mor in the early Iron Age.

Figure 3.27:12 is a nearly intact jug whose handle extends from a well-everted rim to a rounded shoulder. It also has a globular body and a flat base. Figure 3.28:10 is a squat juglet with a red slip; except for its rim, it closely resembles a jug from Stratum VI (see Fig. 3.27:11). A juglet similar in shape, but without the slip, was found at Ashdod in Stratum Xb (Dothan and Porath 1982: Fig. 3:5).

Pilgrim Flasks (Fig. 3.29)

A dozen pilgrim flasks were recovered from relatively secure contexts in various strata at Tel Mor. The earliest flask was among the grave goods of Burial 152 from Stratum IX (Fig. 3.29:1; see also Fig. 2.12:2). It is characterized by the following morphological features: an everted, bowl-shaped rim; a short neck; small, flattened handles attached to the neck by spreading the clay, which creates a triangular space below the rim; and a lentoid, slightly asymmetrical body. Red-painted concentric circles, which were carefully executed, adorn the body. Parallels for this common Late Bronze

Age flask type, particularly in terms of the short neck and handle attachment, may be found, for example, at Tel Yoqne'am in Stratum XIXa (Ben-Ami and Livneh 2005: Fig. IV.21:3), Palmaḥim in Tomb 26 (Singer-Avitz and Levi 1992: Fig. 3:5), Tel Afeq in Stratum X-12–13 (Kochavi, Gadot and Yannai, forthcoming: Pl. 50:3 [Type F1]) and Tell Abu Hawam in Stratum VA (Hamilton 1935: Pl. 42:255).

Two pilgrim flasks were found in Room 71 at an elevation assigned to Stratum VI. The body of Fig. 3.29:3 is large and—characteristic of flasks from Iron I—globular. The rim, neck and handles are not preserved. The bottom, which also does not survive, was probably slightly pointed, similar to large flasks from Stratum III (Fig. 3.29:11, 12). The decoration consists of the usual red concentric circles on an unslipped body.

Figure 3.29:2 is a small, lentoid flask with a single handle and slight protuberance in the middle of both sides of the body (see also M. Dothan 1972: Pl. 7:3). In addition to concentric circles, three painted lines radiate haphazardly from the lower handle attachment. This single-handled variety imitates Cypriot Base Ring and Red Lustrous Ware flasks (e.g., Åström 1972b: Pl. 55:4 [Type VII]). Canaanite imitations have been discovered thus far only in funerary contexts, as at Deir el-Balaḥ (T. Dothan 1979: Ills. 85, 92 [Tomb 116], 129, 135 [Tomb 118]) and Lakhish (Tufnell 1958: Pl. 81:872 [Tomb 216], 874 [Tomb 501], 875 [Tomb 556]).

Pit 17 from Stratum III produced nine flasks (Fig. 3.29:4–12). The fill of this pit also contained restorable storage jars (see Fig. 3.26:1–3), 'Aegean-style' cooking jugs (see Fig. 3.32:18, 19) and an amphoroid krater (see Fig. 3.16:8). With the exception of Fig. 3.29:10, the flasks may be divided into the following two groups based on the shape of the body: small and lentoid (Fig. 3.29:4–9) or large (maximum diameter 18 cm) and globular (Fig. 3.29:11, 12). Regarding the large variety, Fig. 3.29:11 has a taller neck and more painted decoration, including horizontal bands on the handles, than Fig. 3.29:12 (see also M. Dothan 1960a: Pl. 3:4; 1960c: Pl. 11:1). Parallels for this general type may be found in early Iron Age contexts at Ashdod in Stratum XI (Dothan and Porath 1993: Fig. 41:8), Gezer in Stratum XIII (Dever 1986: Pl. 33:5) and Bet She'an in Stratum 4 (Yadin and Geva 1986: Fig. 27:13). The body of Fig. 3.29:10 is transitional in that it is medium in size and slightly lentoid in shape (see also M. Dothan 1960a: Pl. 3:4; 1960c: Fig. 5:6, Pl. 11:1). It has a tall neck; long, almost diagonal, strap handles; and is decorated with many closely grouped, concentric circles.

Most of the small lentoid flasks have tall necks and long strap handles (Fig. 3.29:4–6). Parallels, with or without decoration, may be found at Ashdod in Stratum XII (Dothan and Porath 1993: Fig. 32:10, 11), Tell Qasile in Stratum X (A. Mazar 1985: Fig. 37:2, 5, 8–15 [Type FL 1]), Tel Zippor in Stratum II (Biran and Negbi 1966: Fig. 5:10) and in an early Iron Age tomb located between Ashdod and Ashqelon (Gophna and Meron 1970: Fig. 2:10). The attachment of the shorter loop handles on Fig. 3.29:7 creates a triangular space below the rim characteristic of Late Bronze Age pilgrim flasks (see also Fig. 3.29:1). Parallels for the short-necked variety (Fig. 3.29:9) are known from Ashdod in Stratum XII (Dothan and Porath 1993: Fig. 32:15) and Tel Dor in the Ir1a(l) horizon (Gilboa and Sharon 2003: Fig. 5:5 [FL 2]). Note also that a sherd preserving the rim, neck and handle of an imported Mycenean LH IIIA2 flask was discovered in an unstratified context at Tel Mor (see Fig. 5.8:7).

Lamps (Fig. 3.30)

Figure 3.30:1 is a seven-spouted lamp that was uncovered in the area of the Stratum XI *bāmāh* (see Fig. 2.3; see also M. Dothan 1960a: Pl. 1:2; 1960c: Pl. 9:2). The lamp was created by folding inward seven sections of the rim of a plain bowl. Blackening appears around three of the spouts where the wicks were placed. Seven-spouted lamps have also been found in MB II cultic and funerary contexts at Tel Haror (Katz 2000: Fig. 16), Jericho (Tomb J7; Kenyon 1960: Fig. 186:13) and Nahariya (M. Dothan 1956: Fig. 4). The lamps from Tel Haror and Jericho have solid disk bases, whereas those from Megiddo(?), Nahariya and Tel Mor have round bases. Seven-spouted lamps disappeared during the Late Bronze Age and became popular again during the early Iron Age (for references, see Oren 1973:110).

The remaining lamps from Strata XII–X are of the standard single-spouted variety (Fig. 3.30:2–6). Morphologically, those with less pinched spouts, rounded bases and simple rims are earlier in date (Fig. 3.30:2, 3). Similar lamps have been published from LB I contexts at the following sites: Tel Batash-Timna in Stratum VIII (Panitz-Cohen and Mazar 2006: Pl. 19:5–7); Lakhish in Tomb 1555 (Tufnell 1958: Pls. 51:35, 73:654 [Class C]); various tombs at Megiddo (Guy

1938: Pls. 17:8, 44:7, 49:7, 52:6); and Hazor in Area D, Stratum 3 (Yadin et al. 1958: Pl. 122:21, 22), as well as in Area H, Stratum 2 (Yadin et al. 1958: Pls. 240:7; 257:1, 2; 267:3).

The flattened rims and bases of Fig. 3.30:4 and 5 indicate a date later in the Late Bronze Age. Parallels for the deeper lamp with the more developed flanged rim (Fig. 3.30:4) may be found at Tel Batash-Timna in Stratum IX (Panitz-Cohen and Mazar 2006: Pl. 26:6), Gezer in Cave I.10A (Seger 1988: Pls. 18:6, 8; 20:15) and Hazor in Area D, Stratum 3 (Yadin et al. 1958: Pl. 122:24, 25) and in Area H, Stratum 2 (Yadin et al. 1989: Pl. 267:5–7). A more deeply pinched and upturned spout characterizes Fig. 3.30:5, which is probably the latest in this group. Similar lamps have been uncovered in LB II contexts at Megiddo in Tomb 877 B 1 (Guy 1938: Pl. 14:4) and Hazor in Area D, Stratum 1 (Yadin et al. 1958: Pl. 125:23, 24). Figure 3.30:6 has a more deeply pinched spout, a rim with a well-developed flange, and a round base. Of the numerous parallels that could be cited for this lamp type, the following are but a few: Ashdod Strata XV–XIV (Dothan and Porath 1993: Fig. 11:25); Gezer Stratum XIII (Dever 1986: Pl. 22:18); and Tel Afeq Stratum X-12 (Beck and Kochavi 1985: Fig. 3:7, 8). Oil lamps are conspicuously absent from the Iron Age strata at Tel Mor (IV–II).

Miscellaneous Ceramic Items (Fig. 3.31)

A small jar(?) was found in Courtyard 118 at an elevation that corresponds to Stratum XI (Fig. 3.31:1). The rim, which slopes downward and is triangular in section, probably once held a lid. Below the rim are bilateral perforations that were created before firing. The body, which was turned on a wheel, is roughly cylindrical in shape with a slight entasis in the middle. The vessel wall thickens toward the base, where there are signs of hand-molded clay similar to many Egyptianized beer jars from later strata (cf. Fig. 4.11). Indeed, Fig. 3.31:1 might be an early type of beer jar thus far unattested in Canaan. In this case, it is another example of early Egyptian influence at Tel Mor along with the Type II.1 slender ovoid jar discovered at a similar elevation in Stratum XI (see Fig. 4.10:1).

Two ceramic loom weights recovered in poorly stratified contexts were assigned to Strata IX (Fig. 3.31:2) and VI (Fig. 3.31:3). Each is roughly rectangular in shape with rounded edges and a perforation in the upper third of the weight. This long-lived type may be found in contexts comparable in date to those of the Tel Mor loom weights, such as Megiddo IX (Loud 1948: Pl. 170:24) and Gezer XIII (Dever 1986: Pl. 57:5). Two perforated stones that probably functioned as weights were also excavated at Tel Mor (see Chapter 10, Perforated Objects).

Figure 3.31:4, which derives from a poor Stratum IX context, appears to be a pierced lug handle attached to a rectangular fragment of terracotta. The three straight sides of the object are intact and exhibit traces of excess clay, whereas the fourth side is broken. There are three incised horizontal(?) lines above(?) the handle. The function of this object is not known, nor have any parallels been found.

It is likely that Fig. 3.31:5, which was discovered in a Stratum VII area, functioned as a funnel. Both the rim, though somewhat uneven, and the spout are intact. A larger funnel (with less complex profile) is known from Ḥazor Stratum 1B of Area C (Yadin et al. 1960: Pl. 123:21).

Two jar stoppers were also unearthed, one in Stratum VII (Fig. 3.31:6) and the other in Stratum VI (Fig. 3.31:7). Their small diameters (c. 5.0 cm) would have precluded them from use with most of the Late Bronze Age storage jars at Tel Mor, the average rim diameter of which is 11.5 cm. They could have been fitted, however, inside the mouth of a jug from this period (see, e.g., Fig. 3.27:11). When still soft, the clay was pressed into the mouth so as to give the stoppers a vaguely conical shape. Both are perforated slightly diagonal to the vertical axis. These perforations probably allowed for the release of pressure from gases emitted during the wine fermentation process (e.g., Gal 1989:283).

Figure 3.31:8 is a spout in the shape of a bull's head that belonged either to a kernos or a zoomorphic vessel (see also M. Dothan 1960c: Pl. 11:2). The horns are broken off, the eyes are made of small beads of clay and the mouth is a narrow circular opening at the end of funnel-shaped snout. Zoomorphic spouts were especially popular during Iron I, which supports the attribution of Fig. 3.31:8 to Stratum V. They may be found—to name only two instances—at Ashdod in Stratum XI (M. Dothan 1971: Fig. 75:5) and Tell Qasile in Strata XI–X (A. Mazar 1980:112, Fig. 41b with further references). Note also that the head of a Base Ring II bull-shaped vessel was recovered from an unreliable Stratum III context (see Fig. 5.4). Figure 3.31:9 is a leg that belonged either to a zoomorphic vessel or a tripod. Its fabric is finely levigated with a

thick gray core and a well-burnished, reddish surface. No close parallels have been found for this sherd.

Canaanite Pottery: Summary

All the common local forms and, to a lesser extent, decoration anticipated for pottery from a site in southern coastal Canaan are present at Tel Mor. This observation is especially apparent when one compares the Tel Mor assemblage to that of the much larger and extensively excavated site of Ashdod, with which, as expected, there is a close correspondence. The relative dearth of restorable vessels from Tel Mor is surprising given that most of the strata (IX, VIII, VII, VI) ended with thick destruction levels. A summary of the relatively few stratigraphically secure contexts and the ceramic finds they yielded appears in Chapter 13, Summary and Historical Conclusions.

The study of the pottery has shown that M. Dothan's dating of the strata from Tel Mor, which he arrived at after the first season of excavation, was essentially correct (M. Dothan 1960c). His conclusions are borne out also by the results of numerous subsequent excavations in the southern coastal plain and the Shephelah (e.g., Lakhish, Tel Miqne-'Eqron, Tel Baṭash-Timna, Tel Afeq). In two respects, however, he was somewhat lacking. First, the poorly stratified pottery of Stratum II is closer in date to the tenth than to the eight century BCE; and second, he failed to recognize the significant amount of Egyptianized pottery in the locally made assemblage (see Chapter 4).

PHILISTINE POTTERY

Philistine pottery appears only in Strata IV and III at Tel Mor. Small amounts of Philistine Bichrome, 'Aegean-style' cooking jugs and Ashdod Ware are present; however, there is no locally made Mycenean IIIC:1b (Myc. IIIC:1b). Altogether about 70 sherds and whole vessels were found, of which 31 came from unstratified contexts.[19] Philistine pottery comprises 6% of the overall assemblage in Strata IV–III; however, given that the excavators appear to have collected all decorated body sherds, this percentage is probably inflated. The color of the Bichrome fabric ranges from red (2.5YR 5/6) to yellowish red (5YR 5/6). Its clay generally contains fine to small white inclusions, less frequently dark and sparkling. The core (when present) is thin and light gray, indicating that the vessels were evenly fired. Decoration typically consists of red (10R 4/4) and dark paint on a white wash or thin slip. Ashdod Stratum XII, Tel Miqne-'Eqron Stratum VI and Tell Qasile Stratum VI provide the majority of parallels discussed below.

Bichrome Ware (Fig. 3.32:1–16)

Figure 3.32:1 is a skyphos or bell-shaped bowl decorated with an antithetic spiral motif. The following features characterize its form: everted and tapered rim; horizontal handles (of which only the stubs remain here) attached at an angle on the upper vessel wall; deep hemispherical body; and flat, concave disk or ring base (not preserved here; see T. Dothan 1982:98–106 [Type 1]; A. Mazar 1985:87–90 [Type BL 16]; Killebrew 2000:236–239 [Form AS 4]; Dothan and Zukerman 2004:8–12 [Type D]). A vertical wavy line separates the spirals, which face the same direction, and there is a painted band adorns the interior and exterior of the rim. The bell-shaped bowl was the most common vessel type during the period of Myc. IIIC:1b production and remained popular throughout the Philistine Bichrome phase. Particularly close parallels, both in terms of form and decoration, may be found, for example, at Ashdod in Strata XII (Ben-Shlomo 2005: Fig. 3.15:4–7) and XI (Ben Shlomo 2005: Fig. 3.46:1, 2, 6), Tel Miqne-'Eqron in Stratum VIA (Dothan and Zukerman 2004: Fig. 8:2; Dothan, Gitin and Zukerman 2006: Fig. 3.29:9, 10) and Tell Qasile in Stratum XI (A. Mazar 1985: Fig. 19:3; see also T. Dothan 1982: Fig. 2:1–5). Figure 3.34:2 and possibly 3 are also bell-shaped bowl rims. The vessel wall of the latter, however, is unusually thick for this vessel type.

The best-preserved example of Philistine Bichrome is Fig. 3.32:4, which is a krater with typical spiral decoration on a white wash (see also M. Dothan 1960a: Fig. 5:5; 1960c: Pl. 3:2). The following features characterize its form: a T-shaped rim that slopes inward; two horizontal loop handles attached to the upper body at an angle; a deep bell-shaped body; and a ring base (not preserved here, but see Fig. 3.32:7). Its decoration consists of a red band on the rim and handles, and horizontal red bands that frame the main register located in the upper body. The metopes contain dark-painted spirals facing the same direction with red filling, and the triglyphs are comprised of alternating dark and red, wavy, vertical lines. Similarly decorated kraters have been discovered at the following sites in

mid- to late twelfth-century strata: Ashdod XII (Dothan and Porath 1993: Fig. 29:3) and XI (M. Dothan 1971: Figs. 2:6, 86:7, Pl. 9:2; see also T. Dothan 1982: Fig. 11.3 [Type 2]); Tel Miqne-'Eqron VI (T. Dothan 1998: Pl. 7:6 [Type IKR3]; Killebrew 1998b: Fig. 12:9); and Tell Qasile XII (A. Mazar 1985: Fig. 13:23 [Type KR 2b]). Figure 3.32:5 and 6 are rims that belong to similar kraters, albeit with less painted decoration preserved. Figure 3.32:8 illustrates the lower and mid-body, including a handle stub, of another krater. Three parallel horizontal bands and part of a spiral motif are faintly visible (for another possible Philistine Bichrome krater, see Fig. 3.16:4 above).

Figure 3.32:9 shows the decorated mid-body, shoulder and neck of either a stirrup jar or strainer-spouted jug (see also M. Dothan 1960c: Pl. 11:5). Groups of parallel red lines that enclose a dark horizontal band of chevrons cover the mid-body (for the chevron motif, see T. Dothan 1982:212–214). On the shoulder are dark concentric semicircles filled with red and joined by vertical chevrons. This combination of motifs has been seen thus far only on stirrup jars as at Bet Shemesh in Stratum III (Grant and Wright 1938: Pl. 60:15), Tell el-Far'ah (S) in Tomb 532 (Petrie 1930: Pl. 22:199) and in an Iron I pit burial at Azor (see T. Dothan 1982: Fig. 17:5).

Many other common Bichrome motifs are recognizable on smaller fragments, all of which probably belong either to kraters or jugs. The earliest Bichrome sherd may be Fig. 3.32:10, which preserves the tail of a water bird, the quintessential Philistine motif. To the left of the tail are four vertical lines belonging to the triglyph. The now-faded red and black paint was applied on a white slip. The curvature and thickness of the vessel wall indicate that this sherd belonged to a krater. According to Trude Dothan, the bird motif is characteristic of the first two phases of Philistine pottery, which correspond to the twelfth and the first half of the eleventh centuries BCE (1982:198; see also Dothan and Zukerman 2004:39–40). The water-bird motif is known on Bichrome kraters at Ashdod in Strata XIIIa (Dothan and Porath 1993: Fig. 22) and XII (Dothan and Porath 1993: Fig. 27:1, 2), at Tel Miqne-'Eqron in Stratum VI (Killebrew 1998a: Ill. II:26:17) and at Tell Qasile in Stratum XI (A. Mazar 1985: Fig. 27:11; for additional sites, see T. Dothan 1982:198–203, Figs. 5–7, 8:1, Pl. 1:3, 13, 19–22).

Figure 3.32:11 contains part of a Maltese cross that serves as a filling motif within a spiral. Not enough of the sherd is preserved to determine whether it belongs to a jug or a krater; however, this motif appears more frequently on the latter. Maltese crosses appear as a filling motif on Bichrome kraters at the following well-stratified sites: Ashdod, Strata XII (Ben-Shlomo 2005: Fig. 3.19:5) and XI (Dothan and Porath 1993: Fig. 40:7); Tel Miqne-'Eqron, Strata VIA (Dothan, Gitin and Zukerman 2006: Fig. 3.29:13) and V (T. Dothan 1998: Pl. 10:6–8); Tell Qasile, Stratum XI (A. Mazar 1985: Fig. 27:11); Tel Baṭash-Timna, Stratum V (Panitz-Cohen and Mazar 2006: Pls. 66:1, 67:19, 68:5, 70:18, 71:21); Gezer, Stratum XIII (Dever 1986: Pl. 24:16); and Tel Afeq, Stratum X-10 (Kochavi, Gadot and Yannai, forthcoming; for additional sites, see T. Dothan 1982:204, Fig. 6:4, Pl. 18:2).

Figure 3.32:12 belongs to the shoulder of a Bichrome vessel, probably some type of jug. The main motif is a crosshatched lozenge or rhombus with four dark wavy lines along the side. Variations of the motif are frequent on Bichrome jugs, as at Ashdod in Stratum XII (Dothan and Porath 1993: Fig. 29:4), Bet Shemesh in Stratum III (Grant and Wright 1938: Pl. 38:21) and Tell el-Far'ah (S) in various tombs (Petrie 1930: Pls. 23:3 [Tomb 542], 8 [Tomb 859]; for the motif in general, see T. Dothan 1982:212, Fig. 70).

The shoulders in Fig. 3.32:13–16 most likely belong to jugs. On Fig. 3.32:13 three red horizontal bands enclose what remains of a scale pattern attached vertically to a triglyph. This motif often fills out a metope otherwise dominated by a water bird, as on a krater from Ashdod Stratum XII (Dothan and Porath 1993: Fig. 28:5). Figure 3.32:14 shows the tops of lotuses or lozenges below a concentric semicircular motif. The space in between was probably originally filled with red horizontal bands that have worn away over time. On Fig. 3.32:15 there is a pendant elongated triangle, partially filled. Provided that this sherd is drawn correctly, it reflects a departure from the customary execution of this motif—namely, with the point of the triangle facing upward (cf. T. Dothan 1982: Figs. 46, 47:1, 2). Figure 3.32:16 shows a vertical band of chevrons, three wavy lines with dots in between, and part of a spiral.

Ashdod Ware (Fig. 3.32:17)

Several body sherds of Ashdod Ware were found at Tel Mor in poor Stratum III contexts (e.g., Fig. 3.32:17). At the eponymous site of Ashdod, this type

of pottery first appears in Stratum X (Iron IIA; e.g., Dothan and Porath 1982:10–11) and continues to be found in secure stratigraphic contexts until Stratum VIII, which was destroyed in the late eighth century BCE (e.g., M. Dothan 1971: Figs. 40:5, 41:27, 43:5). Recently a substantial quantity of this pottery was excavated in well-defined, late ninth/early eighth-century BCE contexts at Tell es-Safi (Temporary Stratum 4; Ben-Shlomo, Shai and Maeir 2004). The excavators' proposed term 'Late Philistine Decorated Ware' (LPDW) is preferable in light of the fact that chemical and petrographic analyses of Ashdod Ware from various sites indicate production in the vicinity of both Ashdod and Tell es-Safi.

Given the proximity of Ashdod, the small amount of LPDW found at Tel Mor is surprising. It is worth noting that, similar to the situation at Ashdod (Dothan and Porath 1982:52), LPDW occurs in contexts (albeit poor) alongside Philistine Bichrome pottery in Stratum III. The chronological range of pottery from this stratum, however, is very broad (see above); therefore, it is possible that the LPDW at Tel Mor belongs to c. 1000 BCE, when the Stratum III settlement apparently was destroyed.

The LPDW at Tel Mor is decorated with the thick red slip (10R 4/6), vertical hand-burnishing and horizontal black and white linear decoration familiar to this ware. The clay, which is yellowish red (5YR 5/6) in color, was studied petrographically by David Ben-Shlomo, who provided the following short report:

Four samples from Tel Mor were analyzed by thin section petrography. The sherds include three examples of LPDW (Fig. 3.32:17; and Reg. Nos. A42/6, A67/11, both not drawn) and one plain carinated bowl (Fig. 3.10:11). All four sherds generally belong to Petrographic Group A1, which is characterized by a coastal alluvium clay with large quantities of bimodal quartz, including rounded coastal sand. Two of the LPDW samples have a more silty matrix, classified as Group A1c, which seems to be typical of LPDW vessels at Ashdod and Tell es-Safi. It is not surprising that the samples from Tel Mor exhibit the same characteristics as most of the LPDW from nearby Tel Ashdod. Because of the proximity of the two sites, unfortunately, it is not possible to determine analytically where exactly the pottery was produced. Given that Ashdod was a major production center for LPDW, however, it is more likely that the LPDW vessels found at Tel Mor were produced at Ashdod.

'Aegean-Style' Cooking Jugs (Fig. 3.32:18–20)

Figure 3.32:18–20 are 'Aegean-style' cooking jugs, which are characterized by the following attributes: an everted rim; a short curving neck and a rounded shoulder; one or occasionally two handles that extend from rim to shoulder; a globular-shaped body; and a flat or low ring base. The surface of both is blackened, which is undoubtedly due to their use as cooking vessels. In Canaan, these jugs frequently appear in strata that also contain Philistine pottery, both Myc. IIIC:1b and Philistine Bichrome. At Ashdod, 'Aegean-style' cooking jugs are found in Strata XIIIb (Dothan and Porath 1993: Fig. 17:4, 5), XIIIa (Dothan and Porath 1993: Fig. 23:5, 6), XII (Dothan and Porath 1993: Fig. 34:2, 7; Ben-Shlomo 2005: Fig. 3.28:7–11) and, to a lesser extent, XI (Ben-Shlomo 2005: Fig. 3.5:6–13); at Tel Miqne-'Eqron, they come from Strata VII (Killebrew 1998b: Fig. 7:19; T. Dothan 1998: Pls. 1:7, 3:14 [Type ICJ]) and VI (Killebrew 1998a:Ill. III:26:12, 13 [Form AS 10]; T. Dothan 1998: Pl. 6:7, 8; see also Killebrew 2000: Fig. 12.3:11–14; Dothan and Zukerman 2004: Fig. 36.6 [Type P]).[20] These jugs have been found also at Tell Qasile in Strata XI (A. Mazar 1985: Fig. 25:17) and X (A. Mazar 1985: Figs. 41:4, 49:10, 12, 13 [Type JG 3]), Bet Shemesh in Stratum III (Grant and Wright 1938: Pl. 61:27–31) and, perhaps, Gezer in Stratum XIII (Dever 1986: Pl. 19:11).

This type of cooking jug occurs slightly earlier on Cyprus at sites that correspond to the Late Cypriot IIC and IIIA periods and at sites in the Aegean region in strata that date to the Late Helladic IIIB and IIIC periods (for references, see Killebrew 2000:242; Dothan and Zukerman 2004:28–30). As demonstrated above, the type appears in Syria-Palestine mainly at Philistine Pentapolis sites during the twelfth and eleventh centuries BCE. In these Iron I strata, both 'Aegean-style' cooking jugs and cooking pots in the Canaanite tradition were in use, as was the case at Tel Mor in Stratum III (see above).

Philistine Pottery: Summary

All the wares, forms and decorative motifs in this limited corpus are familiar from the Philistine pottery assemblage as known from such sites as Ashdod and, increasingly, Tel Miqne-'Eqron. As noted above, Philistine Bichrome, 'Aegean-style' cooking jugs and LPDW are all present at Tel Mor in Strata IV–III. Mycenean IIIC:1b, however, is conspicuously absent (for a possible exception, see Fig. 5.8:2). Bell-shaped bowls (Fig. 3.32:1–3), kraters (Fig. 3.32:4–8) and jugs (Fig. 3.32:9) comprise the Philistine Bichrome sub-assemblage. Although no clear examples of strainer jugs were discerned by the present author, the excavators report the existence of this vessel type at Tel Mor as well (referred to as 'beer jugs'; M. Dothan 1993). Among the unattested forms are stirrup jars, kylikes, pyxides, feeding bottles and kalathoi/basins. Beyond the ubiquitous straight and wavy lines that frame the metopes and form the triglyphs, the most common motif is the antithetic spiral, which appears on both bell-shaped bowls (Fig. 3.32:1–3) and kraters (Fig. 3.32:4, 5, 8). There are also single instances of chevron bands, concentric semicircles (Fig. 3.32:9), a water bird (Fig. 3.32:10), a Maltese cross (Fig. 3.32:11), a cross-hatched lozenge (Fig. 3.32:12) and a scale pattern (Fig. 3.32:13).

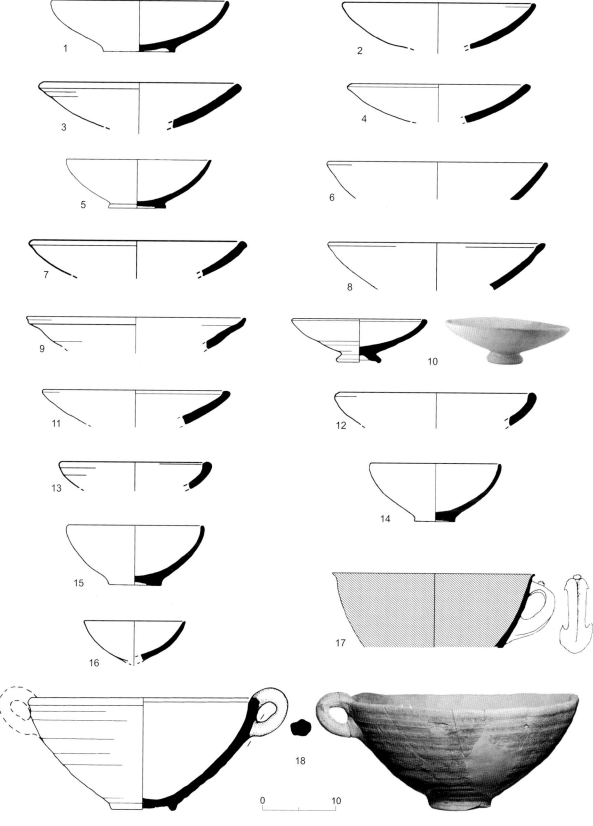

Fig. 3.1. Strata XII–X uncarinated bowls.

◀ **Fig. 3.1**

No.	Reg. No.	Context (Stratum)	Elevation (m)*	Description
1	B345/10	Courtyard 118 (XII)	19.00/18.70	Surface: 7.5YR 6/6 (reddish yellow); fabric: same; core: none; inclusions: many fine to large white, few fine voids, few fine dark
2	B356/11	Courtyard 118 (XII)	18.70/18.60	Burnish; surface: 2.5YR 6/6 (light red); fabric: same; core: none; inclusions: few medium voids, few fine sparkling, few small red
3	B317/9	Courtyard 118 (XII)	N/A	Surface (self-slip): 7.5YR 7/3 (pink); fabric: 10R 5/6 (red); core: light gray; inclusions: very many fine sparkling, few small voids, few fine to small white
4	B256/15	Courtyard 118 (XI)	20.40/20.25	Surface: 7.5YR 8/2 (pinkish white); fabric: 7.5YR 5/6 (strong brown); core: gray; inclusions: few fine white, very few fine sparkling, few small voids
5	B328/61	Courtyard 118 (XII)	19.10/18.90	Surface: 5YR 6/6 (reddish yellow); fabric: same; core: none; inclusions: few medium white, many fine dark
6	B253/26	Courtyard 118 (XI)	19.80/19.60	Surface (self-slip): 5YR 6/4 (light reddish brown); fabric: 5YR 5/6 (yellowish red); core: thin, light gray; inclusions: few fine sparkling, many fine white, few fine dark
7	B345/9	Courtyard 118 (XII)	19.00/18.70	Surface: 10R 5/6 (red); fabric: same; core: light gray, middle and interior; inclusions: very many fine sparkling, many fine white, very few fine voids
8	B259/30	Courtyard 118 (XI?)	19.25/19.10	Surface: 10YR 7/7 (very pale brown); fabric: 2.5YR 5/8 (red); core: thick, light gray; inclusions: many fine to small dark, few fine voids, few fine white
9	B266/19	Courtyard 118 (XII)	19.50	Surface: 2.5YR 6/6 (light red); fabric: same; core: thick, light gray; inclusions: many fine dark, few fine sparkling, few small to medium white
10	B356/5	Courtyard 118 (XII)	18.70/18.60	Wet-smooth marks; surface: 7.5YR 6/4 (light brown); fabric: 5YR 6/6 (reddish yellow); core: N/A; inclusions: many fine to small dark, few fine voids
11	B356/4	Courtyard 118 (XII)	18.70/18.60	Surface: 2YR 6/8 (light red); fabric: 5YR 6/6 (reddish yellow); core: gray; inclusions: very few large white
12	B75/3	Probe 117 (X)	20.40/20.15	Surface: 2.5YR 7/6 (light red); fabric: same; core: none; inclusions: N/A
13	B288/8	Courtyard 118 (XII)	19.10/19.05	Surface: 2.5YR 6/6 (light red); fabric: same; core: thick, gray; inclusions: few small white
14	B211/1	Sq N22 (XI–IX)	20.15	Surface (self-slip): 5YR 5/6 (yellowish red); fabric: 7.5YR 6/6 (reddish yellow); core: thin, light gray; inclusions: many fine white, few fine dark, few fine sparkling
15	B209/1	Courtyard 118 (XI–IX)	20.10	Surface: 7.5YR 5/6 (strong brown); fabric: same; core: thick, gray; inclusions: few fine voids, few fine dark
16	B346/2	Courtyard 118 (XII?)	19.00/18.00	Surface: 5YR 6/4 (light reddish brown); fabric: same; core: none; inclusions: few fine sparkling, few fine to small voids, few small white
17	B365/2	Pit 166 (XII)	18.65/17.90	Burnish; surface (slip): 10R 4/6 (red); fabric: 5YR 6/6 (reddish yellow); core: thick, gray; inclusions: few fine sparkling
18	B128/1	Courtyard 118 (XII–XI?)	N/A	Rilling, wet-smooth marks; surface: 10R 5/6 (red); fabric: same; core: thick, gray; inclusions: many fine dark, many fine sparkling, few fine voids

* The discrepancies in elevation between the figure tables and the list of loci and walls (Appendix 2) are a result of the excavators' errors in record-keeping.

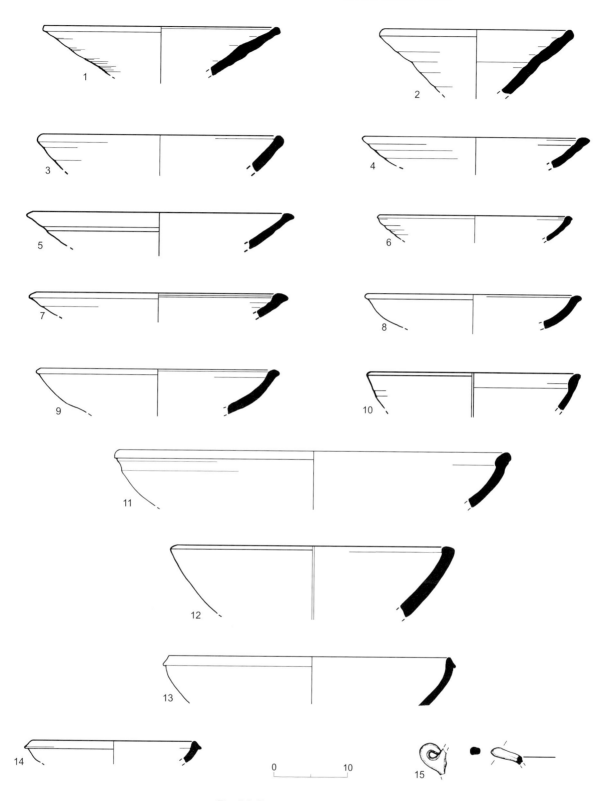

Fig. 3.2. Strata XII–X uncarinated bowls.

◄ **Fig. 3.2**

No.	Reg. No.	Context (Stratum)	Elevation (m)	Description
1	B93/4	Courtyard 118 (XI–IX)	20.10	Rilling; surface: 2.5YR 7/6 (light red); fabric: same; core: thick, gray; inclusions: many small voids
2	B93/5	Courtyard 118 (XI–IX)	20.10	Rilling; surface: 7.5YR 6/6 (reddish yellow); fabric: same; core: thick, dark gray; inclusions: many medium to large white, many small voids
3	B289	Courtyard 118 (XII)	19.00/18.90	Rilling; surface: 10R 6/6 (light red); fabric: same; core: light gray; inclusions: few fine dark, few fine white, few fine sparkling
4	B281/1	Courtyard 118 (XII)	19.10	Rilling; surface: 2.5YR 5/6 (red); fabric: 10R 4/6 (red); core: light gray, middle and interior; inclusions: few medium white, few medium dark, few fine voids, few fine sparkling
5	B345/8	Courtyard 118 (XII)	N/A	Rilling; surface (self-slip): 10R 6/4 (pale red); fabric: 10R 5/6 (red); core: light gray; inclusions: many fine to small white, many fine voids
6	B259/13	Courtyard 118 (XI?)	19.25/19.10	Rilling; N/A
7	B316	Courtyard 118 (XII)	19.30/18.80	Rilling; surface: 10R 6/4 (pale red); fabric: same; core: thin, light gray; inclusions: few fine voids, very few fine sparkling
8	B328/16	Courtyard 118 (XII)	19.10/18.90	Surface: 10R 6/4 (pale red); fabric: same; core: thick, dark gray; inclusions: very many fine sparkling, few fine voids, very few fine white
9	B328/3	Courtyard 118 (XII)	19.10/18.90	Surface (self-slip): 10R 6/6 (light red); fabric: 5YR 6/4 (light reddish brown); core: none; inclusions: few fine to small voids, few fine white
10	B281/2	Courtyard 118 (XII)	19.10	Surface: 2.5YR 6/6 (light red); fabric: same; core: gray; inclusions: N/A
11	B77/16	Courtyard 118 (X)	20.50/20.30	Surface: 5YR 6/8 (reddish yellow); fabric: same; core: light gray, middle and interior; inclusions: few fine sparkling
12	B235/27	Courtyard 118 (XI?)	19.80/19.65	Surface: 5YR 7/6 (reddish yellow); fabric: same; core: none; inclusions: many medium to large voids
13	B256/18	Courtyard 118 (XI?)	20.40/20.25	Surface (self-slip): 7.5YR 7/4 (pink); fabric: 5YR 5/8 (yellowish red); core: thick, gray; inclusions: very many fine to small dark, many fine voids, many small white
14	B87/5	Courtyard 118 (XI–X)	20.20	Surface: 10R 6/6 (light red); fabric: 7.5YR 5/6 (strong brown); core: none; inclusions: many fine to small white, many medium to large dark
15	B265/3	Courtyard 118 (XII)	19.10	Surface: 7.5YR 7/4 (pink); fabric: 2.5YR 6/6 (light red); core: none; inclusions: few fine sparkling, few small dark

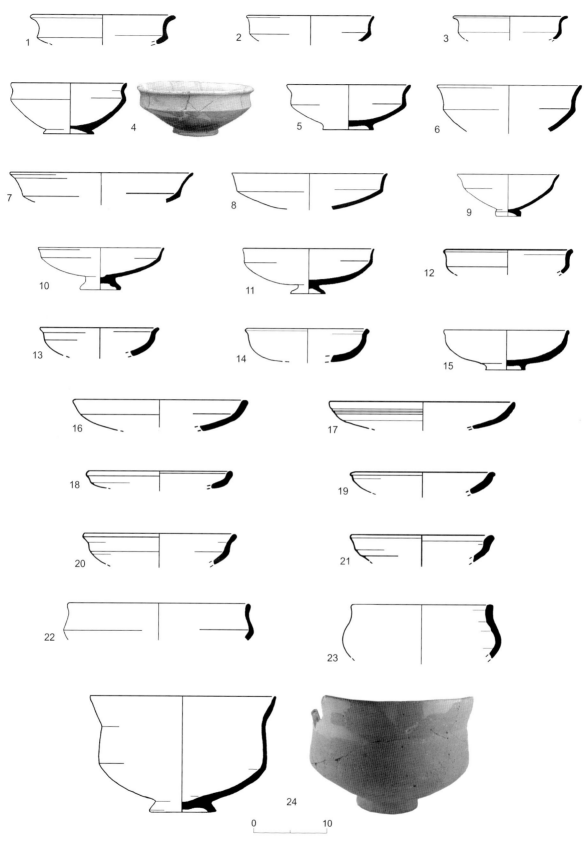

Fig. 3.3. Strata XII–X carinated bowls.

◄ **Fig. 3.3**

No.	Reg. No.	Context (Stratum)	Elevation (m)	Description
1	B328/20	Courtyard 118 (XII)	19.10/18.90	Surface: 5YR 6/4 (light reddish brown); fabric: same; core: gray; inclusions: many fine voids
2	B292/2	Courtyard 118 (XII?)	19.30	Surface: 10YR 7/4 (very pale brown); fabric: same; core: thick, light gray; inclusions: many small white
3	B346/27	Courtyard 118 (XII)	19.00/18.00	Surface: 10YR 7/3 (very pale brown); fabric: same; core: none; inclusions: very few fine to small white
4	B316/23	Courtyard 118 (XII)	19.30/18.80	Surface (self-slip): 10R 7/3 (very pale brown); fabric: 2.5YR 7/6 (light red); core: N/A; inclusions: very many small white, many fine to small dark
5	B316/4	Courtyard 118 (XII)	19.30/18.80	Surface: 10R 6/5 (pale red); fabric: same; core: thick, gray; inclusions: few medium white, few medium voids, many fine dark
6	B212/60	Sq M22–N22 (XI–IX)	20.10/20.00	Surface: 7.5YR 5/6 (strong brown); fabric: same; core: thick, gray; inclusions: many fine sparkling, few fine white
7	B259/1	Courtyard 118 (XI?)	19.25/19.10	Surface: 2.5YR 6/6 (light red); fabric: same; core: thin, gray; inclusions: N/A
8	B253/24	Courtyard 118 (XI?)	19.80/19.60	Surface: 2.5YR 6/6 (light red); fabric: same; core: none; inclusions: N/A
9	B247/27	Courtyard 118 (XII–XI)	19.60	Surface: 10YR 7/2 (light gray); fabric: same; core: none; inclusions: few fine dark, few fine voids
10	B287/1	Courtyard 118 (XII)	19.10/18.90	Surface: 10R 6/6 (light red); fabric: same; core: none; inclusions: few, fine, dark
11	B273/1	Courtyard 118 (XI)	19.40	Surface: 5YR 6/6 (reddish yellow); fabric: same; core: none; inclusions: many fine dark
12	B131/8	Courtyard 118 (XI)	20.00/19.65	Surface (self-slip): 5YR 7/4 (pink); fabric: 5YR 6/8 (reddish yellow); core: light gray; inclusions: many fine to small white
13	B292/1	Courtyard 118 (XII?)	19.30	Surface (self-slip): 7.5YR 7/3 (pink); fabric: 2.5YR 6/6 (light red); core: thin, light gray; inclusions: few fine white
14	B342	Courtyard 118 (XII)	18.80	Surface: 2.5YR 6/6 (light red); fabric: same; core: thick, 7.5YR 5/4 (brown); inclusions: many fine voids, many fine dark
15	B265/1	Courtyard 118 (XII?)	19.10	N/A
16	B317/3	Courtyard 118 (XII?)	N/A	Surface (self-slip): 5YR 7/4 (pink); fabric: 10R 6/6 (light red); core: thick, light gray; inclusions: very many small to medium white
17	B319/1	Courtyard 118 (XII?)	N/A	Surface: 2.5YR 6/6 (light red); fabric: same; core: none; inclusions: few fine dark, few fine to small voids
18	B328/12	Courtyard 118 (XII)	19.10/18.90	Surface (self-slip): 2.5YR 7/3 (light reddish brown); fabric: 2.5YR 6/6 (light red); core: gray; inclusions: N/A
19	B296/8	Courtyard 118 (XII)	N/A	Surface: 2.5 YR 6/6 (light red); fabric: same; core: gray; inclusions: many fine to small white
20	B348/17	Courtyard 118 (XI–IX)	N/A	Surface: 2.5YR 7/4 (light reddish brown); fabric: same; core: 5YR 6/6 (reddish yellow); inclusions: few fine voids
21	B287/13	Courtyard 118 (XII)	19.10	Surface: N/A; fabric: 2.5YR 7/6 (light red); core: gray; inclusions: N/A
22	B245/1	Courtyard 118 (XII–XI)	19.95	Surface: 2.5YR 6/8 (light red); fabric: same; core: thin, light gray; inclusions: N/A
23	B224/5	Courtyard 118? (XI–IX?)	20.00/19.90	Surface: 2.5YR 5/6 (red); fabric: same; core: thick, 7.5YR 6/8 (reddish yellow); inclusions: many small white
24	B70/1	Probe 116 (X)	20.40	Surface: 5YR 7/6 (reddish yellow); fabric: same; core: thick, dark gray; inclusions: very many small white, many fine to small voids, few small red

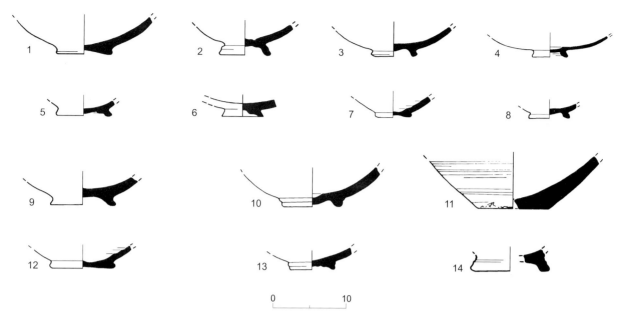

Fig. 3.4. Strata XII–X bowl bases.

No.	Reg. No.	Context (Stratum)	Elevation (m)	Description
1	B248/5	Courtyard 118 (XII–XI?)	19.45	Surface: 2.5YR 6/6 (light red); fabric: same; core: thick, gray; inclusions: many small to medium white, many small to medium voids
2	B365/5	Pit 166 (XII)	18.65/17.90	N/A
3	B356/2	Courtyard 118 (XII)	18.70/18.60	Surface: 2.5YR 6/6 (light red); fabric: same; core: none; inclusions: few fine voids, few fine sparkling, few fine dark
4	B292/5	Courtyard 118 (XII)	19.30	Surface: 10YR 10/3 (very pale brown); fabric: same; core: none; inclusions: few small white, few small red
5	B256/24	Courtyard 118 (XI?)	20.40/20.25	Surface: 10R 6/4 (pink red); fabric: same; core: thick, gray; inclusions: few small red, few fine sparkling, few small white
6	B240/32	Courtyard 118 (XI)	19.65/19.55	Surface: 2.5YR 6/8 (light red); fabric: 7.5YR 6/8 (reddish yellow); core: none; inclusions: very few fine to small white
7	B114/15	Courtyard 118 (XI?)	19.95	Surface: 7.5YR 7/6 (reddish yellow); fabric: same; core: gray; inclusions: none
8	B247/20	Courtyard 118 (XII–XI)	19.60	Surface: 10R 6/6 (light red); fabric: 7.5 YR 4/4 (brown); core: none; inclusions: N/A
9	B259/33	Courtyard 118 (XI?)	19.25/19.10	Surface: 2.5YR 6/6 (light red); fabric: same; core: thick, gray; inclusions: many fine dark, many fine white, few medium red, few fine voids
10	B114/16	Courtyard 118 (XI?)	19.95	Surface: 7.5YR 7/4 (pink); fabric: same; core: thick, dark gray; inclusions: many fine to small voids, few fine red
11	B131/33	Courtyard 118 (XI)	20.00/19.65	Wet-smooth marks; surface: 10YR 7/7 (very pale brown); fabric: same; core: light gray; inclusions: many medium white, few fine sparkling, many medium voids, few fine to small red
12	B124/12	Courtyard 118 (XI–IX)	20.10	Surface: 2.5YR 7/6 (light red); fabric: 10R 6/8 (light red); core: thick, 5YR 6/8 (reddish yellow); inclusions: many fine white
13	B77/37	Courtyard 118 (X?)	20.50/20.30	Surface (self-slip): 5YR 8/3 (pink); fabric: 10R 6/8 (light red); core: gray; inclusions: N/A
14	B72/3	Probe 116 (XI)	N/A	Surface: 10YR 8/4 (very pale brown); fabric: same; core: none; inclusions: N/A

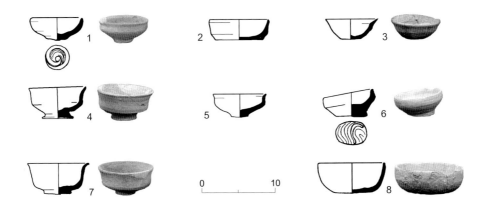

Fig. 3.5. Strata XII–X miniature bowls.

No.	Reg. No.	Context (Stratum)	Elevation (m)	Description
1	B271/1	N/A (XII?)	N/A	Surface: 10YR 7/3 (very pale brown); fabric: 10R 5/6 (red); core: N/A; inclusions: few fine to medium voids; string-cut base
2	B333	Courtyard 118 (XII)	18.80	Surface (self-slip): 2.5Y 7/3 (pale yellow); fabric: 7.5YR 7/6 (reddish yellow); core: none; inclusions: few small white, few fine sparkling
3	B106/1	Courtyard 118 (XI)	19.95	Surface: 7.5YR 7/4 (pink); fabric: 7.5YR 6/6 (reddish yellow); core: thick, gray; inclusions: many fine dark, many fine voids
4	B109	Courtyard 118 (XI)	19.95	Surface (self-slip): 7.5YR 7/4 (pink); fabric: 7.5YR 6/6 (reddish yellow); core: thick, gray; inclusions: many fine voids, few small dark
5	B110	Courtyard 118 (XI)	19.95	Surface: 7.5YR 7/4 (pink); fabric: same; core: N/A; inclusions: many small white, many fine to small voids
6	B102	Courtyard 118 (XI)	19.95	Surface (self-slip): 10R 6/3 (pale brown); fabric: 2.5YR 5/4 (reddish brown); core: N/A; inclusions: many fine to small dark, many fine white, few fine sparkling; string-cut base
7	B103	Courtyard 118 (XI)	19.95	Surface: 5YR 6/4 (light reddish brown); fabric: same; core: N/A; inclusions: many small voids, many small dark
8	B105	Courtyard 118 (XI)	19.95	Surface: 7.5YR 7/4 (pink); fabric: 7.5YR 6/6 (reddish yellow); core: N/A; inclusions: many fine to small dark

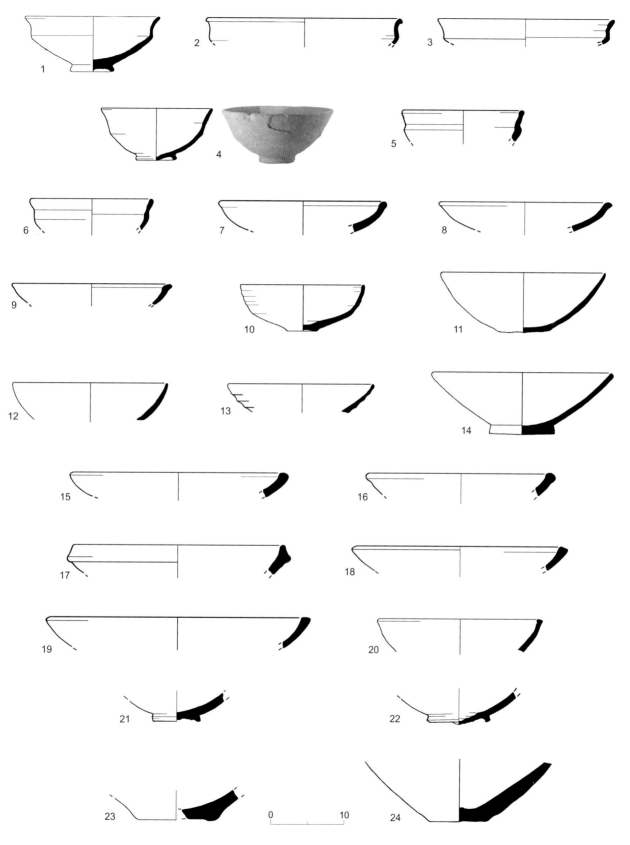

Fig. 3.6. Stratum IX bowls.

◄ **Fig. 3.6**

No.	Reg. No.	Context	Elevation (m)	Description
1	B313/1	Room 137?	20.40	Surface: 7.5 YR 6/6 (reddish yellow); fabric: same; core: thick, gray; inclusions: few small to large voids, very few fine sparkling
2	B251/2	Room 111	20.70/20.63	Surface: 10R 6/8 (light red); fabric: same; core: light gray; inclusions: few small white
3	B325/12	Room 111	20.60/20.20	Surface: 2.5YR 6/8 (light red); fabric: same; core: thick, dark gray; inclusions: few small white, very few fine sparkling
4	B249	Burial 152	9.20/8.80	Wet-smooth marks; surface: 2.5YR 6/4 (light reddish brown); fabric: same; core: N/A; inclusions: many fine to medium dark, many medium to large voids, many fine sparkling
5	A684/4	Subfloor fill of Room 75	21.20/20.90	Surface: 10R 5/8 (red); fabric: same; core: light gray; inclusions: many small to medium white
6	B325/6	Room 111	20.60/20.20	Surface: 2.5YR 5/6 (red); fabric: same; core: none; inclusions: many small white, few fine sparkling
7	B327/3	Room 111	20.80/20.60	Surface: 2.5 YR (6/6) (light red); fabric: same; core: thin, gray; inclusions: N/A
8	B242/5	Room 111	22.65/21.55	Surface: 10YR 8/3 very pale brown; fabric: 2.5YR 7/6 (light red); core: thin, gray; inclusions: N/A
9	A684/6	Subfloor fill in Room 75?	21.20/20.90	Surface: 5YR 5/8 (yellowish red); fabric: same; core: none; inclusions: few small to medium white, few fine sparkling
10	B2 18/1	Burial 152	12.15	N/A
11	A656/10	Subfloor fill in Room 75?	21.20/20.90	N/A
12	B251/3	Room 111	20.70/20.63	Surface: 7.5YR 6/6 (reddish yellow); fabric: same; core: gray; inclusions: few small to medium white, few small dark
13	B290/1	Room 137	21.70/21.05	Rilling; surface: 5YR 5/4 (reddish brown); fabric: same; core: thick, gray; inclusions: few small white
14	B323/1	Room 140	20.90/20.70	Wet-smooth marks; surface: 7.5 YR 6/6 (reddish-yellow); fabric: same; core: dark, gray; inclusions: many small to medium voids, very few small to medium white; string-cut base
15	B285/2	Room 111?	21.20/20.90	Surface: 5YR 6/6 (reddish yellow); fabric: same; core: thick, dark gray; inclusions: N/A
16	B327/18	Room 111	20.80/20.60	Surface: 10YR 7/3 (very pale brown); fabric: same; core: none; inclusions: N/A
17	A688/3	Area 85	N/A	Surface (self-slip): 7.5YR 5/2 (brown); fabric: 7.5YR 4/6 (strong brown); core: thick, gray; inclusions: few fine sparkling
18	A684/3	Subfloor fill in Room 75?	21.20/20.90	Surface: 7.5YR 4/6 (strong brown); fabric: same; core: none; inclusions: few fine sparkling
19	B143/5	Courtyard 118	20.54/20.34	Surface: 10R 6/6 (light red); fabric: same; core: gray; inclusions: N/A
20	B251/1	Room 111	20.70/20.63	Surface: 7.5YR 5/6 (strong brown); fabric: same; core: none; inclusions: few fine sparkling, very few small white
21	A631/8	Area 85	20.55	Surface: 2.5YR 8/2 (pinkish white); fabric: 10R 6/8 (light red); core: thick, 10YR 4/2 (dark grayish brown); inclusions: few small to medium white, few medium dark
22	B51/3	Room 111	20.90	Surface: 2.5YR 6/8 (light red); fabric: same; core: gray; inclusions: N/A
23	A688/1	Area 85	N/A	Surface: 5YR 6/6 (reddish yellow); fabric: same; core: thick, dark gray; inclusions: few fine sparkling
24	A637/5	Subfloor fill(?) in Room 75	21.35/21.25	Surface (self-slip): 5YR 7/4 (pink); fabric: 5YR 5/6 (yellowish red); core: dark gray; inclusions: many medium voids, many fine sparkling

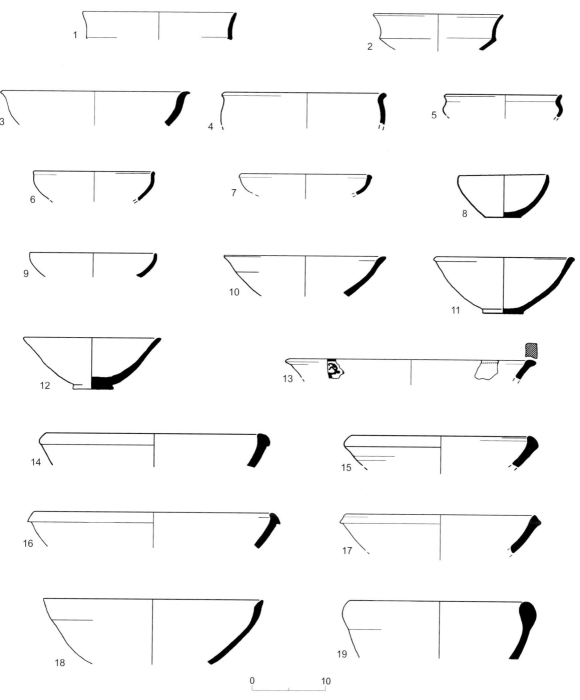

Fig. 3.7. Strata VIII–VII bowls.

◀ **Fig. 3.7**

No.	Reg. No.	Context (Stratum)	Elevation (m)	Description
1	B216/15	Fill above Room 111 (VIII?)	22.00/21.54	Surface: 5YR 6/6 (reddish yellow); fabric: same; core: thick, dark gray; inclusions: few fine voids, few small to medium white
2	B237/10	Fill above Room 111 (VIII?)	21.65/21.55	N/A
3	A305/3	Area 41 (VII)	22.30	Surface (self-slip): 2.5Y 7/3 (pale yellow); fabric: 5YR 6/8 (reddish yellow); core: thick, dark gray; inclusions: few medium voids, few small white, straw
4	A630/2	Room 75 (VIII?)	21.55/21.30	Surface: 7.5YR 5/4 (brown); fabric: same; core: none; inclusions: very few fine sparkling
5	B237	Fill above Room 111 (VIII?)	21.65/21.55	Surface: 7.5YR 7/3 (pink); fabric: 2.5YR 5/8 (red); core: thick, gray; inclusions: very few large white
6	A720/2	Room 92? (VIII?)	N/A	Surface: 5YR 6/6 (reddish yellow); fabric: same; core: thin, light gray; inclusions: very few large white
7	A472/15	Area 59 (VII–VI)	22.25/22.15	Surface: 10YR 6/4 (light yellowish brown); fabric: same; core: none; inclusions: few small white, few fine sparkling
8	A581/14	Area 80 (VII)	N/A	Surface: 2.5YR 6/6 (light red); fabric: 10YR 4/6 (dark yellowish brown); core: thin, gray; inclusions: few small to medium white
9	B217/2	Room 132 (VIII)	22.30/21.90	Surface: 5YR 7/3 (pink); fabric: 10R 6/6 (light red); core: thick, gray; inclusions: few fine to small white
10	A310/23	Area 41 (VII)	22.25	Surface: N/A; fabric: N/A; core: N/A; inclusions: N/A
11	A653	Sq L18 (VII)	N/A	Surface: 5YR 6/6 (reddish yellow); fabric: same; core: none; inclusions: many fine dark
12	B191/1	Area 128 (VII)	22.80	Surface: 2.5YR 5/4 (reddish brown); fabric: 5YR 5/8 (yellowish red); core: thin, gray; inclusions: many fine to medium white, many medium voids
13	A461/3	Area 59 (VII–VI)	22.35–22.25	Paint: 10R 5/4 (weak red); surface: 10YR 7/3 (very pale brown); fabric: 5YR 7/6 (reddish yellow); core: none; inclusions: many fine to small white
14	A272/3	Area 41? (VII)	22.80–22.50	Surface: 10YR 5/4 (yellowish brown); fabric: same; core: none; inclusions: few fine to small white, very few fine red
15	B29/12	Room 108 (VII)	22.50	Surface: 5YR 4/4 (reddish brown); fabric: same; core: thick, dark gray; inclusions: many fine sparkling
16	A530/1	W66 (VIII)	21.26/20.60	Surface: 5YR 5/8 (yellowish red); fabric: same; core: thick, gray; inclusions: few fine to small white
17	B37/2	Room 111 (VII)	N/A	Surface: 2.5YR 5/8 (red); fabric: same; core: dark gray; inclusions: many medium voids, many small white
18	A305/4	Area 41 (VII)	22.30	Surface (self-slip): 2.5Y 6/3 (light yellowish brown); fabric: 2.5 YR 6/8 (light red); core: thick, gray; inclusions: very many medium voids, many fine to small white
19	B268/4	W134? (VII)	22.45	Surface: 2.5Y 7/3 (pale yellow); fabric: 10R 5/8 (red); core: thick, gray, middle and interior; inclusions: many fine voids

Fig. 3.8 ▶

No.	Reg. No.	Context (Stratum)	Elevation (m)	Description
1	A708/1	Room 71 (VI)	N/A	Surface (self-slip): 2.5Y 7/3 (pale yellow); fabric: 10YR 6/4 (light yellowish brown); core: 2.5Y 7/3 (pale yellow); inclusions: many medium voids, very few small white
2	A495/8	Room 71 (VI)	22.10?	Surface (self-slip): 7.5YR (6/4 (light brown); fabric: 5YR 5/6 (yellowish red); core: thin, light gray; inclusions: very few fine dark
3	A195/1	Sq N19 (V–IV)	23.95	N/A
4	A723/1	Pit in Room 71 (VI)	N/A	N/A
5	A203	Sq M19 (V)	23.70	Surface (self-slip): 5Y 7/3 (pale yellow); fabric: 5YR 6/8 (reddish yellow); core: thick, 10YR 4/2 (dark grayish brown); inclusions: many fine to small white, few medium to large white
6	A273/1	Sq M18 (VI)	23.20/23.10	Paint: 10R 5/4 (red); surface: 5YR 6/6 (reddish yellow); fabric: same; core: thin, light gray; inclusions: many fine to small white, few small to medium dark, few straw
7	A377/2	Sqs K–L18 (V)	23.00	Surface: 10YR 6/4 (light yellowish brown); fabric: same; core: dark gray, middle and interior; inclusions: very few fine white
8	A184/1	Room 25 (V)	23.85	Surface: 10YR 6/4 (light yellowish brown); fabric: same; core: dark gray, middle and interior; inclusions: very few fine white
9	A724/1	Pit in Room 71 (VI)	N/A	White wash (interior); surface: 5YR 6/6 (reddish yellow); fabric: N/A; core: N/A; inclusions: few small to medium white, few small to medium voids
10	A189/16	Room 34 (V)	23.70/23.60	Surface: 5YR 6/4 (light reddish brown); fabric: 10YR 6/6 (brownish yellow); core: thin, gray, interior; inclusions: very few fine white
11	A448/2	Area 59 (VI)	22.35?	Wash; surface: 10YR 6/3 (pale brown); fabric: same; core: none; inclusions: many small white, few fine sparkling
12	A311/2	Pit 35 (VI)	22.90	Surface (self-slip): 5YR 7/4 (pink); fabric: 2.5YR 6/8 (light red); core: thick, dark gray; inclusions: many small to medium voids, many fine to small white
13	A201/1	Area 28 (V)	23.70/23.50	N/A
14	A189/1	Room 34 (V)	23.70/23.60	Surface: 7.5YR 6/3 (light brown); fabric: 10YR 5/4 (yellowish brown); core: none; inclusions: few fine voids
15	A236/1	Area 28 (VI)	23.55	Burnish; paint: N/A; surface: 5YR 5/6 (yellowish red); fabric: same; core: 7.5YR 6/6 (reddish yellow); inclusions: many small to medium white

Fig. 3.9 ▶▶

No.	Reg. No.	Context	Elevation (m)	Description
1	A484/1	Room 71	N/A	Rope impressions; surface: 2.5YR 6/6 (light red); fabric: same; core: none; inclusions: very many medium voids
2	A500/1	Room 71	N/A	Rope impressions; surface; N/A
3	A708	Room 71	N/A	Rope impressions, burnish; surface: 2.5YR 4/6 (red); fabric: same; core: 2.5YR 3/4 (dark reddish brown); inclusions: very many fine to small voids
4	A450/1	Room 64	22.10	Rope impressions; surface: 2.5YR 5/8 (red); fabric: same; core: 2.5YR 6/6 (light red); inclusions: many small to medium white
5	A552	Room 71	N/A	Rope impressions; surface (self-slip): 10YR 7/2 (light gray); fabric: 2.5YR 6/6 (light red); core: thick, 5YR 6/8 (reddish yellow); inclusions: many small to medium voids

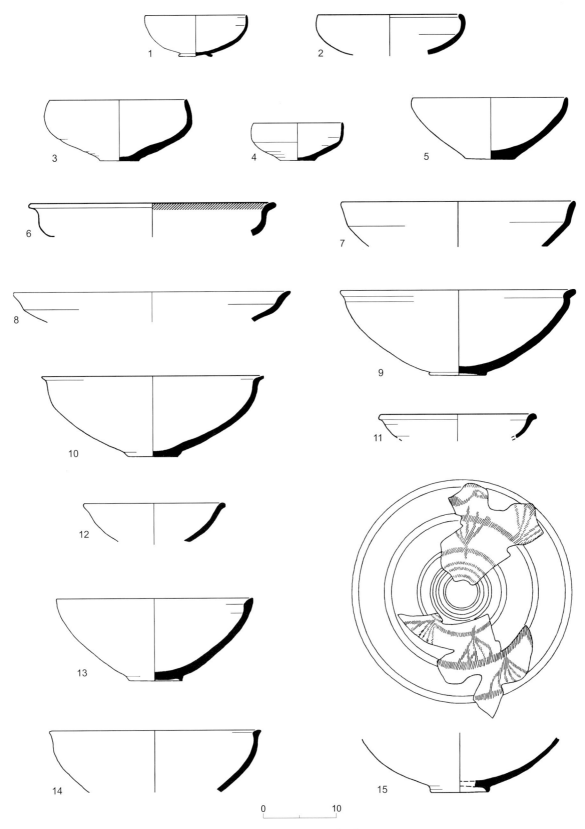

0   10

Fig. 3.8. Strata VI–V bowls.

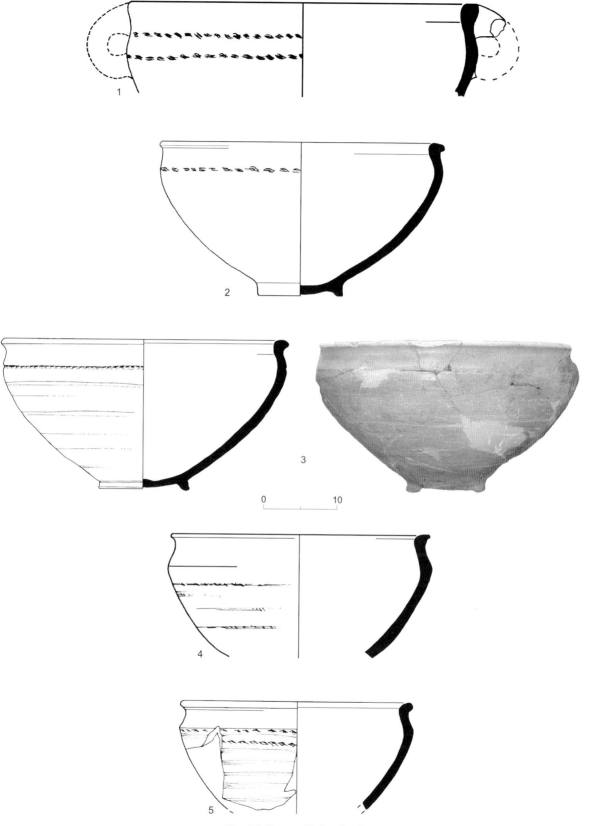

Fig. 3.9. Stratum VI deep bowls.

Fig. 3.10 ▶

No.	Reg. No.	Context (Stratum)	Elevation (m)	Description
1	A64/7	Area 10 (III)	24.56	Paint: 10R 5/4 (weak red); surface: 7.5YR 6/4 (light brown); fabric: 7.5YR 5/6 (strong brown); core: none; inclusions: few fine white, few fine dark
2	A86/1	Area 19? (III)	24.52/24.40	Paint: 10R 4/3 (weak red), wash; surface: 7.5YR 6/4 (light brown); fabric: 7.5YR 5/6 (strong brown); core: light gray; inclusions: few fine to small white, very few fine to small dark
3	A64/11	Area 10 (III)	24.56	Paint: 10R 4/3 (weak red); surface: 2.5YR 5/6 (red); fabric: same; core: none; inclusions: few fine white, very few small red
4	A92/1	Area 10 (III)	24.40/24.30	Paint: 10R 4/3 (weak red); surface (slip): 2.5Y 7/3 (pale yellow); fabric: 7.5YR 6/6 (reddish yellow); core: none; inclusions: many fine to small white, many fine voids
5	A105/16	Sq L19 (IV)	24.06	Paint: 10R 5/4 (weak red); surface: 10YR 7/3 (very pale brown); fabric: 7.5YR 5/4 (brown); core: none; inclusions: few fine white, few fine dark
6	A165/1	Room 25 (IV)	24.30/23.95	Surface: 2.5YR 5/6 (red); fabric: 5YR 5/6 (yellowish red), core: gray; inclusions: few fine dark
7	A103/1	Sq M19 (IV)	24.55/24.38	Surface: 7.5YR 8/3 (pink); fabric: 2.5YR 5/8 (red); core: 7.5YR 5/3 (brown); inclusions: very many fine white, few fine voids
8	A177/1	Area 10 (III)	N/A	White wash; surface: 7.5YR 4/3 (brown); fabric: same; core: N/A; inclusions: many fine voids, many fine dark
9	A73/2	Area 10 (III)	24.52	Surface: 10R 6/4 (pale red); fabric: same; core: thin, light gray; inclusions: many fine to small white
10	A111/1	Sq M18 (III)	24.40	Surface (self-slip): 10YR 7/4 (very pale brown); fabric: 5YR 5/6 (yellowish red); core: 7.5YR 6/6 (reddish yellow); inclusions: many fine voids
11	A177	Area 10 (III)	N/A	Surface (wash): 7.5YR 4/3 (brown); fabric: 5YR 5/6 (yellowish red); core: none; inclusions: few fine to small white, few medium white
12	A64/8	Area 10 (III)	24.56	Surface (self-slip): 10YR 7/3 (very pale brown); fabric: 5YR 5/6 (yellowish red); core: none; inclusions: few fine sparkling, few fine white, few small dark
13	A140/1	Pit 17 (III)	23.80	Surface: 5YR 7/4 (pink); fabric: same; core: thick, light gray; inclusions: few fine to small voids, many fine dark
14	A355/2	Sqs M18–19 (II)	25.00/24.60	Paint: 10R 4/3 (weak red); surface (self-slip): 2.5Y 7/3 (pale yellow); fabric: 10YR 5/4 (yellowish brown); core: none; inclusions: few small white, very few fine red, few fine sparkling
15	A29/16	Sq K18 (II)	24.90/24.75	Surface: 2.5YR 5/4 (reddish brown); fabric: same; core: thick, light gray; inclusions: very few large white, few fine to small voids

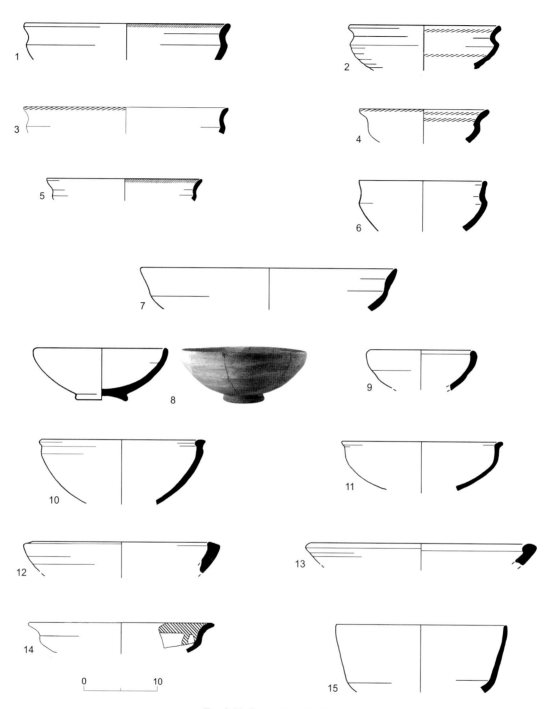

Fig. 3.10. Strata IV–II bowls.

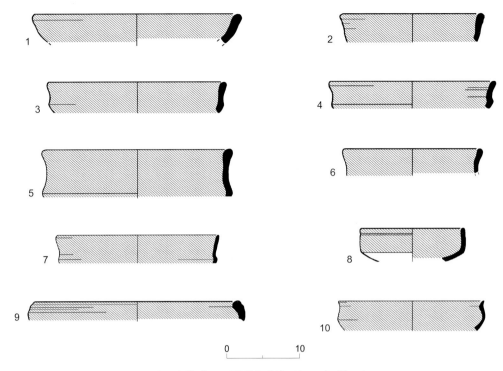

Fig. 3.11. Strata IV–II Red Slip Burnished bowls.

No.	Reg. No.	Context (Stratum)	Elevation (m)	Description
1	A56/3	Area 10 (III)	24.52	Burnish; surface (slip): 10YR 4/6 (red); fabric: same; core: thick, 7.5YR 4/4 (brown); inclusions: few small to medium voids, many fine to small white
2	A56/7	Area 10 (III)	24.52	Burnish; surface (slip): 10YR 4/6 (red); fabric: same; core: thick, 7.5YR 4/4 (brown); inclusions: few small to medium voids, many fine to small white
3	A56/10	Area 10 (III)	24.52	Burnish; surface (slip): 10R 4/6 (red); fabric: 5YR 5/6 (yellowish red); core: none; inclusions: few small white, few small dark
4	A13/1	Sq M19 (II?)	25.50/25.35	Burnish; surface (slip): 10R 5/6 (red); fabric: 5YR 6/8 (reddish yellow); core: thick, gray; inclusions: few fine sparkling, very few fine to small white
5	A156/2	Pit 17 (III)	23.70	Burnish; surface (slip): 10R 4/6 (red); fabric: 7.5YR 5/6 (strong brown); core: none; inclusions: few fine to small white
6	A64/2	Area 10 (III)	24.56	Surface (slip): 10R 4/6 (red); fabric: 2.5YR 4/6 (red); core: thin, gray; inclusions: few fine sparkling
7	A64/1	Area 10 (III)	24.56	Burnish; surface (slip): 10R 4/6 (red); fabric: 5YR 5/6 (yellowish red); core: none; inclusions: few small white, few small dark, many fine voids
8	A30/1	Sq L18 (II)	25.00/24.85	Burnish; surface (slip): 10R 5/6 (red); fabric: 5YR 5/6 (yellowish red); core: thick, 2.5Y 6/4 (light yellowish brown); inclusions: few fine white, very few fine sparkling
9	A56/1	Area 10 (III)	24.52	Burnish; surface (slip): 10R 4/6 (red); fabric: 2.5YR 4/6 (red); core: thin, 2.5YR 4/4 (reddish brown); inclusions: very few fine dark
10	A209/1	*Tabun* 10A (III)	24.50/24.35	Burnish; surface (slip): 10R 4/6 (red); fabric: 5YR 5/8 (yellowish red); core: light gray; inclusions: few fine to small white, very few fine to small dark

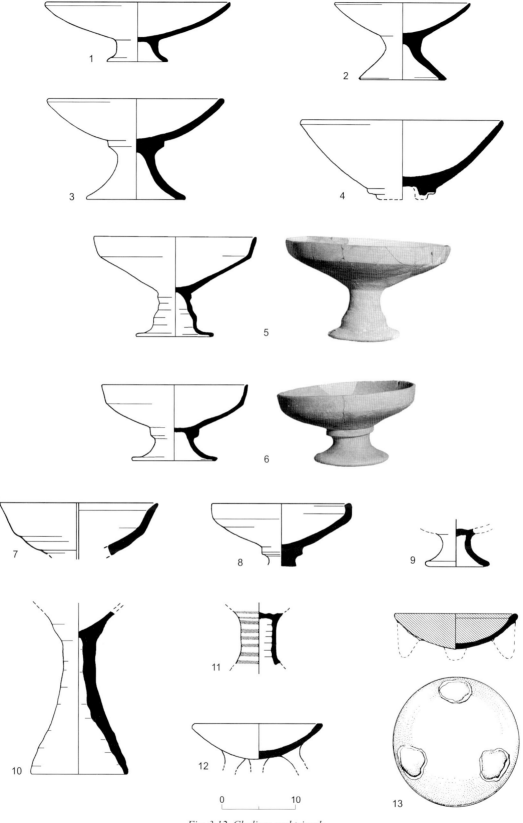

Fig. 3.12. Chalices and tripods.

◀ **Fig. 3.12**

No.	Object	Reg. No.	Context (Stratum)	Elevation (m)	Description
1	Chalice	B247/10	Courtyard 118 (XII–XI)	19.60	Surface: 2.5YR 7/8 (light red); fabric: same; core: thick, 2.5Y 6/4 (light yellowish brown); inclusions: none
2	Chalice	B306/1	Room 137 (IX)	20.60	Surface: 7.5YR 6/6 reddish yellow; fabric: same; core: thick, gray; inclusions: N/A
3	Chalice	B300/19	Room 137 (IX)	20.80/20.60	Surface: 7.5YR 6/6 reddish yellow; fabric: same; core: gray; inclusions: few small voids, very few large red
4	Chalice	B245/2	Courtyard 118 (XI)	19.95	Surface: 7.5YR 6/4 (light brown); fabric: 7.5YR 5/6 (strong brown); core: middle and interior, light gray; inclusions: many fine to small white, many medium to large dark
5	Chalice	B91	Courtyard 118 (XI–IX)	20.10	Surface: 5YR 6/8 (reddish yellow); fabric: 7.5YR 6/6 (reddish yellow); core: none; inclusions: few fine to small dark, few small white
6	Chalice	B112	Courtyard 118 (XI)	19.95	N/A
7	Chalice?	B346/9	Courtyard 118 (XII)	19.00/18.00	Surface: 2.5YR 7/7 (light red); fabric: same; core: gray; inclusions: few fine to small white, very few fine red
8	Chalice	A561/1	Room 79 (VI)	22.30	Surface: 7.5YR 7/6 (reddish yellow); fabric: same; core: none; inclusions: many small to medium white, many medium red
9	Chalice	B259/55	Courtyard 118 (XI)	19.25/19.10	Surface: 7.5YR 6/4 (light brown); fabric: same; core: thick, gray; inclusions: many small voids, few fine to small white
10	Chalice	B80	Courtyard 118 (XI–IX)	20.30	Surface: 7.5YR 6/6 (reddish yellow); fabric: same; core: thick, dark gray; inclusions: many fine dark
11	Chalice	A127/21	Sqs K–L18 (III)	24.35/24.20	Paint: 2.5YR 4/4 (reddish brown); surface (slip): 10YR 8/3 (very pale brown); fabric: 2.5YR 5/8 (red); core: none; inclusions: many fine white and dark
12	Tripod	B309	Room 139 (IX)	20.40	Burnish; surface (slip?): 10R 6/8 (light red); fabric: same; core: thick, dark gray; inclusions: few fine white, few fine voids
13	Tripod	B332	Courtyard 118 (XII)	18.70	Surface (slip): 10R 5/6 (red); fabric: 2.5YR 5/6 (red); core: gray; inclusions: very many fine to small white

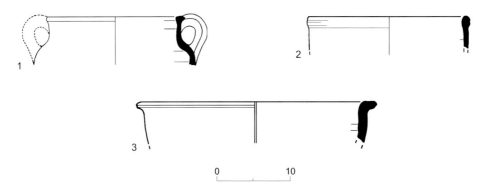

Fig. 3.13. Stratum IX kraters.

No.	Reg. No.	Context	Elevation (m)	Description
1	B282/5	Room 111	21.20	Surface: 2.5YR 6/6 (light red); fabric: same; core: thick, dark gray; inclusions: few medium white, few fine sparkling
2	B51/1	Room 111	20.90	Surface: 5YR 7/6 (reddish yellow); fabric: same; core: thick, gray; inclusions: N/A
3	B243/5	Room 111	N/A	Surface (self-slip): 10R 6/6 (light red); fabric: 2.5YR 5/8 (red); core: thick, dark gray; inclusions: N/A

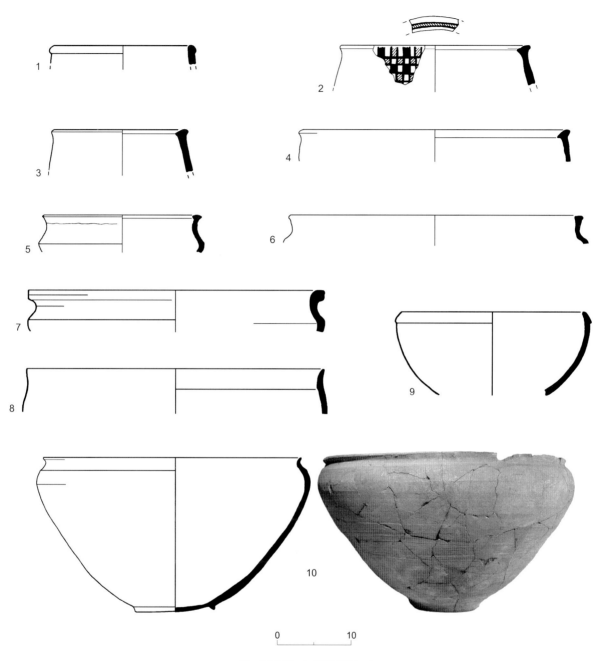

Fig. 3.14. Strata VIII–VII kraters.

◀ **Fig. 3.14**

No.	Reg. No.	Context (Stratum)	Elevation (m)	Description
1	A616/4	Room 83 (VIII)	21.40/21.30	Surface: 2.5YR 6/8 (light red); fabric: same; core: thick gray; inclusions: very many small to medium white, few fine sparkling
2	A720/4	Room 92? (VIII)	N/A	Paint: black and red; surface: 10YR 4/1 (dark gray); fabric: same; core: none; inclusions: few fine white, many fine voids
3	A720/4	Room 92? (VIII)	N/A	Surface: 10YR 4/1 (dark gray); fabric: same; core: none; inclusions: few fine white, many fine voids
4	A310/6	Area 41 (VII)	22.25	N/A
5	B33/2	Room 108 (VII)	22.32	Surface (self-slip): 2.5Y 6/2 (light brownish gray); fabric: same; core: thick, light gray; inclusions: many fine to medium white, few small to medium dark, very few fine red
6	A601/1	Room 63 (VII)	22.00/21.85	Surface: 5YR 5/6 (yellowish red); fabric: same; core: gray; inclusions: many small to medium voids, few small white
7	B218/14	Area 128 (VII)	23.20/23.00	Surface: 7.5YR 5/4 (brown); fabric: same; core: thick, dark gray; inclusions: none
8	B255/17	Area 128 (VII)	22.60/22.55	Surface: 7.5YR 5/4 (brown); fabric: same; core: thick, gray; inclusions: few fine voids, very few small white
9	A581/14	Area 80 (VII)	N/A	Surface: 2.5YR 6/6 (light red); fabric: 10YR 4/6 (dark yellowish brown); core: thin, gray; inclusions: few small to medium white
10	B215/1	Room 132 (VIII)	22.00	Wet-smooth marks; surface: 10R 5/6 (red); fabric: same; core: thick, gray; inclusions: few small white

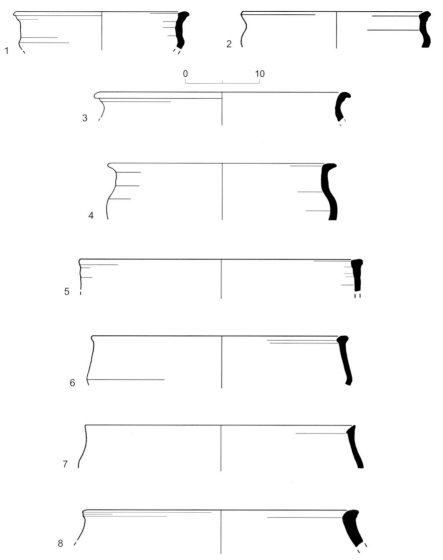

Fig. 3.15. Strata VI–V kraters.

No.	Reg. No.	Context (Stratum)	Elevation (m)	Description
1	A317/5	Area 40 (V)	23.30	Surface: 2.5YR 6/6 (light red); fabric: same; core: 7.5YR 6/4 (light brown); inclusions: few fine white
2	A453/3	Area 65 (V)	22.75	Surface: 10YR 7/3 (very pale brown); fabric: 7.5YR 4/6 (strong brown); core: gray; inclusions: very few fine white
3	A223/2	Area 36 (VI)	23.55/23.40	Surface: 5YR 5/6 (yellowish red); fabric: same; core: thin, gray; inclusions: many medium voids, very many fine sparkling, many small white
4	A371/1	Sq L18 (V)	23.00	Surface: 2.5YR 6/3 (light reddish brown); fabric: 2.5YR 6/8 (light red); core: thick, gray; inclusions: many medium voids, many small to medium white
5	A455/4	Area 59 (VI)	22.35/22.25	Surface: 2.5YR 6/8 (light red); fabric: same; core: thin, gray; inclusions: few fine sparkling
6	A404/16	Sq L18 (VI)	22.40	Surface (self-slip): 10YR 7/3 (very pale brown); fabric: 10R 5/6 (red); core: N/A; inclusions: few small to medium voids, few small to medium white
7	A182/11	Area 26 (V)	23.75/23.65	Surface: 7.5YR 5/6 (strong brown); fabric: same; core: light gray; inclusions: none
8	A455/14	Area 59 (VI)	22.35/22.25	Surface: 7.5YR 5/3 (brown); fabric: same; core: thin, light gray; inclusions: many medium voids

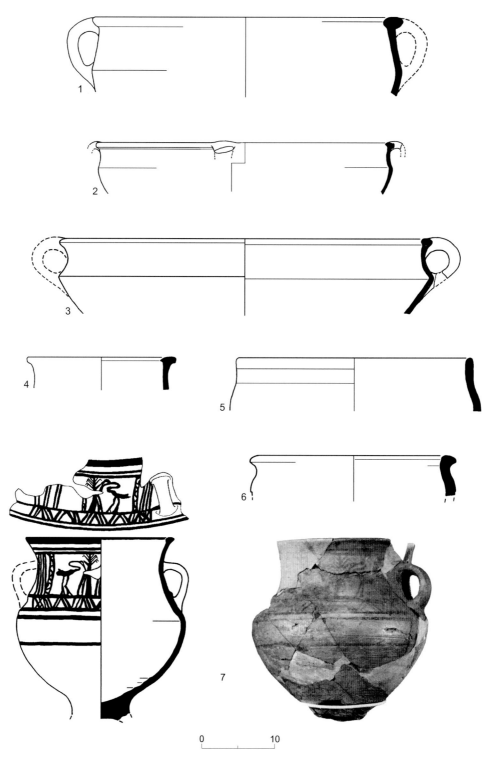

0   10

Fig. 3.16. Stratum III kraters.

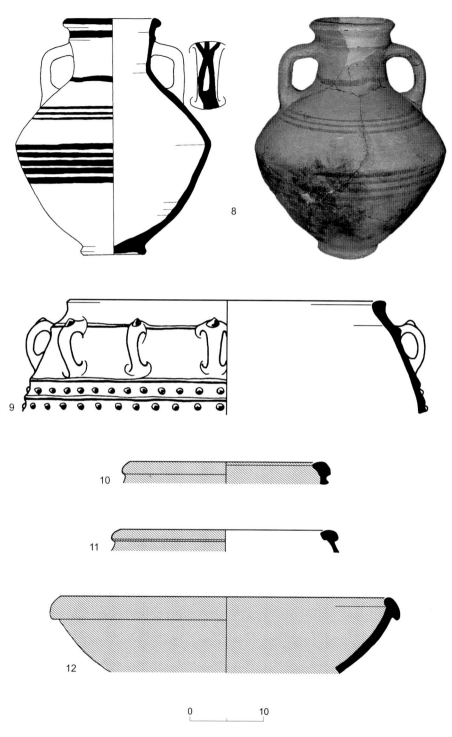

Fig. 3.16 (cont.). Stratum III kraters.

◄ **Fig. 3.16**

No.	Reg. No.	Context (Stratum)	Elevation (m)	Description
1	B180/4	Pit 126	24.55	Surface: 2.5YR 4/4 (reddish brown); fabric: same; core: thick, gray; inclusions: many fine white, few fine to small voids, few fine dark
2	A177/2	*Ṭabun* 10A	N/A	Surface: 5YR 5/6 (yellowish red); fabric: same; core: light gray; inclusions: few fine voids, few fine white
3	A359/3	Sqs L–M18	24.30	Surface (self-slip): 2.5Y 7/3 (pale yellow); fabric: 10YR 5/2 (grayish brown); core: thick, 2.5YR 6/8 (light red); inclusions: many small to medium voids
4	A67/2	Area 13	24.70/24.60	Surface (self-slip): 2.5YR 5/4 (reddish brown); fabric: 2.5YR 5/8 (red); core: thick, light gray; inclusions: many fine white
5	A64/12	Area 10	24.56	Surface: 7.5YR 7/4 (pink); fabric: 5YR 5/6 (yellowish red); core: gray; inclusions: many small to medium white
6	A84	Area 13	24.60	Surface (self-slip): 10YR 6/3 (pale brown); fabric: 7.5YR 5/4 (brown); core: none; inclusions: many fine to small voids, few small white
7	A83/1	Area 13	24.60	Paint; N/A
8	A112/1	Pit 17	24.23	Paint: 10R 4/4 (weak red); surface: 2.5YR 6/4 (light reddish brown); fabric: N/A; core: N/A; inclusions: very many fine to small dark, many fine sparkling, few small to medium white
9	B177/1	Pit 126	24.60/24.05	Molded decoration; surface (self-slip): 7.5YR 7/2 (pinkish gray); fabric: 2.5YR 6/6 (light red); core: thick, black; inclusions: very many medium voids, few fine to small white, straw
10	A20/5	Sq L18	25.25/25.00	Burnish; surface (slip): 2.5YR 4/3 (reddish brown); fabric: 10YR 5/4 (yellowish brown); core: gray; inclusions: few fine white, few fine sparkling
11	A86/8	Area 19?	24.52/24.40	Burnish; surface (slip): 10R 4/4 (weak red); fabric: 7.5YR 4/4 (brown); core: thin, light gray; inclusions: few fine white, few fine dark
12	A118/1	Pit 17	24.00	Burnish; surface (slip): 10R 4/6 (red); fabric: 5YR 5/6 (red); core: light gray; inclusions: few small white, few small dark, many fine voids

Fig. 3.17 ▶

No.	Reg. No.	Context (Stratum)	Elevation (m)	Description
1	B365/69	Pit 166 (XII)	18.65/17.90	Surface: 2.5YR 4/3 (reddish brown); fabric: same; core: thick, dark gray; inclusions: very many small to medium white, few fine sparkling, few small voids
2	B296/33	Courtyard 118 (XII)	N/A	Surface (self-slip): 7.5YR 4/6 (strong brown); fabric: same; core: light gray; inclusions: many small to medium white, many fine to small dark
3	B365/73	Pit 166 (XII)	18.65/17.90	Surface: 2.5YR 4/3 (reddish brown); fabric: same; core: thick, gray; inclusions: many small to medium white
4	B274/3	Courtyard 118 (XII)	18.27	Surface: 2.5YR 6/6 (light red); fabric: 7.5YR 5/6 (strong brown); core: none; inclusions: few medium white, many fine to small dark
5	B274/4	Courtyard 118 (XII)	18.27	Surface: 5YR 3/2 (dark reddish brown); fabric: same; core: thin, dark, interior; inclusions: many small to medium white, few small voids, many small to medium dark
6	B266/33	Courtyard 118 (XII)	19.50	Surface: 2.5YR 6/4 (light reddish brown); fabric: same; core: thick, dark gray; inclusions: many small to medium dark, many small to medium white
7	B107	Courtyard 118 (XI)	19.95	Surface: 2.5YR 5/4 (reddish brown); fabric: same; core: N/A; inclusions: many medium to large white, few small to medium voids
8	B81/1	Courtyard 118 (XI–IX)	20.30	N/A
9	B240/27	Courtyard 118 (XI)	19.65/19.55	Surface: 7.5YR 7/4 (pink); fabric: same; core: thick, dark gray; inclusions: many fine sparkling, few small white, few small voids, few small dark
10	B256/31	Courtyard 118 (XI)	20.40/20.25	N/A
11	B256/33	Courtyard 118 (XI)	20.40/20.25	Surface: N/A; fabric: 5YR 6/4 (light reddish brown); core: thick, gray; inclusions: N/A
12	B77/22	Courtyard 118 (X)	20.50/20.30	Surface (self-slip): 2.5YR 6/4 (light reddish brown); fabric: 2.5YR 5/8 (red); core: thick, dark gray; inclusions: N/A
13	B77/24	Courtyard 118 (X)	20.50/20.30	Surface: 10R 6/6 (light red); fabric: same; core: thick, dark gray; inclusions: many small to medium white
14	B86/2	Courtyard 118 (X)	20.30	N/A

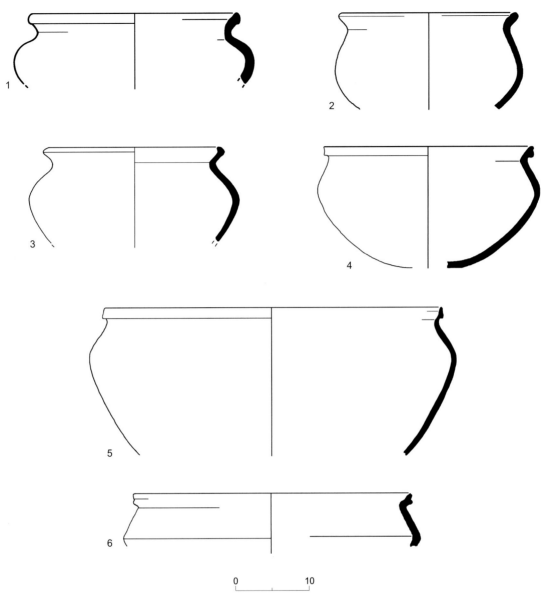

Fig. 3.17. Strata XII–X cooking pots.

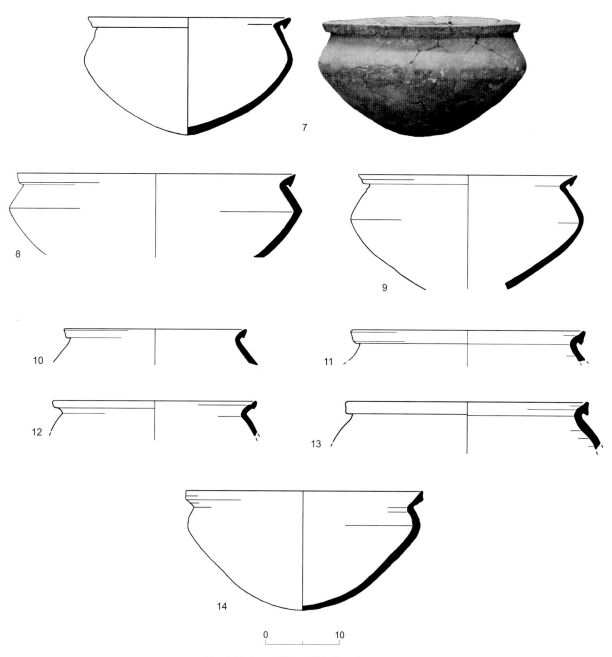

Fig. 3.17 (cont.). Strata XII–X cooking pots.

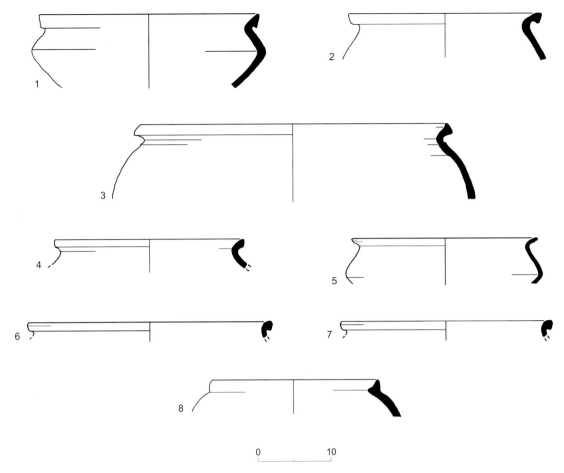

Fig. 3.18. Stratum IX cooking pots.

No.	Reg. No.	Context (Stratum)	Elevation (m)	Description
1	B197/28	Sqs M–N22 (XI–IX)	20.20	Surface: 5YR 7/6 (reddish yellow); fabric: same; core: thick, gray; inclusions: many small to medium white, few medium voids
2	B83/8	Courtyard 118 (XI–IX)	20.23	Surface (self-slip): 5YR 4/4 (reddish brown); fabric: 5YR 5/8 (yellowish red); core: 7.5YR 6/6 (reddish yellow); inclusions: many small to medium dark, many fine to small white
3	B90	Courtyard 118 (IX)	20.30	Surface: 2.5YR 4/6 (red); fabric: same; core: thick, dark gray; inclusions: many medium and large voids, many small to medium white, few fine sparkling
4	A631/10	Area 85 (IX)	20.55	Surface: 2.5YR 6/6 (light red); fabric: same; core: dark gray; inclusions: many small to medium white, few fine sparkling
5	A631/12	Area 85 (IX)	20.55	N/A
6	B224/13	Courtyard 118 (XI–IX)	20.00/19.90	Surface: 7.5YR 7/4 (pink); fabric: same; core: thick, dark gray; inclusions: many small to medium white
7	B285/10	Room 111 (IX)	21.20/20.90	Surface: 2.5YR 5/6 (red); fabric: same; core: thick, dark gray; inclusions: many small to medium white
8	B165/13	Sqs M–N22 (IX)	21.00/20.83	Surface (self-slip): 10R 6/4 (pale red); fabric: 5YR 5/6 (yellowish red); core: none; inclusions: many small to medium white, few small dark

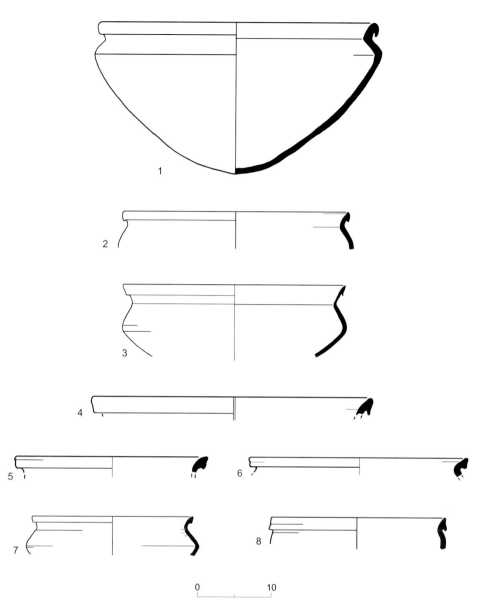

Fig. 3.19. Strata VIII–VII cooking pots.

No.	Reg. No.	Context (Stratum)	Elevation (m)	Description
1	B231/1	Room 132 (VIII)	22.00	N/A
2	B189/1	Area 128 (VII)	22.80/22.65	Surface: 5YR 6/6 (reddish yellow); fabric: same; core: thick, gray; inclusions: very few small white, few fine to small voids
3	A634/15	Sq L19 (VIII–VII?)	21.36/21.26	N/A
4	A720/5	Room 92 (VIII)	N/A	Surface: 2.5YR 5/4 (reddish brown); fabric: same; core: thick, black; inclusions: many small to medium white, few fine sparkling
5	A616/11	Room 83 (VIII)	22.65/22.60	N/A
6	A616/12	Room 83 (VIII)	21.40/21.30	N/A
7	B43/5	Subfloor fill(?) for Room 111 (VIII)	21.90	Surface: 2.5YR 6/3 (light reddish brown); fabric: same; core: none; inclusions: many small to medium white, few fine sparkling
8	B250/7	Area 128 (VII)	22.65/22.60	Surface: 5YR 6/6 (reddish yellow); fabric: same; core: thick, gray; inclusions: many small to medium white, few fine to small voids

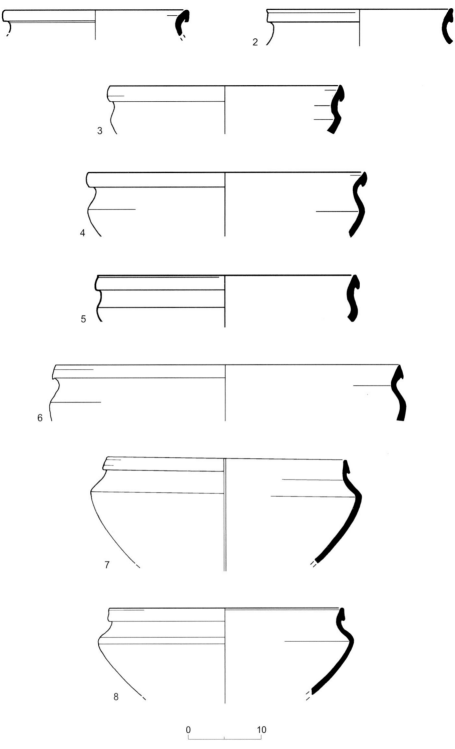

Fig. 3.20. Strata VI–II cooking pots.

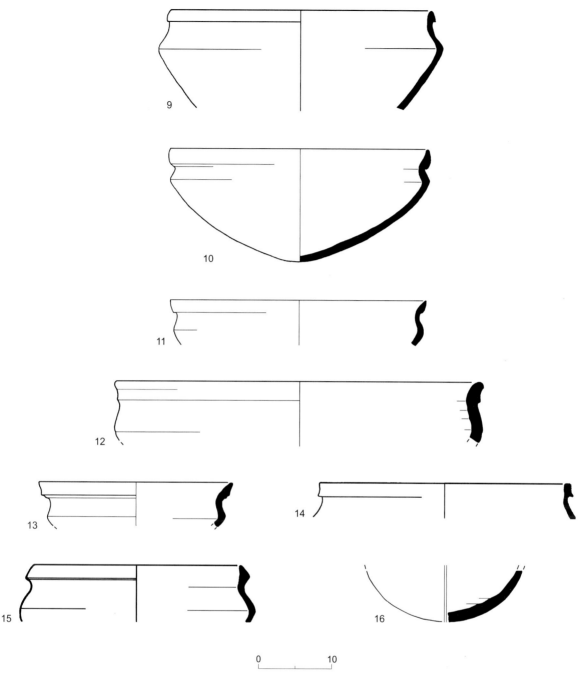

Fig. 3.20 (cont.). Strata VI–II cooking pots.

◀ **Fig. 3.20**

No.	Reg. No.	Context (Stratum)	Elevation (m)	Description
1	A472/21	Area 59 (VI)	22.25/22.15	Surface: 5YR 6/8 (reddish yellow); fabric: same; core: thick black; inclusions: many small to medium white, very few small red
2	A236/4	Subfloor fill(?) of Room 34 (VI)	23.55	Surface: 7.5YR 4/6 (strong brown); fabric: same; core: dark gray; inclusions: many medium white, few fine dark
3	A243/2	Area 36 (VI)	23.55/23.33	Surface: 7.5YR 6/6 (reddish yellow); fabric: same; core: thick, dark gray; inclusions: few small to medium white, few fine to small voids
4	A229/7	Area 36 (VI)	23.50/23.35	Surface: 7.5YR 4/6 (strong brown); fabric: same; core: dark gray; inclusions: many medium white, few fine dark
5	A229/8	Area 36 (VI)	23.50/23.35	Surface: 7.5YR 4/6 (strong brown); fabric: same; core: dark gray; inclusions: many medium white, few fine dark
6	A497/2	Room 71 (VI)	N/A	Surface: 5YR 5/6 (yellowish red); fabric: same; core: gray; inclusions: many small to medium voids, many medium white
7	A486/15	Room 71 (VI)	N/A	Surface: 7.5YR 4/2 (brown); fabric: same; core: thick, gray; inclusions: many medium to large white
8	A478/1	Room 71 (VI)	N/A	Surface: 7.5YR 4/2 (brown); fabric: same; core: thick, gray; inclusions: many medium to large white
9	A497/1	Room 71 (VI)	N/A	Surface: 2.5YR 5/4 (reddish brown); fabric: same; core: thick, gray; inclusions: many medium to large white
10	A202	Area 28 (V)	23.50	Surface: 5YR 5/6 (yellowish red); fabric: same; core: thin, gray; inclusions: many small to medium white, few medium dark
11	A167/8	Area 28 (V)	23.80/23.65	Surface: 5YR 6/6 (reddish yellow); fabric: 10YR 5/4 (yellowish brown); core: gray; inclusions: very many small to medium white
12	A718	*Ṭabun* 24? (V?)	N/A	Surface: 5YR 5/6 (yellowish red); fabric: same; core: none; inclusions: many small white, many medium dark
13	A118/13	Pit 17 (III)	24.00	Surface: 5YR 5/6 (yellowish red); fabric: same; core: thick, dark gray; inclusions: many small dark, very few small white
14	A128/7	Sq K19 (III)	24.45/24.25	Surface: 7.5YR 6/6 (reddish yellow); fabric: same; core: none; inclusions: very many medium dark, many small white, few medium red
15	A28/12	Sq K18 (II)	24.90/24.77	N/A
16	A126/6	Pit 18? (III)	N/A	Surface: 2.5YR 6/4 (light reddish brown); fabric: same; core: thin, light gray; inclusions: few fine white and dark

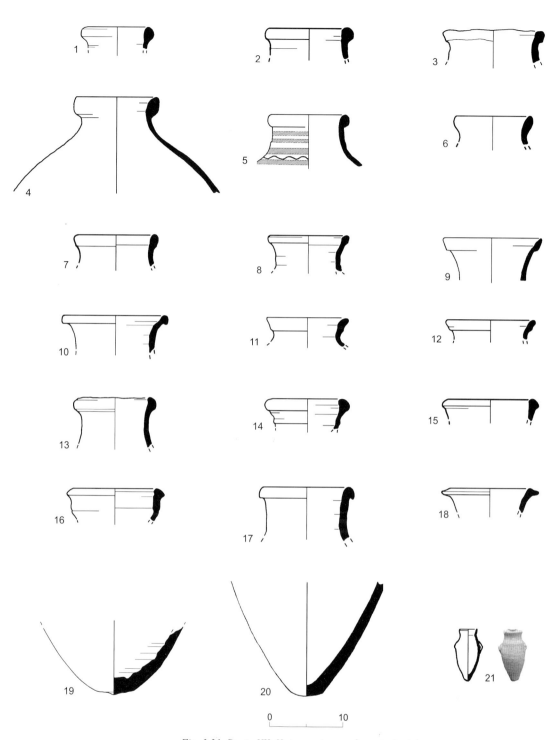

Fig. 3.21. Strata XII–X storage jars and an amphoriskos.

◀ **Fig. 3.21**

No.	Reg. No.	Context (Stratum)	Elevation (m)	Description
1	B114/4	Courtyard 118 (XI)	19.95	Surface: 7.5YR 7/4 (pink); fabric: same; core: none; inclusions: none
2	B77/28	Courtyard 118 (X)	20.50/20.30	Surface (self-slip): 2.5Y 7/3 (pale yellow); fabric: 2.5YR 7/8 (light red); core: thick, dark gray; inclusions: few fine voids
3	B265/15	Courtyard 118 (XII)	19.10	Surface: 7.5YR 8/4 (pink); fabric: same; core: thick, gray; inclusions: many fine dark, few fine to small voids
4	B92/1	Courtyard 118 (XI–IX)	20.10	Surface: 5YR 5/6 (yellowish red); fabric: same; core: thin, gray; inclusions: many small to medium white, many fine dark
5	B224/16	Courtyard 118 (XI–IX)	20.00/19.90	Paint: 10R 5/8 (red) and 10R 3/1 (dark reddish gray); surface: 10R 4/8 (red); fabric: same; core: middle and interior, 10YR 4/4 (dark yellowish brown); inclusions: very many fine to small white, few small to medium white
6	B288/17	Courtyard 118 (XII)	19.10/19.05	Surface: 10R 6/6 (light red); fabric: 10R 4/8 (red); core: thin, gray; inclusions: few fine sparkling, few fine to small dark
7	B93/1	Courtyard 118 (XI–IX)	20.10	Surface: 10R 4/6 (red); fabric: same; core: none; inclusions: few fine white, few fine dark, very few fine sparkling
8	B235/45	Courtyard 118 (XI)	19.80/19.65	Surface: 7.5 YR 7/4 (pink); fabric: same; core: none; inclusions: few fine to small white
9	B256/40	Courtyard 118 (XI)	20.40/20.25	Surface (self-slip): 2.5YR 7/4 (light reddish brown); fabric: 10R 4/6 (red); core: light gray, middle and interior; inclusions: many small to medium white, many small to medium voids, very few large red
10	B131/17	Courtyard 118 (XI)	20.00/19.65	Surface: 10R 5/4 (weak red); fabric: same; core: thin, gray; inclusions: many small to medium white, many small dark, very many small voids
11	B78/5	Test Probe 117 (XI)	20.15/19.85	Surface: 2.5YR 7/6 (light red); fabric: same; core: gray; inclusions: few fine to small white
12	B235/43	Courtyard 118 (XI)	19.80/19.65	Surface: 10YR 7/4 (very pale brown); fabric: same; core: none; inclusions: few small white
13	B265/14	Courtyard 118 (XII)	19.10	Surface: 7.5YR 8/4 (pink); fabric: same; core: gray; inclusions: many small to medium voids, few fine sparkling, few small dark
14	B252/18	Courtyard 118 (XI)	19.50/19.40	Surface: 5YR 7/6 (reddish yellow); fabric: same; core: thin, gray; inclusions: many small white
15	B77/27	Courtyard 118 (X)	20.50/20.30	Surface: 10R 7/8 (light red); fabric: 7.5YR 6/8 (strong brown); core: thin, dark gray; inclusions: N/A
16	B235/15	Courtyard 118 (XI)	19.80/19.65	Surface: 7.5YR 7/6 (reddish yellow); fabric: same; core: none; inclusions: few fine to small voids, very few medium red
17	B131/18	Courtyard 118 (XI)	20.00/19.65	Surface: 2.5YR 6/6 (light red); fabric: same; core: none; inclusions: very many fine sparkling, few small to medium white, few small dark
18	B77/26	Courtyard 118 (X)	20.50/20.30	Surface (self-slip): 2.5YR 6/6 (light red); fabric: 7.5YR 4/2 (brown); core: none; inclusions: very few fine white
19	B240/42	Courtyard 118 (XI)	19.65/19.55	Surface: 10R 4/4 (weak red); fabric: same; core: thick, gray, middle and interior; inclusions: very many small white, many fine voids, few fine sparkling
20	B93/15	Courtyard 118 (XI–IX)	20.10	Surface: 5YR 6/8 (reddish yellow); fabric: 7.5YR 6/6 (reddish yellow); core: thick, dark gray; inclusions: many fine to small dark
21	B307/1	Courtyard 118 (XII)	N/A	Surface (self-slip): 2.5Y 7/3 (pale yellow); fabric: 5YR 5/6 (yellowish red); core: N/A; inclusions: many small to medium white

Fig. 3.22 ►

No.	Vessel	Reg. No.	Context	Elevation (m)	Description
1	Storage jar	B310	Room 139	20.40	N/A
2	Storage jar	N/A	Building A	N/A	N/A
3	Storage jar	B298/14	Room 137	21.00/20.60	Surface: 7.5YR 6/4 (light brown); fabric: same; core: none; inclusions: few fine to small voids
4	Storage jar	B251/11	Room 111	20.70/20.63	Surface: 10R 6/6 (light red); fabric: 10R 4/8 (red); core: thin, gray; inclusions: few fine sparkling, few fine to small dark
5	Storage jar	B327/11	Room 111	20.80/20.60	Surface: 2.5YR 5/8 (red); fabric: same; core: thin, gray; inclusions: many small to medium white, few fine sparkling
6	Storage jar	B242/6	Room 111	22.65/21.55	Paint: 10R 5/1 (reddish gray); surface: 10R 5/8 (red); fabric: same; core: none; inclusions: N/A
7	Storage jar	B47/6	Room 111	21.40?	Surface: 10R 7/6 (light red); fabric: same; core: thick, gray; inclusions: N/A
8	Storage jar	B251/8	Room 111	20.70/20.63	Surface: 5YR 6/8 (reddish yellow); fabric: same; core: none; inclusions: N/A
9	Storage jar	B297/11	Room 138	21.00/20.60	Surface (self-slip): 10YR 7/3 (very pale brown); fabric: 2.5YR 6/6 (light red); core: none; inclusions: many fine white
10	Storage jar	B285/7	Room 111	21.20/20.90	Surface (self-slip): 7.5YR 7/6 (reddish yellow); fabric: 7.5YR 5/8 (strong brown); core: none; inclusions: N/A
11	Storage jar	B325/11	Room 111	20.80/20.60	Surface: 10R 6/8 (light red); fabric: same; core: thick, 7.5YR 6/6 (reddish yellow); inclusions: few small to medium white, few fine sparkling
12	Storage jar	B50/1	Room 111	20.90	Surface: 2.5YR 6/6 (light red); fabric: same; core: thin, gray; inclusions: many fine to small voids
13	Storage jar	B47/8	Room 111	21.40?	Surface (self-slip): 10R 6/6 (light red); fabric: 7.5YR 6/4 (light brown); core: thin, gray; inclusions: N/A
14	Storage jar	B327/1	Room 111	20.80/20.60	Surface: 7.5YR 7/4 (pink); fabric: same; core: none; inclusions: many fine to small white
15	Storage jar	B47/9	Room 111	21.40?	Rilling; surface (self-slip): 5YR 7/3 (pink); fabric: 7.5YR 5/6 (strong brown); core: thin, light gray; inclusions: few medium white, very few medium dark
16	Storage jar	B297/12	Room 138	21.00/20.60	Surface: 7.5YR 7/3 (pink); fabric: same; core: none; inclusions: many small to medium white
17	Storage jar	A678/5	Area 85	N/A	Surface: 7.5YR 7/6 (reddish yellow); fabric: same; core: none; inclusions: few fine sparkling
18	Storage jar	B236/1	Burial 152	11.85/11.60	N/A
19	Storage jar	B326/1	Room 111	20.80	Surface: 5YR 7/6 (reddish yellow); fabric: same; core: very thick, gray; inclusions: few medium white
20	Storage jar	B313	Room 137?	20.40	Surface (self-slip): 5YR 5/3 (reddish brown); fabric: 7.5YR 6/6 (reddish yellow); core: thick, middle and interior; inclusions: many fine to small voids, very few fine sparkling
21	Storage jar	B327	Room 111	20.80/20.60	Surface: 5YR 6/6 (reddish yellow); fabric: same; core: thin, light gray; inclusions: few fine to small voids, few small white
22	Storage jar	B326	Room 111	20.80	Surface (self-slip): 5YR 5/4 (reddish brown); fabric: 7.5YR 7/6 (reddish yellow); core: middle and interior, 10YR 4/4 (dark yellowish brown); inclusions: very many fine to small dark, few fine sparkling
23	Storage jar	B242/3	Room 111	22.65/21.55	Surface: 5YR 5/6 (yellowish red); fabric: same; core: thin, gray; inclusions: few fine sparkling, few small dark and white
24	Pithos	A696/1	Subfloor fill(?) in Room 75	N/A	Rilling; surface: 7.5YR 7/4 (pink); fabric: same; core: thick, dark gray; inclusions: few medium to large voids, few small to medium dark
25	Pithos	A48/12	Room 111	22.40	Rilling; surface: 5YR 5/3 (reddish brown); fabric: 5YR 5/8 (yellowish red); core: none; inclusions: many fine sparkling
26	Pithos	A621/3	Area 85	20.90	Rilling; surface: 5YR 6/8 (reddish yellow); fabric: same; core: dark gray; inclusions: few fine sparkling, very few small to medium white

Fig. 3.22. Stratum IX storage jars and pithoi.

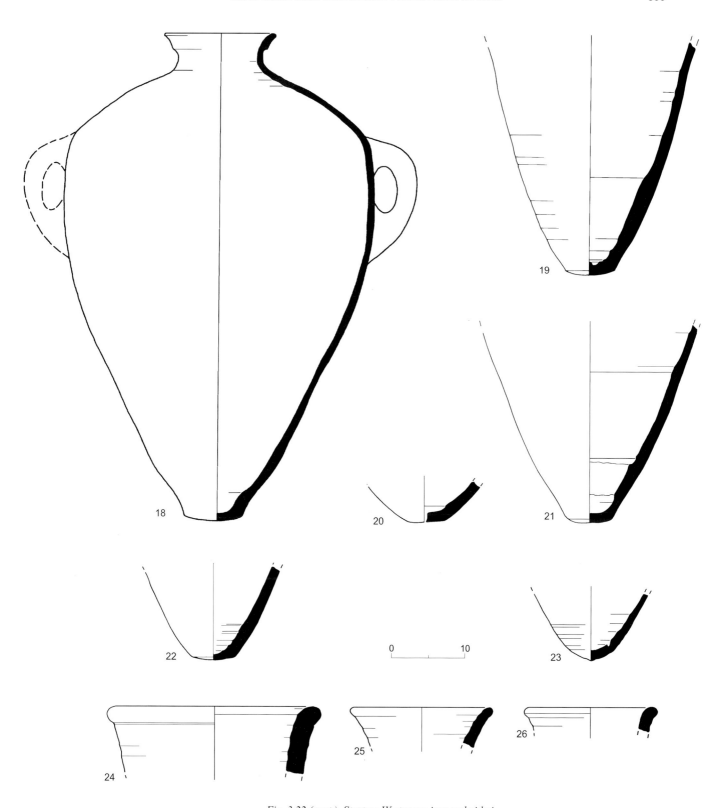

Fig. 3.22 (cont.). Stratum IX storage jars and pithoi.

Fig. 3.23 ▶

No.	Reg. No.	Context (Stratum)	Elevation (m)	Description
1	A616/16	Room 83 (VIII)	21.40/21.30	Surface: 5YR 7/6 (reddish yellow); fabric: same; core: none; inclusions: many fine sparkling
2	A616/15	Room 83 (VIII)	21.40/21.30	Surface: 5YR 7/6 (reddish yellow); fabric: same; core: thick, 10YR 7/6 (very pale brown); inclusions: many small to medium voids
3	B277/6	Area 128 (VIII–VII)	N/A	Surface: 5YR 7/4 (pink); fabric: same; core: thick, gray; inclusions: many fine to small white, many fine to small red
4	A586/1	Room 75 (VII)	21.80/21.65	Surface: 7.5YR 7/3 (pink); fabric: same; core: light gray; inclusions: very many fine to small white, many fine to small dark
5	B258/10	Room 132 (VIII)	20.70	Surface (self-slip): 2.5Y 8/2 (very pale yellow); fabric: 10R 5/8 (red); core: none; inclusions: many fine white
6	B196/2/3	Area 128 (VII)	22.60/22.40	Surface: 5YR 7/4 (pink); fabric: same; core: none; inclusions: few small to medium red
7	A305/25	Area 41 (VII)	22.30	Surface: 7.5YR 7/6 (reddish yellow); fabric: same; core: light gray, middle and interior; inclusions: few small white, very few small red
8	A310/27	Area 41 (VII)	22.25	Surface (self-slip): 5Y 8/2 (pale yellow); fabric: 5YR 7/4 (pink); core: thick, light gray; inclusions: N/A
9	A303/8	Area 43 (VII)	22.50/22.35	N/A
10	B94/2	Sub-floor fill(?) for Room 108 (VIII)	21.70	N/A
11	B29/8	Room 108 (VII)	22.50	Surface: 5YR 5/8 (yellowish red); fabric: same; core: none; inclusions: many fine to small dark
12	B33	Room 108 (VII)	22.32	Incised; N/A
13	B258/12	Room 132 (VIII)	20.70	Surface: 2.5YR 6/6 (light red); fabric: same; core: gray, middle and interior; inclusions: few small to medium white
14	B237	Room 111 (VIII–VII)	21.65/21.55	Surface: 10YR 7/3 (very pale brown); fabric: same; core: thick, gray; inclusions: many small white
15	A272/20	Area 41 (VII)	22.80/22.50	Surface: 10YR 7/3 (pink); fabric: 5YR 6/6 (reddish yellow); core: N/A; inclusions: N/A
16	B217/17	Room 132 (VIII)	22.30/21.90	Surface (self-slip): 7.5YR 7/3 (pink); fabric: 5YR 7/6 (reddish yellow); core: thick, gray, middle and interior; inclusions: many small to medium white, many fine to small dark
17	B33/3	Room 108 (VII)	22.32	Surface: 5YR 6/8 (reddish yellow); fabric: same; core: thick, light gray; inclusions: many fine sparkling, few small red
18	A272/19	Area 41 (VII)	22.80/22.50	Surface: 7.5YR 6/6 (reddish yellow); fabric: 2.5YR 6/3 (light reddish brown); core: thick, gray; inclusions: few fine to small white, few small voids
19	B196/2/2	Area 128 (VII)	22.60/22.40	N/A
20	B238/13	Area 128 (VII)	22.70	N/A

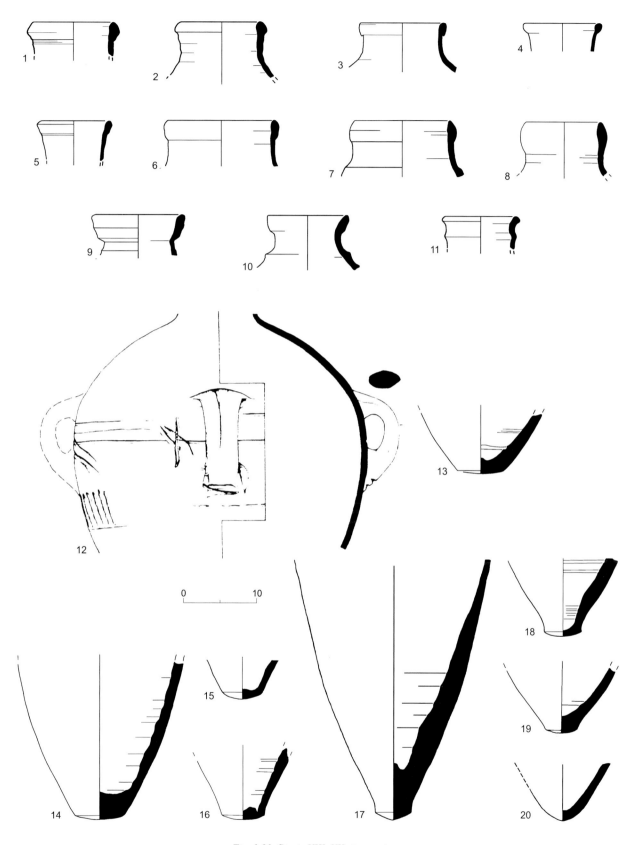

Fig. 3.23. Strata VIII–VII storage jars.

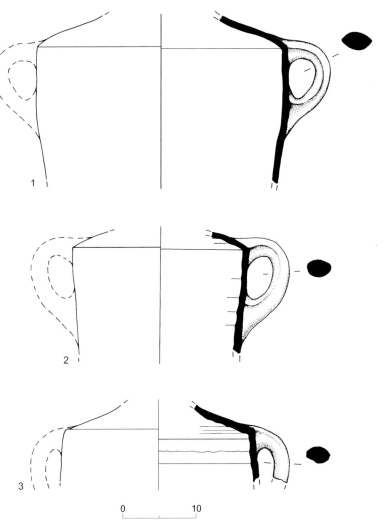

Fig. 3.24. 'Canaanite jars'

No.	Reg. No.	Context (Stratum)	Elevation (m)	Description
1	B33	Room 108 (VII)	22.32	Surface: 2.5Y 7/2 (light gray); fabric: same; core: light gray, interior; inclusions: many medium to large white
2	A425/1	Area 62 (VII–VI)	22.40	Surface: 10YR 7/3 (very pale brown); fabric: same; core: none; inclusions: very many fine to small red, few small to large white
3	A480/1	Room 71 (VI)	N/A	Surface: 7.5YR 6/4 (light brown); fabric: same; core: light gray; inclusions: many fine voids

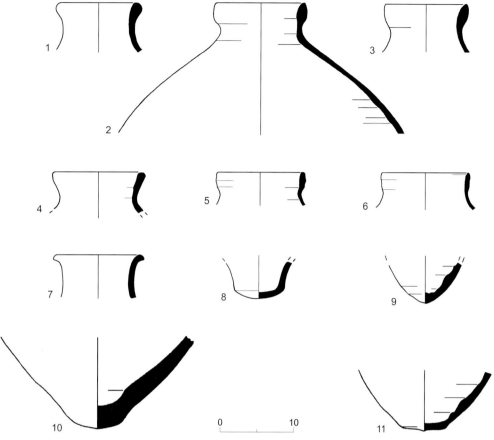

Fig. 3.25. Strata VI–V storage jars.

No.	Reg. No.	Context (Stratum)	Elevation (m)	Description
1	A482	Room 71 (VI)	N/A	Surface: 7.5YR 7/4 (pink); fabric: same; core: very few fine red, few fine voids
2	A229/18	Area 36 (VI)	23.50/23.35	Surface: 5YR 6/6 (reddish yellow); fabric: same; core: thick, gray; inclusions: few fine white, very few fine dark, very few small voids
3	A482/1	Room 71 (VI)	N/A	Surface: 2.5YR 7/8 (light red); fabric: 10YR 7/4 (very pale brown); core: none; inclusions: few small white, few small dark
4	A285/15	Area 40 (V)	23.30	Surface (self-slip): 7.5YR 8/2 (pinkish white); fabric: 5YR 6/6 (reddish yellow); core: 7.5YR 5/3 (brown); inclusions: few fine sparkling, few fine white
5	A708/8	Room 71 (VI)	N/A	Surface: 10YR 6/3 (pale brown); fabric: same; core: thick, gray, middle and interior; inclusions: many fine to small voids
6	A204/13	Room 34 (V)	23.50	Surface: 5YR 6/6 (reddish yellow); fabric: same; core: none; inclusions: few fine voids, few fine to small white, very few fine red
7	A317/3	Area 40 (V)	23.30	Surface: 5YR 5/6 (yellowish red); fabric: same; core: none; inclusions: many fine white
8	A306/28	Area 40 (V)	23.30	Surface (self-slip): 10YR 7/4 (very pale brown); fabric: 5YR 5/6 (yellowish red); core: thick, gray, middle and interior; inclusions: many small dark, few small voids
9	A325/10	Area 40 (V)	23.20/23.00	Surface: 10YR 7/6 (yellow); fabric: same; core: 10YR 6/4 (light yellowish brown); inclusions: few medium voids, few small to medium white
10	A724/3	Room 71 (VI)	N/A	Surface: 5YR 7/6 (reddish yellow); fabric: same; core: thick, gray, interior and middle; inclusions: very many fine to medium white, many fine to small voids
11	A385/16	Sq K18 (VI)	22.90/22.60	Surface: 2.5YR 5/4 (reddish brown); fabric: 2.5YR 5/8 (red); core: thin, dark gray; inclusions: few fine voids, few small dark

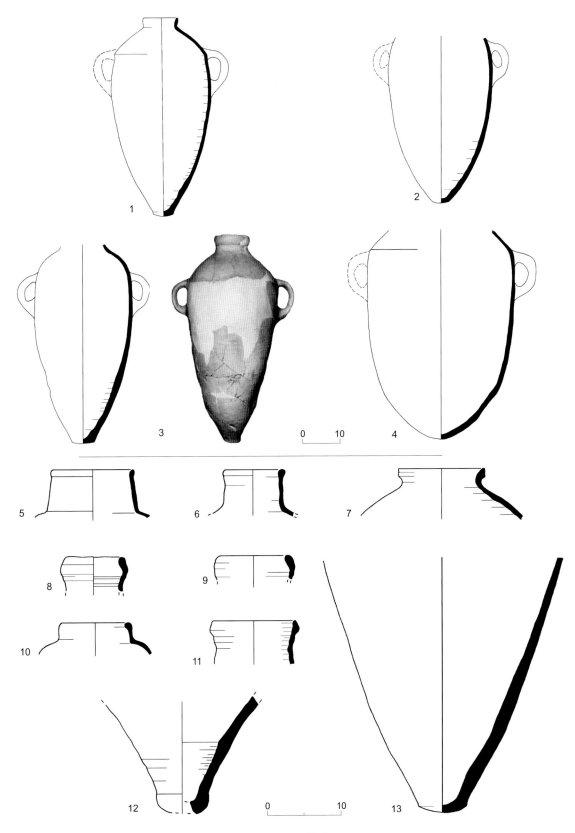

Fig. 3.26. Strata III–II storage jars.

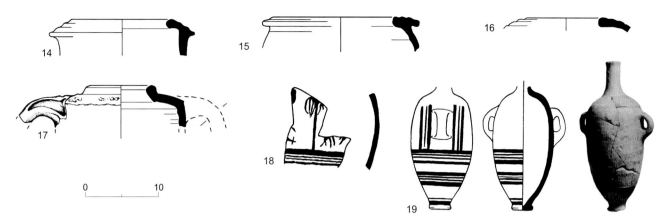

Fig. 3.26 (cont.). Strata III–II storage jars.

No.	Reg. No.	Context (Stratum)	Elevation (m)	Description
1	A123	Pit 17 (III)	24.00	Surface: 7.5YR 6/4 (light brown); fabric: same; core: very thin, light gray; inclusions: few small white and dark, few large dark
2	A118	Pit 17 (III)	24.00	N/A
3	A118/14	Pit 17 (III)	24.00	Surface: 5YR 6/8 (reddish yellow); fabric: same; core: light gray, interior; inclusions: many small to medium dark, few small to medium red
4	A63/1	Pit 18 (III)	24.60	N/A
5	A156/6	Pit 17 (III)	23.70	Surface: 2.5YR 5/6 (red); fabric: same; core: light gray; inclusions: many fine to small white, few fine dark
6	A140/4	Pit 17 (III)	23.80	Surface: 2.5YR 5/4 (reddish brown); fabric: same; core: thin, light gray; inclusions: many fine white, many fine dark
7	A108/1	Sq M18 (III)	24.40	Surface: 5YR 6/6 (reddish yellow); fabric: same; core: none; inclusions: very few fine to small white
8	A118/12	Pit 17 (III)	24.00	Surface: 2.5YR 5/4 (reddish brown); fabric: same; core: thin, light gray; inclusions: many small dark, very few fine sparkling
9	A74/1	Area 10 (III)	24.40	Surface (self-slip): 10YR 7/3 (very pale brown); fabric: 10R 6/4 (pale red); core: thin, light gray; inclusions: very few fine white
10	A60/17	Sq L18 (II)	24.75/24.65	Surface: 5YR 6/4 (light reddish brown); fabric: same; core: thick, gray, middle and interior; inclusions: very few fine white
11	A32/7	Sq M19 (II)	25.00/24.80	Surface: 10YR 7/3 (very pale brown); fabric: 2.5YR 5/6 (red); core: thick, gray; inclusions: many fine to small white
12	A63	Area 13 (III)	24.60	Surface: 7.5YR 5/4 (brown); fabric: same; core: thick, gray; inclusions: many fine to small dark
13	A104/4	Area 19 (III)	24.40	N/A
14	B249/2	Sq N21 (unstratified)	N/A	N/A
15	B7/8	Sq M20 (unstratified)	24.55/24.15	Surface (self-slip): 10YR 7/3 (very pale brown); fabric: 2.5YR 5/8 (red); core: thick, gray; inclusions: very few fine sparkling
16	B150/1	Sq L21 (unstratified)	24.83/23.86	Rilling; N/A
17	A421/6	Sq J20 (unstratified)	22.60	Surface: 5YR 5/6 (yellowish red); fabric: same; core: none; inclusions: few fine white, few fine sparkling
18	A83/2	Area 13 (III)	24.60	Paint: 10R 4/4 (weak red); surface: 10YR 7/4 (very pale brown); fabric: 5YR 6/6 (reddish yellow); core: none; inclusions: few fine sparkling
19	A96/1	L13 (III)	N/A	Paint: 10R 4/4 (weak red); surface (slip): 7.5YR 8/3 (pink); fabric: 7.5YR 4/2 (brown); core: thin gray; inclusions: few small to medium white

Fig. 3.27 ▶

No.	Reg. No.	Context (Stratum)	Elevation (m)	Description
1	B331	Courtyard 118 (XII)	N/A	Surface: 10 YR 7/3 (very pale brown); fabric: same; core: N/A; inclusions: N/A
2	B299/3	Courtyard 118 (XII)	N/A	Surface: 7.5YR 6/8 (reddish yellow); fabric: 5YR 6/6 (reddish yellow); core: none; inclusions: few sparkling
3	B280/2	Courtyard 118 (XII)	19.10	Burnish; paint: 10R 4/2 (weak red) and black; surface (slip): 10YR 6/3 (pale brown); fabric: 2.5Y 4/1 (dark gray); core: none; inclusions: many fine white
4	B252/11	Courtyard 118 (XI)	19.50/19.40	White wash; paint: 2.5YR 3/1 (dark reddish gray); surface: 2.5YR 8/4 (pink); fabric: 2.5YR 7/8 (light red); core: none; inclusions: many fine dark, few fine to small white
5	B240/39	Courtyard 118 (XI)	19.65/19.55	Paint: 10YR 5/4 (yellowish brown); surface (slip): 10YR 8/3 (very pale brown); fabric: 10YR 6/1 (gray); core: N/A; inclusions: very many fine to small white
6	B283/12	Room 135 (IX)	20.45	Paint: 5YR 3/3 (dark reddish brown) and 10R 5/6 (red); surface (self-slip): 2.5YR 7/2 (light gray); fabric: 7.5 YR 5/3 (brown); core: none; inclusions: many fine dark, few fine red, very many fine to small voids, very many fine to small white
7	A310/1	Area 41 (VII)	22.25	Surface: 2.5Y 8/2 (pale yellow); fabric: 5YR 5/6 (yellowish red); core: none; inclusions: many fine white
8	A236/2	Area 28 or Room 34 (V)	23.55	Surface: 2.5YR 6/6 (light red); fabric: N/A; core: N/A; inclusions: many small voids, few medium dark
9	A483	Room 71 (VI)	N/A	Surface: 2.5YR 5/6 (red); fabric: same; core: thick, light gray; inclusions: many medium voids, few small white, few small dark
10	A370/24	Sq K18 (V)	23.00	Paint: 10R 5/6 (red); surface: 2.5YR 6/8 (light red); fabric: same; core: light gray; inclusions: few small to medium white
11	A292	Pit 35 (VI)	23.10	Surface: 5Y 7/2 (light gray); fabric: N/A; core: N/A; inclusions: many fine to small white, few fine dark
12	A117/1	Pit 17 (III)	24.00	Surface: 5YR 5/6 (yellowish red); fabric: same; core: none; inclusions: very many small to medium dark, many medium voids (straw)

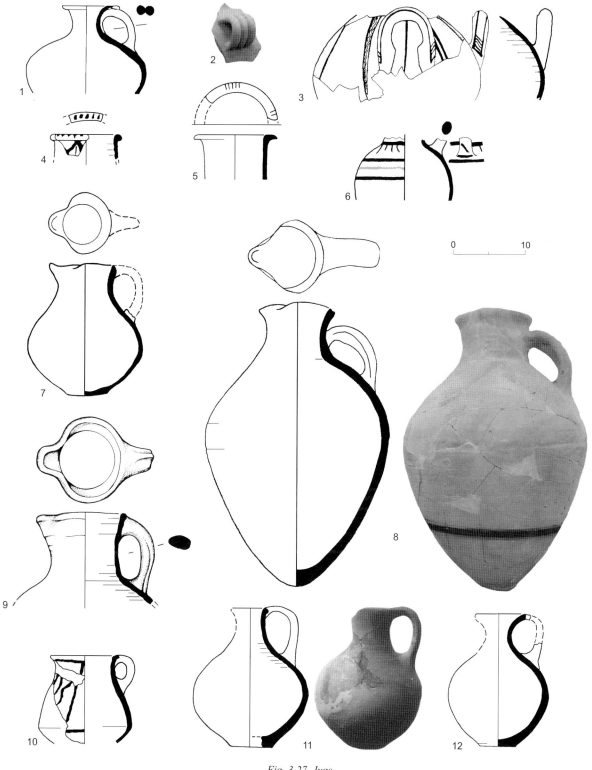

Fig. 3.27. Jugs.

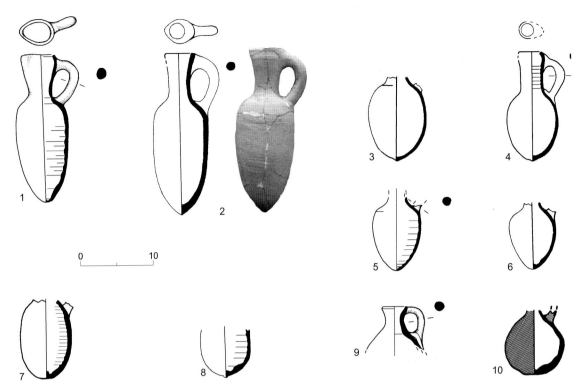

Fig. 3.28. Juglets.

No.	Reg. No.	Context (Stratum)	Elevation (m)	Description
1	B329	Courtyard 118 (XII)	18.90	N/A
2	B318/1	Courtyard 118 (XII)	N/A	Wet-smooth marks; surface (self-slip): 10YR 7/4 (very pale brown); fabric: 2.5YR 5/6 (red); core: N/A; inclusions: many small to medium white, few small red, few fine sparkling
3	B272/1	Courtyard 118 (XII–XI)	N/A	Surface (self-slip): 7.5YR 7/3 (pink); fabric: 2.5YR 5/8 (red); core: thick, 7.5YR 6/6 (reddish yellow); inclusions: many small voids, many fine dark, many fine to small white
4	B355/1	Courtyard 118 (XII)	18.70	Burnish; surface (self-slip): 10YR 7/3 (very pale brown); fabric: 5YR 5/6 (yellowish red); core: dark gray; inclusions: many medium voids, many fine sparkling
5	B335	Courtyard 118 (XII)	18.80	Surface: 10YR 7/4 (very pale brown); fabric: same; core: none; inclusions: very few fine to small white
6	B344	Courtyard 118 (XII)	N/A	Surface: 5YR 7/6 (reddish yellow); fabric: same; core: thick, 10YR 7/4 (very pale brown), middle and interior; inclusions: N/A
7	B252/20	Courtyard 118 (XI)	19.50/19.40	Surface (self-slip): 7.5YR 7/3 (pink); fabric: 7.5YR 6/6 (reddish yellow); core: thick, gray; inclusions: few fine sparkling, few fine to small white
8	B142/1	Courtyard 118 (IX)	20.34	Surface: 5YR 7/6 (reddish yellow); fabric: same; core: none; inclusions: very few fine white
9	A448/23	Area 59 (VI)	22.35?	Shaved(?); surface: 5Y 7/4 (pale yellow); fabric: same; core: none; inclusions: few small voids, very few small dark
10	A80/1	Area 10 (III)	24.40	Burnish; surface (slip): 10R 5/8 (red); fabric: 5YR 5/6 (yellowish red); core: none; inclusions: few small dark

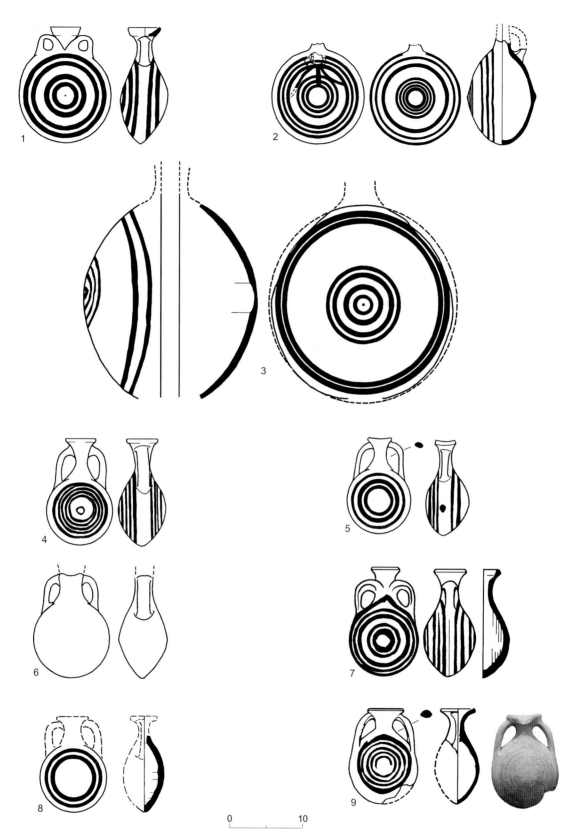

Fig. 3.29. Pilgrim flasks.

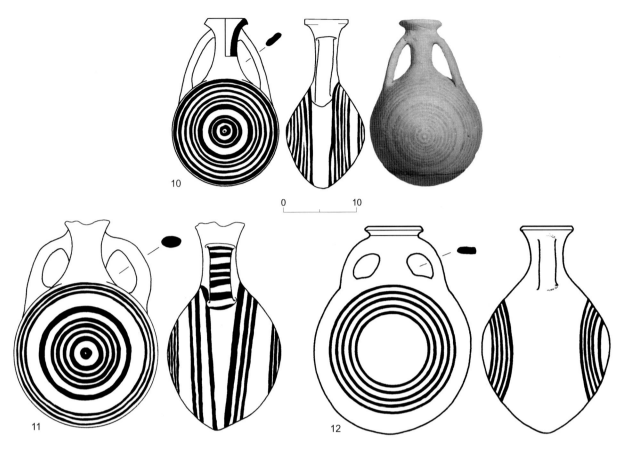

Fig. 3.29 (cont.). Pilgrim flasks.

No.	Reg. No.	Context (Stratum)	Elevation (m)	Description
1	B247/1	Burial 152 (IX)	N/A	Paint; N/A
2	A503/1	Room 71 (VI)	N/A	Paint: 10R 4/4 (weak red); surface: 2.5YR 5/4 (reddish brown); fabric: same; core: none; inclusions: many fine to small white, few fine to small dark
3	A499/1	Room 71 (VI)	N/A	Paint: 10R 4/6 (red); surface: 2.5YR 6/4 (light reddish brown); fabric: same; core: none; inclusions: few fine to small white, few small voids, few small red
4	A114/1	Pit 17 (III)	24.20	Paint; N/A
5	A113/1	Pit 17 (III)	24.20	Paint: 10R 4/4 (weak red); surface (slip): 5Y 7/3 (pale yellow); fabric: 5YR 7/8 (reddish yellow); core: none; inclusions: few fine white, few fine dark
6	A116/1	Pit 17 (III)	24.00	N/A
7	A75/1	Pit 17 (III)	24.40	Paint; N/A
8	A120/1	Pit 17 (III)	24.00	Paint: 10R 4/4 (weak red); surface: 5YR 6/8 (reddish yellow); fabric: same; core: gray, interior; inclusions: few fine to small white
9	A76/2	Pit 17 (III)	24.40	Paint: 10R 4/4 (weak red); surface: 5YR 5/6 (yellowish red); fabric: same; core: gray, interior; inclusions: very many small to medium white
10	A120/2	Pit 17 (III)	24.00	Paint: 10R 4/4 (weak red); surface (self-slip): 10YR 7/3 (very pale brown); fabric: 7.5YR 6/6 (reddish yellow); core: thin, light gray, interior; inclusions: few small white, very few medium red
11	A115/1	Pit 17 (III)	24.00	Paint: 10R 4/4 (weak red); surface (slip?): 5YR 6/8 (reddish yellow); fabric: same; core: thick, 10YR 6/4 (brownish yellow); inclusions: many fine to small voids
12	A122/1	Pit 17 (III)	24.00	Paint: 10R 4/4 (weak red); surface (slip): 10R 5/6 (red); fabric: 5YR 6/6 (reddish yellow); core: light gray, interior; inclusions: many fine dark

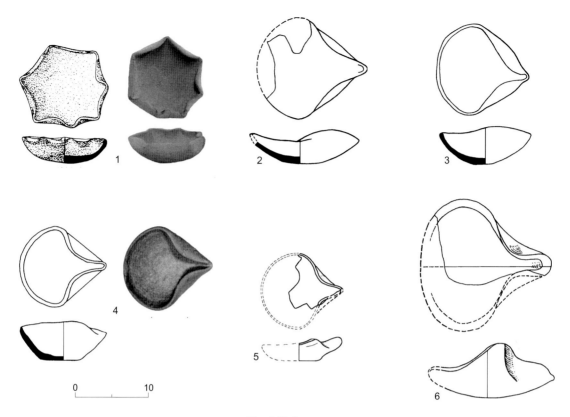

Fig. 3.30. Lamps.

No.	Reg. No.	Context (Stratum)	Elevation (m)	Description
1	B104	Courtyard 118 (XI)	19.95	Surface: 5YR 6/4 (light reddish brown); fabric: same; core: N/A; inclusions: few medium to large dark, few fine voids, few small white
2	B86/1	Courtyard 118 (X)	20.30	Surface: 2.5YR 5/6 (red); fabric: same; core: thin, light gray; inclusions: many fine to small white, many fine dark
3	B213/1	Sqs M–N22 (XI–IX?)	20.13	Surface: 7.5YR 7/3 (pink); fabric: same; core: N/A; inclusions: few small dark
4	B142/2	Courtyard 118 (IX?)	20.34	N/A
5	B77/2	Courtyard 118 (X)	20.50/20.30	Surface: 2.5YR 5/6 (red); fabric: same; core: none; inclusions: few medium dark
6	A708/5	Room 71 (VI)	N/A	Surface: 10YR 7/3 (very pale brown); fabric: 5YR 6/6 (reddish yellow); core: none; inclusions: few fine sparkling, few fine white, few fine voids

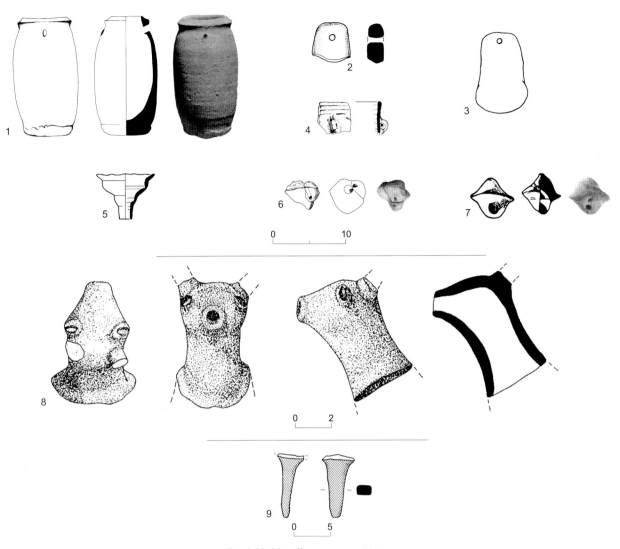

Fig. 3.31. Miscellaneous ceramic items.

No.	Object	Reg. No.	Context (Stratum)	Elevation (m)	Description
1	Jar?	B136	Courtyard 118 (XI)	19.80	Surface: 5YR 7/4 (pink); fabric: same; core: N/A; inclusions: few medium red, few small to medium dark, few small white
2	Weight	A620/26	Sq H20 (IX)	20.90/20.30	Surface: 2.5YR 6/4 (light reddish brown); fabric: same; core: none; inclusions: many fine to small white, few fine to small dark, few fine to small voids
3	Weight	A301/1	Sq J18 (VI)	22.60/22.50	N/A
4	Unknown	B165/16	Sqs M–N22 (IX)	21.00/20.83	Surface: 5YR 6/6 (reddish yellow); fabric: same; core: none; inclusions: very few fine sparkling, very few fine white
5	Funnel?	B255/18	Area 128 (VII)	22.60/22.55	Surface: 10YR 7/3 (very pale brown); fabric: same; core: none; inclusions: very few small white
6	Stopper?	A494/22	Room 75? (VII)	22.10	N/A
7	Stopper	A730	(VI)	N/A	N/A
8	Kernos	A284	Sq L18 (V)	23.60	N/A
9	Zoo-morphic vessel?	B254/6	Sq N21	21.30	Burnish; surface: 2.5YR 5/6 (red); fabric: same; core: thick, dark gray; inclusions: few fine to small voids, few fine sparkling, few fine dark

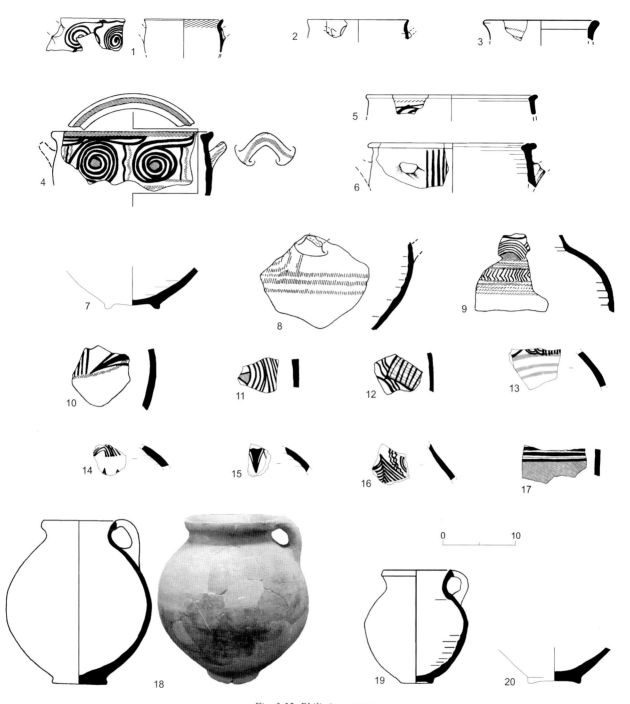

Fig. 3.32. Philistine pottery.

◀ **Fig. 3.32**

No.	Object	Reg. No.	Context (Stratum)	Elevation (m)	Description
1	Bowl	A563/1	Sqs G–H18	21.70/21.40	Paint; N/A
2	Bowl	A90/4	Area 13 (III)	24.40	N/A
3	Bowl	A92/6	Area 10 (III)	24.40/24.30	Paint: 10R 4/3 (weak red); surface (slip): 10YR 8/2 (very pale brown); fabric: 10R 4/8 (red); core: 2.5YR 5/6 (red); inclusions: many fine to small white, few fine sparkling
4	Krater	A142	Sq M19 (IV)	24.18	Paint and wash; N/A
5	Krater	A226	Sq K18 (IV–III)	24.00/23.85	Paint: 10R 4/6 (red) and black; surface (slip): 7.5YR 7/3 (pink); fabric: 7.5YR 5/6 (strong brown); core: none; inclusions: none
6	Krater	A181/1	Sq K18 (III)	24.20/24.05	Paint: 5YR 4/4 (reddish brown); surface: 7.5YR 8/3 (pink); fabric: 5YR 5/6 (yellowish red); core: thin, gray; inclusions: few fine white, few fine voids
7	Krater	A231/32	Sq K18 (IV–III)	23.90/23.74	N/A
8	Krater	A118/18	Pit 17 (III)	24.00	Paint: 10R 5/4 (weak red); surface (slip): 10YR 7/2 (light gray); fabric: 5YR 4/4 (reddish brown); core: N/A; inclusions: few small to medium white, few fine dark
9	Jug	A226/18	Sq K18 (III)	4.00	Paint and wash: 5YR 2.5/1 (black) and 10R 4/4 (weak red); surface (wash): 10YR 8/2 (very pale brown); fabric: 2.5YR 5/6 (red); core: light gray; inclusions: few small to medium voids (some straw), few fine white
10	Krater	A173/14	Sq K18 (III)	24.25/24.00	Paint: 7.5YR 8/6 (reddish yellow) and 5YR 3/3 (dark reddish); surface (slip): 10YR 8/2 (very pale brown); fabric: 2.5YR 4/4 (reddish brown); core: none; inclusions: very many fine white, very many fine voids
11	Jug?	A100/10	Sqs K–L18 (III)	24.32/24.22	Paint: 10YR 4/2 (dark grayish brown); surface: 10YR 8/3 (very pale brown); fabric: 2.5YR 5/6 (red); core: gray; inclusions: few fine voids, few fine white
12	Jug?	A188/31	Sq K18 (IV)	24.05/23.95	Paint: 10R 4/4 (weak red); surface: 7.5YR 4/6 (strong brown); fabric: same; core: none; inclusions: few small white, few medium dark
13	Jug?	A232/9	Sq K18 (IV–III)	23.90/23.70	Paint; N/A
14	Jug?	A188/32	Sq K18 (IV)	24.05/23.95	Paint: 10YR 4/2 (dark grayish brown); surface (slip): 2.5Y 8/2 (pale yellow); fabric: 7.5YR 5/6 (strong brown); core: light gray, interior; inclusions: very few fine voids, many fine white
15	Jug?	A188/30	Sq K18 (IV)	24.05/23.95	Paint: 10YR 4/2 (dark grayish brown); surface (slip): 2.5Y 8/2 (pale yellow); fabric: 7.5YR 5/6 (strong brown); core: light gray, interior; inclusions: very few fine voids, many fine white
16	Jug?	A88/3	Sqs K–L18	24.75/24.45	Paint; N/A
17	Jug?	A128/16	Sq K19 (III)	24.45/24.25	Vertical burnish; paint: black and white; surface (slip): 10R 4/8 (red); fabric: 5YR 5/6 (yellowish red); core: thick, light gray; inclusions: few fine voids, very few large white
18	Jug	A119/17	Pit 17 (III)	24.00	Surface: 7.5Y 7/3 (pale yellow); fabric: 2.5YR 5/8 (red); core: N/A; inclusions: few fine to small white
19	Jug	A118/6	Pit 17 (III)	24.00	Surface (self-slip): 5Y 7/3 (pale yellow); fabric: 2.5Y 4/2 (dark grayish brown); core: N/A; inclusions: many small to medium white, few fine dark
20	Jug	A209/5	Area 10 (III)	24.50/24.35	Surface: 5YR 5/6 (yellowish red); fabric: same; core: thin, light gray; inclusions: many fine sparkling

NOTES

[1] I am grateful to Nava Panitz-Cohen and Amihai Mazar who generously made available to me then-unpublished pottery plates from Tel Baṭash-Timna Strata XII–V (Middle Bronze Age to Iron I). I wish to thank also Yuval Gadot who provided me with the pottery plates for Strata X-14 to X-8 from Pirhiya Beck and Moshe Kochavi's unpublished excavations at Tel Afeq.

[2] Typological parallels from Tel Ḥarasim are cited in this report despite the problematic interpretation of the site's stratigraphy (Givon 1995; 1996; 1997; 1998; 1999). For example, Stratum IV is dated to the tenth and ninth centuries BCE. Notwithstanding, Tel Ḥarasim provides useful comparative material, especially for Iron I (Tel Mor Strata V–III; e.g., Fig. 3.10:10).

[3] These vessels are described here as 'deep bowls' rather than kraters in order to maintain consistency with the scholarly literature (e.g., Killebrew 1998a:83, 84). Note, however, that a similar vessel from Stratum VIII is grouped with the kraters (see Fig. 3.14:10).

[4] The closely related Ashdod Ware also makes its initial appearance in this stratum (see below).

[5] Note that the radiometric dates obtained from early Iron Age pottery from Tel Dor support a low chronology, according to which the conventional high chronology is lowered by approximately 100 years (Gilboa and Sharon 2003: Table 21). Thus Area B1, Phase 9 is assigned the absolute dates of 900–850 BCE.

[6] For several complete and nearly intact deep bowls (which are typologically similar to kraters), found in reasonably secure Stratum VI contexts, see Fig. 3.9.

[7] There are no well-preserved, undecorated kraters from secure Stratum IV contexts. For Philistine Bichrome kraters, either from Stratum IV or Strata IV–III, see Fig. 3.32:4–7.

[8] Unfortunately the present author was not able to locate this krater and, therefore, could not check for the depiction of a second animal. The photograph seems to indicate the presence of a quadraped, in which case the animal would most likely be an ibex (cf. Tufnell, Inge and Harding 1940: Pl. 48:250).

[9] According to the renewed excavations, this krater belongs to Stratum VA–IVB (Finkelstein, Zimhoni and Kafri 2000: Fig. 11.31:5).

[10] To err on the side of caution, most vessel types (including cooking pots) that were assigned broadly to Strata XI–IX are discussed as part of the Stratum IX assemblage. It is not clear what separates an attribution to Strata XI–IX as opposed to Stratum IX in Courtyard 118.

[11] The intact, Egyptianized, slender ovoid jar, which was found in the area of the Stratum XI bāmāh, is a notable exception (see Figs. 4.10:1).

[12] It was not possible to determine the registration number of Fig. 3.22:2, nor was the present author able to locate the vessel and its drawing. According to a preliminary report, however, this storage jar was found in Building A (M. Dothan 1960c: Fig. 4:8, Pl. 10:4). Morphological considerations confirm this Stratum IX attribution (see below).

[13] Scholarship on this vessel type, especially regarding its use as a marker of Israelite ethnicity, is voluminous. For recent discussions with further bibliography, see the articles by Cohen-Weinberger and Wolff (2001); Gilboa (2001); Herr (2001); Killebrew (2001); Raban (2001).

[14] As with all vessel types, Stratum IV produced very few storage jars, fragmentary or intact.

[15] The photograph of Fig. 3.26:3 shows a short neck and thickened rim absent in the drawing. Apparently, this vessel was drawn before it was fully restored. Indeed, none of the restorable storage jars from Stratum III, in addition to many other vessel types from the rest of the strata, were in the same condition as originally depicted.

[16] Note that the fill from the Roman well (L55) contained some Persian pottery (see Chapter 2). It is likely that the Persian-period pottery at Tel Mor arrived by way of Nebi Yunis, located close to the mouth of the Naḥal Lakhish and inhabited at this time (see Chapter 1).

[17] In the photograph of the vessel, which was taken in 1960, the neck is either preserved or was reconstructed, perhaps by analogy with the parallels described below. When the vessel was subsequently drawn, the neck, for whatever reason, was not depicted.

[18] For the unusual double-coil handle with a button on a deep, red-slipped bowl, see Fig. 3.1:17.

[19] The statistics for the Philistine and imported pottery are based on straight diagnostic sherd counts, which include rims, handles, bases and decorated body sherds. Because of the likelihood that numerous sherds belong to a single vessel, these statistics are almost certainly inflated.

[20] 'Aegean-style' cooking-jug rims have been found in great quantity also at Ashqelon in strata characterized by Philistine Bichrome pottery (L.E. Stager, pers. comm.).

CHAPTER 4

EGYPTIAN AND EGYPTIANIZED POTTERY

MARIO A.S. MARTIN AND TRISTAN J. BARAKO

The considerable quantity of Egyptian, and, particularly, Egyptianized pottery[1] found in Late Bronze Age and early Iron Age strata (mainly VIII–V)[2] at Tel Mor, strongly suggests the presence of Egyptians at the site. The locally produced Egyptianized pottery, which is far more numerous, imitates both Egyptian shapes and production techniques. Because of Tel Mor's location near the coast, the assemblage of Egyptian imports, although small in number (11 vessels; see Fig. 4.9), is large and diverse compared to that of other Egyptian garrison sites such as Bet She'an.[3]

Although sporadic Egyptian imports suggest a trade connection with Egypt, they do not necessarily imply an impact expressed by actual Egyptian presence. Locally produced Egyptianized pottery, on the other hand, when found in Canaan in large quantities and in a variety of vessel types, can be regarded as evidence for the presence of Egyptian administrative or military personnel. Such assemblages, which comprise mostly bowls but also various kinds of jars (especially beer jars), have been found mainly at Deir el-Balaḥ, Tel Sera', Tell el-Far'ah (S), Tell el-'Ajjul, Yafo (Jaffa; unpublished), Bet She'an, Tell es-Sa'idiyeh and Tel Afeq (see Figs. 4.2, 4.3).[4] At many of these sites the discovery of Egyptian and Egyptian-style buildings, architectural elements, statues, stelae, inscriptions (hieroglyphic and hieratic), burial practices (e.g., anthropoid coffins) and a variety of small finds further signals an Egyptian presence (Weinstein 1981; Oren 1984). On the strength of its Egyptian-style architecture (i.e., Building B) and abundant Egyptianized pottery, it is argued here that Tel Mor functioned as an Egyptian garrison during the thirteenth century and the first half of the twelfth century BCE (Strata VIII–V).

Recently Carolyn Higginbotham (2000; for a previous discussion, see Redford 1990) has argued that Egypt administered Canaan through the appointment of Egyptian circuit officials rather than resident governors. Furthermore, she proposes that most Egyptian or Egyptianized material culture in Canaan was a result of

emulation by local élites and not, contrary to the traditional view, brought to or produced in Canaan by Egyptians living and serving abroad. Unfortunately, this élite emulation model does not adequately explain the presence of large quantities of locally produced, Egyptianized coarse wares, especially at sites like Bet She'an, Deir el-Balaḥ and now, Tel Mor. Higginbotham (2000:129–132) is partly aware, however, of this problem and prefers the 'Direct Rule' model for such sites as Bet She'an, Gaza, Deir el-Balaḥ and Timna. This latter model should also be applied to other sites with such assemblages (i.e., Tel Sera', Tell el-Far'ah [S], Tell el-'Ajjul, Jaffa, Tell es-Sa'idiyeh, Tel Afeq), leaving few sites where Canaanites might have emulated Egyptian élites.

In addition to a presentation of the Egyptian and Egyptianized pottery from Tel Mor, this chapter contains a discussion of vessel typology and chronology, pottery production techniques and, finally, the nature of the Egyptian presence at Tel Mor during the Late Bronze and early Iron Ages. Because Strata VIII–V are essentially four phases within two main strata—Stratum VIII–VII and Stratum VI–V—the pottery therein will be grouped together in the plates. If the specific phase of a sherd or vessel is known, then that information will be indicated in the 'Context' column of the figure description. In any case, the following discussion is arranged according to vessel type and not stratum.

The imported Egyptian and locally produced Egyptianized pottery are presented together here in order to demonstrate the complete repertoire of Egyptian shapes present at Tel Mor. Egyptian sites with parallel material are shown in Fig. 4.1. It should be assumed that pottery is Egyptianized, which comprises the overwhelming majority of the combined assemblage presented in this chapter, unless a sherd or vessel is specifically described as an import. Classifying pottery as Egyptianized is sometimes difficult: For example, traditional Canaanite forms are occasionally made with heavily straw-tempered fabric typical of Egyptian forms (see, e.g., Fig. 3.9). Furthermore, simple Egyptian

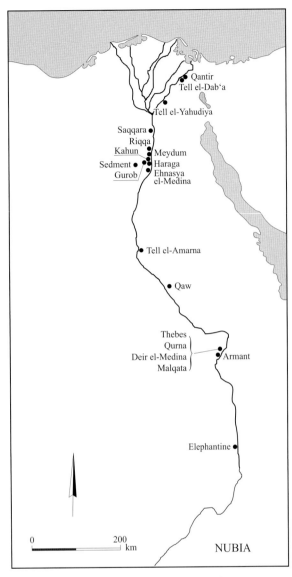

Fig. 4.1. Sites in Egypt mentioned in the text.

bowl shapes, such as straight-sided bowls and, even more so, bowls with rounded walls and a plain rim, are such basic types that they may have evolved in both regions with little or no relationship between them. In such cases, a combination of all factors (i.e., surface treatment, clay fabric, decoration) may tip the balance in favor of an Egyptianized classification.

FABRICS AND PRODUCTION TECHNIQUES

Egyptian Marl Clays

The analysis of fabric is based on visual examination (with the aid of a magnifying glass) of freshly broken pottery. In general, laboratory analyses confirm the identification of Egyptian Marl Clay pottery first made on the basis of visual inspection. The identifications of all the Egyptian Marl sherds from Tel Mor made by the authors were corroborated by David Aston. It should be noted from the outset, however, that it was sometimes difficult to differentiate Marl F from certain Levantine fabrics described by Egyptologists as 'P-30' (Aston, Aston and Brock 1998:142–143), and elsewhere classified as 'IV.07.05' (Aston 1998:70) and 'III.10' (Nicholson and Rose 1985:138).

Marl C

The clay matrix of Marl C fabrics is characterized by abundant, somewhat decomposed, limestone particles of medium to coarse size, which gives the fabric a speckled appearance. The groundmass is fine and dense, and the inclusions consist of fine and medium sand particles, added as temper, particles of unmixed marl clay and micaceous components. Most vessels made of this fabric have very thick walls. Marl C fabrics first appear during the Middle Kingdom at the latest, and become rare after the early XVIIIth Dynasty. Marl C vessels appear mainly in the Memphis–Fayoum region, where this fabric may originate and, less commonly, in the Delta region (Nordström and Bourriau 1993:179–181; Bader 2001, 2002).

The *zîr* from Tel Mor (Fig. 4.9:11) is probably composed of Marl C Variant 2 (B. Bader, pers. comm.; cf. Bader 2001: Pl. IVb, c). A red (10R 4/6) to reddish-yellow fabric (5YR 6/6) and a grayish-white self-slip characterize this subgroup (Nordström and Bourriau 1993:180). Relatively low firing conditions distinguish Marl C2 from other variants of the fabric group.

Marl D

Marl D is a very hard and dense fabric that probably derives from the Memphis–Fayoum region (Aston 1998:65–66; Aston, Aston and Brock 1998:139–140). The color of the fabric generally ranges from red (2.5YR 4/8) to grayish brown (2.5Y 5/2) to olive (5Y 5/3), very often also dark brown (Color Pl. 1.1).[5] Occasionally there are bands of red on either side at the inner and outer surfaces, and sometimes the entire section is red. A thick creamy slip (10YR 8/3) covers the surface. Most characteristic of the Marl D fabric is a large amount of irregular limestone particles scattered throughout the matrix, resulting in a gritty texture. Finer inclusions such as sand, fine mineral particles,

Color Pl. 1. Magnified cross section views of Marl D and F Wares (1 and 2, respectively) and Egyptianized fabric (3).

and sometimes a small amount of fine chaff, as well as the occasional air hole, are also attested. With the exception of 'meat jars', most Marl D pottery was at least partly burnished. In the Tel Mor assemblage traces of horizontal burnishing are discernible on the two Marl D storage-jar ('amphora') rims (Fig. 4.9:8, 9; see below), whereas the large globular jar (Fig. 4.9:7) shows no signs of burnishing.

Beyond its region of origin, Marl D vessels are common in the Eastern Delta and appear as far south as Elephantine from the mid-XVIIIth Dynasty onwards (Aston 1999:5). The fabric is variously known by the following names: 'Marl D' according to the Vienna system of classication (Bourriau 1981:14–15); 'Ba.I' as at Malqata (Hope 1989:67–68); 'IV' (Hope, Blauer and Riederer 1981:161), 'III.3' and 'III.6' (Nicholson and Rose 1985:136–137) as at Tell el-Amarna; 'H1' as at Saqqara (Bourriau and Aston 1985:38–39); and 'II.D.01–02' as at Qantir (Aston 1998:65, 66).

Vessels of either Marl D or the closely related 'mixed marl-and-silt clay' have been found outside Egypt at the following sites: Tel Mor, the vessels discussed here (Fig. 4.9:7–9); Deir el-Balaḥ in Tomb 114, a slender amphora (T. Dothan 1979: Ill. 16; Yellin, Dothan and Gould 1990 ['White Burnished Slip Ware']); Tel Afeq in Stratum X-12, an amphoriskos (Beck and Kochavi 1985: Fig. 2:5); Bet She'an, in contexts contemporary with Strata VII–VI, a wide-bodied amphora (Martin 2006a:201, Pl. 1:1) and a few handled cups (Martin 2006a:206–207); and Tell Abu Hawam, a meat-jar rim (Martin 2006a: Fig. 5:2). Unpublished amphorae and meat-jar fragments come from 'Akko and Tel Nami (M. Artzy, E. Marcus and R. Stidsing, pers. comm.). On the island of Crete a flask and several storage-jar fragments were found in Late Minoan III:A1–2 strata at Kommos (Watrous 1992: Fig. 73, Pls. 54, 55). Hala Sultan Tekke on Cyprus yielded several fragments of transport containers from a Late Cypriot IIIA1 context (1190–1175 BCE; Eriksson 1995:202–203).

Marl F
Marl F has been recovered in large quantities at Tell el-Dab'a (Bietak 1991a:328 [an early variant termed 'IIc']; Aston 2001:174–175) and Qantir (Aston 1998:66) in the Eastern Delta, the most likely region of its origin. At sites in this region, Marl F was used for a variety of shapes, including several open forms, whereas elsewhere in Egypt, as at Saqqara (Fabric H14; Bourriau and Nicholson 1992:51), Tell el-Amarna

(Fabric III.2, 5, 8, 9; Nicholson and Rose 1985:136–138), Thebes (Aston, Aston and Brock 1998:140) and Elephantine (Aston 1999:5), almost exclusively elongated amphorae with a pointed base appear in this fabric. At Qantir four varieties of Marl F were discerned (i.e., II.F.01–04), II.F.02 being by far the most common. The fabric in general ranges from pale brown to brown to reddish brown (Color Pl. 1:2). A white (5Y 8/2) to pale yellow (5Y 8/3) self-slip or, occasionally, a thick cream slip, covers the exterior (Aston 1998:66). Sand, limestone grits and, occasionally, pebbles, ocher, grog and lumps of unmixed marl are the typical inclusions.

Egyptian Nile Clay? (Nile B or E)

Unfortunately it was not possible to analyze a fabric section of the globular cooking jar shown in Fig. 4.9:10. Its external appearance, however, strongly suggests that it was made of Egyptian Nile B.02 or E fabric. Nile clays in general are ferrugineous siliceous clays created by riverine deposits during the Upper Pleistocene and Pliocene Eras (Aston 1998:61–63). Under oxidizing conditions they fire to a reddish or brownish color. Chaff, sand, mica, quartz and, rarely, a few limestone particles characterize Nile B.02 fabric. Abundant inclusions of fine- and medium-rounded sand particles distinguish Nile E fabrics.

Local Egyptianized Fabric

The bulk of the locally produced Egyptianized forms are above all characterized by a large amount of organic temper, which causes the fabric to be brittle and porous. The clay of these forms is generally silty and mineral inclusions are not abundant throughout the matrix. In general the fabric's color ranges from red (2.5YR 5/6) to yellowish red (5YR 5/6) to strong brown (7.5YR 5/6) (Color Pl. 1:3). The organic temper consists of chopped straw, which, when completely burnt out, leaves elongated voids in the fabric and on the surface of the vessel. Often the straw has not been combusted entirely and appears as white fibers (silica skeletons). Commonly the Egyptianized vessels exhibit a dark brown, gray or black core of varying thickness, another indication that not all the organic temper was fully oxidized. This core is found primarily where the vessel wall is thickest (e.g., beer-jar bases).

The addition of straw serves many practical purposes: (1) it enhances the plasticity of the clay; (2) it allows the vessel to dry more quickly, evenly and with less shrinkage (Arnold 1993:105); (3) it decreases the amount of raw material (i.e., clay) required; and (4) it decreases the amount of fuel needed because of the increased porosity of the clay, which reduces firing time. Temper in general facilitates the penetration of hot gases through the vessel wall, thereby creating better-fired pottery. It also allows steam to escape, which reduces the likelihood of bursting. In short, straw is an ideal temper for mass-produced vessels like the Egyptianized bowls and jars from Tel Mor and elsewhere.

The reasons behind the use of this fabric at Tel Mor and other sites, however, probably had more to do with cultural background than functional advantage. Whereas the admixture of organic temper occurs occasionally with Canaanite pottery over time, it is a very common feature of Egyptian Nile clays (e.g., Nile B, C and E groups; for the 'Vienna system', see Nordström 1986:629–634; for the 'Tell el-Dab'a system', see Bietak 1991a:324), especially when occurring in large amounts.

The use of heavy organic temper with typical Egyptian forms is also common at Deir el-Balaḥ (Gould, forthcoming), Tel Sera' (Martin, forthcoming a), Tel Afeq (Martin, Gadot and Goren, forthcoming) and Bet She'an (Martin 2006b; forthcoming b). Thus it is very likely that this method of clay preparation was an attempt to replicate Nile Silt pottery.[6] It is significant that characteristic Egyptian Nile Silt forms and not Marl Clay forms are locally repoduced in Canaan. Furthermore, it is likely that the potters involved in the production of the Egyptianized vessels were Egyptian, or, at the very least, intimately familiar with Egyptian ceramic styles and modes of production.

An examination of a representative sample of fresh breaks of Canaanite pottery from Tel Mor using a ×20 magnifying stereomicroscope indicates that in general a large amount of straw temper is rare, whereas mineral inclusions are common. More specifically, heavy straw temper is virtually absent in Canaanite pottery from strata prior to the appearance of Egyptianized pottery (Strata XII–X), but does occasionally appear in bowls and kraters in strata with Egyptianized assemblages (Strata IX–V).

Based on the fact that Canaanite forms with heavy straw temper appear only in clearly 'Egyptianized' strata, it is reasonable to conclude that foreign Egyptian pottery-production techniques had spread to the indigenous Canaanite population. The agents of this ceramic innovation must have been Egyptian

potters. This phenomenon can also be observed at Bet She'an and Tel Sera', where straw temper gradually appears in larger amounts and in more vessels between the fifteenth and twelfth centuries BCE, along with an increase of Egyptian influence and a higher percentage of Egyptianized vessels (James and McGovern 1993:245; Martin, forthcoming b).[7]

Large amounts of straw temper were occasionally used with kraters at both Tel Mor (Strata VI–V; see Fig. 3.9) and Bet She'an during the twelfth century BCE (Strata S-4 and S-3; Martin 2006b:141–142; forthcoming b). These kraters occasionally bore rope impressions, another characteristic trait of Egyptian manufacture and a further indication of a strong Egyptian influence.

Furthermore, Frances James and Patrick McGovern observed that pottery artifacts at Bet She'an, including Egyptian and Canaanite pottery forms from Levels VIII and VII, were fired at a lower temperature (500–700°C) than wares from the previous Level IX (1993:245; see also Cohen-Weinberger 1998:409). They attributed this lower firing temperature to an Egyptian influence on the pottery tradition at Bet She'an. In Egypt, Nile Silt pottery was also fired at a low temperature (600–800°C). The finer Egyptian Marl pottery, on the other hand, was fired at a higher temperature (800–1050°C) and for a longer time (Aston 1998:37). As noted above, only characteristic Nile Silt forms are reproduced locally in Canaan. Although no refiring studies were carried out on the Tel Mor pottery, it is noteworthy that often there are large amounts of non-combusted straw rods, which suggests a low firing temperature for this pottery as well. The same phenomenon was observed at Tel Afeq (Martin, Gadot and Goren, forthcoming) and at Bet She'an in Strata S-5 to S-3 (Martin, forthcoming b). Citing Mackenzie (1957), Nordström and Bourriau note that in an oxidizing atmosphere the combustion of organic matter takes place at temperatures between 380 and 600°C (1993:155).

Surface Treatment

Apart from having no decoration at all, which is the case with the bulk of the material at Tel Mor, the surface treatment most commonly found on Egyptianized pottery is a red (10R 5/6) band painted on the rims of simple bowls (e.g., Fig. 4.6:5–8, 12, 13). In Egypt such red-rimmed bowls first appear during the XVIIIth Dynasty, particularly starting with the reign of Tuthmosis III, and become more popular during the Ramesside period, especially the XXth Dynasty (Aston 1999:18). In broad terms this trend is borne out at Tel Mor, where the overwhelming majority of red-rimmed bowls (34 out of 51, or 67%) derive from Stratum VI contexts.

Red paint on bowl rims is a feature also of Canaanite pottery throughout many periods, as at Megiddo during the Middle Bronze Age in Stratum XIV (Loud 1948: Pls. 14:6 [Tomb 3143], 14:17 [Tomb 3148]). This type of decoration is common also during the Late Bronze Age, as at Gezer in Strata XVII–XVI (e.g., Seger 1988: Pls. 13:8, 32:15). Therefore, in order to define more accurately the corpus of Egyptianized pottery at Tel Mor and elsewhere, it is important to consider also other factors.

Often in Egypt a red slip covered the interior and/or exterior of bowls (Aston 1998:220). Such red-slipped bowls are common at Bet She'an in Level VII (James and McGovern 1993: Figs. 12:9, 12, 36:3, 41:2), as well as in the corresponding strata of the Hebrew University excavations (Martin, forthcoming b). At Tel Mor, however, only one fully slipped Egyptianized bowl rim was found (A290/1, not drawn). A large bowl was slipped inside and out (Fig. 4.7:6), and a neck-less storage jar was slipped on the exterior (Fig. 4.10:4).

Much of the Egyptianized pottery at Tel Mor bears a faint, grayish white self-slip, which, because of the underlying reddish fabric, often appears pinkish white (e.g., 5YR 8/2). Finally, as noted above, a thick, creamy slip covers imported Marl D wares.

Typology

Bowls

Most of the Egyptianized pottery of Canaan in general and of Tel Mor in particular consists of shallow to medium-deep bowls with straight to rounded walls. In the scholarly literature they are variously referred to as 'shallow bowls' (Pritchard 1980:3), 'saucer bowls' (T. Dothan 1979:12; Oren 1973:103–104), 'V-shaped bowls' (only for the straight-sided variety; T. Dothan 1979:55–57) or, more generally, 'coarse ware bowls' (T. Dothan 1979:39; Oren 1973:104). The majority of these bowls derive from LB II and early Iron I contexts. In New Kingdom Egypt (Kelley 1976) and Nubia (Holthoer 1977), bowls similar in terms of form, fabric and manufacturing techniques comprise the largest

component of every ceramic assemblage. Canaanite sites with these bowls are shown in Fig. 4.2.

The three main bowl shapes are as follows: (1) shallow, straight-sided bowls with a plain rim (Fig. 4.5:1, 2); (2) shallow bowls with straight or slightly curved walls and an everted or flaring rim (Fig. 4.5:3–5); and (3) bowls with rounded walls and a plain rim (Fig. 4.6). As always, there are bowls that are transitional between the various groups. In general the bowls have a flat, round or, rarely, low disk base, all of which are in marked contrast to the ring and developed disk bases typical of LB II Canaanite assemblages (Gould, forthcoming).[8] Strangely, in Canaan most of these bowls have flat bases, whereas in Egypt during the XIXth

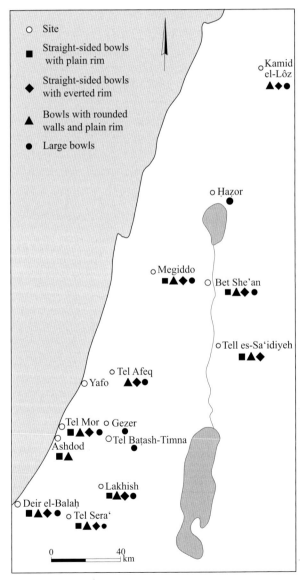

Fig. 4.2. Canaanite sites yielding Egyptianized bowls.

and XXth Dynasties, when Egyptianized material culture was most widespread in Canaan, round bases are equally common.[9] Complete bowls with round or rounded bases from Bet She'an (e.g., Fitzgerald 1930: Pl. 41:3, 6, 7; James and McGovern 1993: Figs. 49:12, 50:8), Tel Afeq (Beck and Kochavi 1985: Fig. 2:1–3), Deir el-Balaḥ (Gould, forthcoming: Bowl Types IA1, IA2 and IB) and Tell es-Saʻidiyeh (Pritchard 1980: Fig. 46A:3), as well as occasionally at Tel Mor (Fig. 4.5:4, 5), attest, however, to the existence of this type in Canaan.

As alluded to above, bowls with straight or rounded sides and a plain rim are so simple and functional that they could have easily evolved independently in both Canaan and Egypt; therefore, it is necessary to consider other factors such as fabric, clay preparation, surface treatment, production techniques, decoration and archaeological context when assigning such vessels to either the Canaanite or Egyptianized assemblage. At Tel Mor, pottery (mostly rim sherds) with much straw temper was classified as Egyptianized, while sherds with little or no straw temper were grouped with the Canaanite assemblage. This rule of thumb was appropriate to the Tel Mor assemblage in that heavy straw temper, a common feature in Egyptian pottery forms, was present very rarely in clearly Canaanite forms.[10] Notwithstanding, bowls with this Egyptianized fabric, but with distinctive Canaanite morphological features (e.g., incurved and internally thickened rim, disk and ring bases; see Beck and Kochavi 1985:33), were classified as Canaanite.

In general the fabric of these Egyptianized bowls is soft, brittle and porous, the lattermost of which is caused by the combustion of organic temper. Above all, a coarse appearance distinguishes Egyptianized bowls. Warped walls and an uneven stance, both of which are common, betray fast and careless mass production. Apart from the occasional wet-smooth marks, there appears to have been little attempt at surface treatment. On the exterior of the base, there are often wheel marks, either concentric circles or an off-center spiral. The latter feature results from cutting the vessel from the wheel with a string (i.e., string-cut base), a sign of fast production. The concentric circles on the base, which are usually accompanied by wheel marks on the exterior of the lower body, indicate that some effort was made to improve the appearance of the bowl. At this stage of production, the vessel, now in a leather-hard state and removed from the wheel, would have been placed back on the wheel, this time upside

down. As the bowl turned on the wheel, excess clay was scraped off the base and lower body with a tool, which produced the aforementioned concentric circles as well as a difference in wall thickness between the lower and upper body.[11] On some bowls the lower body was trimmed, yet the string-cut marks remain.

Both string-cut marks and concentric circles appear on the bases of Egyptianized bowls at Tel Mor. A third type of base, characterized by a well-smoothed surface, is also common at Tel Mor. As at other sites in Canaan under direct Egyptian control such as Bet She'an and Tel Seraʻ, the diameter of Egyptianized bowl bases at Tel Mor varies between 6 and 11 cm, with an average of approximately 8 cm.

Another characteristic feature of these Egyptianized bowls is a red band on the rim (Figs. 4.5; 4.6:5–8, 12, 13), hence their occasional designation as 'lipstick-bowls' (Cohen-Weinberger 1998:406). Sometimes a red slip covers the interior and/or exterior of the bowl. Most of the surface area on bowls from Tel Mor, however, is left undecorated.

Straight-Sided Bowls with Plain Rim (Fig. 4.5:1, 2)
These shallow bowls have straight walls and a plain rim, which is usually rounded at the end, but sometimes slightly pointed or squared-off, the result of having been shaped with a tool. At Tel Mor this bowl type has a flat base and its rim diameter ranges between 18 and 28 cm. In Egypt these vessels are commonly found throughout the entire New Kingdom period (Table 4.1). They were usually made of Nile B or E clay and, in terms of decoration, were red slipped (on one or both sides), had a red band on the rim or were undecorated.

They have been discovered at numerous sites in Canaan (Table 4.1; see also Killebrew 1998a:141–142 [Form EG1a]). At Tel Mor they appear throughout Strata IX–V, mostly undecorated, though some have a red band on the rim. Compared to the next two bowl types, straight-sided bowls with a plain rim are rare at the site.

Straight-Sided Bowls with Everted Rim (Fig. 4.5:3–5)
This generally shallow bowl is characterized by an everted rim, elsewhere described as 'flaring' or 'splaying/splayed'. Because the degree of rim eversion varies, bowls with only slightly everted rims resemble bowls with a plain rim (see above). Bowls with a clearly pronounced eversion in the rim first became popular in Egypt during the later XVIII Dynasty, while in Canaan such bowls do not appear until the

Table 4.1. Straight-Sided Bowls with Plain Rim in Egypt and Canaan

Site	Date/Stratum	Reference
Egypt		
Qantir	Late Second Intermediate Period	Aston 1998: Nos. 20, 21, 64–70
	XIXth Dynasty	Aston 1998: No. 719
	XXth to XXIst Dynasties	Aston 1998: No. 2404
Tell el-Dab'a	Late XVIIIth Dynasty (Stratum b)	Aston 2001: Figs. 11:1; 13:1
Saqqara	Late XVIIIth Dynasty	Aston 2001: Fig. 6 (Tomb of Haremhab)
Thebes	XXth Dynasty	Aston, Aston and Brock 1998: No. 347 (KV 1, Tomb of Ramesses VII)
Deir el-Medina	New Kingdom	Nagel 1938: Pls. 12, 13: Type XVIII
Elephantine	XXth to XXIst Dynasties	Aston 1999: Nos. 169, 220
Nubia	New Kingdom	Holthoer 1977: Pl. 27: Type PL3
Canaan		
Megiddo	Stratum VIII	Loud 1948: Pl. 61:11
Bet She'an	Levels VII–VI	James 1966: Fig. 57:4 (Level VI); Yadin and Geva 1986: Fig. 22:7 (Level VI); James and McGovern 1993: Fig. 41:2 (Level VII); Martin, forthcoming b (Type BL70b)
Tell es-Sa'idiyeh	Thirteenth/twelfth centuries BCE	Pritchard 1980: Fig. 9.2 (Tomb 105)
Ashdod	Strata XV–XIV	Dothan and Porath 1993: Fig. 11:1–3
Lakhish	Fosse Temple III	Tufnell, Inge and Harding 1940: Pl. 37:25
Tel Sera'	Strata XI–IX	Oren 1984: Fig. 4:1
Deir el-Balah	Stratum IX–V?	Killebrew 1998a: Ill. III:38:7, 14, 16; Gould, forthcoming: Type ID2

thirteenth century BCE. As with Egyptianized bowls in general (see above), these bowls most commonly have flat bases in Canaan, as opposed to Ramesside Egypt, where round bases predominate. Bowls with low disk bases are attested in the Stratum VI Acropolis Temple assemblage and other twelfth-century BCE contexts at Lakhish (Clamer 2004a; Yannai 2004). Like bowls with a plain rim, these everted-rim bowls are undecorated, red slipped or have a red band on the rim, the lattermost of which is very common in both Egypt and Canaan.

Parallels may be found at virtually every site in Egypt dating to the latter part of the XVIIIth, XIXth and XXth Dynasties (Table 4.2). Everted-rim bowls first appear in significant amounts at Tel Mor in Strata VIII–VII.[12] Strata VI–V produced more and better preserved examples of this bowl type.[13] The rim diameters of everted-rim bowls at Tel Mor vary between 18 and 26 cm, a range that accords well with the evidence from Egypt.

As noted above, bowls with a pronounced rim eversion initially become popular in Egypt toward the end of the XVIIIth Dynasty. In Area H/VI at Tell

el-Dab'a, for example, such bowls first occur in local Stratum b, dated to the period between Amenophis III and Tutankhamun, and in large numbers only in Stratum a, which corresponds to the reign of Haremhab (D. Aston, pers. comm. and observations by M. Martin). In Canaan, however, a survey of sites where this bowl type has been recovered from secure contexts suggests that, with a few possible exceptions (i.e., Deir el-Balah; see, however, Killebrew, Goldberg and Rosen 2006), everted-rim bowls do not appear in large numbers until the (late?) thirteenth century BCE and are most widely distributed during the twelfth century BCE. Because of this bowl type's potential as a chronological indicator, the evidence from Canaan is summarized here.

Lakhish. Besides several sherds from questionable contexts, everted-rim bowls do not appear in considerable amounts until the twelfth century BCE in Stratum VI (as noted by Yannai 2004), when the Egyptian influence at Lakhish is strongest.[14] It seems, then, that the appearance of everted-rim bowls is correlated with a stronger Egyptian influence at Lakhish.

Table 4.2. Straight-Sided Bowls with Everted Rim in Egypt

Site	Date/Stratum	Reference
Qantir	XIXth Dynasty (Strata B3/2)	Aston 1998: Nos. 624, 626, 629, 641,691–698, 707–717, 722–728, 755–766, 1022, 1023, 1034–1044
	Late XIXth Dynasty (Strata Bb–c)	Aston and Pusch 1999: Nos. 18, 29, 51, 55, 60, 74–76
	XXth to XXIst Dynasties (Stratum B1)	Aston 1998: Nos. 2307, 2389–2395, 2405
Tell el-Dab'a	Late XVIIIth Dynasty	Aston 2001: Figs. 11:1, 13:1
Saqqara	Late XVIIIth to XIXth Dynasties	Aston 2001: Fig. 6; Bourriau and Aston 1985: Pl. 35:5, 6; Aston 1991: Pl. 47:3–6; Aston 1997: Pl. 112:11, 14
Gurob	XVIIIth to XIXth Dynasties	Petrie 1890: Pl. 20:4; Brunton and Engelbach 1927: Pl. 33: Types 2H, 3A.
Tell el-Amarna	Late XVIIIth Dynasty	Rose 1984: Fig.10.1:6
Thebes	Late XIXth Dynasty	Petrie 1897: Pl. 17:8, 19 (foundation deposit of Tausret-Siptah)
	XXth Dynasty	Aston, Aston and Brock 1998: Nos. 326, 346 (KV 1, Ramesses VII)
Deir el-Medina	New Kingdom	Nagel 1938: Pls. 8: Type X (round base), 15: Type XXII (flat base)
Malqata	Late XVIIIth Dynasty	Hope 1989: Fig. 1: g
Armant	New Kingdom	Mond and Myers 1940: Pl. 51:A2
Elephantine	XVIIIth/XIXth Dynasties (Phase 1)	Aston 1999: No. 15
	XXth to XXIst Dynasties (Phase 2a)	Aston 1999: Nos. 31, 81–87, 107, 193–195
Nubia	New Kingdom	Holthoer 1977: Pl. 27: Type PL1

Tel Afeq. A collection of these bowls was found in the Governor's Residence of Stratum X-12 (Beck and Kochavi 1985: Fig. 2:1, 2), which was destroyed no earlier than the last third of the thirteenth century BCE. Synchronisms between the careers of two known officials mentioned in an Akkadian tablet found in the destruction layer establish this unusually precise date (Owen 1981; Singer 1983). Israel Finkelstein (1995:230, n. 15) notes that this letter serves only as a *terminus post quem*; therefore, the destruction may have occurred later.

Bet She'an. Although Bet She'an had been under Egyptian hegemony as early as the second half of the XVIIIth Dynasty (A. Mazar 1997:67–68), everted-rim bowls probably do not appear until Level VII (James and McGovern 1993:235–236),[15] which dates to the thirteenth century BCE. The Hebrew University excavations confirm the popularity of this form in strata that correspond to Levels VII to Lower VI (Killebrew 1998a: Ill. II:69:1; Martin 2006b: BL73, forthcoming b). In the twelfth-century BCE Strata S-4 and S-3, everted-rim bowls comprise as much as 14–16% of the entire assemblage and up to 26–29% of the Egyptianized assemblage (Martin, forthcoming b).

Tell es-Sa'idiyeh. Everted-rim bowls (Pritchard 1980: Fig. 46A, Types 1–3, 6) were retrieved from numerous tombs in the cemetery at Tell es-Sa'idiyeh (T103, T104, T105L, T109S, T117, T118, T121, T136, T137, T139, T141). The funerary assemblage of tombs T109S and T117 included Myc. IIIB pottery, thus suggesting a thirteenth- or very early twelfth-century BCE date for these tombs (Pritchard 1980:28–29).

Megiddo. Everted-rim bowls first appear in well-stratified contexts in Stratum VIIB (Loud 1948: Pl. 65:20; Finkelstein and Zimhoni 2000:242–243), which was destroyed either at the end of the thirteenth (Finkelstein 1996:171) or beginning of the twelfth century BCE (Bietak 1991b:49, Fig. 4). Everted-rim bowls are also present in Stratum VIIA (Loud 1948: Pl. 65:19, 20).[16]

Kamid el-Lôz. Of the small amount of Egyptianized pottery published from this site, several everted-rim bowls appear in Temple Phases T2 and T3b/a (Metzger 1993: Pls. 83:1, 5; 87:5–10; 88:1–11; 96:3–9; 156:7, 8). Phase T2 was dated to the thirteenth century BCE, whereas T3b/a spans the period from the second half of the XVIIIth Dynasty through most of the XIXth Dynasty (Hachmann 1996:17–26). Because no examples of everted-rim bowls were found in palace strata contemporary with the XVIIIth Dynasty (Miron 1990; Frisch, Mansfeld and Thiele 1985), it is safe to assume that the bowls from Temple Phase T3b/a belong to the XIXth Dynasty.

Deir el-Balaḥ. As noted above, Deir el-Balaḥ may be the only site in Canaan to possess everted-rim bowls prior to the thirteenth century BCE. The bowl type first appears in Stratum IX (Killebrew 1998a: Ills. II:37:3, 38:12, 13, 15, 17, 42:8; Gould, forthcoming: Fig. 1:9 [Type ID1], 12 [Type ID2]), which is dated by the excavators to the Amarna period (T. Dothan, pers. comm.).[17] Note, however, that a thirteenth-century BCE date is also possible (Killebrew 1998a:52, n. 22; Killebrew, Goldberg and Rosen 2006). Geographic proximity and cultural affinity to Egypt would explain an earlier appearance of everted-rim bowls at Deir el-Balaḥ.

Ashdod. Because of its proximity to Tel Mor, the excavation results from Ashdod are especially instructive, even as negative evidence. Of the small amount of Egyptianized pottery from Strata XV–XIV (LB II), there are no shallow bowls with clearly everted rims (M. Dothan 1971: Figs. 1:1, 81:14; Dothan and Porath 1993: Fig. 11:1–5, 24). In the subsequent Stratum XIIIb (early Iron I), which is characterized by the introduction of locally produced Myc. IIIC pottery, there is no Egyptianized pottery. The absence of everted-rim bowls in Strata XV–XIV can be explained by reference to sites like Lakhish (see above), where these bowls do not occur in considerable quantities until Stratum VI (twelfth century BCE). Their absence at Ashdod during the twelfth century BCE, however, at a time when this bowl type reached its height of popularity in Canaan, requires further explanation.

The Low Chronology proposed by Israel Finkelstein, according to which Stratum XIIIb should be dated to the late twelfth century BCE, provides one solution.[18] Because the last vestiges of Egyptian hegemony in all of Canaan had disappeared by this time (Weinstein 1981:22, 23), it is to be expected that Stratum XIIIb contains no Egyptianized material culture.

The widely accepted Middle Chronology, according to which strata containing massive amounts of locally produced Myc. IIIC pottery (i.e., Ashdod XIII, Tel Miqne-'Eqron VII) correspond to the Philistine settlement of *c.* 1175 BCE, offers another solution

(e.g., Bietak 1993; Stager 1995). Egyptianized material culture (including everted-rim bowls) does not appear during the twelfth century BCE at Ashdod because the Philistines, a people hostile to Egypt, settled there instead (Barako, in press b). Two observations based on pottery illustrate this point: (1) everted-rim bowls, which are a distinct feature of twelfth-century BCE sites in Canaan that possess Egyptianized material culture, are absent at Ashdod yet common at Tel Mor (especially in Strata VI–V); and (2) locally produced Myc. IIIC, which is the hallmark of the initial Philistine settlement in southern coastal Canaan, is abundant at Ashdod yet completely absent from Tel Mor (see Chapter 3; see also Barako, in press a).

Bowls with Rounded Walls and Plain Rim (Fig. 4.6)
Medium-deep to deep bowls with rounded walls and plain rim are the most common Egyptianized vessel type at Tel Mor and other sites in Canaan under direct Egyptian control (Table 4.3). In Ramesside Egypt this bowl type appears with a flat or round base, the former being much more popular in Canaan. These semi-hemispherical bowls have been recovered in great quantity from virtually every New Kingdom site in Egypt (Table 4.3). The simple shape of this bowl is familiar also from pottery assemblages in Canaan, where it is usually mounted on a disk or ring base. Because of the ubiquity of the shape, it is often difficult to determine whether these bowls belong to the Egyptianized or Canaanite tradition, especially when only sherds remain; therefore, it is necessary to rely upon other factors such as surface treatment and fabric. The bowls do not seem to have undergone any morphological development over time; therefore, they cannot be used for more than general dating purposes.

At Tel Mor, bowls with rounded walls and a plain rim appear throughout Strata VIII–V and comprise the largest percentage of all the Egyptianized pottery. Their rim diameters generally fall within the range of 18 to 26 cm, which approximates the data from Egypt. The base diameters of the bowls range between 6.5 and 11 cm.

Large Bowls (Fig. 4.7)
There are two subtypes of these large open bowls at Tel Mor. A ledge below the rim, a feature well known in Egypt during the New Kingdom (Aston and Pusch 1999:41; Aston 2001:169), characterizes the more common type. The ledge is created either by folding over the rim (Fig. 4.7:1–3) or by shaping a ridge

Table 4.3. Bowls with Rounded Walls and Plain Rim in Egypt and Canaan

Site	Date/Stratum	Reference
Egypt		
Qantir	XVIIIth/XIXth Dynasties (Stratum Bd)	Aston and Pusch 1999: No. 84
	XIXth Dynasty (Strata B3/2)	Aston 1998: Nos. 785, 788, 791
	Late XIXth Dynasty (Stratum Bb)	Aston and Pusch 1999: Nos. 19–28, 52–54
	XXth–XXIst Dynasties (Stratum B1)	Aston 1998: No. 2396
Tell el-Dabʻa	Amarna period (Stratum b)	Aston 2001: Fig. 11:5
Saqqara	XIXth Dynasty	Aston 1997: Pl. 112:18–21
Tell el-Amarna	Late XVIIIth Dynasty	Rose 1984: Fig. 10.1:5
Thebes	XIXth Dynasty	Aston, Aston and Brock 1998: Nos. 25, 45–48 (KV 8, Merenptah)
	XXth Dynasty	Aston, Aston and Brock 1998: Nos. 92, 121–159 (KV 2, Ramses IV)
Deir el-Medina	New Kingdom	Nagel 1938: Pls. 1: Type II; 2: Type IV; 9–10: Type XIV
Malqata	Late XVIIIth Dynasty	Hope 1989: Fig. 1: h–k
Elephantine	XVIIIth/XIXth Dynasties (Phase 1)	Aston 1999: Nos. 17, 18
	XXth to XXIst Dynasties (Phase 2a)	Aston 1999: Nos. 88–90, 128–130, 105, 106, 406
Nubia	New Kingdom	Holthoer 1977: Pls. 25: Type CU1; 26: Type CU4
Canaan		
Megiddo	Strata VIII–VIIA	Loud 1948: Pls. 61:10; 65:6; 68:14
Bet Sheʼan	Levels IX–VI	James and McGovern 1993: Figs. 8:1–3, 48:1–10; James 1966: Figs. 49:9, 57:2; Martin forthcoming b; Mullins 2006
Tell es-Saʻidiyeh	Thirteenth/twelfth centuries	Pritchard 1980: Fig. 9:3 (Tomb 105)
Tel Afeq	Stratum X-12	Beck and Kochavi 1985: Fig. 2.3
Ashdod	Strata XV–XIII	Dothan and Porath 1993: Figs. 11:6–12; 16:1
Tel Seraʻ	Stratum IX	Oren 1984: Fig. 4:3
Deir el-Balaḥ	Strata IX–IV	Gould, forthcoming: Type IC

below the rim (Fig. 4.7:4, 5, 7–11). On drawings, these different techniques are often not distinguishable. Bowls of this type usually have a ring base.

In Egypt ledged-rim bowls are common in the XVIIIth and XIXth Dynasties and seem to have disappeared by the XXth Dynasty (Table 4.4; Aston and Pusch 1999:41). The slight evidence from Tel Mor accords well with the Egyptian data: This type appears mainly in Stratum IX, less so in Strata VIII–VII, and seemingly disappears in Strata VI–V.[19]

The profiles of ledged-rim bowls found at Tel Mor vary: The vessel wall can be roughly straight, slightly rounded or carinated at the point of the ledge. These ledged-rim bowls occasionally differ in terms of fabric (little or no straw temper) and surface appearance from other typical Egyptianized vessels. Their appearance at sites without strong Egyptian influence (e.g., Ḥazor; see Table 4.4) is also noteworthy. For these reasons, therefore, it is perhaps better to regard this vessel type

as the result of general Egyptian influence rather than presence.

The second subtype has no distinct ledge but has an externally thickened rim. It is represented by only one specimen (Fig. 4.7:6), which has rope impressions on its walls (not drawn) and bears faint traces of red slip inside and out. Rope impressions are very common on large bowls in Egypt. The ropes that created the impressions held larger vessels together during the drying process (Aston 1998:110). When they appear on large Egyptian-style bowls at other sites in Canaan under direct Egyptian control, such as Bet Sheʼan (Martin 2006b: BL80), they clearly can be interpreted as an Egyptian manufacturing trait. Their occasional appearance on Canaanite kraters at Tel Mor and Bet Sheʼan is also best explained as reflecting Egyptian influence, particularly when these vessels contain a heavy straw temper, as they commonly do (see above, Local Egyptianized Fabric).

Table 4.4. Large Bowls in Egypt and Canaan

Site	Date/Stratum	Reference
Egypt		
First Subtype		
Qantir	XIXth Dynasty (Strata B3/2)	Aston 1988: Nos. 333, 428–447, 729
	Late XIXth Dynasty (Stratum Bb)	Aston and Pusch 1999: No. 31
Saqqara	Late XVIIIth Dynasty	Bourriau, Aston, Raven and van Walsem, forthcoming
Tell el-Amarna	Late XVIIIth Dynasty	Peet and Woolley 1923: Pl. 47: ix, No. 242
Deir el-Medina	New Kingdom	Nagel 1938: Pl. 7: K.2.123
Thebes	Early XVIIIth Dynasty	Aston, Aston and Ryan 2000: Nos. 14, 46, 47
	Late XIXth Dynasty	Petrie 1897: Pl. 17:10 (Tomb of Queen Tausret)
Malqata	Late XVIIIth Dynasty	Hope 1989: Fig. 1: n
Nubia	New Kingdom	Holthoer 1977: Pl. 26, Type CU6/IR/0/h-I
Second Subtype		
Qantir	Late XIXth Dynasty (Stratum Bb)	Aston and Pusch 1999: No. 32
Thebes	XVIIIth Dynasty	Aston, Aston and Ryan 2000: Nos. 42–45 (KV 45).
Deir el-Medina	New Kingdom	Nagel 1938: Pl. 7: Type IX (M19, M17, K2.131)
Malqata	Late XVIIIth Dynasty	Hope 1989: Fig. 1l
Canaan (Both Subtypes)		
Kamid el-Lôz	Temple T2c–a	Metzger 1993: Pl. 90:9–11
Ḥazor	Stratum XV	Yadin et al. 1961: Pl. 157:29, 31
Megiddo	Level F-9	Ilan, Hallote and Cline 2000: Fig. 9.10:26
Bet She'an	Stratum 4; Level VII	Yadin and Geva 1986: Fig. 35:1; Killebrew 1998a: Ill. III:20:12 (Form EG 6)
Tel Afeq	Strata X-14 and X-12	Martin, Gadot and Goren, forthcoming
Gezer	Strata XIV–XIII	Dever 1986: Pl. 18:2, 21
Tel Baṭash-Timna	Stratum IX	Panitz-Cohen and Mazar 2006
Lakhish	Fosse Temple III; Level S-3	Tufnell, Inge and Harding 1940: Pl. 38:55, 56 (Type 55); Yannai 2004: Fig. 19.6:1 (Group B-22)
Tel Sera'	Strata X–IX	Martin, forthcoming a
Deir el-Balaḥ	N/A	Beit-Arieh 1985: Fig. 5:13 (Tomb 108); Gould, forthcoming: Type IG

'Spinning Bowl' (Fig. 4.8:1)

At Tel Mor, a single 'spinning bowl' handle fragment, with part of the attached side-wall, originated in a poorly stratified, Stratum III context. The fabric does not contain the heavy straw temper characteristic of most Egyptianized pottery from Tel Mor. Spinning bowls are deep bowls with one to four (usually two) loop handles attached to the interior bottom of the vessel. The undersides of the handles usually bear deeply cut grooves, which are related to the bowls' use (see below). They have disk, flat, ring or rounded bases. Trude Dothan (1963), Vogelsang-Eastwood (1987–1988) and Allen (1997) have discussed at length the distribution and use of this type of vessel.

In Egypt, spinning bowls are known from representations on funerary wall scenes from the late XIth Dynasty through the New Kingdom (Allen 1997: Table 1) and from tomb models from the XIth and XIIth Dynasties (Allen 1997: Table 2). The bowls themselves date from the XIIth Dynasty through the Late Period, and are most commonly found in New Kingdom contexts (Allen 1997:33–36 [Appendix 2]). Depictions, models and the bowls themselves indicate that spinning bowls were used to spin thread from flax roves, which were placed inside or beside the vessel, and/or to ply yarn from an already spun thread.

In Canaan spinning bowls have been discovered only in contexts dating from LB II through the seventh century BCE (for references, see T. Dothan 1963). Most of these bowls came from early Iron Age contexts, as at Bet She'an in Stratum VI, Megiddo in Stratum VIIA, Tell Qasile in Strata XII–X and Bet Shemesh in Level IIA. The production of spinning bowls in the southern Levant for centuries after the final withdrawal of the Egyptian administrative presence shows that this distinctive Egyptian vessel type was fully adopted into local Levantine (i.e., Canaanite, Israelite[20] and Philistine) pottery assemblages. The period of its introduction (LB II) and its early distribution in Canaan (especially at sites in Canaan under direct Egyptian control such as Deir el-Balaḥ, Tell el-'Ajjul and Bet She'an) is undoubtedly related to the intensification of Egyptian activity in the region during the XIXth and XXth Dynasties.

Flanged-Rim Bowl(?) (Fig. 4.8:2)
Two rims that may belong to Egyptianized bowls with a flanged rim and flat or rounded base were found in Stratum VII (e.g., Fig. 4.8:2). Such flanged-rim bowls are known from various sites in both Egypt and Canaan (Table 4.5).

Imported Egyptian Bowls (Fig. 4.9:1–3)
At Tel Mor three rim fragments were attributed to possibly imported, Egyptian Marl Ware bowls. Macroscopic analysis of fresh breaks suggested that they probably belong to the Marl F group. Unfortunately it was not possible to confirm this identification by petrographic or chemical analyses. If, indeed, these bowls were made of Marl F clay, they are the first open

vessel, New Kingdom marl imports found thus far in Canaan. Even closed vessel, Egyptian imports are rare (see below, Table 4.10); thus, the imported assemblage at Tel Mor is a welcome addition to the limited regional corpus.

All three rim fragments derive from Stratum VII. Figure 4.9:1 and 2 have flaring rims and a white–pale yellow self-slip. The closest parallels from sites in Egypt are made of Marl A fabric, such as outside the tomb of Merneptah in the Valley of the Kings (Aston, Aston and Brock 1998: No. 68) and Elephantine in Phase 2a (XXth to XXIst Dynasties; Aston 1999: No. 188). Figure 4.9:3 has rounded walls and an internally thickened rim. It is covered on the exterior and interior with a light gray self-slip. In Egypt bowls similar in terms of form occur in Marl A, D, F and Mixed Clay Wares. Usually these bowls have a round or ring base. Parallels are known at Qantir in XIXth (Strata B3/2; Aston 1998: Nos. 1650–1652, 1704–1707 [Marl D]) and XXth to XXIst Dynasty contexts (Stratum B1; Aston 1998: Nos. 2128, 2129, 2515, 2518, 2519 [Mixed Clay]), Tell el-Dab'a in the Ramesside period (D. Aston, pers. comm.) and Elephantine during the XXth and XXIst Dynasties (Aston 1999: No. 357 [Marl A]).

Most Egyptian imports probably appear at sites overseas because of the commodities they contained. If indeed of Egyptian Marl F fabric, these bowls from Tel Mor, however, must have been imported for their inherent value—namely, they were used as fine tableware.

Table 4.5. Flanged-Rim Bowls in Egypt and Canaan

Site	Date/Stratum	Reference
Egypt		
Qantir	XIXth Dynasty	Aston 1998: Nos. 416–419
Gurob	XVIIIth to XIXth Dynasties	Brunton and Engelbach 1927: Pl. 33:4E
Tell el-Amarna	N/A	Rose 1984: Fig. 10.1:6 (lower vessel)
Deir el-Medina	New Kingdom	Nagel 1938: Pl. 8: Type XI
Elephantine	XXth to XXIst Dynasties	Aston 1999: Nos. 259, 365, 398
Canaan		
Bet She'an	Levels VII–VI	Fitzgerald 1930: Pl. 54:3; Oren 1973: Figs. 43:15, 47a:2, 48a:4; James and McGovern 1993: Figs. 50:6; 51:1, 2; Martin 2006b: BL74
Tel Afeq	Stratum X-12	Beck and Kochavi 1985: Fig. 2:2
Deir el-Balaḥ	Strata VIII–VI	Gould, forthcoming: Type IB

Jars

Slender Ovoid Jar with Everted Rim (Fig. 4.10:1)

An intact, ovoid jar with a round base and an everted, slightly thickened rim was found at Tel Mor in Stratum XI (Fig. 4.10:1; see also M. Dothan 1960c: Pl. 9:1). Trimming or wheel marks encircle the lower body, and there are three concentric grooves around the neck. The grooves were probably created with a pointed tool while the vessel was still on the wheel and, as is often the case on similar jars from sites in Egypt, served a decorative purpose. The wheel marks on the lower body result from a similar production process as that described for the Egyptianized bowls (see above).

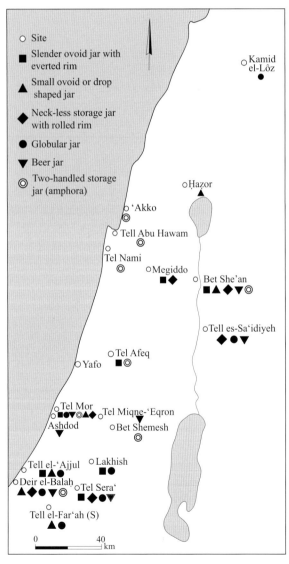

Fig. 4.3. Canaanite sites yielding Egyptianized jars.

Because the jar is fully preserved, it was not possible to inspect a cross section of the vessel wall; however, based on its outer appearance, it can be identified as a local product.

In Egypt this well-known type appears most frequently in Hyksos-period and XVIIIth Dynasty contexts (Table 4.6). According to Holthoer's typology, Fig. 4.10:1 corresponds to Type JO 1, described as an ordinary 'round based ovoid jar' (1977: Pls. 35–37; see especially Variant IP/1/i–k). In Canaan these jars appear during the early part of the Late Bronze Age, thus corrobating their chronological range in Egypt (Fig. 4.3; Table 4.6). Regarding the decorative grooves around the neck, Petrie argued a century ago that they do not appear prior to the reigns of Amenophis II and Thutmosis IV (1906:16). This prescient observation seems now to be corroborated at Haruba (Site-345) in the Northern Sinai (D. Aston, pers. comm.).

Small Ovoid or Drop-Shaped Jars (Fig. 4.10:2)

Small ovoid jars were long-lived and very popular in Egypt, appearing in great numbers at virtually every New Kingdom site (Table 4.7). During the XIXth and particularly the XXth Dynasties, the maximum body diameter tends to be lower, thus giving the jar its drop shape (Killebrew 1998a:152).

In Canaan small ovoid or drop-shaped jars are less common, appearing at only a handful of sites (Table 4.7). Tel Mor Stratum VI produced one nearly complete example (Fig. 4.10:2; see also M. Dothan 1960c: Pl. 11:6). The vessel has a slightly everted rim and a rounded base, and its maximum body diameter is located in the lower third of the vessel, but not as low as on the numerous XXth Dynasty examples from Bet She'an. Note also that most of the jars at Bet She'an found in XXth Dynasty contexts show a slight carination at the point of the maximum body diameter, whereas the jar from Tel Mor is well rounded.

As with the slender ovoid jar (Fig. 4.10:1), it was not possible to examine the fabric; however, based on the yellowish surface color, it is safe to suppose that it was made locally. There are wheel marks on the lower part of the vessel, which indicates that the vessel was trimmed on the wheel in a secondary stage of production. Traces of red on the vessel's surface indicate that it was originally red slipped, a very common form of decoration for this jar type at Bet She'an (Martin, forthcoming b).

Table 4.6. Slender Ovoid Jars with Everted Rim in Egypt and Canaan

Site	Date/Stratum	Reference
Egypt		
Qantir	XVIIIth Dynasty	Aston and Pusch 1999: No. 97
Riqqa	XVIIIth to XIXth Dynasties	Engelbach 1915: Pl. 35 (Type 25)
Meydum	XVIIIth Dynasty	Petrie, Mackay and Wainwright 1912: Pl. 19:88–91
Gurob	XVIIIth to XIXth Dynasties	Brunton and Engelbach 1927: Pls. XXXIV–XXXV (Type 25); Loat 1905: Pl. I:21–26
Haraga	XVIIth to XVIIIth Dynasties	Engelbach 1923: Pls. 42:23C, E–G, H2, I; 43:24C–F, J, L, O, P–R, T–V; 43:25F, K, L, O
Sedment	XVIIIth Dynasty	Petrie and Brunton 1924: Pls. 60:24; 62:92, 93, 96–100; 63:24M2
Ehnasya el-Medina	XVIIIth Dynasty	Petrie 1905: Pl. 37
Tell el-Amarna	Late XVIIIth Dynasty	Frankfort and Pendlebury 1933: Pl. LIII:XV/13
Thebes	Amenophis II and Thutmosis IV	Petrie 1897: Pls. 5:1, 7:12
Deir el-Medina	New Kingdom	Nagel 1938: Figs. 39:1, 2 [T1145]; 43:4 [T1153–55]; 53:2 [T1161]; 70:3 [T1169]
Qurna	XVIIIth Dynasty	Petrie 1909: Pl. 41:704
Malqata	Late XVIIIth Dynasty	Hope 1989: Fig. 2: g, h
Canaan		
Megiddo	Stratum VIII	Guy 1938: Pl. 57:9 (T26); Loud 1948: Pl. 60:7
Bet She'an	Stratum R1	Mullins 2006: Fig. 3:8
Tel Afeq	Stratum X-14	Martin, Gadot and Goren, forthcoming
Lakhish	Fosse Temple I	Tufnell, Inge and Harding 1940: Pl. LIV (Type 335)
Tell el-'Ajjul	Late Bronze Age (old excavations); Stratum H3 (new excavations)	Petrie 1931: Pl. XLII.31H7 (T168), H8 (T194); 1932: Pl. XXIX.31H3 (T1500); 1933: Pl. XXXII.31H8 (T370, T411); 1934: Pl. XLVIII.31K19 (TCT 920); Fischer 2001:228, Fig. 6
Tel Sera'	Stratum XI	Martin, forthcoming a

Neck-Less Storage Jars with Rolled Rim
(Fig. 4.10:3–5, 9)
This storage jar is a characteristic Egyptian Nile Silt vessel type throughout the Ramesside period, particularly during the XXth Dynasty (Table 4.8). Unfortunately, because of their considerable size, few intact jars of this type have survived. Slender, tall and 'bag-shaped' variants are known,[21] many of which are covered with a red slip.

These jars have been found at several sites in Canaan (Table 4.8). At Tel Mor four rim fragments of this type were recovered throughout Strata VIII to VI. Three are made from the characteristic fabric with heavy straw temper used for Egyptian forms (Fig. 4.10:3–5) and the fourth (Fig. 4.10:9), which bears a creamy (self-) slip, is of an unknown fabric. One of the examples is red slipped.

Large Neck-Less Storage Jar with Rolled Rim
(Fig. 4.10:6)
A rim sherd belonging to a large, neck-less, locally produced storage jar with a rolled rim was recovered from a poorly stratified, Stratum V context at Tel Mor. The projected size and shape of this jar recall the so-called Egyptian 'meat jars', a common Marl and Mixed Clay vessel type of the Ramesside period that first appeared in the late XVIIIth Dynasty (Aston 1998:44; Aston and Pusch 1999:45–46); however, as noted above (see Imported Egyptian Bowls), Egyptian Marl types were generally not imitated locally in Canaan.[22] Although the rim is similar in shape to the neck-less storage jar, which in Ramesside Egypt is typically a Nile Silt vessel, jars with such large rim diameters and thick side-walls are not characteristic of this type. A potential parallel for the Tel Mor rim sherd is a large, possible

Table 4.7. Small Ovoid or Drop-Shaped Jars in Egypt and Canaan

Site	Date/Stratum	Reference
Egypt		
Qantir	XIXth to XXIst Dynasties	Aston 1998: Nos. 1312, 1313, 1436, 2456; Aston and Pusch 1999: Nos. 35, 78, 80, 81
Tell el-Yahudiya	XXth Dynasty	Griffith 1890: Pl. XV:4
Saqqara	Ramesses II	Aston 1997: Pl. 119:50–51
Gurob	XVIIIth to XIXth Dynasties	Brunton and Engelbach 1927: Pl. XXXIV:20E, H, O–P, R; 22F, H
Kahun	XXth Dynasty	Petrie 1891: Pl. XXVII:29, 34
Tell el-Amarna	Late XVIIIth Dynasty	Rose 1987: Fig. 10.4:63109
Deir el-Medina	New Kingdom	Nagel 1938: Fig. 2:30, 32; T356
Malqata	Late XVIIIth Dynasty	Hope 1989:22, Fig. 2: d
Qurna	XVIIIth Dynasty	Petrie 1909: Pl. XLI:680–689
Elephantine	XXth to XXIst Dynasties (Phase 2a)	Aston 1999: Nos. 115–117
Canaan		
Ḥazor	Stratum XV	Ben-Tor et al. 1997: Fig. III:16.15
Bet She'an	Levels VII–VI	James and McGovern 1993: Fig. 10:6; Martin, forthcoming b
Tell el-'Ajjul	N/A	Petrie 1931: Pl. XLII:31K3; 1933: Pl. XXXII:31K9
Tell el-Far'ah (S)	N/A	Starkey and Harding 1932: Pl. LXXXVIII: 75N1 (T905); 75N4 (T967)
Deir el-Balaḥ	N/A	Gould, forthcoming: Type II

Table 4.8. Neck-Less Storage Jars with Rolled Rim in Egypt and Canaan

Site	Date/Stratum	Reference
Egypt		
Qantir	XIXth Dynasty	Aston 1998: Nos. 999–1008
	XIXth/XXth Dynasties	Aston and Pusch 1999: Nos. 10, 41
Saqqara	XIXth Dynasty	Aston 1991: Pl. 48:45
Qaw	XIXth Dynasty	Brunton 1930: Pl. 27:71
Thebes	XXth Dynasty	Anthes 1939: Pls. 56, 58 (foundation deposit of Ramesses IV)
	XXth Dynasty	Aston, Aston and Brock 1998:162, 209, Pl. 43:373 (tomb of Ramesses VII)
Elephantine	XXth Dynasty	Aston 1999: No. 198 (inscribed with titulary of Ramesses IX)
Canaan		
Megiddo	Stratum VII	Guy 1938: Pl. 57:10 (Tomb 26); Loud 1948: Pl. 65:3 (Type 118)
Bet She'an	Levels VII–VI	Yadin and Geva 1986: Fig. 35:4 (Stratum 4); Killebrew 1998a: Ill. III:22:5, 7; Martin 2006b: TJ76C
Tell es-Sa'idiyeh	Thirteenth/twelfth centuries BCE	Pritchard 1980: Fig. 15.5 (Tomb 110, Type 63)
Tel Sera'	Stratum IX	Martin, forthcoming a
Deir el-Balaḥ	LB II	Gould, forthcoming: Type III:2–4, 6

meat-jar imitation in Nile B.02 Clay from a XXth to XXIst Dynasty context at Elephantine (Aston 1999: No. 492). It is difficult to determine whether the rim sherd from Tel Mor is part of a local imitation of an Egyptian Marl clay meat jar or an unusually large, local variant of the neck-less storage jar. There is little doubt, however, that based on its general shape, this rim belongs to an Egyptianized form.

Globular Jars

Three types of necked jars with globular body were discerned at Tel Mor: (1) locally produced, necked, globular jars; (2) a possibly imported (Nile B.02 or E clay) globular jar, which probably served as a cooking pot; and (3) an imported, large globular jar of Marl Ware. (The parallels in Table 4.9 refer to the first two subtypes only.)

Locally Produced Globular Jars (Fig. 4.10:7, 8). Three rims of locally produced, Egyptianized globular jars were found at Tel Mor; two belong to Strata VIII–VII (e.g., Fig. 4.10:7) and one to Stratum V (Fig. 4.10:8). The rims resemble beer-jar rims except for their relatively long necks (cf. Fig. 4.11:6, 8, 9, 12, 14).

Globular Cooking Jar, Possibly Imported (Nile B/E) (Fig. 4.9:10). A nearly complete, necked, globular jar with rounded base was uncovered in Stratum V at Tel Mor (see also M. Dothan 1960c: Pl. 11:4). The neck is bulging and slants outward slightly, similar to the rim shown in Fig. 4.10:8. Its blackened surface suggests that the jar was used for cooking,[23] as were many such globular jars in Egypt (e.g., Rose 1987: Fig. 10.3:63573). If so, then this jar is a rare example of an Egyptian or Egyptianized cooking vessel excavated in Canaan. Although it was not possible to inspect the fabric closely, it appears that this globular jar is composed of Nile B.02 or E Clay, which would place it in a small group of imported Nile Silt vessels found in Canaan.

According to David Aston, the globular jar from Tel Mor can confidently be dated to the period of the XXth Dynasty, where the closest parallels can be found at Qantir in Stratum B1 (Aston 1998: Nos. 2252, 2483). In Egypt, necked globular jars of different sizes used for storage or cooking have been excavated in various New Kingdom contexts (Table 4.9).

Table 4.9. Globular Jars in Egypt and Canaan

Site	Date/Stratum	Reference
Egypt		
Qantir	XXth/XXIst Dynasties (Stratum B1)	Aston 1998: Nos. 2226, 2252, 2320, 2321, 2448, 2449, 2483
Tell el-Yahudiya	XXth Dynasty	Griffith 1890: Pl. 15:5
Gurob	XVIIIth to XIXth Dynasties	Brunton and Engelbach 1927: Pl. 36: Type 36
Tell el-Amarna	Late XVIIIth Dynasty	Rose 1987: Fig. 10.3:63573, 62026, 62041
Thebes	XXth Dynasty	Aston, Aston and Brock 1998: No. 244
Deir el-Medina	New Kingdom	Nagel 1938: Figs. 43:1, 2 (T1150); 86:17 (T1176); 97:15 (T1193)
Elephantine	XXth/XXIst Dynasties	Aston 1999: Nos. 63, 214, 449
Nubia	New Kingdom	Holthoer 1977: Pl. 34 (Type GJ 1, especially IR/0/d, e)
Canaan		
Kamid el-Lôz	Temple T2a	Metzger 1993: Pl. 117:1–5
Tell es-Saʿidiyeh	Thirteenth/twelfth centuries BCE	Pritchard 1980: Figs. 6:4 (Type 60, T104); 9:9 (Type 56, T105 Lower); 18:1 (Type 60, T116)
Lakhish	Level P1	Clamer 2004a: Fig. 20.10:11
Tell el-ʿAjjul	N/A	Petrie 1934: Pl. 52:41V, T (T1632)
Deir el-Balaḥ	LB II	Killebrew 1998a: Ill. III:21:9, 10 (Form EG11)
Tel Seraʿ	Stratum IX	Martin, forthcoming a
Tell el-Farʿah (S)	N/A	Duncan 1930: Type 41

Large Globular Jar, Marl D (Fig. 4.9:7). The rim and shoulder of a large globular jar were found at Tel Mor in Stratum VI. Its distinctive creamy pink slip, as well as the appearance of the fabric, clearly place it in the Marl D group. It is the first such import of this type identified at a site in Canaan. In Egypt parallels have been found at Qantir in Stratum B3/2 (XIXth Dynasty; Aston 1998: Nos. 1749, 1751, 1755) and Malqata in a late XVIIIth Dynasty context (Hope 1989: Fig. 5k). A similar jar type, but composed of a Mixed Clay fabric, is known from Tell el-Amarna, also in a late XVIIIth Dynasty context (Rose 1984: Fig. 10.1:14 [left]).

Two-Handled Storage Jars ('Amphorae')
(Fig. 4.9:4, 5, 8, 9)
Egyptian two-handled storage jars, referred to in the Egyptological literature as 'amphorae' (e.g., Aston and Pusch 1999:43–45; Aston 2001:174–175; Hope 1989:87–125; see also Wood 1987), appear in Canaan mostly as imports; however, they imitate what was originally a Canaanite form (Grace 1956:86; T. Dothan 1979:10; Hope 1989:87). New Kingdom Egyptian amphorae have a slender, tapering or broad ovoid body. They frequently have bulging rolled rims, their necks are longer than those of Canaanite storage jars, and their shoulders are rounded. Egyptian amphorae were made mainly of Marl A, D and F, Mixed Clay and, rarely, Nile Silt fabrics (Aston and Pusch 1999:43–45; Aston 1998:66). Most of the imported Egyptian amphorae found in Canaan were composed of Marl D (Table 4.10).

Of four amphora rims at Mor, two certainly belong to the Marl D fabric group (Fig. 4.9:8, 9), and two can very likely be assigned to the Marl F group (Fig. 4.9:4, 5;[24] D. Aston, pers. comm.). The two Marl D sherds bear the characteristic creamy slip and show traces of vertical burnishing. A pale yellow self-slip covers the possible Marl F sherds. If Fig. 4.9:4 was indeed made of Marl F, then it is an ironic example of a 'Canaanite Jar' produced in Egypt.

'Zîr' (Fig. 4.9:11)
A Marl C fabric (probably C2) *zîr* rim was found at Tel Mor in Stratum IX, which corresponds to the latter part of the XVIIIth Dynasty. *Zîr*s are very large storage jars with a rounded base, bag-shaped body and thick, everted rim. They are made of either Marl C or F fabric and take their name from the large water containers still used in parts of Egypt today. The body of ancient *zîr*s was handmade, whereas the neck and rim were wheel-made. *Zîr*s first became common during the Middle Kingdom and disappeared by the end of the XVIIIth Dynasty (Aston 2001:181). It seems that Marl C *zîr*s fell out of use earlier than those made of Marl F (B. Bader, pers. comm.). *Zîr*s appear in Egypt in Second Intermediate Period and early New Kingdom contexts at Tell el-Dab'a (Stratum b; Aston 2001: Fig. 13:11 [Marl F])[25] and Memphis (Bader 2001: No. 315 [Second Intermediate Period/New Kingdom]; No. 322 [late Second Intermediate period] [both Marl C]). In addition to Tel Mor, *zîr*s are known from an early XVIIIth Dynasty context at Tell el-'Ajjul (Petrie 1933: Pl. 33: Type 31Y20 [Marl C]).

Small Conical Jar ('Crucible') (Fig. 4.10:10)
An intact small conical jar, currently displayed in the Eretz-Israel Museum in Tel Aviv, was discovered at Tel Mor in Stratum VII (Fig. 4.10:10). Such small conical jars appear in Egypt as early as the Second Intermediate Period and as late as the XVIIIth Dynasty. Because several of these jars from Tell el-Amarna have a blackened exterior, the excavators supposed that they had been used as crucibles (Peet and Woolley 1923:138,

Table 4.10. Imported Egyptian Amphorae in Canaan

Site	Date/Stratum	Reference
'Akko	LB IIA	Ben-Arieh and Edelstein 1977: Fig. 10:9; Pl. 13:8 (Tomb C1, Nile B)
	LB IIB	M. Artzy and E. Marcus, pers. comm. (mainly Marl D)
Tell Abu Hawam	Level V	Balensi 1980: Pl. 12:7 (Mixed Clay)
Tel Nami	LB IIB	M. Artzy and R. Stidsing, pers. comm. (Marl D and Mixed Clay)
Bet She'an	Stratum N-4	Killebrew 1998a: Ill. III:23:2 (Marl D)
Tel Afeq	Stratum X-12	Martin, Gadot and Goren, forthcoming (Marl D)
Bet Shemesh	N/A	Grant 1929: Pl. 173:2 (Tomb 1, fabric unknown)
Deir el-Balaḥ	LB IIB	T. Dothan 1979: Ills. 14, 16 (T114, Marl D?)

Pl. 50 [Type XXIX:8–11, 13]; see also Frankfort and Pendlebury 1933:113, Type XXI.3). In the recent excavations at the site, these vessels are classified as Type 27 and belong to the Nile Clay fabric group (Rose 1984:138, Fig. 10.1:27). Typically the lower body bears vertical, knife-paring marks.

The relationship between these small conical jars and similarly shaped alabaster vessels, which are common in Egypt (e.g., Brunton and Engelbach 1927: Pls. 22:46, 47; 26:38; B. Aston 1994:155–156, Nos. 188, 191), is not clear. These alabaster vessels, generally with flat bases, were recovered from a number of tombs at Tell el-'Ajjul (e.g., Petrie 1931: Pl. 25:38 [Tomb 36]; 1932: Pl. 23:43 [Tomb 1156]; 1934: Pl. 39:84 [Tomb 1766]).

Insofar as Stratum VII at Tel Mor corresponds approximately to the XIXth Dynasty, and that its stratigraphic context (Area 128) is relatively secure, it is probable that Fig. 4.10:10 functioned at the site as an heirloom. There are knife-paring marks on the lower body, as is common on these vessels in Egypt. Based on a macroscopic examination alone, it is not possible to determine whether the vessel is a local product or an import from Egypt.

Miscellaneous Jar Fragments (Figs. 4.9:6, 4.10:11, 12)
For several sherds, because of their small size and/or non-diagnostic quality, an unequivocal designation as Egyptian or Egyptianized was not possible. Form, fabric, or both, however, make this designation likely. The first sherd is a large flat base of a jar or jug with pale yellow (self-) slip that was found in Stratum VII (Fig. 4.9:6). The fabric may be Marl F; thus, the vessel is a possible Egyptian import. Two rounded to slightly pointed bases of probable Egyptianized storage jars were found in Strata VI and V (Fig. 4.10:11, 12). Both vessels were made of the typical, straw-tempered, Egyptianized fabric. Figure 4.10:11 may belong to a funnel-necked jar (cf. Aston 1998: Nos. 918, 2377) and Fig. 4.10:12, based on an old drawing of a more complete vessel, looks like a type of short-necked, ovoid jar.

Beer Jars (Fig. 4.11)
Holthoer first coined the term 'beer bottle' to describe a distinctively shaped jar characterized by careless manufacture, commonly with deep fingerprints near its heavy, flat base (1977:86–87; for further discussions of this type, see Aston 1996:12–13, 2001:169–171; Aston and Pusch 1999:42).[26] Based on various indirect lines of

evidence, he concluded that these jars were associated with beer in a symbolic or ritual context. Because beer jars were occasionally uncovered in contexts with so-called 'flowerpots', which are deep, conical bowls with a heavy, flat base that closely resemble bread molds as depicted in Old Kingdom tomb reliefs (e.g., Steindorff 1913: Pl. 84), Holthoer speculated that flowerpots and beer jars were the archaeological correlates of the bread and beer, respectively, often mentioned in the *htp dj nsw* offering formulae (1977:83, 86; for bread and beer in the offering formulae, see Barta 1968). Unfortunately, this theory founders on the non-contemporaneity of most flowerpots and beer jars; however, it may succeed on other grounds as described below.

Holthoer divided beer bottles into four subtypes, of which only the 'ordinary' BB 4 is relevant to a discussion of the Tel Mor Egyptianized pottery assemblage. The other three subtypes date to the early and mid-XVIIIth Dynasty, prior to the appearance of Egyptianized pottery at Tel Mor; whereas BB 4 first appeared in the early XVIIIth Dynasty, became very common in the XIXth Dynasty, and continued with slight modifications well into the Third Intermediate Period (Table 4.11).

Evidence of the crude manufacture of beer jars includes a string-cut base and, usually, the aforementioned fingerprints, which were probably created by the abrupt removal of the vessel from the wheel by hand (Bourriau and Aston 1985:34–35). Rilling is prominent on the exterior and interior of the vessel (e.g., Fig. 4.11:8). The variance in diameter of the lower half of the body and base has chronological significance, which will be discussed briefly below. Usually there is no surface treatment; however, occasionally a red slip was used, as at Qantir (Aston 1998: Nos. 905–910) and Deir el-Balaḥ (Gould, forthcoming). There are no morphological differences between beer jars found in Egypt and Canaan (Table 4.11). 'Egyptian' beer jars are always made of Nile Silt (mostly Nile B and E), whereas 'Canaanite' beer jars are composed of local clays. Thus far no imported Egyptian beer jars have been discovered in Canaan.

Because the base is distinctive and durable, it tends to be the only part of the beer jar that survives. A classification problem arises, however, in that beer-jar bases closely resemble those of flowerpots. Fortunately, flowerpot bases tend to be wider and their side-walls slant outwards more from the base. Also, flowerpots were more common during the middle of the XVIIIth

Table 4.11. Beer Jars in Egypt and Canaan

Site	Date/Stratum	Reference
Egypt		
Qantir	XIXth Dynasty	e.g., Aston 1998: Nos. 525–528, 538–548
	XXth Dynasty	Aston 1998: No. 2447; Aston and Pusch 1999: No. 2
Tell el-Dabʿa	Stratum a (Haremhab)	Aston 2001: Fig. 2:5
Saqqara	XIXth Dynasty	Aston 1997: Pls. 113:45–47; 115:103, 104
Deir el-Medina	New Kingdom	Nagel 1938: Pls. 20:19, 46:246 (T359); 107:7 (T1176); 121:26
Elephantine	XIXth Dynasty	e.g., Aston 1999: Nos. 4–12
	XXth to XXIst Dynasties	Aston 1999: Nos. 57, 58
Nubia	New Kingdom	Holthoer 1977: Pl. 18 (Type BB 4)
Canaan		
Bet Sheʾan	Levels VIII–VI	Fitzgerald 1930: Pls. 42:11, 14; 45:7; James 1966: Fig. 49:6; Yadin and Geva 1986: Fig. 35:3; James and McGovern 1993: Fig. 12:4
Tell es-Saʾidiyeh	Thirteenth/twelfth centuries BCE	Pritchard 1980: Fig. 7:5 (T104)
Ashdod	Strata XV–XIV	M. Dothan 1971: Fig. 81:14, Pl. 75:3; Dothan and Porath 1993: Fig. 11:24, Pl. 33:14
Tel Miqne-ʿEqron	Stratum IX, Phase D	Killebrew 1996: Pl. 4:22
Tel Seraʿ	Stratum IX	Martin, forthcoming a
Deir el-Balaḥ	LB II	Yellin, Dothan and Gould 1986: 68–73, Fig. 1; Gould, forthcoming: Type VI

Dynasty, already becoming rare by the reign of Amenophis III, and disappearing after the Amarna period (Williams 1992:34–35). On the other hand, BB 4 beer jars were most popular during the XIXth and XXth Dynasties. For these morphological and chronological reasons, the Tel Mor bases were classified as beer jars.

Evidence from other Canaanite sites confirms the chronology of flowerpots and beer jars. The excavations at Bet Sheʾan provide the best data for the chronological distribution of both: Several flowerpots but no beer jars were found in XVIIIth Dynasty strata (Mullins 2006), whereas numerous beer jars but no flowerpots were found in XIXth and XXth Dynasty strata (Martin 2006b:147).

Approximately 50 fragmentary beer-jar bases and rims were excavated at Tel Mor. Eight came from Stratum IX loci defined as 'areas' or from probable Stratum VIII subfloor fills. Of the remainder, 4 belong to Stratum VIII, 18 to Stratum VII, 15 to Stratum VI and 4 to Stratum V. Based on data from Egyptian sites, particularly Tell el-Dabʿa, Aston observes that beer-jar base diameters range between 10 and 12 cm during the XVIIIth Dynasty, 7 and 9 cm during the XIXth Dynasty and occasionally decrease to 6 cm or less during the XXth Dynasty (pers. comm.). This tendency is also borne out in Canaan at Tel Mor and Bet Sheʾan.

Base diameters at Tel Mor vary between 6 and 11 cm and average 8.80 cm. Apart from one specimen, all measurable examples belong to Strata IX–VII, which date to the late XVIIIth and XIXth Dynasties. Beer-jar base diameters from Bet Sheʾan Strata S-5 to S-3 range between 5.5 and 9.5 cm, with an average of 7 cm. Most bases belong to Strata S-4 and S-3, both of which correspond to the XXth Dynasty. It is not surprising that there is a greater tendency for beer-jar base diameters to decrease at Bet Sheʾan given that the assemblage at Bet Sheʾan is later than that of Tel Mor.

Beer-jar rim diameters at Tel Mor vary between 10 and 12 cm, as is the case in Egypt. Except for a single vertical rim, all beer-jar rims at Tel Mor slant inward. It is possible that some of the rims belong to short-necked jars, which have the same upper body and coarse surface treatment (i.e., rilling) as beer jars, but are characterized by a well-finished, rounded base (e.g., Fig. 4.11:8; Holthoer 1977: Pl. 33 [Type FU2]). Because body and rim sherds of these short-necked jars are indistinguishable from those of beer jars, the two jar types are often grouped together (Aston 2001:169, n. 22), as they are here. The fabric of most of the beer jars at Tel Mor contains an unusually large amount of straw temper, a feature also of beer jars from Bet Sheʾan (Martin, forthcoming b).

Beer-jar bases from sites throughout Canaan (including Tel Mor) and Egypt were often perforated pre- or post-firing.[27] At Tel Mor and Bet She'an in Area S at least a third of the bases have perforations. What function might these perforated vessels have served? The following observations regarding the distribution and production of beer jars suggest a possible answer: (1) at virtually every New Kingdom site in Egypt and at sites in Canaan under direct Egyptian control (i.e., Deir el-Balaḥ, Tel Mor and Bet She'an) a large number of beer jars have been found; (2) in Canaan most beer jars derive from settlement contexts,[28] whereas in Egypt they appear in both funerary and settlement contexts; and (3) in both Canaan and Egypt beer jars were carelessly produced (see above). Based on these observations it is reasonable to conclude that beer jars were a mass-produced, widely used, utilitarian coarse ware.

Regarding the perforations, a hole in the base rules out use as a storage container, the function typically associated with jars. Petrie's excavation of the cemetery at Rifeh might offer a solution to the puzzle of perforated beer jars. A pressed cake of barley mash and grains was found in a large conical bowl—almost certainly a flowerpot—with a hole in the bottom (1907:23). As opposed to Holthoer's bread mold theory (see above), Petrie suggested that vessels of this type were used to squeeze out the fermented beer from the grain. Gould, in her forthcoming study of the Egyptianized assemblage from Deir el-Balaḥ, proposes that perforated beer jars were used in a similar fashion.[29]

In Egypt, beer brewing is depicted on the walls of numerous Old, Middle and New Kingdom tombs (for references, see Lucas and Harris 1962:13). Among the processes shown are the making and baking of bread, the mixing and filtering of beer, and the pouring of the beer into jars (Lutz 1922:72–96; Lucas and Harris 1962:10–16; Helck 1971:15–42, 1975:790–791). Based on these scenes and by analogy to traditional methods employed by Nubians today to make *bouza*, it is possible to reconstruct the following process: first, beer loaves are baked; next, these loaves are broken into pieces, soaked and (during the New Kingdom) placed in a large fermentation vat; then the mash is pressed through a sieve into a collection container; finally, the fermented beer is poured into large jars. For small-scale production, perforated beer jars might have replaced fermentation vats and larger sieves. A potsherd or piece of cloth might have been placed over the perforation in order to reduce the flow of the fermented beer. As

for beer jars with unperforated bases, they could have served as collection or storage containers.

It is clear from ancient Egyptian texts that beer was a staple food item in Egypt, a fact that easily accounts for the presence of beer jars at virtually every New Kingdom site. It appears that five loaves of bread and two jars of beer were the daily subsistence minimum (Erman 1900; Helck 1975:791). In the Middle Kingdom story of the 'eloquent peasant', however, the protagonist receives ten loaves of bread and two jars of beer (Gardiner 1923:10). Beer also appears frequently among offerings to the deceased and the divine (for references, see Helck 1975:791).[30]

DISCUSSION

Overview of the Assemblage

The slender ovoid jar from Stratum XI (Figs. 4.10:1) is the earliest Egyptian vessel type found at Tel Mor. In light of its singular appearance, it is better to view this jar as evidence of occasional contact with Egypt during LB I than as an indication of an Egyptian presence at Tel Mor, as during LB II and early Iron I.

Egyptianized pottery first appears at Tel Mor in poorly stratified Stratum IX contexts. More than 40 sherds or partially mended vessels of Egyptianized fabric, mostly bowls (n = 32) and beer jars (n = 7; see Fig. 4.11:1–5), were recovered primarily from area loci or Stratum VIII subfloor fills (Table 4.12). The appearance of beer jars in Stratum VIII subfloor fills indicates that Egyptianized pottery preceeded, however briefly, the construction of Building B. Also many of the ledged-rim bowls were found in Stratum IX (Fig. 4.7:1, 2, 4, 5, 7).

The quantity of Egyptianized pottery more than doubled in the subsequent Strata VIII–VII (n = 110), 90% of which belongs to Stratum VII. Again, the assemblage is comprised primarily of bowls (n = 72) and beer jars (n = 21; Fig. 4.4). Five of the eleven imports found at the site derive from these two combined strata. The significant amount of Egyptianized pottery in Strata VIII–VII associated with an Egyptian-style building (B) strongly indicates an Egyptian presence at Tel Mor beginning in the thirteenth century BCE.

The size of the Egyptianized assemblage increases more than twofold once more in Strata VI–V (n = 238). In these combined strata, bowls comprise approximately 90% of all Egyptian and Egyptianized pottery, as

Table 4.12. Distribution of Egyptian and Egyptianized Pottery by Stratum

Stratum	Total Registered Sherds	Egyptian and Egyptianized Sherds	% Egyptian and Egyptianized
IX	1202	43	4
IX–VII	41	0	0
VIII	245	11	4
VIII–VII	232	4	2
VII	1046	91	9
VII–VI	113	4	4
VIII–VII Subtotal	1636	110	7
VI	945	146	15
VI–V	117	1	1
V	688	85	12
V–IV	58	6	10
VI–V Subtotal	1808	238	13
IV	138	2	1
IV–III	50	0	0
III	509	5	1
IV–III Subtotal	697	7	1
Total	5384	398	7

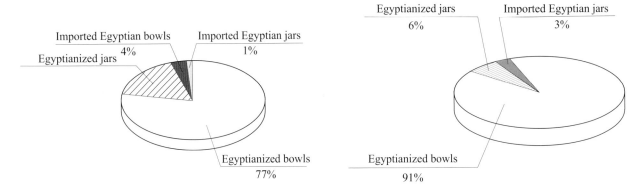

Fig. 4.4. Percentages of Egyptian and Egyptianized pottery from Strata VIII–VII (left) and Strata VI–V (right), according to vessel type. Only sherds and vessels with a preserved rim were included in these counts.

opposed to the previous Strata VIII–VII, in which they accounted for only *c.* 75% (Fig. 4.4). There is a similar percentage of bowls at Bet She'an, where they comprise between 80 and 95% of the Egyptianized assemblage throughout Strata S-5 to S-3 in Area S (Martin, forthcoming b).

After the destruction of Building F sometime during the second half of the twelfth century BCE, Egyptianized pottery was no longer made and Egyptian pottery ceased to be imported to Tel Mor. The few Egyptianized sherds from the ephemeral Stratum IV, as well as from the pits and open area of Stratum III, must derive from earlier strata.

Chronological Implications

With the exception of a single vessel (Fig. 4.10:10), which may have been an heirloom, the stratigraphic contexts of the Egyptian and Egyptianized pottery from Tel Mor conform to the well-established ceramic chronology from Egypt. Furthermore, this corpus of data corroborates the dates previously assigned to Strata XI–V by the excavators. The slender ovoid jar from Stratum XI (Fig. 4.10:1) appears in Egypt only during the XVIIIth Dynasty, probably after the reign of Thutmosis III and before the end of the Amarna period, which corresponds roughly to the LB I date assigned to this stratum.

The Egyptian and Egyptianized pottery assemblage from Stratum IX, despite its small size, has the following chronological indicators: (1) ledged-rim bowls (Fig. 4.7), which first became common in Egypt during the Amarna period; (2) the *zîr* (Fig. 4.9:11), which is a form that disappears from sites in Egypt after the Amarna period at the latest;[31] (3) the absence of everted-rim bowls, which are a hallmark of Egyptianized assemblages in Canaan during the period of the XIXth Dynasty; and (4) the absence of neck-less storage jars with rolled rims, which in Egypt are a classic Ramesside vessel type that first appear during the XIXth Dynasty.

The combined Strata VIII–VII assemblage is typically Ramesside in character; more specifically, the overall evidence suggests a XIXth Dynasty date. In contrast to Stratum IX, everted-rim bowls (Fig. 4.5:3–5) and neck-less jars (Fig. 4.10:3–5, 9) are now present. As noted above, the small conical jar or 'crucible' is out of place (Figs. 4.10:10) insofar as such jars in Egypt probably did not outlast the XVIIIth Dynasty.

The Strata VI–V assemblage is very similar to that of the preceeding Strata VIII–VII. Only the following ceramic developments might suggest that Strata VI–V belong to the XXth and not the XIXth Dynasty: a larger number of everted-rim bowls, a characteristic of twelfth-century BCE sites with Egyptianized pottery in Canaan (see above); and, more significantly, the imported(?) globular cooking jar of Stratum V (Fig. 4.9:10), a clear XXth Dynasty form.

Comparative Analysis

In addition to describing the types of Egyptian and Egyptianized pottery present at Tel Mor, it is important also to note which types are absent and to attempt an explanation of why. Such a comparison should be made both with Canaanite sites (especially Bet She'an and Deir el-Balaḥ), as well as with sites in Egypt.

Compared to other Canaanite sites, most of the typical forms are well represented at Tel Mor with the following possible exceptions, which are either rare or absent: funnel-necked jars (see, however, Fig. 4.10:11); imported handled cups (see, however, Fig. 4.9:5); and spinning bowls (see, however, Fig. 4.8:1, which was found in a later stratum). The rarity or complete absence of these types might be attributable to the selection process of the excavators and the relatively small size of the overall Tel Mor assemblage.

A diachronic comparison of sites under direct Egyptian control reveals a similar trend in the percentage of Egyptianized material culture throughout the XVIIIth to XXth Dynasties. At all sites there was a low percentage of Egyptianized pottery in strata that correspond to the XVIIIth Dynasty (e.g., less than 5% at Bet She'an; Mullins 2006). There was a marked increase during the XIXth Dynasty, as at Bet She'an (more than half of the overall assemblage; Martin, forthcoming b) and Tel Afeq and Tel Sera' (both roughly one third; Martin, Gadot and Goren, forthcoming; Martin, forthcoming a). By the XXth Dynasty the percentage of Egyptianized pottery at these sites was even higher. A very similar trend is now borne out at Tel Mor. The best estimate of the percentage of Egyptianized pottery over time is as follows (Table 4.12): XVIII Dynasty (Stratum IX), 4%; XIXth Dynasty (Strata VIII–VII), 7%; and XXth Dynasty (Strata VI–V), 13%.

Only vessel types made of Nile Silt Clays in Egypt, which are typically household ware, were replicated locally in Canaan, whereas types made of Egyptian Marl Clays appear in Canaan only as imports. Marl Clay forms found abroad tend to be larger transport vessels (mainly amphorae) or small vessels, which probably held precious ointments (handled cups). Transport containers are mainly distributed along the coast, such as at Tel Mor, while they are rare at inland Egyptian garrison sites. Only three have been found in thirteenth- and twelfth-century strata at Bet She'an (Martin, forthcoming b) and none are known from Tel Sera' (Martin, forthcoming a). The possible Marl Clay bowls from Tel Mor are anomalous in Canaan (Fig. 4.9:1–3).

Important Egyptian forms that are missing or altogether absent at Canaanite sites are cooking wares, such as cooking pots and bread molds. In Egypt these forms were typically made of Nile Silt. During the XIXth and XXth Dynasties, necked globular jars and large carinated bowls were used as cooking vessels in Egypt, both of which are extremely rare in Canaan when used in this way. In Canaan the former has been found at Tel Mor (Fig. 4.9:10) and the latter at Bet She'an (Killebrew 1998a: Ill. II:70:3).[32] In contrast, Canaanite cooking pots in the Late Bronze Age tradition are well represented in strata characterized by Egyptianized pottery. At Tel Mor, for example, the number of Canaanite cooking pots appears to be roughly constant throughout the pre-Egyptianized (XII–IX) and Egyptianized strata (VIII–V; see Figs. 3.17–3.20).

A very different trend in regard to foreign cooking vessels has been observed at nearby, contemporaneous, Philistine sites. In strata corresponding to the initial Philistine settlement, characterized by the appearance of massive amounts of locally made Mycenean IIIC pottery (e.g., Tel Miqne-'Eqron VII), so-called 'Aegean-style' cooking jugs largely supplant Canaanite cooking pots (Barako 2000:523). The abandonment versus retention of traditional styles of food preparation by an intrusive population may reveal information about that population's composition, especially in regard to gender. Given that food preparation was primarily the domain of women in the ancient world (e.g., Watterson 1991:128–134; Holaubek 1992:44; King and Stager 2001:64–65), the distribution of cooking-vessel types in twelfth-century BCE Canaan is revealing. There is strong evidence that women were part of the Philistine migration and settlement (e.g., Barako 2003:32); in contrast, Egyptians stationed at Canaanite garrisons must have been mainly male administrators and soldiers.

Egyptian-style bread molds are virtually absent in Canaan. So far only a few possible candidates have been found at Bet She'an (James and McGovern 1993: Figs. 115:1, 2; 118:1). Two factors might explain their scarcity at Canaanite sites: (1) because bread molds are made of a friable fabric, only small fragments tend to survive, and were not properly identified during older excavations; and (2) since bread was often made in large bakeries outside the main settlements in Egypt (Spalinger 1986; Aston 1999:56), bread molds appear less commonly in domestic contexts. Similar bakeries might have operated outside Egyptian garrisons in Canaan.

Egyptian Presence or Influence?

The Egyptianized character of a significant amount of locally produced pottery from Tel Mor Strata VIII–V is clear. The question remains, however, who produced this pottery? Two explanatory scenarios may be put forth: (1) it was made by Egyptians for Egyptians living in garrisons in Canaan (James and McGovern 1993:245; Cohen-Weinberger 1998:411; Killebrew 1998a:275); or (2) it was made by Canaanites for Canaanite elites who emulated Egyptian material culture in an attempt to partake of Egyptian prestige and authority (Higginbotham 2000). Based on the available evidence from Tel Mor and other sites in Canaan with

similar assemblages (e.g., Bet She'an, Deir el-Balah), actual Egyptian presence is the more likely scenario. The reasons for this conclusion, although based largely on ceramic evidence, go beyond the facile 'pots equals people' formulation. By studying the types of Egyptian pottery imitated locally (mainly coarse ware) and how it was produced, it is possible to infer more about the cultural background of the people who made and used Egyptianized pottery than simply by noting its presence and amount. Furthermore, the incorporation of corroborating evidence derived, for example, from architectural styles and ancient texts strengthens the argument.

The vast majority of Egyptianized pottery found at Tel Mor and elsewhere in Canaan is comprised of coarse household wares. For example, bowls and beer jars comprise 95% of the Egyptianized assemblage at Tel Mor. These coarse wares served certain basic needs such as food consumption and, possibly, production. Unlike fine wares, they were less likely to have been objects of trade or emulation. Egyptianized pottery not only imitated Egyptian forms, but the following aspects of Egyptian pottery production as well, which, although discussed above, bear repeating here: The addition of organic temper to the clay; hasty and careless mass production; red-painted bands on bowl rims (see Figs. 4.5, 4.6:5–8, 12, 13); rope impressions on large bowls (Fig. 4.7:6); fingerprints and perforations on beer-jar bases (Fig. 4.11); and, perhaps, a relatively low firing temperature. Any one of these aspects considered in isolation is insufficient grounds for the proposal that Egyptian potters resided in Canaan. Indeed, red bands on large bowl rims are also characteristic of Canaanite pottery; however, the co-occurrence of numerous aspects gives persuasive force to an argument for Egyptian presence.

The close correlation between Egyptian assemblages in Egypt and Egyptianized assemblages in Canaan in terms of range of forms, as well as adherence to form, is further evidence in favor of Egyptian presence. If Canaanite potters had been emulating Egyptian pottery, then one would expect to find more hybrid forms at sites in Canaan under direct Egyptian control.[33] Moreover, morphological developments over time in Egypt find parallels in Egyptianized assemblages from Canaan, an indication of the close contact that must have existed between the Egyptian homeland and the outlying regions under her hegemony.

As with the pottery, buildings at Tel Mor were constructed according to Egyptian architectural styles and practices. With its exterior salients and recesses and interior arrangement of space, Building B of Strata VIII–VII resembles Egyptian granaries and administrative buildings (see Chapter 2). Also, the mudbrick walls of both Buildings B and F (Strata VI–V) were founded on a layer of sand, a common Egyptian building practice (Spencer 1979:120).

Although no hieratic or hieroglyphic inscriptions were found at Tel Mor, part of an inscribed, larger than lifesize, Ramesside statue made of limestone was discovered during a surface survey of the area between Tel Ashdod and Tel Mor carried out by the IDAM (Leclant 1971:259). As for hieratic ostraca, which have been found at several sites in Canaan under direct Egyptian control (for a recent summary, see Higginbotham 2000:59–63), the excavators easily could have missed them. Another category of evidence missing from Tel Mor is anthropoid coffins known thus far from Bet She'an, Deir el-Balaḥ, Tell el-Farʻah (S) and Lakhish (for descriptions and bibliography, see T. Dothan 1982:252–279). If more of the Late Bronze Age cemetery at the base of the mound is ever excavated, such Egyptian-style burials might also be found at Tel Mor.[34]

Ancient Egyptian inscriptions testify to the establishment of Egyptian outposts at Canaanite sites during the Ramesside period. The Bet She'an stelae of Seti I (Rowe 1930: Fig. 5, Pls. 41, 47:3; Kitchen 1993: §2 [Sethos I]) and Ramesses II (Rowe 1930: Pl. 46; Kitchen 1996: §6), which were discovered in a secondary context in Lower Level V (eleventh to tenth centuries BCE), strongly suggest that there was an Egyptian garrison at the site during their reigns. In Lower Level VI (early twelfth century BCE) a door lintel inscribed with the titulary of Ramesses Weser-Khepesh, a resident high official in the court of Ramesses III, was found near the Egyptian-style Building 1500 (Ward 1966: Figs. 96:1, 97:1). In Jaffa parts of two door jambs bearing the names and titles of Ramesses II were discovered in Stratum IVb (thirteenth century BCE; Kaplan 1972: Fig. 8; Kitchen 1996: §148, A). These jambs might have stood at the entrance to the royal granary referred to in Amarna letter 294 (Moran 1992:337), if it was still in existence.

In a general sense, textual evidence also attests indirectly to the physical presence of Egyptians in Canaan during the Ramesside period. First, Egyptianized material culture begins to appear in Canaan in large amounts at the start of the thirteenth century BCE, at a time when Egyptian involvement in Canaan intensified. The evidence includes battle reliefs (see recently Murnane 1990) and stelae (Tell es-Shihâb: KRI I, 17; Tell Nebi Mend/Kadesh: KRI I, 25; Tyre: KRI I, 117; Bet She'an: KRI I, 11, 12, 15, 16) from the reign of Seti I, as well as stelae (Nahr el-Kalb: Kitchen 1996: §§1, 2, 5; Bet She'an: §6) and letters (Owen 1981) from the reign of Ramesses II. Conversely, Egyptianized material culture effectively disappears before the last quarter of the twelfth century BCE, by which time there is no inscriptional evidence for Egyptian activity in Canaan (Weinstein 1981:22, 23; Bietak 1991b).

The Hebrew University excavations at Bet She'an best illustrate this cessation of material culture. Egyptianized pottery comprises roughly half of the total Stratum S-3 assemblage. In the following Stratum S-2, which was probably established shortly after the heavy destruction of S-3 (A. Mazar, pers. comm.), this percentage drops to c. 10%, most of which are small sherds that probably derive from earlier strata (Martin, forthcoming b). In the ephemeral Strata IV and III at Tel Mor, Egyptianized pottery comprises no more than 1% of the total assemblage (seven sherds in total), down from 12% in Stratum V (see Table 4.12). If Canaanite potters had indeed been emulating Egyptian pottery, then it beggars the imagination to suppose that they stopped doing so abruptly at the time when the Egyptians are known to have withdrawn from Canaan.

In summary, the ceramic and architectural data from Tel Mor in particular, along with the textual evidence pertaining to Canaan in general, strongly suggest that Egyptians were present at the site at the end of the Late Bronze Age. The types and quantity of Egyptian and Egyptianized pottery indicate that this presence was especially strong during the thirteenth and first half of the twelfth centuries BCE, which correspond to the XIXth and early XXth Dynasties (Strata VIII–V). There is little reason to push this presence back into the fourteenth century (Stratum IX) or extend it into the latter half of the twelfth century BCE (Stratum IV).

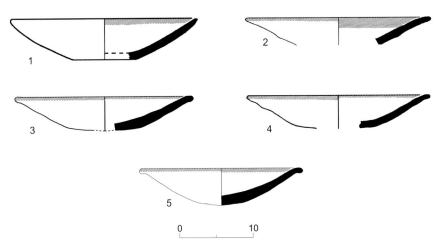

Fig. 4.5. Straight-sided bowls with plain (Nos. 1, 2) or everted (Nos. 3–5) rims.

No.	Reg. No.	Context (Stratum)	Elevation (m)	Description
1	A468/1	Area 59 (VI)	22.20	Paint: 10R 5/4 (weak red); surface (self-slip): 5YR 7/2 (pinkish gray); fabric: 2.5YR 5/8 (red); core: 5YR 6/8 (reddish yellow); inclusions: few fine to small white, few small voids
2	A404/10	Sq L18	22.40	Paint; N/A
3	A448/22	Area 59 (VI)	22.35	Paint: 10R 5/4 (weak red); surface: 10R 6/6 (light red); fabric: same; core: thick, dark gray; inclusions: very many medium voids, many small to medium white
4	A481/1	Room 71 (VI)	N/A	Paint: 10R 5/4 (weak red); surface: 5YR 6/8 (reddish yellow); fabric: 10YR 6/6 (brownish yellow); core: thin, gray; inclusions: many medium voids, few fine white
5	A712/1	Sq H18 (VIII–VII)	21.35/21.00	Paint: 10R 5/6 (red); surface: 2.5YR 6/6 (light red); fabric: same; core: thick, 7.5YR 5/6 (strong brown); inclusions: many small to medium voids

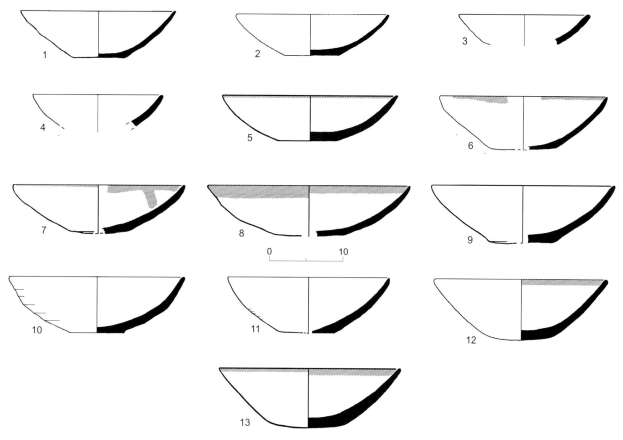

Fig. 4.6. Bowls with rounded walls and plain rim.

No.	Reg. No.	Context (Stratum)	Elevation (m)	Description
1	A600/1	Sq L19 (VII)	N/A	Surface (self-slip): 5Y 7/3 (pale yellow); fabric: 10R 5/8 (red); core: 5YR 4/4 (reddish brown); inclusions: few medium voids, few medium dark, few small white
2	B268/1	Sq L20 (VII)	22.45	Surface: 10R 5/8 (red); fabric: same; core: thick, black; inclusions: few small to medium white, few medium voids, very few fine sparkling
3	A574/9	Area 80 (VII)	22.00/21.20	Surface (self-slip): 5YR 6/8 (reddish yellow); fabric: same; core: thick, dark gray; inclusions: few small to medium voids, few fine to small white
4	A397/15	Area 59 (VII)	22.50/20.75	Surface: 5YR 5/8 (yellowish red); fabric: same; core: none; inclusions: few medium voids, very few fine sparkling
5	A722/2	Room 71 (VI)	N/A	Paint: 10R 5/4 (weak red); surface: 5YR 6/8 (reddish yellow); fabric: 10YR 6/6 (brownish yellow); core: thin, gray; inclusions: many medium voids, few fine white
6	A495/2	Room 71 (VI)	22.10?	Paint: 10R 5/4 (weak red); surface (self-slip): 5YR 7/4 (pink); fabric: 2.5YR 6/8 (light red); core: none; inclusions: many medium voids, very few small white
7	A495/1	Room 71 (VI)	22.10?	Paint: 10R 5/4 (weak red); surface: 2.5YR 6/4 (light reddish brown); fabric: 5YR 5/6 (yellowish red); core: none; inclusions: few small to medium voids
8	A406/1	Sq L18 (VI)	22.40	Paint: 10R 5/4 (weak red); surface: 10R 5/8 (red); fabric: 2.5YR 6/8 (light red); core: thick, gray; inclusions: very many medium voids, many fine to small white
9	A495/6	Room 71 (VI)	22.10?	Surface (self-slip): 5YR 7/2 (pinkish gray); fabric: 2.5YR 5/8 (red); core: 5YR 6/8 (reddish yellow); inclusions: very many fine white, many small to medium voids
10	A293/1	Pit 35 (VI)	23.30/23.10	Surface (self-slip): 5YR 6/8 (reddish yellow); fabric: 10YR 6/6 (brownish yellow); core: thin, gray; inclusions: many medium voids, few fine white
11	A214/1	Pit 35 (VI)	23.40	Perforated; surface: 2.5YR 6/8 (light red); fabric: same; core: gray; inclusions: very many medium voids
12	A578	Room 71 (VI)	22.05	Paint: 10R 5/4 (weak red); surface: 2.5YR 6/8 (light red); fabric: same; core: gray; inclusions: very many medium voids
13	A577	Room 71 (VI)	N/A	Paint: 10R 5/4 (weak red); surface: 5YR 6/8 (reddish yellow); fabric: 10YR 6/6 (brownish yellow); core: thin, gray; inclusions: many medium voids, few fine white

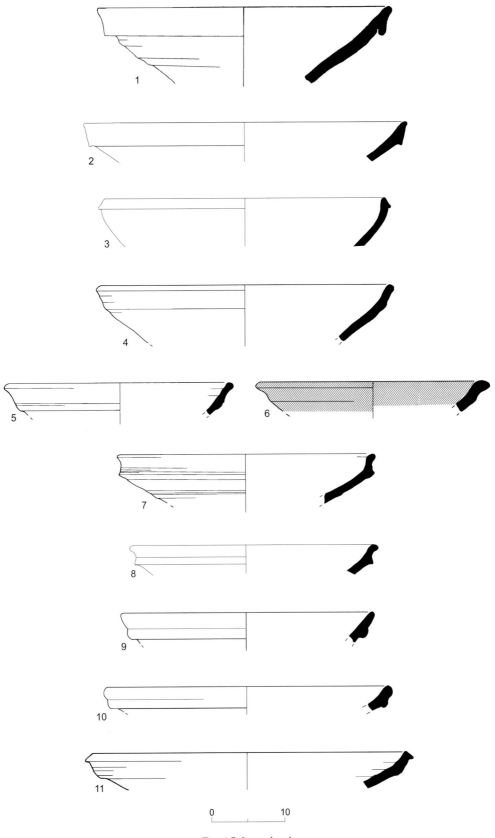

Fig. 4.7. Large bowls.

◀ **Fig. 4.7**

No.	Reg. No.	Context (Stratum)	Elevation (m)	Description
1	B93/2	Courtyard 118 (XI–IX)	20.10	Surface (self-slip): 7.5YR 6/3 (light brown); fabric: 7.5YR 5/4 (brown); core: thick, gray, middle and interior; inclusions: few fine to small voids, very few small white
2	B83/4	Courtyard 118 (XI–IX)	20.23	Surface: 2.5YR 6/6 (light red); fabric: same; core: thick, gray; inclusions: many fine to small voids
3	B256/18	Courtyard 118 (XI?)	20.40/20.25	Surface (self-slip): 7.5YR 7/4 (pink); fabric: 5YR 5/8 (yellowish red); core: thick, gray; inclusions: many fine voids, many fine white
4	B293/1	Room 138 (IX)	21.00/20.90	Surface: 5YR 6/8 (reddish yellow); fabric: 7.5YR 5/6 (strong brown), core: none; inclusions: none
5	B325/9	Room 111 (IX)	20.60/20.20	Surface (self-slip): 5YR 6/6 (reddish yellow); fabric: 10YR 5/4 (yellowish brown); core: thin, very light gray; inclusions: few small white, very few fine sparkling
6	A310/14	Area 41 (VII)	22.25	Rope impression; surface (slip): 10R 5/4 (weak red); fabric: 7.5YR 5/8 (strong brown); core: dark gray; inclusions: few medium voids, few fine sparkling
7	B297/1	Room 138 (IX)	21.00/20.60	Surface: 5YR 6/8 (reddish yellow); fabric: 7.5YR 5/6 (strong brown), core: none; inclusions: none
8	B255/2	Area 128 (VII)	22.60/22.55	Surface: 5YR 7/4 (pink); fabric: same; core: gray; inclusions: very few fine white
9	A435/1	Sq H20 (VII)	21.50	Surface: 7.5YR 6/4 (light brown); fabric: 2.5YR 5/8 (red); core: thick, gray; inclusions: none
10	A442/3	Sq L18 (VII)	22.35/22.10	Surface: 2.5YR 5/6 (red); fabric: same; core: thick, gray; inclusions: many fine white
11	A193/1	Sq M18 (VI)	23.60/23.40	Surface: 5YR 5/3 (reddish brown); fabric: same; core: thick, dark gray; inclusions: few, fine red

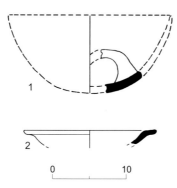

0   10

Fig. 4.8. 'Spinning bowl' (No. 1) and flanged-rim bowl (No. 2).

No.	Reg. No.	Context (Stratum)	Elevation (m)	Description
1	A54/10	Sq M18 (III)	24.80/24.70	Surface: 2.5YR 5/6 (red); fabric: same; core: thin, light gray; inclusions: few fine white, few fine dark
2	B29/2	Room 108 (VII)	22.50	White slip; surface: 7.5 YR 6/8 (reddish yellow); fabric: same; core: none; inclusions: many medium voids

Fig. 4.9 ▶

No.	Object	Reg. No.	Context (Stratum)	Elevation (m)	Description
1	Bowl	A333/2	Area 41 (VII)	22.25	Surface (self-slip): 2.5Y 7/3 (pale yellow); fabric: 7.5YR 6/4 (light brown); core: none; inclusions: many fine to small voids, few small white, very few large red
2	Bowl	A331/3	Area 43 (VII)	22.25/22.14	Surface (self-slip): 5Y 8/1 (white); fabric: 5YR 5/4 (reddish brown); core: none; inclusions: few small white, very few small red
3	Bowl	A442/1	Sq L18 (VII)	22.35/22.10	Surface (self-slip): 5Y 7/2 (light gray); fabric: 2.5YR 5/6 (red); core: thick, light gray; inclusions: many medium to large white
4	Storage jar	A310/28	Area 41 (VII)	22.25	Surface (self-slip): 10YR 7/3 (very pale brown); fabric: 7.5YR 5/3 (brown); core: none; inclusions: very many fine to small white, few fine sparkling
5	Storage jar	A328/28	Sq K18 (V)	23.20/23.07	N/A
6	Jar?	A333/12	Area 41 (VII)	22.25	Surface (self-slip): 2.5Y 7/3 (pale yellow); fabric: 5YR 6/6 (reddish yellow); core: none; inclusions: few small to medium voids
7	Globular jar	A722/1	Room 71 (VI)	N/A	Surface (slip): 10YR 7/3 (very pale brown); fabric: 10R 5/6 (red); core: none; inclusions: very many small voids, very many small white
8	Storage jar ('amphora')	A502/1	Room 71 (VI)	N/A	Burnish; surface (slip): 2.5YR 7/3 (pale yellow); fabric: 2.5YR 4/6 (red); core: none; inclusions: very many fine to small white, very few medium dark
9	Storage jar ('amphora')	A548/4	Installation 74 (VI)	21.90	Burnish; surface (slip); N/A
10	Cooking jar	A189/22	Room 34 (V)	23.70/23.60	Blackened; surface: 2.5YR 6/3 (light reddish brown); fabric: N/A; core: N/A; inclusions: very many medium voids, few fine sparkling
11	*Zîr*	B291/13	Room 136 (IX)	21.70/21.25	Surface (self-slip): 5Y 7/2 (light gray); fabric: 10R 4/6 (red); core: none; inclusions: N/A

Fig. 4.9. Egyptian imports: (1–6) Marl F Ware; (7–9) Marl D Ware; (10) Nile B/E Ware; (11) Marl C Ware.

Fig. 4.10 ▶

No.	Object	Reg. No.	Context (Stratum)	Elevation (m)	Description
1	Jar	B111	Courtyard 118 (XI)	19.95	Grooved; surface: 7.5YR 6/4 (light brown); fabric: 10R 6/6 (light red); core: N/A; inclusions: many small to medium voids, many fine to small dark, many small to medium white
2	Jar	A311/1	Pit 35 (VI)	22.90	Surface (slip): 2.5YR 5/6 (red); fabric: N/A; core: N/A; inclusions: many medium voids, few fine to small white
3	Storage jar	A658/2	Room 63 (VIII)	21.45/21.30	Surface (self-slip): 2.5YR 6/3 (light reddish brown); fabric: 2.5YR 5/8 (red); core: gray; inclusions: N/A
4	Storage jar	A724/4	Room 71 (VI)	N/A	Surface (slip): 10R 5/4 (weak red); fabric: 2.5YR 5/8 (red); core: none; inclusions: many small to medium voids
5	Storage jar	A663	Room 71 (VI)	21.90	Surface (self-slip): 2.5YR 5/6 (red); fabric: same; core: none; inclusions: many small to medium voids, many fine to small white
6	Storage jar	A358/7	Sq K18 and Sq L18 (V)	23.90/23.60	Surface (self-slip, except rim): 10YR 7/3 (very pale brown); fabric: 10R 5/8 (red); core: dark gray; inclusions: many small to medium voids, many small white
7	Jar	A418/13	N/A (VIII–VII)	N/A	Surface (self-slip): 2.5YR 6/3 (light reddish brown); fabric: 10R 5/8 (red); core: none; inclusions: many small to medium voids, few fine white
8	Jar	A366/19	Sq K18 and Sq L18 (V)	23.60/23.30	N/A
9	Storage jar	A634/16	Sq L19 (VIII–VII?)	21.36/21.26	Surface (self-slip): 2.5Y 7/3 (pale yellow); fabric: 10R 6/6 (light red); core: none; inclusions: many fine white
10	Crucible	B190/1	Area 128 (VII)	21.65	Knife pared; N/A
11	Jar	A458/6	Room 71 (VI)	22.95/22.33	Surface: 2.5YR 5/6 (red); fabric: same; core: thin, gray; inclusions: many small to medium voids, few small white
12	Jar	A189/17	Room 34 (V)	23.70/23.60	Surface: 2.5YR 5/6 (red); fabric: same; core: dark gray; inclusions: many small to medium voids, few small white

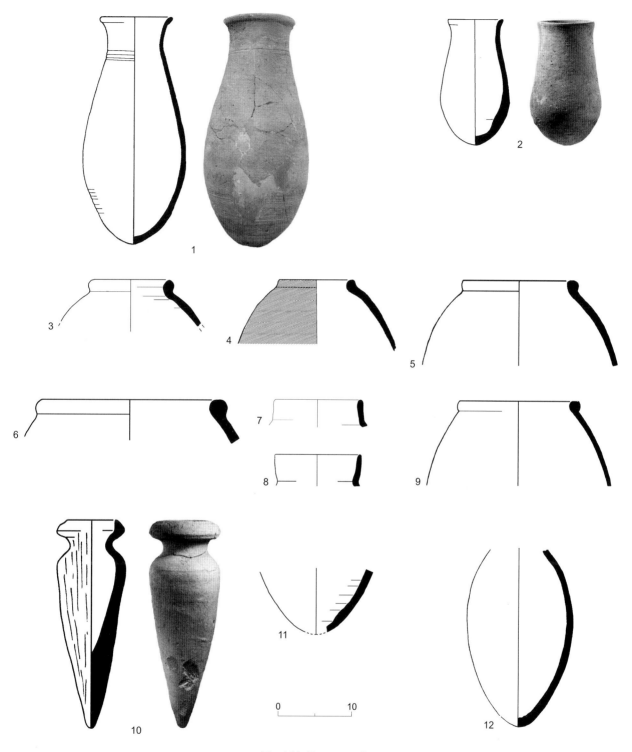

Fig. 4.10. Egyptianized jars.

Fig. 4.11 ▶

No.	Reg. No.	Context (Stratum)	Elevation (m)	Description
1	A655/9	Area 86 (IX)	21.10/20.95	Surface: 10R 6/6 (light red); fabric: same; core: thick, gray; inclusions: many small voids; base perforated pre-firing?
2	A655/10	Area 86 (IX)	21.10/20.95	Surface (self-slip): 7.5YR 6/3 (light brown); fabric: 5YR 6/6 (reddish yellow), core: gray; inclusions: many small to medium voids; base perforated post-firing
3	A652/1	Subfloor fill for Room 75 (IX)	21.20/20.70	Surface: 5YR 5/6 (yellowish); fabric: same; core: dark gray; inclusions: many small to medium voids, few small white, few small sparkling; base perforated pre-firing
4	A652/12	Subfloor fill for Room 75 (IX)	21.20/20.70	Surface: 2.5YR 5/8 (red); fabric: red; core: thick, dark gray; inclusions: many small to medium voids, very few medium to large white; probably perforated
5	A652/11	Subfloor fill for Room 75 (IX)	21.20/20.70	Surface (self-slip): 2.5Y 8/3 (pale yellow); fabric: 2.5YR 6/8 (light red); core: very thick, black; inclusions: many small to medium white, few fine sparkling; base perforated pre-firing
6	B268/2	Room 134 (VIII)	22.45	Surface (self-slip): 5YR 6/8 (reddish yellow); fabric: same; core: 7.5YR 6/4 (light brown); inclusions: many small to medium voids; base perforated pre-firing
7	A616	Room 83 (VIII–VII)	21.40/21.30	Surface (self-slip): 10YR 6/3 (pale brown); fabric: 7.5YR 6/4 (light brown); core: thick, gray
8	A687	Room 63 (VIII–VII)	20.80	Rilling; surface: N/A; fabric: N/A; core: N/A; inclusions: N/A; base perforated
9	A670/9	Room 63 (VIII–VII)	21.20	Surface: 2.5YR 5/6 (red); fabric: same; core: none; inclusions: many small to medium voids
10	B37/7	Room 111 (VIII–VII)	N/A	Surface (self-slip): 2.5YR 5/6 (red); fabric: 7.5YR 6/8 (reddish yellow); core: thin, gray; inclusions: many fine sparkling; base perforation created by string cutting
11	B186/14	Area 128 (VII)	23.30/22.80	Surface (self-slip): 7.5YR 5/6 (strong brown); fabric: same; core: thin, gray; inclusions: many medium voids; base not perforated
12	A580/1	Room 71 (VI)	N/A	Surface (self-slip): 5YR 6/6 (reddish yellow); fabric: 5YR 5/8 (yellowish red); core: 10YR 6/4 (light yellowish brown); inclusions: very many fine to small voids
13	A504/1	Room 71 (VI)	N/A	Rilling; surface: 10R 6/6 (light red); fabric: same; core: thick, gray; inclusions: many small voids; base perforated pre-firing
14	A579/4	Room 71 (VI)	22.05	Rilling; surface (self-slip): 10YR 7/2 (light gray); fabric: same; core: thick, 10R 7/6 (light red); inclusions: many small to medium voids.
15	A723/2	Room 71 (VI)	N/A	Rilling; surface: 2.5YR 6/6 (light red); fabric: same; core: thick, 7.5YR 5/6 (strong brown); inclusions: very many medium voids, very few small white; base perforated post-firing?
16	A503/2	Room 71 (VI)	N/A	Rilling; surface (self-slip): 5YR 8/2 (pinkish white); fabric: 5YR 5/6 (yellowish red); core: gray, 10R 7/6 (light red); inclusions: many small voids; base perforated pre-firing
17	A281/11	Sq J18 (VI)	23.00/22.80	Surface: 2.5YR 5/8 (red); fabric: same; core: thick, black, middle and interior; inclusions: many medium voids; base perforated

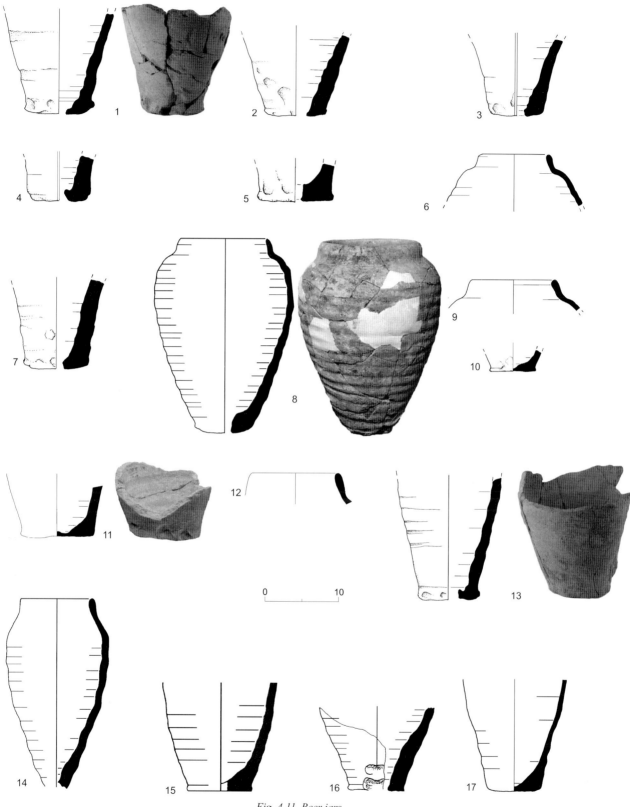

0   10

Fig. 4.11. Beer jars.

NOTES

[1] The authors wish to thank David Aston, Bettina Bader, Manfred Bietak, Amihai Mazar and Eliezer Oren for their assistance with this corpus of pottery and for making available unpublished material from their own sites.

[2] A slender ovoid jar, probably produced locally, was found in Stratum XI (see Fig. 4.10:1) and approximately 45 sherds from Egyptianized vessels (mostly bowls and beer bottles) were recovered from poorly stratified Stratum IX contexts.

[3] For an overview of the Egyptian garrison at Bet She'an (Strata IX–VI), see A. Mazar 1993; for the Egyptian and Egyptianized pottery from the Ramesside period see Martin 2006b, forthcoming b.

[4] For an overview of these sites and their Egyptianized assemblages, see, for instance, Killebrew 1998, 2005; Higginbotham 2000; Martin 2004, 2005, 2006b.

[5] The images of the Marl and Egyptianized fabrics were created by placing a freshly broken piece of pottery on a flatbed scanner and scanning at 800 dpi.

[6] For a similar phenomenon during the EB I period, see Goren 2000.

[7] A similar process seems to have occurred at Lakhish during the late thirteenth and twelfth centuries BCE, when there was a stronger Egyptian influence on the material culture, including an increased use of straw as temper (Clamer 2004b; Yannai 2004).

[8] Ring bases appear in Egypt on these simple bowl types only in the first half of the XVIIIth Dynasty (D.A. Aston, pers. comm.).

[9] Flat bases in Egypt are common and round bases rare, however, during the first half of the XVIIIth Dynasty (Aston 2001:169).

[10] At other sites (i.e., Bet She'an, Tel Sera', Ashqelon), however, the reverse was true—namely, heavy straw temper was commonly present in Canaanite forms—which necessitated a purely morphological approach (Martin 2005; forthcoming a, b). Because of these different methodologies, comparative analyses between the percentages of Egyptian forms at Tel Mor as opposed to other sites should be treated with some reservation.

[11] Replication studies (conducted by Martin) involving both manufacturing techniques (i.e., string cutting and tool scraping) produced these same distinctive features.

[12] Five rim sherds attributed to Stratum IX come from very unreliable loci.

[13] Based on rim count, everted-rim bowls comprise 20.9% (n = 18) of the Egyptianized pottery assemblage in Strata VIII–VII, 23.8% (n = 25) in Stratum VI and 25.4% (n = 18) in Stratum V.

[14] The authors wish to thank David Ussishkin, director of the renewed excavations at Lakhish, who made the Strata VII–VI pottery from Areas S and P available for study. The Egyptianized pottery from Area S has been published by Yannai (2004) and from Area P, by Clamer (2004a; 2004b).

[15] Four Egyptianized 'bowls with everted rim' found in Area R of the renewed excavations date to the latter part of the XVIIIth Dynasty (Mullins 2006). These bowls, however, are somewhat unlike the characteristic everted-rim bowls of the thirteenth and twelfth centuries BCE in that they have thicker, slightly ribbed side-walls (Martin, forthcoming b).

[16] Both vessels originate from Room 2131, which was attributed to Stratum VIIB by the Chicago Expedition but reassigned to VIIA by Finkelstein and Zimhoni (2000: 233–234).

[17] The authors wish to thank Trude Dothan for sharing with us the unpublished results from her excavations at Deir el-Balah.

[18] For the most complete exposition of the Low Chronology as it pertains to Iron I, see Finkelstein 1995; for its application specifically to the site of Ashdod, see Finkelstein and Singer-Avitz 2001.

[19] In light of the small size of the ledged-rim bowl sherds found in Strata VI–V, and their generally poor stratigraphic contexts, it is possible that they are residual.

[20] For a spinning bowl fragment from 'Izbet Ṣarṭah Stratum III, which was dated between the late thirteenth and first half of eleventh centuries BCE, see Finkelstein 1986: Fig. 8.11.

[21] These variants are determined by a 'vessel index', which is calculated by multiplying the maximum body diameter by 100 and dividing the result by the vessel's height. 'Slender' is defined by an index smaller than 50, 'tall' is between 50 and 90, and 'bag-shaped' refers to when the maximum body diameter is located in the lowest third of the vessel (Aston 1996:12).

[22] An imported Marl D meat-jar rim fragment was found at Tell Abu Hawam (Balensi 1980: Pl. 12:6).

[23] There is no indication that the room (34) and building (H) in which this jar was found ended in fiery destruction, a situation that might otherwise explain the signs of burning on the exterior of the vessel. That the entire surface of the jar was evenly blackened is a further indication of its use as a cooking vessel.

[24] The latter may belong to an imported, small-handled cup. In Egypt these cups were usually made of Marl A or D, but appear also in Marl F, Mixed Clay and, during the XXth Dynasty, occasionally even in Nile Silt (Aston 1996:65; Aston 1998: Nos. 1686–1690 [Marl D], 1974–1981 [Marl F], 2145, 2146 [Mixed Clay], 2496 [Marl A4]; 1999: No. 145b [Nile B]). Handled cups appear at the following Canaanite sites exclusively as imports: Deir el-Balah (T. Dothan 1979: Ills. 24, 29 [Tomb 114]); Tell el-'Ajjul (Petrie 1931: Pl. 44:34E2 [Tomb 808]; 1932: Pl. 30:34E4 [Tomb 1506]; 1933: Pl. 11:67 [Tomb 419]; 1934: Pl. 49:34E2 [Tomb 1687]); Tell es-Sa'idiyeh (Pritchard 1980: Figs. 5:1, 52:6 [Tomb 102]); Bet She'an (Killebrew 1998a: Ill. II:71; Martin, forthcoming b; Oren 1973: Figs. 46:19, 74:11 [Tomb 227]); and Megiddo (Loud 1948: Pl. 67:15).

[25] According to David Aston, however, this type is more common in Strata c and d, which date to the reign of Tuthmosis III (pers. comm.).

[26] The term 'beer bottle' refers to the earliest appearances of this type (early to mid-XVIIIth Dynasty), which tended to have a slender body and tall neck. By the late XVIIIth and XIXth Dynasties, however, they assumed more of a jar shape and, consequently, became known as 'beer jars'.

[27] Egyptianized bowls were also occasionally perforated, as at Deir el-Balaḥ (T. Dothan 1979: Figs. 126, 127, 133, 134 [Tomb 118]) and Tel Mor in Stratum VI (Fig. 4.6:11).

[28] A few beer jars have been found, however, in funerary contexts at Tell es-Saʿidiyeh in Tomb 104 (Pritchard 1980: Fig. 7:5), Tell el-Farʿah (S) in Tomb 939 (Starkey and Harding 1932: Pl. 88:94) and at Deir el-Balaḥ (Yellin, Dothan and Gould 1986:69).

[29] The authors benefited from the insights of Galit Litani on the subject of beer production in the ancient Near East.

[30] Spot testing for calcium oxalate ('beerstone') carried out by Margie Burton at the Scripps Institution of Oceanography at the University of California on a Stratum IX beer jar from Tel Mor (Fig. 4.11:1) produced negative results.

[31] Marl C *zîr*s might disappear even earlier. Also the Tel Mor *zîr* rim could have been reused as a stand, which is a common phenomenon in Egypt (B. Bader, pers. comm.).

[32] Note, however, that there are no signs of exposure to fire on the carinated bowl from Bet Sheʾan. So-called Egyptian-style 'firedogs', which have also been found at Bet Sheʾan (James and McGovern 1993: Fig. 94), were probably used as supports for cooking vessels placed over a hearth (Aston 1989; Martin, forthcoming b).

[33] Hybrid forms are almost completely absent from Egyptianized assemblages in Canaan (Killebrew 1998a:275). A possible exception is an ovoid Egyptian-style storage jar with a typical Canaanite stump base found at Deir el-Balaḥ (Killebrew 1998a: Ill. III:22:3, 4 [Type EG14]).

[34] Burial 152, which contained mostly Cypriot pottery (see Fig. 2.12), probably corresponds in date to Stratum IX, thus prior to the true advent of Egyptianized material culture at the site.

CHAPTER 5

CYPRIOT AND MYCENEAN POTTERY

CYPRIOT POTTERY

Approximately 300 Cypriot whole vessels and diagnostic sherds were found at Tel Mor.[1] Many of these imports (n = *c.* 70) belong to the earliest strata (XII–X). The majority of these early imports are Base Ring (BR) I and Monochrome bowls. Indeed, several bowls appeared in the deepest levels (19.00–17.90 m) of Courtyard 118 and Pit 166 (see Figs. 5.1:1, 3; 5.3:1, 3–5). Of the nearly 50 sherds and partially restorable vessels of Cypriot pottery recovered from Stratum IX, most are BR II and White Slip (WS) II bowls. The same is true for the approximately 40 Cypriot imports found in Strata VIII–VII and the 20 from Strata VI–V. In light of their generally poor stratigraphic contexts, it is likely that most of the sherds from Strata VI–V derive originally from earlier strata.

What follows is a description of the better preserved and unusual Cypriot imports from Strata XII–V. They are arranged first according to ware (i.e., Monochrome, Red-on-Black, BR, WS, White Shaved, Bichrome) and then vessel type. Whenever possible, the Swedish Cyprus Expedition's typology is utilized here (Åström 1972b; Popham 1972; see also Gittlen 1977). Within this framework, the imports are presented from earliest to latest following the Late Cypriot (LC) relative chronology.

Monochrome (Fig. 5.1)

In terms of surface treatment and fabric, Monochrome and BR I bowls are very similar. The main differences between the two are morphological—namely, the generally inturned rim and concave base of Monochrome bowls as opposed to the slightly everted rim and ring base of BR I bowls. Monochrome pottery was recovered from the deepest Stratum XII levels of Courtyard 118 and Pit 166. For example, Fig. 5.1:1 is a Type IF bowl, which is characterized by an everted

rim, wishbone handle and concave base. Such bowls first appear at Canaanite sites during MB IIC, but were more common in LB IA (Oren 1969:140–142). They have been discovered in securely dated MB IIC contexts at Tell el-ʿAjjul in Palace II–I and City III–II, Ḥazor in Stratum 3 and Megiddo in Tomb 1100A–D (for references, see Oren 1969:142). The type has been found in LB I contexts at Tel Yoqneʿam in Stratum XXa (Ben-Ami and Livneh 2005: Fig. IV.20:1, 2). Figure 5.1:2, which belongs to Stratum XI, is probably another Type IF bowl (cf. Åström 1972b: Fig. 45:4).

Figure 5.1:3 and 4 are Type IJ Monochrome bowls, which are characterized by slightly carinated side-walls and concave bases (Åström 1972b: Fig. 45:7, 8). Such bowls first appeared in significant quantities in Canaan during LB I and continued to be imported throughout LB IIA (for references, see Gittlen 1977:330–332). Thus far the only possible Type IJ from a Middle Bronze Age context is from Ḥazor in Stratum IV (Yadin et al. 1960: Pl. 115:8).[2] It is noteworthy that this type of bowl was discovered at Tel Mor in the lowest levels of Stratum XII, which probably dates to MB IIC. Other Type IJ bowls were retrieved in Strata IX (Reg. No. B297/3) and VI (Reg. No. A432/3; neither drawn). The latter sherd derives from a poor stratigraphic context and is therefore probably residual. Moreover, it is likely that Type I Monochrome bowls were no longer exported to Canaan by the end of LB IIB (Gittlen 1977:320, Charts 40, 41).

Figure 5.1:5 may be a Type VIII Monochrome jug (cf. Åström 1972b: Fig. 46:10), a Cypriot import rarely found in Canaan (Gittlen 1977:321, 334). An ovoid body, almost angular shoulder, and handle that pierces the vessel wall characterize this particular Type VIII jug. The neck and rim are not preserved; however, based on similar vessels found elsewhere, it is likely that the former widened upward and the latter was trefoil shaped.[3]

Red-on-Black (Fig. 5.2)

Several examples of Cypriot Red-on-Black Ware were discovered at Tel Mor in various strata.[4] All bear the distinctive red parallel or cross-hatched lines on a dark base. The earliest and best preserved is Fig. 5.2:1, a spouted bowl with a slightly upraised, horizontal loop handle (see also M. Dothan 1972: Pl. 4:3; 1973: Fig. 4:4, Pl. 3A; Johnson 1982: Fig. 7.P1). The majority of Red-on-Black pottery was produced on Cyprus during the Middle Cypriot III period and tapered off during the Late Cypriot I period (Åström 1964:78). Accordingly, Red-on-Black pottery, including spouted bowls, is found at Canaanite sites in MB IIC and LB I contexts, particularly at Tell el-ʿAjjul in levels associated with Cities III, II and above (Petrie 1932: Pl. 27:10U; 1933: Pl. 30:10U2, 10W; Bergoffen 1989: Cat. Nos. 409–416). Late Bronze Age I tombs from Megiddo (Tomb 77; Guy 1938: Pls. 42:14, 140:32) and Lakhish (Tomb 4004; Tufnell 1958: Pl. 79:816) have also produced close parallels for Fig. 5.2:1.

The Red-on-Black bowl rim (Fig. 5.2:2) from a questionable Stratum XI context resembles sherds from Ashdod Stratum XXIIa (MB IIC; Dothan and Porath 1993: Fig. 3:12) and Lakhish Fosse Temple I (Tufnell, Inge and Harding 1940: Pl. 64:3). The rest of the Red-on-Black pottery from Tel Mor derives from residual contexts and/or is non-diagnostic.

Base Ring (Figs. 5.3, 5.4)

The smoothed and burnished surface of the Base Ring Ware found at Tel Mor is typically mottled, ranging in color from red (2.5YR 5/6) to dark reddish gray (2.5YR 4/1). The well-levigated fabric is often red (2.5YR 5/8) with a thick gray core and few fine to small white inclusions.

Figure 5.3:1 is a rare BR I bowl with some of the distinctive molded decoration preserved—namely, two vertical relief bands that descend from the shoulder to the lower body (see also M. Dothan 1973: Fig. 4:5). In terms of the form, it has an everted rim and hemispherical body. Neither the curved fork handle nor the ring base survives. Few bowls possessing both this form and decoration are known from Canaan or Cyprus, where it is classified as Type IAg (Åström 1972b:138–139). In Canaan this type has been recovered thus far only at Tell el-ʿAjjul (Bergoffen 1989: Cat. No. 542). Excavations at Megiddo (LB IIB; see Sjöqvist 1940:

Fig. 6 [Type 3]) and Alalakh (Level IV; Bergoffen 2004: Cat. No. B1) have produced the conical version of this bowl (Type IBb; Åström 1972b: Fig. 47:6).

Figure 5.3:2–5 are also Type IA hemispherical bowls, but without any relief decoration preserved. Thus far, these bowls have been found at the following Canaanite sites: Tell el-ʿAjjul in Palace II (for references, see Bergoffen 1989:415–419), Lakhish in Fosse Temple I (Tufnell, Inge and Harding 1940: Pl. 44:169) and Megiddo in Tomb 217C (Guy 1938: Pl. 11:8). The majority of BR I pottery (including Type IA bowls) in Canaan dates to LB IA (Late Cypriot IA2); however, it is possible that it began to arrive at coastal sites, particularly Tell el-ʿAjjul, as early as MB IIC (Bergoffen 2001a:44–46). The presence of Type IA bowls (especially Fig. 5.1:3) in the basal level at Tel Mor, which probably dates to MB IIC, supports this tentative conclusion (see also M. Dothan 1973:8, n. 21).

Figure 5.3:6 and 7 are probably Type IB BR I bowls, which are characterized by an everted rim, straight neck, fork handle, carinated side-wall, conical lower body and ring base (Åström 1972b:139–141, Fig. 47:8, 9). No relief line decoration is visible on either sherd. The importation of Type IB bowls into Canaan began in LB I, peaked during LB IIA and died out by LB IIB (Gittlen 1977:117, Charts 28–30). The undecorated subtypes (IBe–f) have been found mostly at Tell el-ʿAjjul and Lakhish in various contexts (for references, see Gittlen 1977:159–161; Bergoffen 1989:415–419).

Figure 5.3:8 is the only Type IC bowl discovered so far in Canaan (see also M. Dothan 1960c: Fig. 4:5). Based on the limited evidence from Tel Mor, therefore, it seems that this bowl type was imported to Canaan during LB I (Stratum XI). On Cyprus, such bowls with a molded wavy line decoration around the upper body are classified as Type IAe (Åström 1972b:138, Fig. 38c, Pl. 47:5). The wavy line on the Tel Mor bowl clearly ends, suggesting that a snake motif was intended (cf. Bergoffen 1989:417, Cat. Nos. 543, 544, Pl. 4 [Tell el-ʿAjjul]). Type IC bowls have forked handles, conical lower bodies and ring bases (Gittlen 1977:117, 161, Pl. ICa:1). Uneven firing conditions produced a mottled surface, ranging from red (lower body) to black (upper body), on Fig. 5.3:8.

Figure 5.3:9 is the base of a Type IF BR II bowl commonly found in Canaan throughout LB II (for references, see Gittlen 1977:194–201, Pl. 7; see also Åström 1972b:175–179, Fig. 52:2–7). The relatively low ring base distinguishes it from the generally higher conical ring bases of BR I bowls. Such Type IF bowls were found, for example, at Ashdod in Strata XVI (Dothan and Freedman 1967: Fig. 18:15, 16) and XV (Fig. 21:2).

Figure 5.3:10 is a strap handle from a BR I jug, perhaps Type VID1d (Åström 1972b:156–159). The unusual incised decoration consists of a row of short diagonal strokes enclosed by two parallel vertical lines. The surface is a highly burnished shade of red (2.5YR 5/6). The same design appears on two jug handle fragments, probably belonging to the same vessel type, recovered during Woolley's excavations at Alalakh (Bergoffen 2004:43, Pls. 24c: B75, B77; 24d; 24e).

The rim, neck and beginning of the handle are preserved in Fig. 5.3:11, which is probably a Type VIA1 jug (cf. Bergoffen 2004: Cat. Nos. B29, B30 [Palace IV]). Its decoration, a single horizontal relief band on a short and relatively wide neck, distinguishes this type from the most common BR I jug type (VID), which has two such bands (Åström 1972b: Fig. 49:9, 10; Gittlen 1977:164–170). Both types date to the end of LB I or the beginning of LB IIA, which corresponds well to the Stratum X context of Fig. 5.3:11. Figure 5.3:12, with its everted rim and cylindrical neck, appears to belong to another Type VI BR I jug, an attribution that matches its context (Stratum XI, LB I). A similar jug rim (Fig. 5.3:13), probably a residual sherd, comes from Stratum VII.

The tapering, slanted neck of Fig. 5.3:14 belongs to a large, Type VID, BR I juglet. Figure 5.3:15 is a smaller, better preserved juglet of this type that was found on the surface, probably washed out from another Late Bronze Age tomb at the base of the tell (see Chapter 2, Stratum IX). They belong to Subtype VID1bθ, which is characterized by a more globular body, two horizontal relief ridges on the neck and two vertical relief ridges on the body opposite the handle (Åström 1972b: Fig. 49:6; Gittlen 1977: Pl. 3).

Among the grave goods from Burial 152 were two BR II jugs and a juglet (Fig. 5.3:16, 18; see also Fig. 2.12:1, 6 see also M. Dothan 1960c: Pl. 9:3).[5] All have the white painted lines on a mottled slip that ranges from grayish to light reddish brown characteristic of BR II pottery. Each strap handle on the jugs bears two incised, vertical, parallel lines. The jugs belong to the ubiquitous Type IXB1d (Åström 1972b: Fig. 53:2), which appears in numerous LB IIA funerary contexts,

particularly at Tell el-'Ajjul and Lakhish (for references, see Gittlen 1977:213–223; Bergoffen 1989:439–445). At nearby Ashdod, for example, this jug type appears in Stratum XV (LB II; Dothan and Freedman 1967: Fig. 21:3, 4). The rim of another Type IXB1d jug (Fig. 5.3:17) is from Pit 119, which was originally assigned to Stratum IX by the excavator (see also M. Dothan 1960c: Fig. 4:10). However, because Pit 119 clearly cut a Stratum IX wall (W122; see Fig. 2.20), the pit and the sherd must belong instead to Stratum VIII or later.

The juglet from Burial 152 (Fig. 5.3:18) is either Type IXB1a or b depending on the base, which is not preserved (Åström 1972b: Fig. 52:13–14; Gittlen 1977: Pl. 8). It has a funnel mouth; high tapering neck, which bulges at the point of the upper handle attachment; a strap handle that extends from the shoulder to the neck; and a piriform body. This juglet has approximately the same chronological and geographical distribution as the Type IXB jugs described above. Figure 5.3:19, which came from a poor Stratum VII context, belongs to Type IXB1b, as indicated by its everted ring base.

Figure 5.3:20 appears to be an imitation of a BR II jug (see also M. Dothan 1972: Pl. 7:1). A thick yellowish-white slip covers the vessel, and groups of diagonal and vertical painted lines decorate its body, which is vaguely biconical in shape. There is a slight bulge at the base of the neck and the ring base is splayed. The loop handle is attached to the exterior of the vessel, unlike imported BR jugs that have strap handles which pierce the vessel wall. Numerous similar imitation BR jugs were found in LB IIB funerary contexts at Lakhish (especially Tomb 532; Tufnell 1958: Pl. 81:896 [Class B]) and Deir el-Balaḥ (Tomb 303; Killebrew 1998a: Ill. III:18.5 [Form CA 35]). Petrographic analysis of imitation BR II jugs recently excavated at Jatt and Naḥal 'Iron (Wadi 'Ara) indicates that they were made somewhere along the Lebanese coast; therefore, it may be better to describe these jugs as 'Levantine' rather than 'local' imitations (Y. Gadot, pers. comm.).

The head of a BR II bull-shaped vessel (Fig. 5.4), which was found in an unreliable Stratum III context, should probably be ascribed also to Stratum IX (see also M. Dothan 1960a: Pl. 2:1; 1960c: Pl. 10:2). It belongs to the group of Type XVIB animal-shaped vases (Åström 1972b: Fig. 53:12, 15) that are known predominantly at Canaanite sites in LB IIA contexts (for references, see Nys 2001:113–116).

White Slip (Fig. 5.5)

White Slip (WS) Ware accounts for approximately half the total number of Cypriot imports at Tel Mor. Importation began on a small scale in Stratum XI, increased by Stratum IX and continued through Stratum VI. Most of the WS imports are bowls; however, two kraters (Fig. 5.5:9, 10) belong to the assemblage as well. Most bear the familiar brown (7.5YR 4/4) or dark reddish-gray paint (10R 3/1) applied on a thick white (7.5YR 8/1) or gray slip (2.5Y 7/1). The color of the fabric tends to be red (2.5YR 5/8) or reddish brown (2.5YR 4/4) with few fine to small white inclusions. Typically there is a gray core visible in the middle and interior side of the vessel wall.

A rim sherd from a Type Iaβ' WS I bowl was found in Courtyard 118 in the area of the Stratum XI *bāmāh* (Fig. 5.5:1; see also M. Dothan 1960c: Fig. 4:3). The main decorative motif is a horizontal row of lozenges framed by two pairs of parallel lines (Gittlen 1977:451, Pl. 14; see also Popham 1972:460). There is also a single wavy line below the rim. Petrie's excavations at Tell el-'Ajjul provide the best comparisons (mostly from City II) for this bowl type, as well as for the majority of WS I pottery found in Canaan (Bergoffen 2001b: Fig. 4:1–7; 2002: Fig. 3). In the new excavations the bulk of the WS I pottery came from Phase H3, which dates to LB IA (Fischer 2001:227–228). More specifically, it seems that the *floruit* of the framed lozenge style, of which Fig. 5.5:1 is an exemplar, dates to LC IB (Bergoffen 2002:30). The discovery of WS I near the *bāmāh* at Tel Mor, then, reinforces an LB I date for Stratum XI.

Most of the WS I pottery known from other Canaanite sites belongs also to LB IA (Gittlen 1977:415). For this reason, the transitional WS I–IIA rim sherd belonging to another Type Ia bowl, which is from a poorly stratified context (Sq H18–19), should probably be attributed also to Stratum XI (Fig. 5.5:2). The sloppily executed, pendant lozenge frieze framed by rows of dots is typical of late WS I pottery (cf. Popham 1972: Fig. 48:4, Pl. 80:2). Similar sherds have been found at Ḥazor in Area H, Stratum 2 (Yadin et al. 1989: Pls. 269:38, 312:6). Figure 5.5:3 has a slightly better executed pendant lozenge frieze, which is surrounded instead by lattice bands, also a characteristic of early WS II pottery (e.g., Popham 1972: Fig. 53:3; cf. Fig. 5.5:5 below). Despite its Stratum XII find-spot, this bowl rim probably dates to no earlier than LB I.

Figure 5.5:4 is a rim sherd from a Type IA WS I bowl with bichrome decoration. Below the rim there is a red wavy line, beneath which are two parallel dark lines. Two vertical dark lines frame another red wavy line. A few WS bowls with bichrome decoration have been found in Canaan in both LB I and II strata (for references, see Gittlen 1977:371, n. 12; more recently, see Fischer 2001:225) and on Cyprus in LC I contexts as, for example, recently at Maroni-Vournes in Stratum I (Cadogan et al. 2001: Fig. 10). In light of the sherd's small size and poor stratigraphic context—it is not clear if 'Wall 66' means near the wall or from among its mudbricks—it is reasonable to suppose that Fig. 5.5:4 was imported to Tel Mor during Stratum XI (LB I/Late Cypriot I), the *floruit* of WS bichrome production.

Figure 5.5:5 belongs to a class of early WS II pottery characterized by a horizontal lattice band painted below the rim with pendant rows of hatched lozenges (Type IA; Popham 1972:464–465). A bowl from a tomb at Arpera has identical decoration, which includes also plain pendant lozenges and a dotted row frieze around the rim (Popham 1972: Pl. 83:7). The type is relatively uncommon in Canaan, where it has been found at Bet She'an in Stratum VII (Type I1A'; Gittlen 1993: Fig. 56:14, Pl. 25g) and Ḥazor in Stratum 1A (Yadin et al. 1958: Pls. 92:16, 161:10, 11).

A noteworthy import is Fig. 5.5:6, a rare WS II Type IB bowl. It is distinguished by a loop handle below the rim (not preserved here) and painted decoration, which includes pendant dotted semicircles below a group of parallel lines (Popham 1972: Pl. 84:9; Gittlen 1977:465). There are also rows of dots on the rim and, unevenly, across the upper body. Tell el-Hesi (Petrie 1891: Pl. 8:156a) is the only other site in Canaan where this bowl type is known.

Figure 5.5:7 and 8 are Type IDβ bowls of the late WS II variety characterized by sloppily drawn, parallel line decoration (see also M. Dothan 1972: Pl. 7:2; for this type in general, see Popham 1972: Figs. 57:3–5, Pl. 86:2, 3; Gittlen 1977: Pl. 18). Type ID bowls represent the end of the WS sequence and appear at Canaanite sites primarily in LB IIB, as at Tel Afeq in Stratum X-12 (Beck and Kochavi 1985: Fig. 2:6), Tel Baṭash-Timna in Stratum VI (Panitz-Cohen and Mazar 2006: Pl. 57:9) and Bet She'an in Stratum N-5 (A. Mazar, pers. comm.). At Ashdod such bowls occur in Strata XV (Dothan and Freedman 1967: Fig. 21:8) and XIV (Dothan and Freedman 1967: Fig. 23:14, Pl. 13:2).

Figure 5.5:9 belongs to a vessel type rarely discovered at Canaanite sites. The presence of a row of hatched lozenges between lattice bands, although a common WS I motif, indicates that it is a Type 3, WS II early krater (Gittlen 1977: Pl. 20; Popham 1972:468). Similar kraters with a tubular spout and two loop handles have been found at Alalakh in Palace IV levels (Bergoffen 2004: Cat. Nos. WE6–8). Two other parallels, both apparently from residual contexts, derive from Bet She'an Stratum VII (Type I1Aβ'; Gittlen 1993: Fig. 56:16) and Gezer Stratum XIV (Dever 1986: Pl. 16:17).

Figure 5.5:10 is another Type 3, WS II early krater (Popham 1972: Fig. 53:4; Gittlen 1977: Pl. 20). The main decorative motif is a faintly visible hatched lozenge frieze between two lattice bands. Along the rim there are vertical strokes. The rim has an unusual triangular profile and the stub of a handle is preserved. The customary white slip has turned black due to firing conditions (cf. Dever 1986:58, n. 109, Pl. 16:17). Given that this WS II early sherd was retrieved from a poor stratigraphic context (Sq K18), it is likely that it, like Fig. 5.5:9, derives originally from Stratum IX.

White Shaved (Fig. 5.6)

Two White Shaved dipper juglets were also among the grave goods of Burial 152. They correspond to Type Ia and are common among LB IIA funerary assemblages (for references, see Gittlen 1977:358–364). Both have the characteristic knife-pared surface and white fabric. Another intact Type Ia juglet (Reg. No. B2 12/1) was recovered from the same square (M30), but at a higher elevation (12.55/12.40 m). It is likely that it belonged to Burial 152 or a nearby grave. At Ashdod these juglets came from Strata XV (Dothan and Freedman 1967: Fig. 21:5) and XIV (Dothan and Freedman 1967: Fig. 23:11, Pl. 13:7).

Bichrome (Fig. 5.7)

Tel Mor yielded approximately 20 sherds and vessels of a specific type of Bichrome pottery. Visual inspection indicates that this small assemblage, comprised almost entirely of kraters and jugs,[6] probably corresponds to Bichrome Wheel-Made Ware. This ware was produced both on Cyprus and in Canaan in the mid-second millennium BCE.[7] At Tel Mor, fittingly, most of this pottery derives from the Strata XII–XI elevations of Courtyard 118, thus MB IIC–LB IA, the *floruit* of

Bichrome Ware in Canaan (see below). Moreover, some of the Bichrome Ware (Fig. 5.7:3, 5, 9) was found in the same basket (B365), which appears to have been collected from a pit, along with Monochrome (Fig. 5.1:1, 3) and BR I (Fig. 5.3:3, 5) pottery.

In general, the Bichrome Ware at Tel Mor is well levigated and evenly fired, and often contains white and red inclusions. The color of the fabric tends toward brownish yellow (10YR 6/6) or light red (2.5YR 6/8). The painted decoration is red (10R 4/6) and black on a well-smoothed, even-polished surface that is sometimes also slipped. The motifs are mostly non-figural, such as joined spoked or solid wheels (Fig. 5.7:1, 2), cross-hatching (Fig. 5.7:3) and cross bands (Fig. 5.7:5); however, there is also a sherd that preserves part of a bird (Fig. 5.7:6). Bichrome Ware motifs, including most of the Tel Mor pottery on which they appear, was previously published by Epstein (1966:118–119).

Figure 5.7:1 is among the best preserved examples of Bichrome Ware excavated at Tel Mor (back cover; see also M. Dothan 1973: Fig. 4:1, Pl. 1B). This krater has the following morphological features: an everted rim; a short neck; a single horizontal handle (not fully preserved), which is attached to a rounded shoulder; globular body; and a ring base (Type A1[b]; see also Epstein 1966: Pl. 6:4). The decoration consists of groups of dark horizontal bands enclosing red bands, both below the rim and at mid-body. Joined spoked wheels, executed also in bichrome, fill the main frieze located in the shoulder zone. Close parallels, both in terms of form and decoration, have been found in Canaan at Lakhish in Fosse Temple I (Tufnell, Inge and Harding 1940: Pl. 39:60), Megiddo in House Z (Loud 1948: Pl. 134:3), Bet Shemesh in Stratum IVa (Grant 1934: Fig. 2:7) and Ras Shamra (Epstein 1966: Pl. 6:1). The krater depicted in Fig. 5.7:2, of which only the shoulder, neck and rim survive, is quite similar to Fig. 5.7.1 except for slight differences in the vessel's shape and decoration (see also M. Dothan 1960c: Fig. 4.4). The rim is flattened with a horizontal flange and is decorated with a dark band. The primary motif in the shoulder zone is a solid rather than a joined spoked wheel (Epstein 1966:63).

Figure 5.7:3 is a krater with an inward sloping neck and a flattened rim (see Epstein 1966: Pl. 19:3). Horizontal bichrome bands decorate the rim and ill-defined neck. The main frieze on the shoulder is comprised of latticed panel triglyphs (Epstein 1966:71–73) and cross lines in the metopes (Epstein

1966:83–87). A sherd with the latticed panel motif was found at Ashdod in Stratum XX (MB IIC/LB I), when Bichrome Ware first appears in large quantities at the site (Dothan and Porath 1993:29, Fig. 5:5, Pl. 31:5; see also Fig. 6:7, Pl. 31:12 [Stratum XIX]). The krater depicted in Fig. 5.7:4 has a gutter rim and a neck that slopes inward. There are bichrome strokes on the rim and horizontal bands on the neck, a combination of motifs common on Bichrome kraters (for references, see Epstein 1966: Pls. 6:1, 2; 16:1; 18:1, 3).

Figure 5.7:5 preserves a common Bichrome motif—namely, a series of hub and spokes set within a band of square frames (see also Epstein 1966: Pl. 16:4). Often this motif was oriented vertically on the shoulder or neck of a jar, as at Lakhish in the Interim LB I phase (Singer-Avitz 2004b: Fig. 18.7:4), Megiddo in Tomb 1100 (Guy 1938: Pl. 147:6) and Ḥazor in Tomb 8130 (Yadin et al. 1989: Pl. 242:1). This motif first appears at Tell el-Dabʻa in Phase D/1, which corresponds to the beginning of the XVIIIth Dynasty (Bietak 2001:177, Fig. 2). Along with Bichrome Ware in general, this motif (the 'union-jack square') is especially common at Tell el-ʻAjjul (e.g., Petrie 1931: Pl. 30:27; 1933: Pls. 42:26, 30, 40, 41; 43:70; 1934: Pl. 43:4).

Figure 5.7:6 preserves the front portion of a bird, which, along with fish, is the most popular figural motif of Bichrome Ware (see also Epstein 1966: Pl. 17:3). All that remain are parts of the beak, breast and three claws of a single leg that rest on a horizontal dark band. As reconstructed, the bird corresponds to Epstein's Category 2, which is characterized by a solid black body, triangular tail and absence of wings (1966:38, 39, Fig. 2). Figural motifs such as birds, similar to more complex linear patterns, also first appear in Phase D/1 at Tell el-Dabʻa (Bietak 2001: Fig. 12, Cat. No. 23).

Figure 5.7:7 is a jug with an ovoid body and flattened handle attached vertically on the shoulder (see also Epstein 1966: Pl. 19:1; M. Dothan 1973: Fig. 4:2). Groups of alternating dark and red bands frame the handle, which bears a reversed feather motif (Epstein 1966:75–76) and an incised 'X' (see Chapter 6, No. 2). Figure 5.7:8 is from the shoulder of another jug. Its preserved decoration consists of two dark wavy lines inside a bichrome-framed band panel (Epstein 1966:80) and part of a cross line motif.[8] Note also that an unusual jug, possibly a local imitation of Bichrome Ware, was found in a Stratum XII level of Courtyard 118 (see Fig. 3.27:3).

Figure 5.7:9 is a well-preserved Bichrome goblet decorated with an unusual stylized floral motif (back cover; see also M. Dothan 1973: Fig. 4:3). It has a conical body with a slight eversion at the rim and a marked carination near the juncture with its tall trumpet base (see Epstein 1966:19 [Type A2b]). The entire vessel is slipped and there are vertical burnish marks on the base. The decoration consists of thick, dark, vertical lines that begin at the point of carination and bifurcate near the rim. Upward-slanting diagonals connect these vertical lines to form a web that covers most of the body, with red paint filling the majority of spaces in between.

No other goblets excavated at Bronze Age Canaanite sites match Fig. 5.7:9 in terms of both form and decoration. Undecorated goblets from the MB II palace at Jericho are similar in shape except for their lack of carination and shorter bases (Garstang 1934: Pls. 21:3, 26:11). It is likely that the stylized floral motif imitates the modeled lotus pattern common on faience chalices found in Egypt beginning in the XVIIIth Dynasty (Davies 1982: Fig. 145; Gould, forthcoming).[9]

Cypriot Pottery: Summary and Discussion

The Cypriot pottery found at Tel Mor in Strata XII–X fits the established chronology and distribution patterns for early imports to Canaan at the end of MB IIC and the beginning of LB I. First, as is well known, Monochrome, Red-on-Black and Bichrome Wares initially appear during MB IIC (Stratum XII) and continue into LB IA (Strata XI–X). Of greater interest is the appearance of BR I pottery also in Stratum XII, in the earliest and best-stratified context of this stratum (Pit 166), resting immediately above bedrock (18.60–17.90 m). Moreover, Monochrome bowls (Fig. 5.1:1, 3) and Bichrome Ware (Fig. 5.7:3, 5, 9) were discovered along with BR I bowls (Fig. 5.3:3, 5) in Pit 166. There is a long-standing debate regarding whether BR I was first imported into Canaan during MB IIC (prior to the XVIIIth Dynasty; e.g., Merrillees 1968:191–192) or LB IA (e.g., Oren 1969:143–145). A re-evaluation of Petrie's excavations at Tell el-ʻAjjul indicates that the importation of BR I began there, at least on a small scale, during MB IIC (City III; Bergoffen 2001a:44–48). It seems, then, that sites in southern coastal Canaan, including Tel Mor, were among the earliest recipients of BR I pottery.

The types of Cypriot imports present at Tel Mor in Stratum IX are to be expected for LB IIA: BR II and WS II predominate, Monochrome continues and Red-on-Black and Bichrome pottery disappear. Moreover, many of the imports derive from funerary contexts (i.e., Burial 152), as was the case at the majority of Canaanite sites. Of note are the Type IA WS II bowl (Fig. 5.5:5) and the early WS II krater (Fig. 5.5:9), both of which are imports rarely found in Canaan.

Nor are the types and quantity of Cypriot pottery from Tel Mor Strata VI–V surprising for the end of the Late Bronze Age. The late WS II Type ID bowls (Fig. 5.5:7, 8) and the imitation of the BR II jug (Fig. 5.3:20) both derive from Stratum VI and are characteristic of LB IIB. It may be that Levantine potters produced more imitations at this time to compensate for the decreasing amounts of Cypriot imports. The limited corpus of Cypriot pottery from Tel Mor in Stratum VI seems to bear out this trend. With the exception of small, probably residual sherds, Stratum V yielded no imported Cypriot pottery. The combined absence of imports in Stratum V and initial appearance of Philistine Bichrome pottery in Stratum IV have important implications for the ongoing Iron I chronological debate (see Chapter 3; see also Barako, in press b).

The quantity and, more significantly, range of Cypriot pottery that was imported to Tel Mor at the end of the Middle Bronze Age and throughout the Late Bronze Age are to be anticipated given the site's location. Possessing one of the few safe anchorages on or near the Levantine coast, Tel Mor was a logical point of entry for foreign wares either for local consumption (i.e., Ashdod) or for distribution farther inland. The same is not true, however, for imported Mycenean pottery, of which there is a relative dearth.

MYCENEAN POTTERY (Fig. 5.8)

Approximately fifteen sherds of imported Mycenean pottery of the Late Helladic III period were recovered from a variety of Late Bronze Age contexts at Tel Mor. With the exception of a single flask (Fig. 5.8:7), the remaining diagnostic sherds belong to jugs and jars. The clay of all the Mycenean pottery is finely levigated and the fabric is evenly fired as is typical of these imports. The color of the clay tends to be reddish yellow (5YR 6/8) and the slip is usually a creamy, very pale brown (10YR 8/4). The paint varies from a lustrous red (10R 4/8) to a matte dark gray (7.5YR 4/1). The

following discussion of this small corpus draws on Mountjoy's updated version (e.g., 1999) of Furumark's (1941) typology.

All but the lower body and base of the jug depicted in Fig. 5.8:1 survive. The following features characterize its form: an everted rim with a rounded lip; a wide, tall neck; a round handle that extends from rim to shoulder; and a globular body. The decoration, which consists of matt dark brown paint on a creamy slip, is entirely linear: a thick horizontal band below the rim, another at the juncture of the neck and shoulder, and three thin bands at mid-body. A wavy line adorns the handle and there is a circle around the lower handle attachment. Apparently the upper body was turned on a wheel, whereas the lower body was handmade.

Figure 5.8:1 corresponds most likely to the medium jug FS 110, which first became popular in LH IIIB1 (Mountjoy 1986:93, Fig. 120); however, a closer parallel, both in terms of form and decoration, belongs to LH IIIC Early (Fig. 176:2 [Mycenae]; see also Mountjoy 1999: Fig. 70:125 [Korakou]). FS 110 is a rare import at Canaanite sites. The single possible attestation of this type in Tomb 117 at Tell es-Sa'idiyeh (Leonard 1994:40, #484), which has a narrower neck and piriform body, may in fact correspond to FS 105 (Pritchard 1980:5, Figs. 21:15, 57:1).

Figure 5.8:2 may belong to a Myc. IIIC:1b trefoil mouth jug. The rim is decorated with a horizontal band in black matt paint, as is typical with these jugs (Killebrew 2000:242, Fig. 12.3.7–9 [Form AS 9]; Dothan and Zukerman 2004:22, Fig. 27:10, 11 [Type H]). If this identification is correct, then this sherd is the only piece of Myc. IIIC:1b found at Tel Mor in any stratum. In terms of morphology, however, there is a discrepancy—the rim is straight and bulbous when it should be everted and triangular. Based strictly on elevation, this sherd should be assigned to Stratum VI, which corresponds approximately to the period of Myc. IIIC:1b production.

Figure 5.8:3 and 4 belong to stirrup jars. All that remains of Fig. 5.8:3 is the top of the false neck and stirrup handle. The neck is narrow, hollowed and slightly concave with a small convex disk at the false mouth. The one partially preserved handle is round. A spiral, executed with reddish matt paint applied directly to the surface, adorns the disk. A small fragment of another false neck was recovered from an unstratified context (Reg. No. A11/9; not drawn). Its disk is decorated with concentric circles in a lustrous dark paint. Part of the false spout and shoulder of a third stirrup jar is shown in Fig. 5.8:4.[10] The narrow spout is thickened slightly where it was inserted into the vessel wall. A thick band of lustrous dark gray paint encircles the base of the spout, and a group of thin, closely spaced curved lines decorate the shoulder.

It is difficult to date precisely these stirrup jars for the following two reasons: (1) their poor state of preservation and (2) the fact that stirrup jars were widely exported throughout Canaan for the entire LB II period (Leonard 1994:50–79). Notwithstanding, aspects of their morphology, decoration, and (albeit poor) stratigraphic context indicate that Fig. 5.8:3 and 4 should be attributed to between the LH IIIB1 and IIIC Early periods. Spiral decoration on a small disk atop the false mouth, and thin bands at the base of tall, narrow, false necks and spouts are all characteristic of stirrup jars of the LH IIIB1 and beyond (Mountjoy 1986:108). As for a *terminus ante quem*, neither jar can be later than LH IIIC Early given their find-spots (i.e., Strata VII and V). They probably correspond to the globular stirrup jar (FS 171, 173), which was the most popular closed shape toward the end of the LH III period (Mountjoy 1999:33, 43).

Figure 5.8:5 belongs to the shoulder of a closed vessel, perhaps a piriform jar, decorated with lustrous, reddish orange paint. Part of a central triglyph filled with horizontal wavy lines (FM 75) is visible. The most common motif of the LH IIIB period is this type of triglyph arranged in a paneled pattern (Mountjoy 1986: Figs. 143:17 [Mycenae], 148:14). In the panel to the left of the triglyph is part of an antithetic spiral (FM 50), and below is a group of horizontal bands. Such framed decorative zones, which first appear in the LH IIIB period, are particularly common on small and medium piriform jars (Mountjoy 1999:33). Figure

5.8:6 is the ring base of a closed vessel. The bottom is decorated with a thick horizontal band of reddish-orange lustrous paint.

Figure 5.8:7 belongs to a flask, a vessel type that was exported to the Levant especially during the LH IIIA2 period (Mountjoy 1986:81). Only the everted, rounded lip and part of a flat handle that attaches to the center of a narrow neck are preserved. The interior of the lip and the exterior of the top of the neck and handle are decorated with reddish lustrous paint. The flask probably corresponds to the horizontal type FS 190 (e.g., Mountjoy 1986: Fig. 96.1 [Mycenae]; 1999: Figs. 69:116 [Corinth], 114:73 [Pylos]), which has been found at several sites in Canaan, including Ḥazor in Stratum 1b (Yadin et al. 1960: Pl. 137:6–8).

All the diagnostic sherds of Mycenaean pottery excavated at Tel Mor belong to closed vessels. The jugs and jars (Fig. 5.8:1–6) were probably exported sometime during the LH IIIB or beginning of LH IIIC periods, which makes the probable LH IIIA2 flask (Fig. 5.8:7) the earliest Mycenaean import at the site. Because of its small size, fragmentary nature and poor stratigraphic context, it is difficult to extract much additional information from this limited assemblage. Of greater value, perhaps, is a comparison with the importation of Cypriot pottery, which was more numerous, diverse and long-lived. A quick examination of the distribution of imports at other southern Levantine sites reveals a similar ratio of Cypriot to Mycenaean pottery. To cite a prominent example, nearly a thousand Cypriot sherds and whole vessels were found at Tell el-'Ajjul (Bergoffen 1989:390–496), but there are less than fifty published Mycenaean imports at the site (Leonard 1994:202). Tel Mor, then, fits the general pattern of import distribution for the region during the Late Bronze Age.[11]

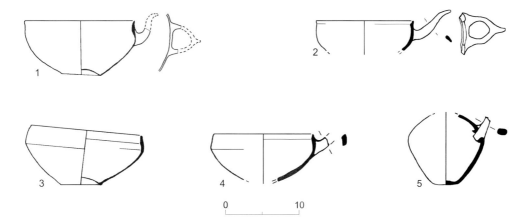

Fig. 5.1. Monochrome Ware.

No.	Object	Reg. No.	Context (Stratum)	Elevation (m)	Description
1	Bowl	B365	Pit 166 (XII)	18.65/17.90	Surface: 2.5YR 7/6 (light red); fabric: 7.5YR 6/6 (reddish yellow); core: none; inclusions: very few fine white
2	Bowl	B259/31	Courtyard 118 (XI)	19.25/19.10	Surface: 2.5YR 4/1 (dark reddish gray); fabric: 2.5YR 5/8 (red); core: none; inclusions: very few fine sparkling
3	Bowl	B365	Pit 166 (XII)	18.65/17.90	Surface: 10R 4/6 (red); fabric: 2.5YR 6/8 (light red); core: none; inclusions: none
4	Bowl	B289/5	Courtyard 118 (XII)	19.00/18.90	Surface: 2.5YR 6/6 (light red) to 2.5YR 4/1 (dark reddish gray); fabric: 5YR 6/6 (light red); core: none; inclusions: very few fine white, few fine to small voids
5	Jug	B191/2	Room 108 (VII)	22.80	N/A

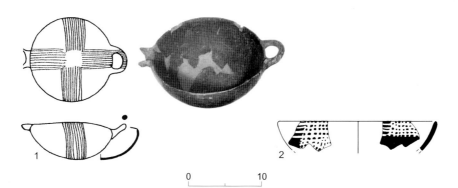

Fig. 5.2. Red-on-Black bowls.

No.	Reg. No.	Context (Stratum)	Elevation (m)	Description
1	B339	Courtyard 118 (XII)	18.80	Paint; N/A
2	B137/1	Sq M22 (XI)	19.70/19.50	Paint: 10R 5/6 (red); surface (slip): 5YR 4/1 (dark gray); fabric: 2.5YR 7/6 (light red); core: none; inclusions: none

Fig. 5.3 ▶

No.	Object	Reg. No.	Context (Stratum)	Elevation (m)	Description
1	Bowl	B355/3	Courtyard 118 (XII)	18.70/18.60	Molded decoration; irregular burnish; surface: 10YR 5/3 (brown); fabric: 5YR 6/6 (reddish yellow); core: thick, gray; inclusions: many fine to small white
2	Bowl	B281/2	Courtyard 118 (XII)	19.10	Surface: 2.5YR 2.5/1 (reddish black); fabric: 2.5YR 5/8 (red); core: N/A; inclusions: N/A
3	Bowl	B365/38	Pit 166 (XII)	18.65/17.90	Burnish; surface: 10R 5/6 (red); fabric: 2.5YR 6/6 (light red); core: none; inclusions: very few fine sparkling
4	Bowl	B342	Courtyard 118 (XII)	18.80	Surface: 2.5YR 3/1 (dark reddish gray); fabric: 5YR 5/1 (gray); core: none; inclusions: very few small white
5	Bowl	B365/70	Pit 166 (XII)	18.65/17.90	Burnish; surface: 2.5YR 3/1 (dark reddish gray); fabric: 5YR 5/1 (gray); core: none; inclusions: very few small white
6	Bowl	B131/1	Courtyard 118 (XI)	20.00	Surface: 10R 4/6 (red) and black; fabric: 2.5YR 5/8 (red); core: none; inclusions: many fine to small white
7	Bowl	B259/27	Courtyard 118 (XI)	19.25/19.10	Surface: 2.5YR 3/1 (dark reddish gray); fabric: 2.5YR 6/8 (light red); core: none; inclusions: none
8	Bowl	A531/1	W66? (VIII)	20.70/20.60	Molded decoration; surface: 10YR 4/1 (dark gray); fabric: 10YR 5/3 (brown); core: none; inclusions: few fine white, very few fine red
9	Bowl	B26/9	Room 108 (VII)	22.80	Surface; N/A
10	Jug	B85/1	Subfloor fill for Room 108 (IX)	22.05/21.85	Incised decoration; burnish; surface: 2.5YR 5/6 (red); fabric: same; core: light gray; inclusions: very few small white
11	Jug	B77/1	Courtyard 118 (X)	20.50/20.30	Molded decoration; surface: 2.5YR 4/2 (weak red); fabric: 2.5YR 5/6 (red); core: thick, gray; inclusions: few fine white, few fine dark
12	Jug	B240/36	Courtyard 118 (XI)	19.65/19.55	Surface: 2.5YR 4/1 (dark reddish gray); fabric: 2.5YR 6/8 (light red); core: thin, gray; inclusions: few fine white
13	Jug	B29/10	Room 108 (VII)	22.50	Surface: 5YR 5/4 (reddish brown); fabric: 10R 5/8 (red); core: thin, light gray; inclusions: few small voids
14	Juglet	B29/22	Room 108 (VII)	22.50	Burnish; surface: 2.5YR 5/8 (red); fabric: same; core: none; inclusions: very many fine to small white
15	Juglet	1955-15	Surface find		Molded decoration; surface: 7.5YR 7/4 (pink); fabric: Gley 2 5/1 (blueish gray); core: none; inclusions: none
16	Jug	B230/1	Burial 152 (IX)	11.85/11.65	Incised; paint: 10YR 8/3 (very pale brown); surface (slip): 2.5YR 6/4 (light reddish brown); fabric: 2.5YR 6/6 (light red); core: 10YR 8/3 (very pale brown); inclusions: very many fine to small voids, many fine white, few fine dark
17	Jug	B95/1	Pit 119 (VIII)	21.40	Paint; N/A
18	Juglet	B251	Burial 152? (IX)	11.75	Paint; N/A
19	Juglet	A322	Area 41 (VII)	22.25/22.15	Slip; N/A
20	Jug	A475/1	Room 71 (VI)	N/A	Paint: 5YR 4/4 (reddish brown); surface (slip): 5YR 7/2 (light gray); fabric: 7.5YR 7/3 (pink); core: N/A; inclusions: many medium to large white, many small to medium voids

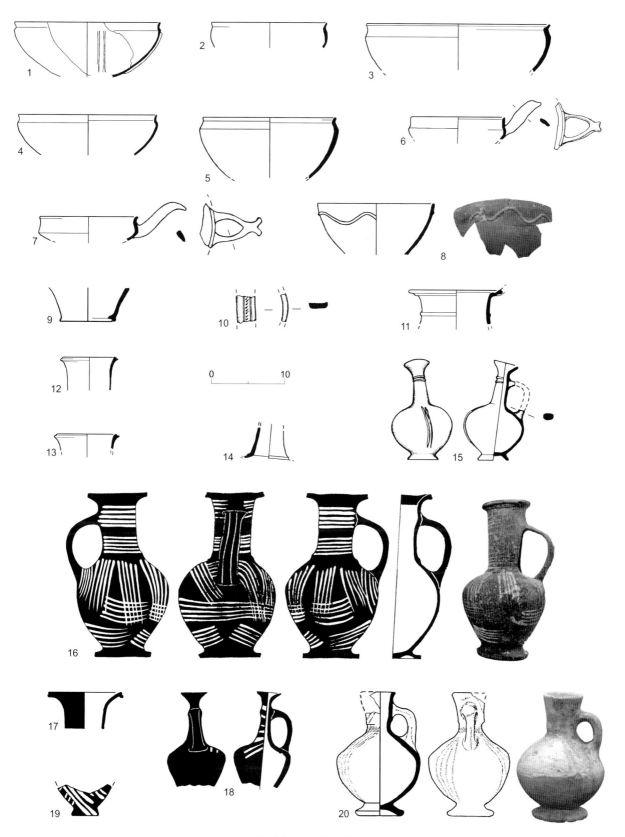

Fig. 5.3. Base Ring Ware.

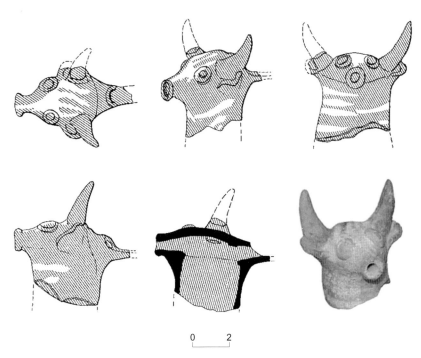

Fig. 5.4. A bull's head from a Base Ring II zoomorphic vessel from Stratum III; possibly to be ascribed to Stratum IX (Reg. No. A68/1; Sq M18, St. III, elevation 24.49).

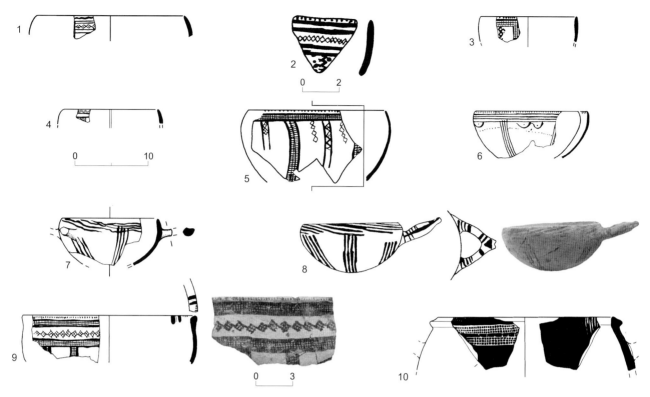

Fig. 5.5. White Slip Ware.

No.	Object	Reg. No.	Context (Stratum)	Elevation (m)	Description
1	Bowl	B108	Courtyard 118 (XI)	19.95	Paint: 10R 3/1 (dark reddish gray); surface (slip): 7.5YR 8/1(white); fabric: 2.5YR 4/4 (reddish brown); core: middle and interior, gray; inclusions: few fine to small white
2	Bowl	A511/2	Sqs H18–19 (N/A)	22.12	Paint: 7.5YR 2.5/1 (black); surface (slip): 10YR 8/2 (very pale brown); fabric: 5YR 5/8 (yellowish red); core: none; inclusions: few fine white
3	Bowl	B266/1	Courtyard 118 (XII)	19.50	Paint: 7.5YR 3/2 (dark brown); surface (slip): 2.5Y 7/3 (pale yellow); fabric: 5YR 5/4 (reddish brown); core: none; inclusions: few fine white
4	Bowl	A555/1	W66 (VIII)	21.40/21.26	Paint: 2.5YR 5/8 (red) and 5YR 3/4 (dark reddish brown); surface (slip): 2.5Y 8/1 (white); fabric: 2.5YR 5/6 (red); core: light gray, interior; inclusions: few fine white
5	Bowl	B81/2	Courtyard 118 (XI–IX)	20.30	Paint: 7.5YR 4/4 (brown); surface (slip): 10YR 8/1 (white); fabric: 5YR 5/6 (yellowish red); core: thick, gray; inclusions: few fine white
6	Bowl	A590/1	Room 63 (VII)	22.00/21.85	Paint: 5YR 4/2 (dark reddish gray); surface (slip): 10YR 7/3 (very pale brown); fabric: 2.5YR 5/1 (reddish gray); core: none; inclusions: very few fine white
7	Bowl	A501/2	Room 71 (VI)	N/A	Paint: 2.5YR 4/3 (reddish brown); surface (slip): 10YR 6/3 (pale brown); fabric: 7.5YR 5/6 (strong brown); core: thick, light gray; inclusions: few fine to small white
8	Bowl	A501/1	Room 71 (VI)	N/A	Paint: 2.5YR 4/4 (reddish brown); surface (slip): 7.5 YR 7/2 (pinkish gray); fabric: 10R 4/8 (red); core: N/A; inclusions: few small voids, few small dark
9	Krater	B204/1	Sqs M–N22 (IX)	20.30/20.10	Paint: 10YR 3/2 (very dark grayish brown); surface (slip): 10YR 8/2 (very pale brown); fabric: 5YR 4/6 (yellowish red); core: gray, middle and interior; inclusions: many fine to small white
10	Krater	A719	Sq K18 (VII–VI)	22.25	Paint: 5YR 4/3 (reddish brown); surface (slip): Gley 12.5/N (black); fabric: 5YR 5/6 (yellowish red); core: thick, gray; inclusions: few fine sparkling

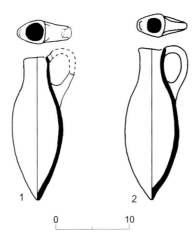

Fig. 5.6. Burial 152 (Stratum IX) White Shaved juglets.

No.	Reg. No.	Elevation (m)	Description
1	B237/1	11.85/11.60	Shaved; N/A
2	B248/1	N/A	Shaved; N/A

Fig. 5.7 ▶

No.	Object	Reg. No.	Context (Stratum)	Elevation (m)	Description
1	Krater	B279/1	N/A	N/A	Paint: 2.5YR 5/8 (red) and 5YR 3/1 (very dark gray); surface (slip): 7.5YR 7/3 (pink); fabric: 2.5YR 6/4 (light reddish brown); core: none; inclusions: many fine dark, many fine voids, few medium white, very few fine sparkling
2	Krater	B76	Probe 117 (X)	19.85	Paint: 10R 4/6 (red) and 2.5YR 3/1 (dark reddish gray); surface (slip): 2.5Y 8/3 (pale yellow); fabric: 10YR 7/6 (yellow); core: none; inclusions: many fine to small white, few fine red
3	Krater	B365/65	Pit 166 (XII)	19.65/19.55	Paint: 10R 4/6 (red) and black; surface: 10R 5/8 (red); fabric: same; core: none; inclusions: few fine to small dark, very few fine to small white
4	Krater	B144/1	Courtyard 118 (XI–IX)	20.25	Paint: 2.5YR 4/8 (red) and black; surface: 7.5YR 7/4 (pink); fabric: same; core: none; inclusions: N/A
5	Krater?	B365/74	Pit 166 (XII)	19.65/19.55	Paint: 10R 4/6 (red); 2.5YR 3/1 (dark reddish gray); surface (slip): 10YR 6/6 (brownish yellow); fabric: same; core: N/A; inclusions: few fine to small red, few fine white
6	Jug	B188/2/1	Sqs M–N22 (IX)	20.40/20.20	Paint; N/A
7	Jug	B366	Courtyard 118 (XII)	N/A	Paint: 10R 3/3 (dusky red) and black; surface: 5YR 6/4 (light reddish brown); fabric: same; core: none; inclusions: few fine voids, few medium to large dark and white
8	Jug	B348/23	Courtyard 118 (XI–IX)	N/A	Paint: 10R 4/6 (red) and 2.5YR 4/1 (dark reddish gray); surface: 2.5YR 6/8 (light red); fabric: same; core: none; inclusions: N/A
9	Goblet	B365	Pit 166 (XII)	18.65/17.90	Paint: 10R 4/6 (red), black; surface (slip): 7.5YR 7/4 (pink); fabric: same; core: N/A; inclusions: many fine dark, few fine white, few small voids

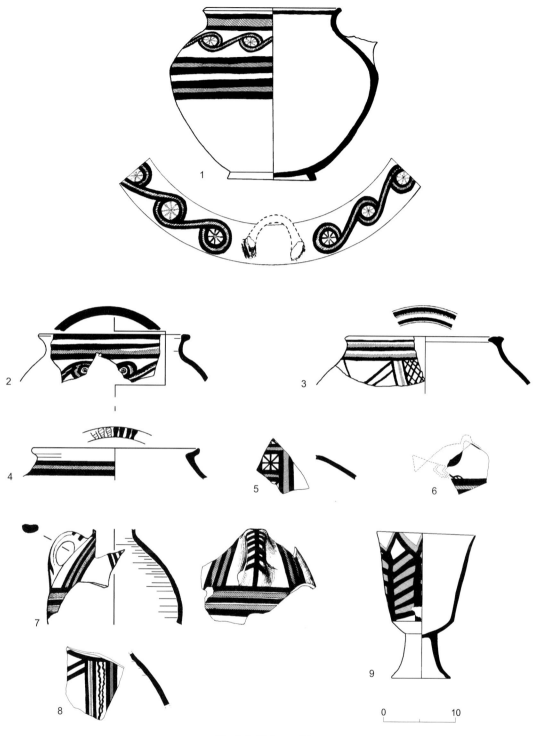

Fig. 5.7. Bichrome Ware.

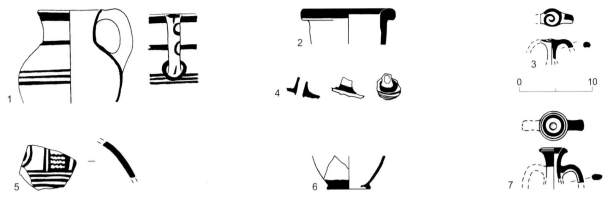

Fig. 5.8. Mycenean pottery.

No.	Object.	Reg. No.	Context (Stratum)	Elevation (m)	Description
1	Jug	A635/1	Sq L19 (VIII–VII?)	21.36	Paint: 7.5YR 3/3 (dark brown); surface (slip): 7.5YR 6/4 (light brown); fabric: same; core: none; inclusions: very few fine to small voids
2	Jug	A388/5	Sq K18 (N/A)	22.90/22.60	Paint: N/A
3	Stirrup jar	A366/6	Sqs K–L18 (V)	23.60/23.30	Paint: 2.5YR 3/6 (dark red); surface: 2.5YR 7/6 (light red); fabric: same; core: none; inclusions: N/A
4	Stirrup jar	A472/24	Sq K18 and Sq L18 (VII)	22.25/22.15	Paint: 5YR 3/1 (very dark gray); surface: 7.5YR 8/3 (pink); fabric: 10YR 7/3 (very pale brown); core: none; inclusions: many fine voids, very few fine white
5	Jar or jug	A393/2	Sq J19	N/A	Paint: 10R 4/8 (red); surface (slip): 7.5YR 8/3 (pink); fabric: 5YR 5/8 (yellowish red); core: none; inclusions: N/A
6	Jar or jug	A588/1	Fill above Room 63 (VI)	22.10/22.05	Paint: 10R 4/8 (red); surface (slip): 10YR 8/4 (very pale brown); fabric: 2.5YR 7/4 (light reddish brown); core: none; inclusions: few fine dark
7	Flask	B117/14	Sq M23	20.20	Paint: 10R 4/8 (red); surface (slip): 7.5YR 8/3 (pink); fabric: 5YR 5/8 (yellowish red); core: none; inclusions: N/A

NOTES

[1] The author benefited from many valuable suggestions offered by Celia Bergoffen regarding the Cypriot imports from all strata at Tel Mor.

[2] Cf. Gittlen, who believes that the bowl may belong to Type IF (1977:338–339, n. 32).

[3] Note also that Åström examined the body of a Stratum VII jug, possibly Type VIII2c(?) Monochrome or Type VIC3b Base Ring I, which was stored in the Rockefeller Museum (1972a:736).

[4] The author wishes to thank Paul Åström for verifying the identification of this small corpus of Red-on-Black pottery.

[5] An additional BR II jug, not drawn here, was also found with the burial; it is currently on display at the Ashdod Museum.

[6] It was not possible to locate the "part of a shallow bowl, Type B2(a)", apparently registered as Basket No. B61/2, that Epstein examined (1966:118, n. 11).

[7] Neutron Activation Analysis indicated that the majority of likely Bichrome Ware sherds sampled from Tel Mor (9 out of 12?) were made of Cypriot clay (Artzy, Asaro and Perlman 1973:460–461).

[8] The registration number of a Cross Line Style jug (not located by the present author) is reported variously by Epstein as B365/77 (1965:49) and B365/72 (1966:118, n. 10). According to the pottery registry, the former corresponds to a carinated bowl, whereas the latter is a jug.

[9] For a Cypro-Minoan potmark on the handle of a possible Plain White Wheel-Made jug, see Chapter 6, No. 1.

[10] It is possible also that this spout belongs to a feeding bottle; however, the shoulder appears to be too straight for this type of vessel (cf. Mountjoy 1986: Figs. 126 [Zygouries], 179 [Perati]).

[11] For the small corpus of Egyptian imports, which is somewhat atypical for Late Bronze Age Canaan, see Fig. 4.9.

CHAPTER 6

POTMARKS

NICOLLE HIRSCHFELD

INTRODUCTION

Twelve potmarks[1] have been recorded among the finds from Tel Mor (Fig. 6.1). They are all simple marks, and only one may possibly be part of a longer inscription. They are incised, mostly into handles. At present, we do not know enough about the potmarking practices of the Late Bronze Age Levant to ascertain whether the assemblage recovered from Tel Mor is typical or unusual.

POTMARKS IN THE LEVANT

Potmarking practices varied widely in the different regions of the Bronze and Iron Age eastern Mediterranean. Pottery circulating within the Late Bronze Age Aegean was almost never marked.[2] However, Egyptians and Cypriots marked the vases they used, though only certain shapes, with certain kinds of marks. Mycenean pottery imported into the Levant occasionally bore incised or painted marks, most likely made by Cypriot traders en route to the Levantine coast (Hankey 1967, 1970; Hirschfeld 2002:108, n. 61). The situation changed in the transition to the Iron Age, when the practice of marking pottery fell off in Cyprus but seems to have gained currency in the Levant.

The marked pottery found at Tel Mor that can be securely dated is mostly from the Late Bronze Age. The extent to which the inhabitants of Late Bronze Age Palestine marked their pottery is not clear. Very few potmarks appear in the published catalogues of local coarse wares from Late Bronze Age strata, a dearth that may simply reflect oversight by archaeologists. In general, potmarks receive attention as a by-product of other studies: when there is some reason to associate the marks with inscriptions or (proto-) writing; and when the marks happen to appear on vases that are under study for other purposes (e.g., imported Mycenean pottery). But many potmarks do not garner such attention. They tend to comprise very simple patterns (i.e., impressed dots, series of parallel grooves, incised X's, crosses) and appear on coarse utilitarian vases.

In every instance where I have been invited to look more closely at the collections or field notes from a Late Bronze Age excavation in Palestine, some potmarks have come to light.[3] Yet at present, we do not know the range of marks, the kinds of vases marked or the distributions of the markings. The topic needs concentrated study. Single-site studies of solitary marks, especially simple ones, rarely tell their own story. Simple potmarks can be understood only through analysis in quantity. The larger pattern of potmarking practices in Late Bronze Age Palestine remains to be understood; this report on the marks found at Tel Mor is a beginning.[4]

THE POTMARK ASSEMBLAGE

The size of potmark assemblages tends to increase when attention is paid to utilitarian wares. The Tel Mor assemblage is a good example. Only one mark appears on a decorated vase (No. 2), another is on a small thin-walled body sherd of a vessel of indeterminate shape and fabric (No. 12), but the rest of the marked finds are plain and coarse.

Number 2 is the only mark that appears on a definite import, a Cypriot Bichrome jug. It is likely that No. 1 is also a Cypriot import; it is possible that some of the marked storage jars are also imported, perhaps also from Cyprus (e.g., Hadjicosti 1988; Jones and Vaughan 1988; Sugerman 2000). Whether a marked vase is an import or a local production is vital in the interpretation of the possible reasons for marking a vessel. The small number and the uncertain origin(s) of the marked vases found at Tel Mor provide evidence neither for nor against a local marking practice. There is no pattern, spatial or chronological, to the find-spots of the potmarks.

Despite the aforementioned limitations of the evidence from Tel Mor, there are points to be made about this material. It should be noted at the outset that it was not possible for me to inspect the marked pottery from Tel Mor firsthand. This report is based solely on examination of digital images and/or drawings, and descriptions provided by the author of this volume. One crucial aspect of the marks cannot therefore be addressed here, namely, whether the marks were made before or after firing. It can be a difficult distinction to make, but it remains an important one, because marks made before firing must have been incised at the place of production. Marks incised into wet clay are easy to identify by a characteristic ridge raised on either side of the incised groove, the result of clay being pushed aside by the incising tool. Even if wear reduces the visibility of the ridge on either side of the incised groove, evidence of the ridge will remain in the junctions. But it is much more difficult to differentiate between signs incised into clay at the leather-hard stage and those cut into fired clay. Ten of the twelve potmarks found at Tel Mor have been photographed; none show evidence of pre-firing ridges. Based solely on visual inspection of the images, it seems likely that seven of these ten marks were made after firing (Nos. 1–6, 8). No determination could be made for the others.

No. 1. Cypriot(?) Plain Jug

Based on the present state of knowledge, Cyprus is the single region in the Late Bronze Age eastern Mediterranean with a potmarking system characterized by large single marks incised into the handles of medium to large closed containers. This marking system is in some way related to Cypro-Minoan, the writing system(s) in use on Late Bronze Age Cyprus, but the exact nature of the relationship is still unclear and not all the marks appearing on pottery can be identified with signs appearing in the formal texts.[5] The potmarking system was used not only on vases circulating within Cyprus, but also appears on vases exported from the island or traveling on cargos passing through Cyprus or through the hands of Cypriot traders (Hirschfeld 2002:108, n. 61).

The mark incised on the handle of No. 1 fits the characteristics of the Cypriot potmarking system and can reasonably be identified as evidence of Cypriot handling of this vase. Although the mark itself cannot be identified with any known sign of the Cypro-Minoan syllabary, its form—especially the 'flag' or 'tick'—accords well with the general character of the

signs attested for Cypriot Late Bronze Age writing.[6] The mark's manner of application and placement also conform to typical Cypriot practice: a single mark, incised into hard clay, conspicuous in its size and location on the vase. Finally, the shape and fabric of this jug recall the most commonly marked vase type in Cyprus (Plain Ware and Plain White Wheel-Made [PWWM] jugs of medium to large size). In fact, its shape and fabric strongly suggest that it should be identified as a Cypriot import (see Dothan 1960: Pl. 10:5); in the absence of firsthand or scientific (e.g. petrographic analysis) verification, this identification must remain a hypothesis.

No. 2. Cypriot Bichrome Jug

An 'X' is incised through the paint and into hard clay on No. 2, and appears to have been made after firing. It is impossible to know whether this mark was cut on Cyprus, at Tel Mor, or somewhere in between. An 'X' is a frequent choice for a mark, regardless of time or place. In both the Bronze Age Levant and Cyprus, however, this particular 'X' would be unusual. In the Levant, there is as yet no clear evidence for the routine marking of pottery of any kind; and in Cyprus, the custom of marking vases did not usually extend to Bichrome jars.

Nos. 3–9. Storage Jars with Single Mark Incised on Handle

The marks on Nos. 3–9 are all simple: a single line, cross, 'X' and pi-shaped mark. Four of the handles can be assigned dates between MB IIC and the end of the Late Bronze Age. The contexts of the remaining three handles are uncertain. While storage-jar handles with large incised marks are ubiquitous at Late Bronze Age sites in Cyprus, the situation on the Levantine coast is not clear.

The marks and jars from Tel Mor fit Cypriot marking practices; thus it is possible that these marked handles may be indicative of some Cypriot connection. Perhaps the jars were imported from Cyprus or Cypriots were involved in some other capacity. But the simple nature of the marks and our uncertain knowledge of the extent to which Canaanites marked their jars preclude definitive conclusions. At this point the primary task is to publish all marked pottery and thus begin to build a corpus on the basis of which it will be possible to delineate the local use of potmarks in Late Bronze Age and Iron Age Palestine.

Number 5 carries its mark at the base of the handle. Most storage-jar handles are marked in the upper third, as if made to be visible when looking down or straight at the jars. Marks at the base of the handle are rare and almost always very simple in form. This suggests that the marks at the bases of handles and those at the top were made for different purposes. Orientation may also indicate the purpose of marks. Where was the inscriber sitting or standing when making the mark, and what does that tell us about its function? Especially in the case of simple marks, it is often impossible to establish a mark's orientation. In those instances when marks on handles can be identified with signs of the Cypriot writing system, the marks are most often oriented along the vertical axis of the handle, with the top of the sign in the direction of the mouth of the jar. Although it is too simple to be certainly identified with any writing system, No. 8 could be the Cypro-Minoan sign 59 or 78, in which case it is perpendicular to the customary orientation.

No. 10. Storage Jar with Multiple Marks

Number 10 (see Fig. 3.23:12) is remarkable for the number of its marks and their distribution: two parallel strokes at the base of the single preserved handle, an 'X' at mid-belly, another mark of undetermined form also at mid-belly and a series of five(?) parallel strokes just below mid-belly. It is unknown whether these marks were incised before or after firing, or whether the incisions were made by the same tool or in the same manner. Thus, questions of whether these marks were all made at the same time for the same purpose, or are traces of marking at various stages of the jar's production, transfer and use, remain unanswerable. Since two of the marks on this jar consist of series of parallel strokes, it is tempting to interpret the marks as numerical in nature.[7]

Most Late Bronze Age potmarks have been preserved singly on the broken handles or bases of vases. Perhaps by accident of discovery/preservation, the general impression received is of a single mark per vase. This impression is substantiated in most of those few instances where complete vases with marks have been recovered. A second substantial category of preserved marks, also suggestive of single-purpose marking, are the multiple marks that have been incised or painted on

the vase as a 'set' or an 'associated series'.[8] The few marked, complete 'Canaanite' storage jars, Cypriot Plain ware jugs and Mycenean decorated vases found in tombs and shipwrecks characteristically display either a single mark or a closely associated set of marks that can be assumed to have been applied simultaneously, for a single purpose. But the archaeological record occasionally preserves traces of different kinds of marks applied to a single vase. So, for example, a piriform jar discovered at Tiryns carries an incised mark on one handle and a painted mark on another.[9] One handle of a coarse ware stirrup jar found in the storerooms of an Egyptian fortress at Zawyet Umm el-Rakham bears two different marks, clearly not cut by the same tool or for the same purpose (pers. obs.). The scattered and disparate appearance of the marks on No. 10 suggests that it may be another example of a jar marked at different times for different purposes; identification (perhaps possible through firsthand visual inspection) of pre- and post-firing marks would support this hypothesis.

No. 11. Handle with Two Marks

A handle fragment partially preserves two incised marks, one of which is probably a simple cross. The sherd comes from a poor context and its date is uncertain. Its identification as a storage jar is also dubious since the section is unusual for this form. The one sign is too simple and the other too fragmentary for a certain identification with any writing or marking system, Late Bronze Age or otherwise.

In the face of these uncertainties, any discussion of this handle in terms of writing practices is highly tenuous. With that proviso firmly in mind, I will nevertheless suggest the possibility that this handle fragment preserves traces of Cypriot writing. The drawing shows grooves of similar dimensions for both marks, and it looks as if the same tool might have been used to cut them. Of course, the actual marks need to be carefully inspected firsthand and under magnification in order to confirm this hypothesis. This detail is important because two marks associated by location and alignment and method of application (ductus) may be indicative of writing.[10] Furthermore, if the handle is Late Bronze Age in date, it is most likely that such an inscription would be based on the Cypriot writing system. In general, inscriptions on vases are very rare in the Late Bronze Age eastern Mediterranean and,

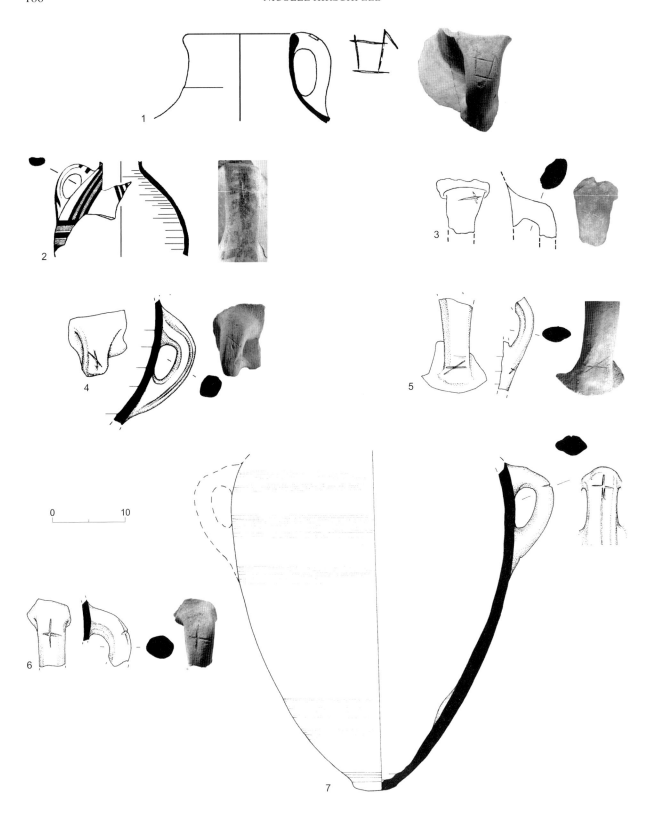

0   10

Fig. 6.1. Potmarks.

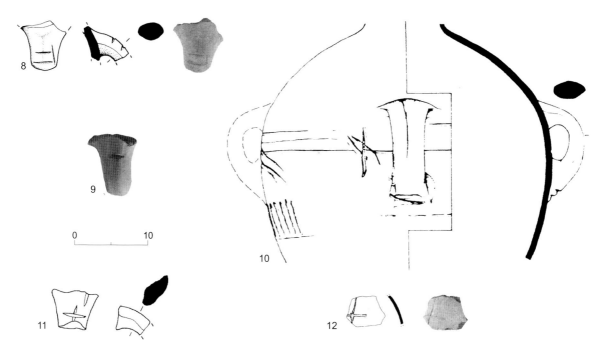

Fig. 6.1 (cont.). Potmarks.

No.	Object	Reg. No.	Context (Stratum)	Elevation (m)	Description
1	Jar	A305	Area 41 (VII)	22.30	N/A
2	Jug	B366	Courtyard 118 (XII)	N/A	See Fig. 5.7:7
3	Storage jar	A30/17	Sq L18 (II)	25.00/24.85	N/A
4	Storage jar	B357/1	Room 63? (VIII?)	N/A	N/A
5	Storage jar	B256/46	Courtyard 118 (XI?)	20.40/20.25	N/A
6	Storage jar	A698/1	Pit 85 (IX)	20.70/20.15	Surface: 2.5YR 7/3 (light reddish brown); fabric: 2.5YR 4/4 (reddish brown); core: dark gray; inclusions: few fine sparkling, few small voids, few small white
7	Storage jar	A699	Pit 35? (VI)	N/A	Surface: 10YR 6/6 (brownish yellow); fabric: same; core: light gray; inclusions: many fine to small voids
8	Storage jar	A375	Pit 55 (Hellenistic)	21.45/20.25	Surface: 10R 7/6 (light red); fabric: same; core: thick, light gray; inclusions: very many fine to small dark, many fine sparkling, few small white
9	Storage jar	B354/4	Subfloor fill(?) under Room 137 (XII–X)	N/A	Self-slip; N/A
10	Storage jar	B33	Room 108 (VII)	22.32	See Fig. 3.23:12
11	Storage jar?	A15/13	Sq L19	25.10/25.00	N/A
12	Jar?	A252	Sq L19 (VI)	23.50/23.35	N/A

when they do occur, they appear on the shoulders or bodies of the vessel. The few inscriptions on handles known to me all follow conventions used by persons employing Cypriot script or Cypriot marking systems. Nothing in the drawing belies an identification of these marks as Cypriot signs, and there is as yet no basis for any alternative explanation within the context of the Late Bronze Age eastern Mediterranean. Identification of the origin of this handle, whether local or imported, is particulary important in interpreting the significance of this possible Cypriot inscription.

The recent publication (Cross and Stager 2006) of 18 potmarks from Late Bronze Age and Iron I contexts at Ashqelon illustrates the impact that a few new discoveries can have on interpretations of the small corpus of known potmarks from the Levant. This is not the forum in which to debate the authors' conclusions, but it is appropriate here to signal one advance and one caution in methodology. Singularly important is the added dimension of petrographic analyses. The origin of a vase is vitally important to defining the possible function(s) of its mark. The Ashqelon study, like the earlier publication of a marked sherd found in Late Bronze Age Tel Afeq (Yasur-Landau and Goren 2004), demonstrates the successful—and here, essential—incorporation of the results of petrographic analysis into potmark inquiry. The caveat lies in the identification of individual marks as signs of writing, or even of a particular script. This can be done only if a mark is complex enough to make identification with a sign of a specific script compelling, or it can be identified as fitting into a coherent marking system with demonstrated (formal and/or historical) ties to a writing system.[11] For the Late Bronze Age Levant, we lack convincing or sufficient raw data to identify the potmarking systems used, much less their relationship to specific scripts.

No. 12. Body Sherd

A small thin-walled body sherd preserves part of an incised mark. The breaks make it impossible to reconstruct the shape of the mark; it may be a simple cross or the edge of a more complex sign. Vase shape and fabric are indeterminate; it appears to be a shoulder fragment. Egyptian amphorae and the Linear B-inscribed stirrup jars from the Aegean regularly carry marks on their shoulders, but otherwise Late Bronze Age vases are rarely marked on their bodies.[12] There is no pattern to the types of mark which do occasionally appear on bodies: five storage jars from the Ulu Burun shipwreck carry incised marks at the sharp shoulder carination;[13] and a few storage jars from terrestrial sites bear a large painted or incised mark on the belly.[14]

CONCLUSIONS

In and of itself, a simple potmark delivers little information. The marks discovered at Tel Mor are simple in form, and the stratigraphic contexts of the marked vases do not clarify the marks' functions or makers. However, as marks at different sites are cataloged, the larger context of the Tel Mor marks will become clearer. The local marking systems of Late Bronze Age Palestine must be recorded in order to understand their regional and chronological limits. This chapter is a contribution to the first step in this process: the publication of the complete corpus of marks discovered at a site.

In closing, two hypotheses can be raised upon examination of the assemblage of marked pottery from Tel Mor. First, marked pottery is rare at Tel Mor and at the other sites in Late Bronze Age Palestine whose potmark assemblages I have examined. No site has a sufficient amount of preserved marks to determine their purpose; there are no significant clusters. Perhaps this scattered distribution is an indication that marks were used for extra-site purposes. In addition, the marks at Tel Mor suggest the possibility of some connection with Cyprus or Cypriots. No single piece of evidence is compelling, but the indications—the Cypriot(?) jug with a characteristically Cypriot mark (No. 1), the imported Cypriot bichrome vase (No. 2), a possible Cypriot inscription (No. 11) and the storage jars marked in characteristic Cypriot fashion (Nos. 3–9)—seem significant when considered together.

Notes

[1] 'Potmark' is a neutral term that can be used to describe a mark applied at any point during the manufacture, exchange, use, purposeful deposit or final discard of a vase. This is different than the term 'potter's mark', which implies that the mark was applied in the course of the vase's manufacture.

[2] The coarse-ware stirrup jars with Linear B inscriptions are the single significant exception.

[3] Again I thank the many excavators (the list is too long to include here) who have generously shared their material and notes with me.

[4] I am grateful to Tristan Barako for the invitation to participate in this study.

[5] For a critique of the commonly cited sign lists proposed in Masson 1974:12–15, Figs. 1–4, see Palaima 1989. For a discussion of the uncertain relationship between Cypriot marks and the Cypriot script, see Hirschfeld 2000:181–182 and 2002:92–94.

[6] For the Cypro-Minoan sign-list, see Masson 1974.

[7] Not enough marked jars with sufficient profile preserved to calculate volume have been recovered to test the hypothesis that 'numerical' marks may record volume. Nor have marked vases been found in clusters, which could support a hypothesis that the marks represent quantities of vases or batch marks. It is difficult to suggest how the hypothesis that these marks represent value ('price') could be confirmed archaeologically.

[8] It is not always clear whether or not multiple marks on a single vase should be considered as separate marks or as an associated series. This is the case with many stirrup jars, piriform jars and 'Canaanite' storage jars with more than one incised handle. I have adopted the following guideline: two or more marks associated by location *and* alignment *and* method of application (ductus) constitute an associated series rather than individual potmarks.

[9] Tiryns 27985, most recently published in Olivier 1988:255, 257, Fig. 4; see also Hirschfeld 2000:177, n. 31 for several other examples.

[10] According to Olivier and Godart (1978:34), 'a group of at least two signs' is the definition of an 'inscription'; see also the discussion in Hirschfeld 2000:164, n. 6.

[11] As, for example, with the marks incised into LH III Aegean vases (Hirschfeld 1992).

[12] This may be partially a happenstance of recovery, as handles and bases are diagnostic sherds and thus are more likely to be examined and/or saved during excavation. Marks on body sherds are much more easily overlooked.

[13] KW 93, 130, 1957, 2343, 2353 (unpublished; I thank C. Pulak for providing access to the material).

[14] Ḥazor FN: C 11083 (Yadin et al. 1958: Pls. 89:7, 158:8); Hala Sultan Tekke F 1200, 1209, 1222, 1261 (Hult 1981:7, 27, 31, Fig. 63); Enkomi 718/7 (Dikaios 1969–1971: vol. II, 596; vol. IIIa, Pls. 77:23, 125:4); Mycenae, Nauplion 11454 (Cline 1994:170, No. 308); Zawyet Umm el-Rakham (unpublished; I thank S. Snape for providing access to this material). It is now possible to add Tel Mor to this list of sites.

References

Cline E. 1994. *Sailing the Wine-Dark Sea: International Trade and the Late Bronze Age Aegean* (BAR Int. S. 591). Oxford.

Cross F. and Stager L.E. 2006. Cypro-Minoan Inscriptions Found in Ashkelon. *IEJ* 56:129–159.

Dikaios P. 1969–1971. *Enkomi: Excavations 1948–1958* I–III. Mainz.

Dothan M. 1960. Excavations at Tel Mor (1959 Season). *BIES* 24:120–132 (Hebrew).

Hadjicosti M. 1988. 'Canaanite' Jars Fragments from Maa-Palaeokastro. In V. Karageorghis and M. Demas eds. *Excavations at Maa-Palaekastro, 1979–1986*. Nicosia. Pp. 340–385.

Hankey V. 1967. Mycenaean Pottery in the Middle East: Notes on Finds Since 1951. *BSA* 62:107–148.

Hankey V. 1970. Mycenaean Trade with the Southeastern Mediterranean. *Mélanges de l'Université Saint-Joseph* 46:11–30.

Hirschfeld N. 1992. Cypriot Marks on Mycenaean Pottery. In J.-P. Olivier ed. *Mykenaïka: Bulletin de Correspondence Hellenique Supplement* 25:315–319.

Hirschfeld N. 2000. Marked Late Bronze Age Pottery from the Kingdom of Ugarit. In M. Yon, V. Karageorghis and N. Hirschfeld eds. *Céramiques mycéniennes* (Ras Shamra-Ougarit XIII). Paris–Nicosia. Pp. 163–200.

Hirschfeld N. 2002. Marks on Pots: Patterns of Use in the Archaeological Record at Enkomi. In J. Smith ed. *Script and Seal Use on Cyprus in the Bronze and Iron Ages* (AIA Colloquia and Conference Papers 4). Boston. Pp. 49–109.

Hult G. 1981. *Hala Sultan Tekke 7: Excavations in Area 8 in 1977* (SIMA 45:7). Göteborg.

Jones R.E. and Vaughan S.J. 1988. A Study of Some 'Canaanite' Jar Fragments from Maa-Palaeokastro. In V. Karageorghis and M. Demas eds. *Excavations at Maa-Palaekastro, 1979–1986*. Nicosia. Pp. 386–398.

Masson E. 1974. *Cyprominoica: Repertoires, documents de Ras Shamra, essays d'interpretation* (SIMA 31:2). Göteborg.

Olivier J.-P. 1988. Tirynthian Graffiti: Ausgrabungen in Tiryns 1982/83. *Archäologischer Anzeiger* 9–10:253–268.

Olivier J.-P. and Godart L. 1978. *Fouilles exécutées à Mallia: le quartier Mu* I: *introduction générale, écriture hiéroglyphique crétoise* (Études crétoises XXIII). Paris.

Palaima T.G. 1989. Cypro-Minoan Scripts: Problems of Historical Context. In Y. Duhoux, T.G. Palaima and J. Bennet eds. *Problems in Decipherment*. Louvain-la-Neuve. Pp. 121–188.

Sugerman M.O. 2000. *Webs of Commerce: The Archaeology of Ordinary Things in Late Bronze Age Israel and Palestine*. Ph.D. diss. Harvard University. Cambridge, Mass.

Yadin Y., Aharoni Y., Amiran R., Dothan T., Dunayevsky I. and Perrot J. 1958. *Hazor* I: *An Account of the First Season of Excavations, 1953*. Jerusalem.

Yasur-Landau A.Y. and Goren Y. 2004. A Cypro-Minoan Potmark from Aphek. *Tel Aviv* 31:22–31.

CHAPTER 7

GLYPTICS

BARUCH BRANDL

INTRODUCTION

Eleven glyptic finds excavated during Moshe Dothan's excavations at Tel Mor are described below.[1] Their presentation order reflects their Israel Antiquities Authority (IAA) registration number sequence. All the Egyptian hieroglyphic signs referred to are designated by square brackets as they appear in Gardiner's Sign List (Gardiner 1973). The author has endeavored to include as many known excavated parallels as possible as a basis for future studies. Where discussion by other scholars regarding specific issues exists, the relevant references are given.

Physical Attributes

Throughout the article a standardized terminology is used in the description of the artifacts' physical attributes. The following abbreviations are employed in reference to physical dimensions: D = diameter; H = height; L = length; T = thickness; and W = width. All the Tel Mor glyptic artifacts made from steatite were glazed.[2] However, due to the chemical conditions in the various destruction or debris layers, the glaze usually survived only in the incisions of the designs on the scarabs' bases and on their sides, and on the flat areas on the beetles' heads. The original glaze colors, which were most probably blue or green, have faded and turned white or yellow (see Keel 1995a:153, §406).

Classification and Typology

There are two main classification systems or typologies relating to the shape of Middle Bronze Age scarabs.[3] The first was published by Alan Rowe (1936: Pls. 32–35 = Keel 1995a: Ills. 44, 46, 67) and the second by Olga Tufnell (1984:31–38, Figs. 12–14 = Keel 1995a:39–57, Ills. 45, 49, 69). There are noticeable discrepancies in the identifications made by the two scholars, and

both works are now outdated. Notwithstanding, the Middle Bronze Age design scarabs are described here according to Tufnell's Design Classification,[4] with the adoption of some later modifications made by Keel (1995a:158–162). As for the Late Bronze Age scarabs and seals, the following publications are essential for their classification: Rowe 1936 for scarabs and Keel 1995a for cowroids (pp. 78–81) and bifacial seals (pp. 84–86, 89–93).

Origin and Dating

An attempt has been made here to determine whether the seals were imported from Egypt or produced locally. Recently, Daphna Ben-Tor has convincingly shown that most of the scarabs found in Palestine that bear an early Middle Bronze Age design were, in fact, local productions ('early Palestinian scarab series'), as were those belonging to the latter part of the same period ('late Palestinian [scarab] series'; Ben-Tor 1997; 1998). I fully agree with Ben-Tor's observation regarding origins, but suggest the use of an alternative terminology, namely, 'Early Middle Bronze [Age] Canaanite Scarabs' (EMBCS) and 'Late Middle Bronze [Age] Canaanite Scarabs' (LMBCS). This is because locally produced imitations of Egyptian scarabs have also been produced and found at Canaanite sites during the Late Bronze Age and later.

I date the EMBCS to the early MB IIB, or 1680–1650 BCE (= Tell el-Dab'a E/3), and the LMBCS to the late MB IIB and MB IIC, or 1650–1530 BCE (= Tell el-Dab'a E/2–D/2). The latter period is subdivided into early LMBCS, which corresponds to 1650–1590 BCE (= Tell el-Dab'a E/2–1), and late LMBCS, which corresponds to 1590–1530 BCE (= Tell el-Dab'a D/3–2). My dating of Ben-Tor's 'early Palestinian scarab series' (my EMBCS), therefore, is later by some 30 years.[5]

DESCRIPTION AND DISCUSSION

1. Scarab (IAA No. 1959-140; Fig. 7.1)
Bibliography. Dothan 1960b: Pl. 10:3 = 1960a: Pl. 3:1;
Keel 1995a:214, §584 = 1997:704, 705 (Aschkelon
No. 39).
Material. Glazed steatite; traces of green glaze in the
incisions above and below the legs.

Dimensions. L 21.50 mm, W 16 mm, H 9.25 mm.
Method of Manufacture. Carving, abrading, drilling,
incising and glazing.
Workmanship. Good to excellent.
Technical Details. Perforated, drilled from both sides;
linear and hollowed-out engraving with hatching.
Preservation. Complete.

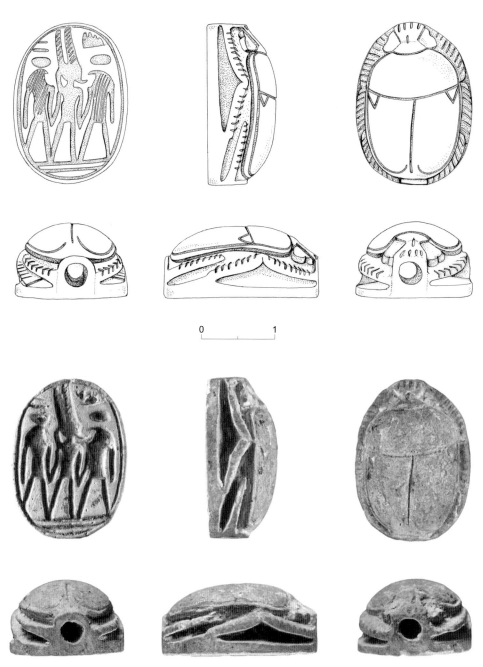

Fig. 7.1. Scarab (No. 1) from Stratum VI.

Scarab Shape. Rowe—HC 12 (XIIth to XXIInd Dynasty), EP 31 (XIIth to *c.* XVIIIth–XIXth Dynasty), Side 27 (XIIIth to XXVIth Dynasty).

Base Design. Three Egyptian gods dressed in short kilts are framed inside a vertical oval. The deities stand holding hands on a common plane defined by a double line.[6] The central anthropomorphic deity is slightly taller than the other two. He has a false beard and can be positively identified as the god Amun based on the distinctive double-plumed crown[7] with the hanging streamer (cf. Ions 1968:33, 101; Petrie 1933: Pl. 3:111 = Giveon 1985:102, 103, No. 122 = Keel 1995a:214, 215, Ill. 442 = 1997:264, 265 [Tell el-'Ajjul No. 479]; Hornung and Staehelin 1976: No. 599; Śliwa 1985:21, No. 9).[8]

The deities on either side are described as mythical creatures with a human body and a falcon's head. Above each is an oval solar disk, the attribute of a sun god.[9] Different hieroglyphic signs fill the spaces above the solar disks: to the right is *mn* ('stability' [Y 5]; see Keel 1995a:171, §457) and to the left is the sign *n* ([N 35]; see Keel 1995a:171, §458) with a stroke above it. It is tempting to interpret these signs as a shortening of the name of the god Amun (see n. 7 above); however, the common appearance of a second solar disk above the first figure indicates otherwise.[10]

Canaanite parallels to the scarab were found at Ashqelon, Bet She'an, Bet Shemesh, Gezer, Lakhish, Megiddo, Tell el-'Ajjul and Tell el-Far'ah (S) (for references, see above). The Gezer exemplar is actually a bulla that was impressed with a parallel scarab (Macalister 1905:190, 191, Pl. 2:1 = 1912, II: 295, Fig. 437:1, 330 [Second Semitic Period, No. 6a]; see Keel 1995a:214, 215, §584; 1997:704, 705 [Aschkelon No. 39]). In Egypt similar scarabs were excavated, for example, at Tell el-Yehudiyeh (Petrie 1906:15, Pl. 11:213) and Soleb (Schiff Georgini 1971:291, Fig. 568).

Typology. Design scarab. According to Keel's addition to Tufnell's design typology, this scarab belongs to the group of 'Human and Mythical Figures. Standing, Human-Headed, Amun' (10A1k; Keel 1995a:162, 214, 215, §§582, 584). According to much older typologies, the scarab belongs to the category of 'Scarabs Bearing Names and Figures of Gods' (Newberry 1906: Pl. 41:17 = 1907: Pl. 9:36315) or 'scarabs with gods' (Petrie 1925: Pl. 15:1044).

Origin. Canaanite. The poor quality of the signs strongly suggests that the scarab was made locally. This hypothesis is further supported by the seemingly local character of the Gezer bulla and the discovery of more parallels in Canaan than in Egypt.

Date. The scarab should be dated to the XIXth Dynasty on the basis of both iconography and excavated parallels. Keel and Uehlinger observe that "… Amun receives strong emphasis on seal amulets only during the Nineteenth Dynasty" (1998:92). As for excavated parallels, all seem to originate in contexts belonging to the thirteenth century BCE. Thus, Keel's attribution of this group to the XIXth and XXth Dynasties is not fully justified (1995a:215).[11]

Archaeological Context. Locus 35 (in Sq M18) is a pit belonging to Stratum VI, which spanned the end of the thirteenth and beginning of the twelfth centuries BCE, according to the excavator of the site (see Chapter 2; Dothan 1993). It seems, then, that the scarab was found in a contemporaneous context, particularly if the pit was filled before the stratum came to an end.

2. Scarab (IAA No. 1959-142; Fig. 7.2)
Material. Glazed steatite; white, coating not preserved.
Dimensions. L 14 mm, W 10 mm, H 7 mm.
Method of Manufacture. Carving, abrading, drilling, incising and glazing.
Workmanship. Excellent.
Technical Details. Perforated, drilled from both sides; linear and hollowed-out engraving.
Preservation. Complete.

Scarab Shape. Rowe—HC 13 (*c.* XIIIth to XVIIIth Dynasties), EP 32 (XVIIIth to *c.* XXVIth Dynasties), Side 27 (*c.* XIIIth to XXVIth Dynasties).

Base Design. Five hieroglyphic signs in two rows are depicted in a vertical oval frame. The three signs in the upper row, *i* ([M 17]; see Keel 1995a:171, §456), *mn* ([Y 5]; see also §457) and *n* ([N 35]; see also §458)], combine to form the name *Imn* ('Amun'; Gardiner 1973:553). In the lower row are the signs *nfr* ('good' [F 35]; see Keel 1995a:172, §459) and *iꜣw* ('old' [A 19]).

These five signs together read *'Imn nfr iꜣwt*,[12] which means 'Amun [gives] a good (or definite) old age'[13] (cf. Hornung and Staehelin 1976: No. 611).[14] A comparable title may be found on a bifacial rectangular plaque from Mitrahineh (Memphis)—'*Imn nfr ḥwn*, 'Amun [gives] a good (or definite) youth' (Reisner 1958: No. 12841; see also Gardiner 1973:580).

Typology. Wish scarab. According to Keel's addition to Tufnell's design typology, this scarab belongs to the group of 'Religious Formulae and Wishes' (11D; Keel 1995a:162 and 246, §651). According to an older typology, the scarab belongs to 'Scarabs Bearing Mottoes, Good Wishes, &c.' (Newberry 1906: Pl. 40).

Origin. Egyptian. The scarab bears a rare formula and is the first of its kind to have been excavated. Thus, it strengthens the authenticity of a parallel scarab formerly of the Fraser Collection and considered unique hitherto (Fraser 1900: No. 411 = Hornung and Staehelin 1976: No. 611).

Date. The scarab should be dated to the XVIIIth Dynasty. According to Rowe's segmented typology, all three scarab features (see above, Scarab Shape) fit within this period only.

Archaeological Context. Locus 118 (in Sqs M–N22) is a courtyard that was in use throughout Strata XII–IX. The scarab was found at an elevation (19.75 m) that corresponds to Stratum XI, in which case it dates to the fourteenth century BCE or LB IIA (see Chapter 2; Dothan 1993). Therefore, it seems the scarab was recovered in a context that approximates the date of its production.

3. Cowroid (IAA No. 1959-143; Fig. 7.3)
Bibliography. Keel 1995a:79, §188.
Material. Glazed steatite; yellowish glaze, mainly in incisions.

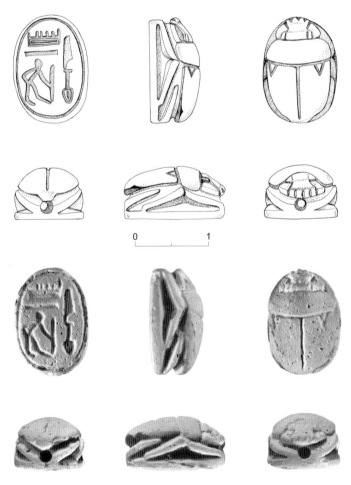

0   1

Fig. 7.2. Scarab (No. 2) from Stratum XI.

Fig. 7.3. Unstratified cowroid (No. 3).

Dimensions. L 10 mm, W 10 mm, H 4.5 mm.
Method of Manufacture. Carving, abrading, drilling, incising and glazing.
Workmanship. Mediocre.
Technical Details. Perforated, drilled from both sides; linear and hollowed-out engraving.
Preservation. Complete.

Seal Shape. Cowroid. The seal belongs to Keel's Type III, *Kauroide mit einem Schnurmuster oder häufiger einem Kerbband, das sich dem rand des Rückens entlag zieht* (Keel 1995a:78, §185, 190–193; cf. Rowe 1936: Nos. 758, 846).[15]

Base Design. Six signs that create the name *Imn-Ra* ('Amun-Re') (cf. Rowe 1936: Nos. 758, 846) with an additional slightly curved base line (cf. Brandl 1999b:17*, 18*, Scarab No. 1).

Typology. According to Keel's addition to Tufnell's design typology, this scarab belongs the group of 'Gods' Names' (11C; 1995a:162, 242, §642). According to an older typology, the cowroid belongs to the category of 'Scarabs Bearing Names and Figures of Gods' (Newberry 1906: Pl. 41:3, 4, 7, 30).

Origin. Canaanite. The mediocre workmanship, especially of the base design, indicates that the seal was locally made.[16]

Date. The cowroid should be dated to the XIXth Dynasty, both on the basis of its shape and workmanship. The one-to-one proportion of its length and width is typical of that dynasty (Keel 1995a:80, §193). The mediocre workmanship is to be expected in the Egyptian province of Canaan during the long *pax Aegyptiaca* of the thirteenth century BCE.

Archaeological Context. The only available information on the find-spot of the cowroid is that it was retrieved in Sq L18 at an elevation of 22.40 m asl.

4. Scarab Impression (IAA No. 1960-1147; Fig. 7.4)
Material. Pottery.
Dimensions. L 16 mm, W 13 mm.
Method of Manufacture. Scarab impression made before firing of vessel.
Workmanship. Mediocre.
Technical Details. Impressed on upper part of storage-jar handle; perpendicular to handle's direction; motifs upside down and in high relief; traces of hatching visible on motifs.
Preservation. Complete.

Impression. Five hieroglyphic signs are depicted in a horizontal oval frame. Two opposing *Hrw* birds that correspond to 'the falcon-god Horus' ([G 5]; see Keel 1995a:171, §454; 175, §467) occupy the lower part of the frame. Behind each of them is an *i'rt* 'uraeus' (cobra) [I 12], and above their heads is the sign *nbw* ('gold' [S 12]; see Keel 1995a:172, §458). This combination is one of the many subgroups of the motif 'falcon between two uraei'.[17]

Scarabs with this design are known from three other Canaanite sites. At Tell el-'Ajjul, one such scarab was found during Petrie's excavations (1934: Pls. 6 [row 6, 8th from left], 7:199 = Tufnell 1984: Pl. 37:2559 = Keel 1989a:316, 317, Ill. 134 = Keel 1997:362–363 [Tell el-'Aǧul No. 759]) and another was obtained from a later surface collection (Keel 1997:522–523 [Tell el-'Aǧul No. 1237 = IAA No. 57-565]). Another scarab, which belongs to the British Museum, is reportedly from Gezer (Giveon 1985:118, 119, No. 27 = Keel 1989b:267, 269, Ill. 80). Burial Cave A2 in the Baq'ah Valley produced another close parallel (Weinstein

1986:284–285 [No. 2], 287, Fig. 93:3, Pl. 38:a [lower left] = Eggler and Keel 2006:150–151 [Dschabal al-Hawayah No. 1, with additional bibliography]); it was found in Layer 2b, which the excavators dated to LB IA (Brown and McGovern 1986:32–44). An impression with the same design was very recently discovered on the body of a combed storage jar in the new excavations at the City of David in Jerusalem (Mazar 2007:29). In Egypt a similar impression, probably of a door sealing made from a Hyksos import, was found at Kerma in Nubia (Reisner 1923:76, Fig. 169:116, 79 [4.a.ii]).[18]

Typology. Design scarab. The scarab belongs to Tufnell's design classes 3B6 ('Symmetric Patterns—GOLD-sign (*nbw*) in Longitudinal Setting'; 1984: Pl.15:1683) and 9C3 ('Animals and Heraldic Beasts.

Cobras Confronted—with Hawk(s)'; Pl. 37:2559). It also belongs to Keel's design class 9H2 (*Paarweise angeordnete Falken*; 1995a:162, 203, §557).

Origin. Canaanite. The extensive use of cross-hatching on the body is one of the most characteristic features of 'Hyksos' scarabs.[19] As such, the scarab and the impression were locally made (see Keel 1997:362–363, 522–523 [Tell el-'Aǧul Nos. 759, 1237, respectively]).

Date. On the basis of the design and the excavated parallel from Tell el-'Ajjul, the scarab that produced the impression should be dated to the latest part of MB II or MB IIC (late LMBCS/1590–1530 BCE, *pace* Keel above).

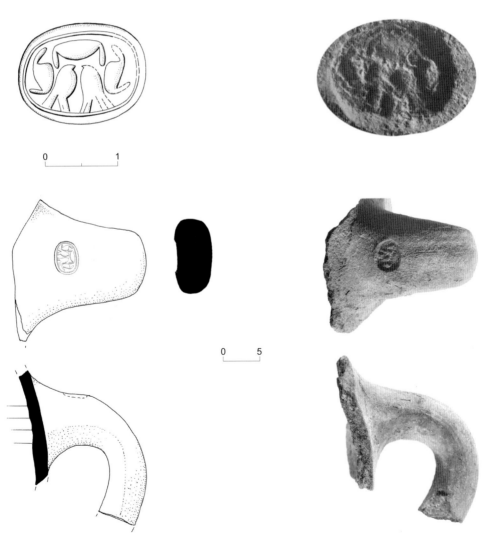

Fig. 7.4. Handle with scarab impression (No. 4) from Stratum XI.

Archaeological Context. Locus 116 is a probe belonging to Stratum XI,[20] which is loosely dated to LB IA (see Chapter 2; Dothan 1993); therefore, it seems that the impressed handle was found in a roughly contemporaneous context.

5. **Scarab Impression** (IAA No. 1960-1148; Fig. 7.5)
Material. Pottery.
Dimensions. L 16 mm, W 13 mm.
Method of Manufacture. Scarab impression made before firing of vessel.
Workmanship. Mediocre.
Technical Details. Impressed on upper part of storage-jar handle, diagonal to handle's direction; motifs in high relief; likely it and previous handle (No. 4) were part of same vessel, or at least impressed by same scarab.
Preservation. Complete.

Base Design. As No. 4.

Typology. As No. 4.

Origin. As No. 4.

Date. As No. 4.

Archaeological Context. Locus 117 is a Stratum X probe located directly above L116 (see Chapter 2), the Stratum XI probe that yielded Scarab Impression No. 4, thus strengthening the supposition that both impressed handles once belonged to the same storage jar.

6. Scarab Impression (IAA No. 1960-1149; Fig. 7.6)
Bibliography. Dothan 1973a:125, Fig. 3:13, 126 = 1973b:6, Fig. 3:13, 8, 9, Pl. 3:D = Leclant 1976:310 (III.2.g—Tell Mor).
Material. Pottery; loessy soil typical of northern Negev and southern Shephelah.[21]
Dimensions. L 19.5 mm, W 13.5 mm.

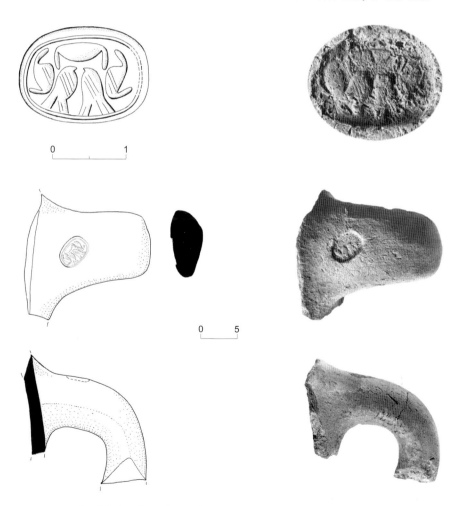

Fig. 7.5. Handle with scarab impression (No. 5) from Stratum X.

Method of Manufacture. Scarab impression made before firing of vessel.
Workmanship. Mediocre.
Technical Details. Impressed vertically on lowest part of jug wall and base; motifs in high relief.
Preservation. Complete.

Base Design. Inside an oval framed by a rope pattern are two *sm3 t3wi* signs ('Union of Upper and Lower Egypt') in a *tête-bêche* arrangement (see Ward 1978:72–74; Keel 1995a:174, §466). The stems of the lotus and papyrus are arranged in a unique form, resembling a bifacial oval plaque from Tomb 1018 at Tell el-Far'ah (S) (Starkey and Harding 1932: Pl. 43:30 = Rowe 1936: S. 19 = Tufnell 1984: Pl. 27:2169).

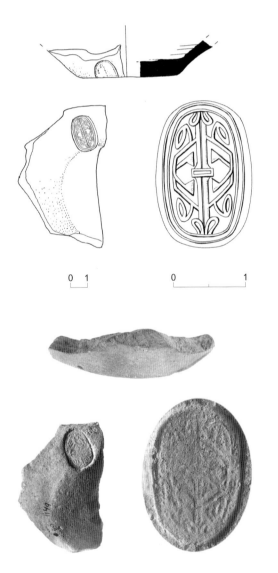

0   1

0   1

Fig. 7.6. Base with scarab impression (No. 6) from Stratum XII.

Typology. Design scarab. The scarab that produced the impression belongs to Tufnell's design classes 3A1 ('Monograms and Varia—Sign of Union, *sm3*'; 1984: Pl. 7:1281, 1282, 1285), 6 ('Coiled and Woven Patterns'; Pl. 27:2169) and 8A ('Rope Borders. Twisted Strand'; Pl. 34).

Origin. Canaanite. The *tête-bêche* arrangement of the *sm3 t3wi* signs seems to reflect local fashion.[22] On Egyptian seals the two signs meet at their bases.[23] The specific location of the impression on the vessel, which seems to be an exclusively Canaanite trait, finds a parallel on a jug base from Jerusalem (R. Reich and E. Shukron, pers. comm. [to be published by the author]).

Date. The scarab that produced the impression belongs to the LMBCS, which corresponds to 1650–1530 BCE. This range may be narrowed further to 1590–1530 BCE on the basis of the Jerusalem jug.

Archaeological Context. Locus 118 belongs to Stratum XII, the earliest period of settlement at the site, dated to the end of MB IIB or MB IIC (Dothan 1993; see also Chapter 2); thus it seems that the impressed jug base was found in a contemporaneous context.

7. Scarab (IAA No. 1960-1150;[24] Fig. 7.7)
Bibliography. Dothan 1973a:125, Fig. 3:12, 126, Pl. 23:3 = 1973b:6, Fig. 3:12, 8, Pl. 3:C = Leclant 1976:310 (III.2.g—Tell Mor).
Material. Feldspar?
Dimensions. L 24 mm, W 17 mm, H 10 mm.
Method of Manufacture. Carving, abrading, drilling and incising.
Workmanship. Good.
Technical Details. Perforated, drilled from both sides; linear engraving.
Preservation. Complete, except for small scar on right side of base plinth.

Scarab Shape. Rowe—HC 1 (XIIth to XXIInd Dynasties), EP 5 (XIIth to XXVIth Dynasties), Side 27 (*c.* XIIIth to XXVIth Dynasties). Tufnell—D3-0-d5.

Base Design. In a vertical oval frame is a hooked scroll border made of three pairs with an open top, and five hieroglyphic signs arranged in a central column. On top is the sign *sšr* ('linen, cloth' [V 33]), below is the sign *kȝ* ('soul, spirit' [D 28]),[25] and at the base are two adorsed papyrus stems growing from the sign *nbw* ('gold' [S 12]; see Keel 1995a:172, §458).[26] The scarab was published erroneously as a Hyksos copy of a royal name (i.e., Amenemhet II; Dothan 1973a:125, Fig. 3:12, 126; 1973b:6, Fig. 3:12, 8; Leclant 1976:310 [III.2.g—Tell Mor]).

Typology. Design scarab. It belongs to Tufnell's design classes 1E2 ('Linear Patterns. Floral Motifs—Two Stems'; 1984: Pl. 2:1051), 3A3 ('Egyptian Signs and Symbols. Varia'; Pls. 8:1352, 8b:1382, 1391) and 7C3 (ii)a ('Scroll Borders. Paired Scrolls, Open—Three Pairs, Oblong, Hooked'; Pl. 32:2369, 2371, 2372).

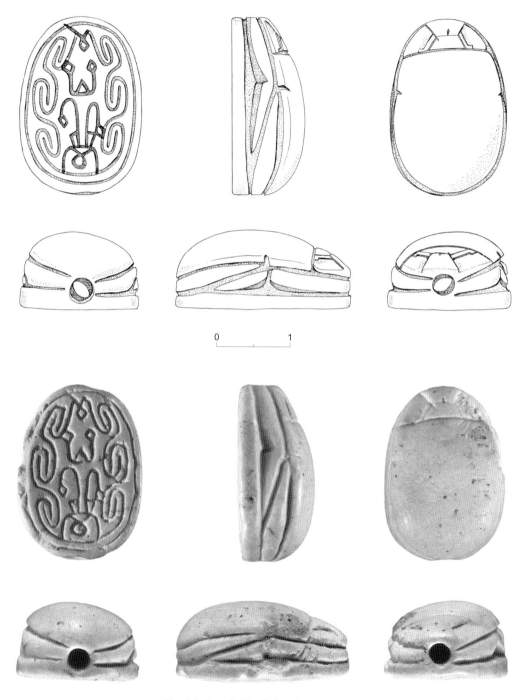

Fig. 7.7. Scarab (No. 7) from Stratum XII.

Origin. Canaanite. It is a typical 'Hyksos', or LMBCS, local product.

Date. As a clear product of the LMBCS, the scarab should be dated to between 1650 and 1530 BCE, preferably in the later part of that period, 1590–1530 BCE.

Archaeological Context. This scarab was found in a poor Stratum XII context (end of MB IIB/*c*. 1600 BCE), which corresponds roughly to the date assigned based on stylistic considerations.

8. Bifacial Rectangular Plaque (IAA No. 1960-1151; Fig. 7.8)

Material. Serpentine.
Dimensions. L 12 mm, W 9.50 mm, T 6.25 mm.
Method of Manufacture. Carving, abrading, drilling and incising.
Workmanship. Good.
Technical Details. Perforated, drilled from both directions; drilling and linear engraving.
Preservation. Complete, but motifs are either worn or unfinished.

Seal Shape. Bifacial rectangular plaque.[27] The seal belongs to Keel's Type III, described as *Rechteckige, beidseitiggravierte Platte, die im Gegensatz zu Typ I und II aus schwärzlichem Stein besteht und keine typische ägyptischen Dekorationsmotive aufweist* (1995a:89, 90, 92, 93, §§216–218, 225–228).[28]

Base Design. The designations 'Face A' and 'Face B' are analogous to a parallel from the Chiha Collection (see below), since both faces are horizontal in arrangement.

Face A contains remnants of a *couchant* griffin including the legs, head and the beginning of a wing.

On Face B there are traces of a landing(?) eagle depicted *en face*. Around the body the neck and the beginnings of wings stretched upward diagonally on both sides, and an open tail and two legs extend downward diagonally on both sides.

Similar rectangular plaques were found in Macalister's excavations at Gezer (1912 II:319 [No. 172], 1912 III: Pl. 207:10 [left]) and at Lakhish (Murray 1953:372, Pls. 44A–45:136). Parallels on Syro-Palestinian cylinder seals are known from Ugarit (Amiet 1992:43, 47, Fig. 16:79).

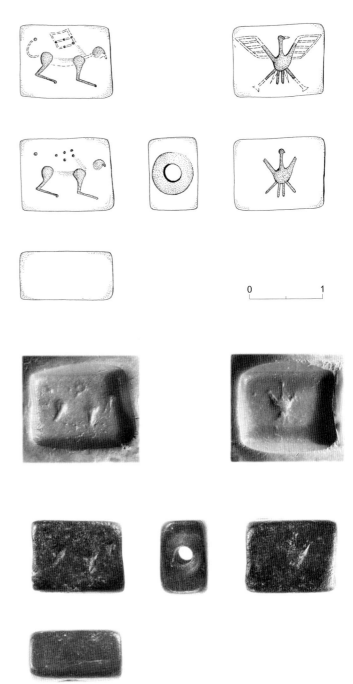

Fig. 7.8. *Unstratified bifacial rectangular plaque (No. 8).*

The only published parallel of such a bifacial rectangular plaque familiar to the author is from the Chiha Collection (Doumet 1992: No. 359).[29] Parallels on Syro-Palestinian cylinder seals are known from the following sites: Gezer (Macalister 1912 II:345 [No. 6], III: Pl. 137:48 = Nougayrol 1939:17 17 [XXXV], Pl. 3: [EG. 9]); Tell Abu Hawam (Hamilton 1934:64,

Pl. 26 [No. 412] = Nougayrol 1939:59 [CXXII], Pl. 1: [AH. 7] = Parker 1949:34, Pl. 23 [No. 154] = Mazar 1978:13, No. 34, 14 = Salje 1990:307 [S(P) 3—Abu Hawam 412], Pl. 21:360); Ugarit (Amiet 1992:42, 43, 45, Fig. 14:65, 66, 48, Fig. 17:80, 81; the first is also in Salje 1990:308 [S(P) 3—RS 8.002], Pl. 21:365); and Tel Baṭash-Timna (Kelm and Mazar 1995:62, Fig. 4.29 [Upper] = Keel 1994:228, 250, Ill. 52; 1995a:125, Fig. 55).

Typology. The plaque belongs to Keel's group (a) of 'The Animal Plaques Group of the LB IIA (*c*. 1400–1300 BCE)' (1994:226–230, 248–250; 1995:36, §66; and 92, §225; 1995a:121–126), or his Type IIIa (1995a:92, §226).

Origin. Keel identified the entire group of Type III seals as Syro-Palestinian in origin.

Date. According to Keel, the group to which this seal belongs dates to the fourteenth century BCE. The group of cylinder seals from Ugarit and several sites in Palestine, which influenced the seal-cutters of the Type IIIa plaques, however, dates more broadly to the fourteenth and thirteenth centuries BCE (Keel 1994:229; 1995b:125 = Amiet 1992:41–49, Nos. 61–91).

Archaeological Context. No stratigraphic information is available for this object. It could originate from any of the strata ranging from Stratum IX to VI.

9. Cylinder Seal (IAA No. 1960-1154; Fig. 7.9)
Material. Faience (or sintered quartz);[30] light blue (or azure) glaze.
Dimensions. H 19 mm, D 8.00–8.25 mm, circumference 25.50 mm.

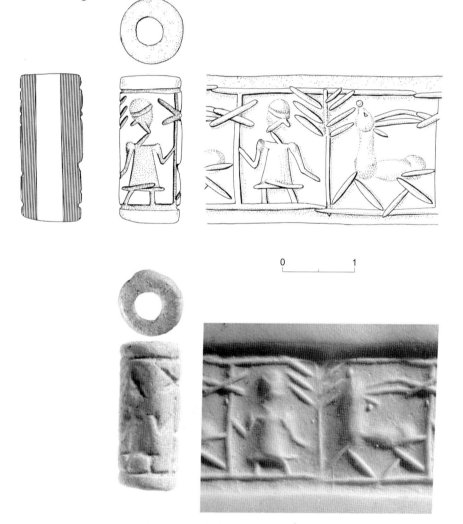

Fig. 7.9. Unstratified cylinder seal (No. 9).

Method of Manufacture. Hand forming,[31] perforating, drilling, impressing, incising and firing.
Workmanship. Good.
Technical Details. Perforated off center, by means of pulling a straw; drilling and linear engraving.
Preservation. Complete, losing its glaze.

Seal Shape. Cylinder seal; typical of mass production techniques.

Seal Design. The seal is comprised of a single scene in one register with borderlines on the top and bottom. The scene has the following three components: (1) on the left is a worshiper who wears long drapery and a turban, and holds a standard surmounted by an x-shaped symbol (a star?) in his right hand; (2) in the center is a (sacred) tree that the worshiper grasps with his left hand; and (3) on the right is a horned animal, probably an antelope.

The Tel Mor cylinder seal belongs to a very small group consisting of one complete parallel and four close parallels. In the close parallels, the standard and tree were changed into poles and an additional terminal was placed above the antelope. The complete parallel was found at Kamid el-Lôz (Salje 1990:41 [No. 71], 90, 175 [KL 66:680], 206 [1.5.71], 232 [S/P 2—KL 66:680], Pls. 4:68, 14:283 = Kühne and Salje 1996:58, 59 [18. KL 66:680], Ill. 6:18, Pl. 5:18, Plan 12:18). The close parallels were discovered at Bet She'an (Parker 1949:15 [No. 39], Pl. 6:39 = Beck 1967:135, 173, Fig. 168:9 = Salje 1990:232 [S/P 2—Beth Shan P 39]), Ugarit (Schaeffer-Forrer et al. 1983:95 [R.S. 7.602] = Salje 1990:208 [1.6.10], Pl. 5:81) and Kamid el-Lôz, the two seals from which are framed within either a feather-shaped (Salje 1990:43 [No. 11], 90, 175 [KL 73:265], 208 [1.6.11], 232 [S/P 2 - KL 73:265], Pl. 10:193 = Kühne and Salje 1996:56, 57 [16. KL 73:265], Ill. 6:16, Pl. 5.16 and Plan 3:16) or net pattern panel (Salje 1990:43 [No. 10a], 90, 175 [KL 80:15], 208 [1.6. 10a], 232 [S/P 2 - KL 80:15] = Kühne and Salje 1996:57, 58 [17. KL 80:15], Ill. 6:17, Pl. 5:17, Plans 6:17, 9:17).

Typology. The seal belongs generally to the Mitannian 'Common Style' (Porada 1947:11–13), which corresponds to the simpler part of Frankfort's 'Popular Style' (1939:279, 280). More specifically, the Tel Mor cylinder seal and its parallel(s) are related to a Syro-Palestinian subgroup of the Mitannian 'Common Style'.[32]

Origin. Based on the typology and distribution of parallels discussed above, it is safe to assume that the seal was produced in a Canaanite workshop.[33]

Date. By reference to the stratigraphic contexts of its parallels, it is possible to date the cylinder seal to the thirteenth century BCE.[34]

Archaeological Context. No stratigraphic information is available for this object.

10. Cylinder Seal (IAA No. 1960-1155; Fig. 7.10)
Material. Faience or sintered quartz (see n. 30 above); light blue or azure glaze.
Dimensions. H 18 mm, D 7.5 mm, circumference 22 mm.
Method of Manufacture. Hand forming (see n. 31 above), perforating, drilling, impressing, incising and firing.
Workmanship. Mediocre.
Technical Details. Perforated by means of pulling a straw; linear and hollowed-out engraving.
Preservation. Complete, losing its glaze.

Seal Shape. Cylinder seal; typical of mass production techniques.

Seal Design. The seal is composed of a single scene in one register with borderlines on the top and bottom. The scene consists of alternating figures and standards, all rendered in a highly schematic and linear fashion. The three worshippers (or dancers) each wear a turban(?) and long drapery that covers the feet. The right hand (actually the left) of the figures rests on the hip and the left hand (actually their right) is raised. The bodies are shown in frontal view, the heads in profile.

The schematic appearance of the figures and their dress resemble cylinder seals from Tell el-Ḥesi (Bliss 1894:79 [No. 128], 80 = Nougayrol 1939:34 [LXXVI], Pl. 11: [T.H. 5] = Parker 1949:25 [No. 109], Pl. 17:109 = Beck 1967:105, 139, Fig. 183:14 = Salje 1990:182, 231 [S(P) 2—T. el Hesi P 109]) and Ugarit (Schaeffer-Forrer et al. 1983:160 [R.S. 28.026]). The hand gestures recall a cylinder seal made of black stone from Ugarit (Amiet 1992:114 [No. 270], 118, Fig. 49:270).

Typology. The seal generally belongs to the Mitannian 'Common Style' (Porada 1947:11–13), which corresponds to the simpler part of Frankfort's 'Popular Style' (1939:279, 280). This seal and its parallels are

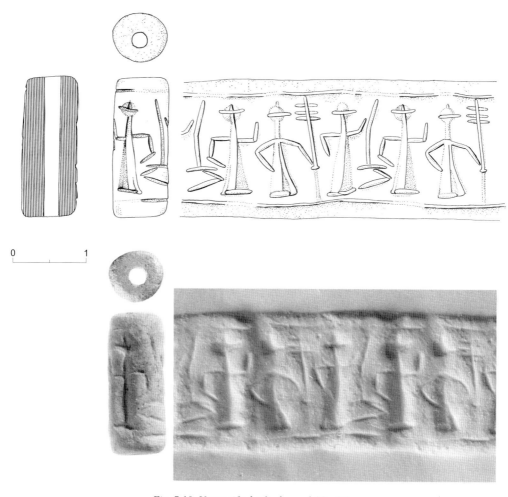

Fig. 7.10. Unstratified cylinder seal (No. 10).

related also to a Syro-Palestinian subgroup of the Mitannian 'Common Style' (see n. 32).

Origin. Based on the typology and distribution of parallels discussed above, it is safe to assume that the cylinder seal from Tel Mor was produced in a Canaanite workshop.

Date. By reference to the stratigraphic contexts of its parallels, it is possible to date the Tel Mor cylinder seal to the thirteenth century BCE.

Archaeological Context. No stratigraphic information is available for this object.

11. Bifacial Rectangular Plaque (IAA No. 1960-1231; Fig. 7.11)
Material. Serpentine.
Dimensions. L 15.50 mm,[35] W 11.50 mm, T 7.75 mm.

Method of Manufacture. Carving, abrading, drilling and incising.
Workmanship. Good.
Technical Details. Perforated off center, drilled from both sides; drill marks visible on edges of perforation; linear and hollowed-out engraving.
Preservation. Complete.

Seal Shape. A bifacial rectangular plaque (see n. 27) belonging to Keel's Type III (see n. 28).

Base Design. Of the two sides, both of which are horizontally arranged, Face A is clearer. It contains parts of a human figure sitting on a chair with what appears to be a footrest under its feet.[36] The figure is bald with a bar-shaped beard and seems to be holding a scepter. Hanging above the figure's shoulder is an object with a corner-like sign in front of it. The combination of these motifs strongly suggests that the figure is an imitation of the Egyptian god Ptah (cf. scarabs in Keel 1989a:290–291, Ill. 30; 300–301, Ills. 65, 66; 302–303, Ills. 71, 75; 307, Ill. 90). In Egyptian iconography that god is frequently represented as a mummified man with a shaved head and false beard, standing on a pedestal

with a *menat* counterpoise hanging on his back (see Ions 1968:105, 106; Lurker 1982:96, 97). The corner-like sign, which usually appears above the deity's head, therefore, probably symbolizes the god's *naos*.[37]

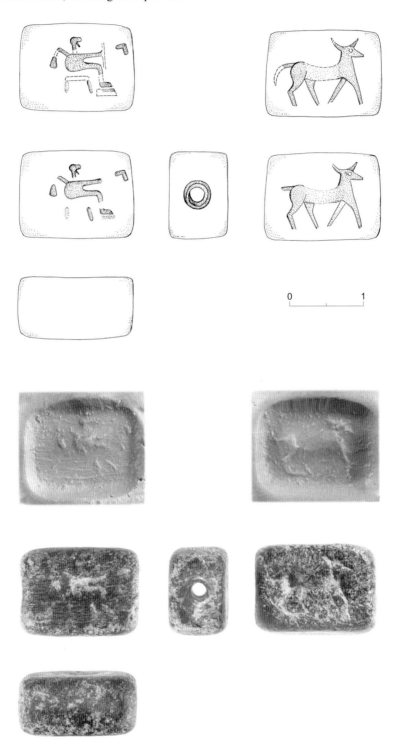

Fig. 7.11. Bifacial rectangular plaque (No. 11) from Stratum VI.

The only known parallel among bifacial rectangular plaques was excavated at Kamid el-Lôz; however, the excavators failed to identify the figure as the Egyptian god Ptah (Kühne and Salje 1996:100, 101 [50. KL 64:438], Ill. 13:50, Pl. 11:50, Plan 10:50). Unrecognized imitations of Ptah also appear on several cylinder seals from Ugarit (Amiet 1992:55 [No. 111], 61, Fig. 22:111; 56 [Nos. 122, 129], 63, Fig. 24:122; 64, Fig. 25:129; 89 [No. 194]; 100, Fig. 36:194).

Face B shows a quadruped, probably a walking bull. Only the excavations at Tell Jarisha (see above) and Tell Abu Hawam (Hamilton 1934:27 [No. 142] = Keel 1994:226, 248, Ill. 41; 1995b:122–123, Fig. 44; 1997:4–5 [Tell Abu Hawam No. 4]) have produced bifacial rectangular plaques with such a motif.[38] A walking bull also appears on the Syro-Palestinian cylinder seal found at Tel Baṭash-Timna, mentioned above in connection with the previous bifacial plaque (Kelm and Mazar 1995:62, Fig. 4.29 [Upper] = Keel 1994:228, 250, Ill. 52; 1995b:125, Fig. 55).

Typology. The plaque belongs to Keel's Group (a) of 'The Animal Plaques Group of the LB IIA (*c.* 1400–1300 BCE)' (1994:226–230, 248–250; 1995a:36, §66; and 92, §225; 1995b:121–126), or his Type IIIa (1995a:92, §226).

Origin. Keel places the origin of the entire group of his Type III seals in Syro-Palestine.

Date. A fourteenth-century BCE date was assigned by Keel to the group to which this seal belongs. The group of cylinder seals from Ugarit and other sites in Palestine that influenced the seal-cutters of the Type IIIa plaques, however, dates more broadly to the fourteenth and thirteenth centuries BCE (Keel 1994:229; 1995b: 125 = Amiet 1992:41–49, Nos. 61–91).

Archaeological Context. The plaque was found in Sq H20 at an elevation that corresponds to Stratum VI, which the excavator dated to *c.* 1200 BCE (Dothan 1993; see also Chapter 2). The date provided by stratigraphy, then, falls within the wide typological/chronological range described above.

SUMMARY AND CONCLUSIONS

The Tel Mor excavations yielded a total of eleven objects that belong to the following five glyptic types: (1) three scarabs (Nos. 1, 2, 7); (2) three scarab impressions (Nos. 4–6); (3) one cowroid (No. 3); (4) two bifacial rectangular plaques (Nos. 8, 11); and (5) two cylinder seals (Nos. 9, 10).

The three scarab impressions are all stamped on pottery vessels, two of them on jar handles (Nos. 4, 5) and one (No. 6) on the lower part of a jug. The remaining eight seals and scarabs are made of four different materials, both natural and man-made. Three objects (scarab Nos. 1, 2 and cowroid No. 3) are made of glazed steatite, all with traces of yellow, white or green glaze. Two (bifacial rectangular plaques Nos. 8, 11) are made of serpentine, two (cylinder seals Nos. 9, 10) of faience/sintered quartz, and one (scarab No. 7) possibly of feldspar.

There are clear differences in the standard of workmanship of the scarabs, the scarab impressions and the cowroid. The workmanship of the LMBCS scarab (No. 7) is good, whereas that of the impressions (Nos. 4–6), which were made from scarabs belonging to the same LMBCS group, is only mediocre. The quality of the XVIIIth Dynasty scarab (No. 2) is better than that of the XIXth Dynasty scarab (No. 1) and cowroid (No. 3). Aside for scarab No. 2, all the items were manufactured locally, namely, in the greater Canaan area, which extended as far north as Ugarit.

Four items (scarab impressions Nos. 4–6 and scarab No. 7) date to MB IIB–C, and, as local products, belong to the LMBCS. The other seven date to the Late Bronze Age. Scarab No. 2 belongs to the fourteenth century BCE, whereas the remaining six items (Nos. 1, 3, 9–11 and most probably No. 8) date to the thirteenth century BCE. The majority of the glyptic items (Nos. 1, 2, 4, 6, 7, 11) correlate well with their archaeological contexts.

Some of the objects are very rare and have only one known parallel. In two instances (Nos. 9, 11) the parallels were excavated at Kamid el-Lôz in Lebanon. Tel Mor can now be added to the list of sites with bifacial rectangular plaques (Keel 1995a:92–93) and Mitanni 'Common Style' cylinder seals (Salje 1990:110, 111). The identification of the figure on one of the plaques (No. 11) as the Egyptian god Ptah contributes a new motif both to the bifacial rectangular plaques and to the several cylinder seals from Ugarit depicting that god. The wide variety of glyptic finds found at Tel Mor probably results from the site's role as an international harbor for the nearby city of Ashdod.

NOTES

[1] I wish to thank Tristan Barako for inviting me to study and publish these finds. I also thank Anat Cohen-Weinberger (IAA petrographer) for the information concerning scarab impression No. 6 (IAA No. 1960-1149). Special thanks are due to Pamela Ullman for editing the first draft. The objects were photographed by Mariana Salzberger, drawn by Carmen Hersch and scanned by Yiftah Shalev, all under the author's guidance. Thanks are due to the editor and the reader of this work for their contributions.

[2] For the different methods of glazing steatite objects in ancient Egypt, see Tite and Bimson 1989.

[3] See the diagrams showing the parts of the scarab beetle in Rowe 1936: Pl. 23; Ward 1978: frontispiece; Uehlinger 1990:62, Fig. 37; and Keel 1995a:20, Fig. 1. Keel is the most detailed, with terms given in German, English, French and Italian.

[4] On the history and development of Tufnell's Design Classification, see Brandl 1986:247, n.4.

[5] For a full discussion, see Brandl 2004:124–125.

[6] The lower line does not create, together with the frame's segment, the sign *nb* (= 'all' or 'lord' [V 30]; see also Keel 1995a:171, §458) as suggested, for example, by Rowe (1936: Nos. 572 and 711). That is clear from two rectangular pieces with domed top from Tombs 641 and 935 at Tell el-Far'ah (S), where the two lines are equal (Petrie 1930: Pl. 31:305; Starkey and Harding 1932: Pl. 53:222, respectively), or a scarab from Ashqelon where the lower line forms a zigzag (Keel 1997:704, 705 [Aschkelon No. 39]).

[7] Macalister's suggestion that this deity be identified with Khnum (1905:190, 191, Pl. 2:1 = 1912 II:295, Fig. 437:1, 330 [Second Semitic Period—No. 6a]), and Rowe's attempt to identify him with *Mnṯw* ('Mont'; 1936: Nos. 572, 711) seem unlikely. In a scarab belonging to the Israel Museum (Ben-Tor 1989:76, No. 27), the name *Imn* 'Amun' appears in the space above and between the central god and the solar deity to his right. Scarabs or plaques where the anthropomorphic Amun is the only deity and is identified by name were excavated at Koptos (Petrie 1896: Pl. 24:45), Soleb (Schiff Giorgini 1971:207, Fig. 384 [T 17 c4]) and Fadrus (Säve-Söderbergh and Troy 1991:91, 95–97, 114, Pl. 16 [185/434:1]). Furthermore, Khnum does not appear with a human head and Mont always has a falcon's head. Cf. the rectangular piece with domed top from Lakhish (Tufnell 1958:123, Pl. 38:317) and two bifacial rectangular plaques from the former von Bissing and Fraser collections (Hornung and Staehelin 1976: Nos. 307, 345).

[8] The same crown with the streamer is worn by two other gods, *Mnw* ('Min') and Onuris. Min, however, is depicted in mummified form, often ithyphallic, with one hand raised and holding a flail (e.g., Petrie 1896: Pl. 18:2 [Koptos]); Lurker 1982:80 [Karnak] and Brissaud 1987:155, Pl. II-a [Tanis]). Onuris is shown dressed in a long robe, also with one hand raised, but lifting a spear (Hornung and Staehelin 1976:321, 322 [No. 662, side A]). Onuris appears without the streamer on one face of a bifacial rectangular plaque from Tell el-

'Ajjul (Petrie 1933: Pl. 4:193 = Giveon 1985:102–103 [No. 123, side 1] = Keel 1997:290–291 [Tell el-'Aǧul No. 554, side A]). Giveon's attempt to identify the Amun figure on the other face as Onuris was rightly rejected by Keel and Uehlinger (1992:104–105, Ill. 116a = 1998:92–93, Ill. 116a; Keel 1995a:214–215, Ill. 443; 1997:290–291 [Tell el-'Aǧul No. 554, side B]).

[9] Cf. a rectangular piece with domed top from Tell el-Far'ah (S) (Petrie 1930: Pl. 31:305) and a scarab from Lakhish (Tufnell 1958:121, Pl. 36:240). There is a possibility that one (Brandl 2000:538–539 [Scarab No. 2]) or both of the figures is Horus (Petrie 1906:15, Pl. 11:213). Alternatively, both figures may represent *Ra* (Lamon and Shipton 1939: Pl. 69:41).

[10] Cf. scarabs from Tell el-Far'ah (S) (Starkey and Harding 1932: Pl. 52:138 = Keel 1994:214–215, Ill. 448), Bet She'an (Rowe 1936: No. 572), Bet Shemesh (No. 711), Lakhish (Tufnell 1958:124–125, Pl. 39:339, 371) and Megiddo (Lamon and Shipton 1939: Pl. 69:41). Rowe's suggestion that the deities on the Bet She'an scarab are *Rʿ* and *Ḥr-ȝḫty* is not convincing, as is his reading of the two upper signs on the Bet Shemesh scarab as *nb* 'all' or 'lord' ([V 30]; see also Keel 1995a:171, §458). It seems more likely that motifs such as an extra solar disk (Loud 1948: Pl. 152:188) or two strokes (Keel 1997:704, 705 [Aschkelon No. 39]) serve as space fillers.

[11] For the misleading use of mixed contests like that of Tomb 934 at Tell el-Far'ah (S) to produce a XXth Dynasty date, see Brandl 2003:251–255.

[12] See Gardiner 1973:550

[13] The title or name 'Amun the old' appears in Papyrus Wilbour (see Otto 1975: Col. 241).

[14] This scarab was originally identified as bearing the private name *Nfr-'Imn* (see Fraser 1900: No. 411).

[15] "Cowroid with a necklace-pattern or, more frequently, a notched strap that is stretched along the edges of the back" (author's translation).

[16] See also Keel 1995b:121. For a somewhat similar parallel from Tell el-Far'ah (S), see Petrie 1930: Pl. 33:342.

[17] For a full discussion, see Brandl 2004: No. 30.

[18] For the Kushite-Hyksos interactions that bypassed Upper Egypt via the Oasis Road, see Yurco 2001:72–76.

[19] Cf. Hayes 1968:35–36, Fig. 17. Very rarely do hatching and cross-hatching appear on earlier scarabs, and if so, these filling motifs are rendered less densely and in between double-lined borders (Tufnell 1975:74, n. 46; Keel 1995a:130, §327).

[20] Ink writing on the handle, from the time of the excavation, assigns this find to Stratum XI. It seems that it was written immediately after the first season, at which point the earliest stratum was Stratum XI (cf. Dothan 1959:271 with 1960a; 1960b:122, 132; 1960c:124).

[21] According to Anat Cohen-Weinberger, "the base from Tel Mor is characterized by a silty calcareous clay. The silty component contains mainly quartz, but also a recognizable

quantity of other minerals including hornblende, minerals of the mica group and feldspar. The silt is well sorted and comprises about 10% of the matrix. The non-plastic components are mainly quartz but also calcareous rock fragments. This sediment is identified as loess soil which occurs in Israel mostly in the northern Negev and the southern Shephelah regions" (pers. comm., July 23, 2003).

[22] This arrangement is first seen on the EMBCS at Jericho (Kirkbride 1965: Fig. 285:5 [Group II] = Ward 1978:73, Fig. 16:21 = Tufnell 1984: Pl. 7:1281 = Keel 1995a:174, Ill. 285:21).

[23] See, for example, seals from Kahun (Petrie 1890: Pl. 10:19; 1891: Pl. 8:81) and Nubt (Petrie and Quibell 1896: Pl. 80:66). Such scarabs were imported to the following Canaanite sites: Megiddo (Guy 1938: Pl. 105:8 = Rowe 1936: No. 197), Lakhish (Tufnell 1958: Pl. 39:362) Tell 'Amr, Tomb 2 (Leibovitch 1982), and one from an unknown provenance (Rowe 1936: No. 73). Note that for Tell 'Amr there is a misleading translation as to the original dating: SIP instead of MK = Ward and Dever 1994:64–65, 97, 101, Fig. 5:1c.65 = Keel 1997: 638–639 [Tell 'Amr No. 2).

[24] This scarab may have been assigned an earlier IAA number (1959-141) that was overlooked.

[25] See also Keel 1995a:171, §456. According to D. Ben-Tor, it is a non-Egyptian form of the sign (1997:171, n. 51, 173, Fig. 4:1–6; 1998:157); however, such a form is attested on Egyptian private name scarabs (Martin 1971: Pls. 3:28 [1709], 19:29 [1675], 27:37 [1698], 34:40 [208]).

[26] For such a *nbw* sign with an oval at the lower part, see two scarabs from Tell el-'Ajjul (Petrie 1933: Pls. 3:38, 4:134 = Tufnell 1984: Pls. 15:1680, 14:1662 = Keel 1997:240, 241, 272, 273 [Tell el-'Aǧul Nos. 407, 500], respectively). For a parallel with three lotus stems emanating from the *nbw* sign, see a scarab from Bet She'an (Rowe 1936: No. 47).

[27] Keel rendered the German *rechteckige platte* (e.g., Hornung and Staehelin 1976:37) as 'rectangular piece' (Keel 1995a:89–93).

[28] "Rectangular piece engraved on both sides that, contrary to Types I and II, is made of blackish stone and does not show any typical Egyptian design motif" (author's translation).

[29] Another parallel from the excavations at Shiqmona will be published by the author. Most recently Keel published a parallel from Weill's excavations at Gezer, but with an

erroneous drawing (Keel 2004:52 [5.2.4.], Pl. 15:2); and see n. 38 below.

[30] For the preference of the description 'sintered quartz' in reference to the artificial material used in the manufacture of cylinder seals during the second and the first millennia BCE, see Collon 1982:5–6; 1987:61–62.

[31] The absence of vertical breaks in the design disproves the suggestion that these seals were made in molds (Collon 1987:62; contra Nougayrol 1939:13 [XXVI n. 1], Pl. 1: [AH. 1] and 27 [LX], Pl. 5: [GR. 4]; Schaeffer 1948:412). For cylinder seals that were produced in bivalve molds, see Brandl 1999a:230–236.

[32] According to H. Kantor, the Canaanite group is a crude subgroup of the 'Common Style', which she refers to as the 'Depleted Style' (1958:82–84; see also Beck 1967:2; Mazar 1978:10; Dabney 1993:228). According to B. Salje's typology, the full parallel from Kamid el-Lôz belongs to her Syro-Palestinian Style Group 2 [S/P 2] (1990:232, 233, Pl. 10:192–196).

[33] Note that there is only one cylinder seal impression out of 1011 at Nuzi that is similar to the small group of cylinder seals to which this seal impression from Tel Mor is a part (Porada 1947:15, 16 [No. 27], Pl. 2:27).

[34] Such a late date is supported also by a 'Common Style' cylinder seal impression on a krater handle from Stratum VI at Shiloh (see Brandl 1993:213–215 [No. 12]).

[35] Note that according to Keel, the average length of the seals belonging to this group is 15.7 mm (1995a: §226; 1995b:124).

[36] Another bifacial plaque with a sitting figure was found at Tell Jarisha (Ory 1926:6, Pl. 3b [left]—J.899, 7 = Keel 1994:227, n. 41, 249, Ill. 46; 1995b:123, n. 47, Fig. 49). Keel mistakenly thought that the plaque had not been published and, subsequently, made a new drawing.

[37] Leibovitch was among the first to identify this sign correctly (1960:5* [No. !0]). For earlier erroneous identifications, see Rowe 1936, Nos. 718, 726. For such a corner-like sign with the god Ptah on a sealing from Memphis, see Petrie, Mackay and Wainwright 1910:43, Pl. 37:48.

[38] A third parallel from the excavations at el-Aḥwaṭ will be published soon by the author. Keel recently published a parallel from Weill's excavations at Gezer with an erroneous drawing (Keel 2004:52 [5.2.4.], Pl. 15:2); and see n. 29 above.

REFERENCES

Amiet P. 1992. *Corpus des cylindres de Ras Shamra-Ougarit* II: *sceaux-cylindres en hematite et pierre diverses* (Ras Shamra-Ougarit IX). Paris.

Beck P. 1967. *Problems in the Glyptic Art of Palestine*. Ph.D. diss. Columbia University. New York.

Ben-Tor D. 1989. *The Scarab: A Reflection of Ancient Egypt* (Israel Museum Catalogue 303). Jerusalem.

Ben-Tor D. 1997. The Relations between Egypt and Palestine in the Middle Kingdom as Reflected by Contemporary Canaanite Scarabs. *IEJ* 47:162–189.

Ben-Tor D. 1998. The Relations between Egypt and Palestine during the Middle Kingdom as Reflected by Contemporary Canaanite Scarabs. In C.J. Eyre ed. *Proceedings of the Seventh International Congress of Egyptologists,*

Cambridge, 3–9 September 1995 (OLA 82). Leuven. Pp. 149–163.

Bliss F.J. 1894. *A Mound of Many Cities or Tell el Hesy Excavated.* London.

Brandl B. 1986. The Scarabs from Field VI at Gezer. In W.G. Dever ed. *Gezer IV: The 1969–71 Seasons in Field VI, the "Acropolis"* (Annual of the Hebrew Union College/Nelson Glueck School of Biblical Archaeology 4). Jerusalem. Pp. 247–257.

Brandl B. 1993. Scarabs and Other Glyptic Finds. In I. Finkelstein ed. *Shiloh: The Archaeology of a Biblical Site* (MSIATAU 10). Tel Aviv. Pp. 203–222.

Brandl B. 1999a. Two First-Millennium Cylinder Seals from Bethsaida (et-Tell). In R. Arav and R.A. Freund eds. *Bethsaida, A City by the North Shore of the Sea of Galilee* II. Kirksville, Missouri. Pp. 225–244.

Brandl B. 1999b. Two Ramesside Scarabs from Jatt (Tel Gat Carmel). *'Atiqot* 37:17*–22*.

Brandl B. 2000. Two Scarabs from Horvat 'Eleq. In Y. Hirschfeld ed. *Ramat Hanadiv Excavations. Final Report of the 1984–1988 Seasons.* Jerusalem. Pp. 537–542.

Brandl B. 2003. The Cape Gelidonya Shipwreck Scarabs Reconsidered. In M. Bietak and E. Czerny eds. *The Synchronisation of Civilisations in the Eastern Mediterranean in the Second Millennium B.C.* II: *Proceedings of the SCIEM 2000—EuroConference, Haindorf, 2nd of May–7th of May 2001.* Vienna. Pp. 249–261.

Brandl B. 2004. Scarabs, Seals, an Amulet and a Pendant. In S. Ben-Arieh. *Bronze and Iron Age Tombs at Tell Beit Mirsim* (IAA Reports 23). Jerusalem. Pp. 123–188.

Brissaud P. 1987. Notes sur le secteur au sud de la porte sud. In P. Brissaud ed. *Cahiers de Tanis* I: *Mission française des fouilles de Tanis* (Éditions Recherche sur les Civilisations "mémoire" 75). Paris. Pp. 155–162.

Brown R.M. and McGovern P.E. 1986. Cave A2. In P.E. McGovern ed. *The Late Bronze and Early Iron Ages of Central Transjordan: The Baq'ah Valley Project, 1977–1981* (University Museum Monographs 65). Philadelphia. Pp. 32–44.

Collon D. 1982. *The Alalakh Cylinder Seals: A New Catalogue of the Actual Seals Excavated by Sir Leonard Woolley at Tell Atchana, and from Neighbouring Sites on the Syrian-Turkish Border* (BAR Int. S. 132). Oxford.

Collon D. 1987. *First Impressions: Cylinder Seals in the Ancient Near East.* London.

Dabney M.K. 1993. The Cylinder Seals. In. F.W. James and P.E. McGovern eds. *The Late Bronze Egyptian Garrison at Beth Shan: A Study of Levels VII and VIII* (University Museum Monographs 85). Philadelphia. Pp. 227–234.

Dothan M. 1959. Notes and News: Tell Mor (Tell Kheidar). *IEJ* 9:271–272.

Dothan M. 1960a. The Ancient Harbour of Ashdod. *CNI* 11:16–19.

Dothan M. 1960b. Excavations at Tel Mor (1959 Season). *BIES* 24:120–132 (Hebrew).

Dothan M. 1960c. Notes and News: Tell Mor (Tell Kheidar). *IEJ* 10:123–125.

Dothan M. 1973a. The End of the Late Bronze Age at Tel Mor and Ashdod. *Eretz Israel* 11:122–133 (Hebrew; English summary, p. 27*).

Dothan M. 1973b. The Foundation of Tel Mor and of Ashdod. *IEJ* 23:1–17.

Dothan M. 1993. Tel Mor. *NEAEHL* 3. Pp. 1073–1074.

Doumet C. 1992. *Sceaux et cylinders orientaux: la collection Chiha* (OBOSA 9). Freibourg–Göttingen.

Eggler J. and Keel O. 2006. *Corpus der Siegel-Amulette aus Jordanien. Vom Neolithikum bis zur Perserzeit* (OBOSA 25). Freiburg–Göttingen.

Frankfort H. 1939. *Cylinder Seals: A Documentary Essay on the Art and Religion of the Ancient Near East.* London.

Fraser G. 1900. *A Catalogue of the Scarabs belonging to George Fraser.* London.

Gardiner A. 1973. *Egyptian Grammar* (3rd rev. ed.). London.

Giveon R. 1985. *Egyptian Scarabs from Western Asia from the Collections of the British Museum* (OBOSA 3). Freiburg–Göttingen.

Guy P.L.O. 1938. *Megiddo Tombs* (OIP 33). Chicago.

Hamilton R.W. 1934. Excavations at Tell Abu Hawām. *QDAP* 4:1–69.

Hayes W.C. 1968. *The Scepter of Egypt. A Background for the Study of the Egyptian Antiquities in the Metropolitan Museum of Art* II: *The Hyksos Period and the New Kingdom (1675–1080 B.C.).* New York.

Hornung E. and Staehelin E. 1976. *Skarabäen und andere Siegelamulette aus Basler Sammlungen* (ÄDS 1). Mainz.

Ions V. 1968. *Egyptian Mythology* (2nd ed., 3rd impression 1975). London.

Kantor H. 1958. The Glyptic. In C.W. McEwan et al. eds. *Soundings at Tell Fakhriyah* (OIP 79). Chicago. Pp. 69–85.

Keel O. 1989a. Der ägyptische Gott Ptah auf Siegelamuletten aus Palästina/Israel. Einige Gesetzmässigkeiten bei der Übernahme von Motiven der Grosskunst auf Miniaturbildträger. In O. Keel, H. Keel-Leu and S. Schroer. *Studien zu den Stempelsiegeln aus Palästina/Israel* II (OBO 88). Freiburg–Göttingen. Pp. 281–323.

Keel O. 1989b. Zur Identifikation des Falkenköpfigen auf den Skarabäen der ausgehenden 13. und der 15. Dynastie. In O. Keel, H. Keel-Leu and S. Schroer. *Studien zu den Stempelsiegeln aus Palästina/Israel* II (OBO 88). Freiburg–Göttingen. Pp. 243–280.

Keel O. 1994. *Studien zu den Stempelsiegeln aus Palästina/Israel* IV (OBO 135). Freiburg–Göttingen.

Keel O. 1995a. *Corpus der Stempelsiegel-Amulette aus Palästina/Israel: Von den Anfängen bis zur Perserzeit, Einleitung* (OBOSA 10). Freiburg/Schweiz-Göttingen.

Keel O. 1995b. Stamp Seals—The Problem of Palestinian Workshops in the Second Millennium and Some Remarks on the Preceeding and Succeeding Periods. In J. Goodnick Westenholz ed. *Seals and Sealing in the Ancient Near East. Proceedings of the Symposium Held on September 2, 1993. Jerusalem, Israel.* Jerusalem. Pp. 93–142.

Keel O. 1997. *Corpus der Stempelsiegel-Amulette aus Palästina/Israel. Von den Anfängen bis zur Perserzeit.*

Katalog I: *Von Tell Abu Farağ bis 'Atlit. With Three Contributions by Baruch Brandl* (OBOSA 13). Freiburg–Göttingen.

Keel O. 2004. The Glyptic Finds: Stamp-Seal Amulets. In A.M. Maeir ed. *Bronze and Iron Age Tombs at Tel Gezer, Israel. Finds from Raymond-Charles Weill's Excavations in 1914 and 1921* (BAR Int. S. 1206). Oxford. Pp. 51–54.

Keel O. and Uehlinger C. 1992. *Göttinnen, Götter und Gottessymbole. Neue Erkenntnisse zur Religionsgeschichte Kanaans und Israels aufgrund bislang unerschlossener ikonographischer Quellen* (QD 134). Freiburg.

Keel O. and Uehlinger C. 1998. *Gods, Goddesses, and Images of God in Ancient Israel*. Edinburgh. [Translation of the German 1992 first edition].

Kelm G.L. and Mazar A. 1995. *Timnah. A Biblical City in the Sorek Valley*. Winona Lake.

Kirkbride D. 1965. Scarabs. In K.M. Kenyon. *Excavations at Jericho* II: *The Tombs Excavated in 1955–8*. London. Pp. 580–655.

Kühne H. and Salje B. 1996. *Kāmid el-Lōz* 15: *Die Glyptik* (SBA 56). Bonn.

Lamon R.S. and Shipton G.M. 1939. *Megiddo* I: *Seasons of 1925–34, Strata I–V* (OIP 42). Chicago.

Leclant J. 1976. Fouilles et travaux en Égypte et au Soudan, 1974–1975. *Orientalia* 45:275–314.

Leibovitch J. 1960. Un choix d'antiquites egyptiennes au Musee Bezalel. *Eretz Israel* 6:1*–6*.

Leibovitch J. 1982. Scarab. In A. Druks. Early Tombs at Tell 'Amr. *'Atiqot (HS)* 8:6 (English summary, p. 1*).

Loud G. 1948. *Megiddo* II: *Seasons of 1935–39* (OIP 62). Chicago.

Lurker M. 1982. *The Gods and Symbols of Ancient Egypt* (1st paperback ed., reprinted 1995). London.

Macalister R.A.S. 1905. Twelfth Quarterly Report on the Excavation of Gezer. *PEFQSt* 38:183–199.

Macalister R.A.S. 1912. *The Excavation of Gezer 1902–1905 and 1907–1909* I–III. London.

Martin G.T. 1971. *Egyptian Administrative and Private-Name Seals. Principally of the Middle Kingdom and Second Intermediate Period*. Oxford.

Mazar A. 1978. Cylinder-Seals of the Middle and Late Bronze Ages in Eretz-Israel. *Qadmoniot* 9:6–14 (Hebrew).

Mazar E. 2007. *Preliminary Report on the City of David Excavations 2005 at the Visitors Center Area*. Jerusalem.

Murray M.A. 1953. Hieroglyphic and Ornamental Seals. In O. Tufnell. *Lachish* III (*Tell ed-Duweir): The Iron Age*. Oxford. Pp. 360–373.

Newberry P.E. 1906. *Scarabs: An Introduction to the Study of Egyptian Seals and Signet Rings*. London.

Newberry P.E. 1907. *Scarab-Shaped Seals* (Catalogue général des antiquités égyptiennes du Musée du Caire, Nos. 36001–37521). London.

Nougayrol J. 1939. *Cylindres-sceaux et empreintes de cylindres trouvés en Palestine (au cours de fouilles réguliérs)* (BAH 33). Paris.

Ory J. 1926. A Bronze-Age Necropolis at Ramath Gan, near Tell el Jerisheh (Jaffa District). *PMJB* 2:6–9.

Ory J. 1940. A Late Bronze Age Tomb at Tell Jerishe. *QDAP* 10:55–57.

Otto E. 1975. s.v. Amun. *LÄ* 1:237–248.

Parker B. 1949. Cylinder Seals from Palestine. *Iraq* 11:1–43.

Petrie W.M.F. 1890. *Kahun, Gurob and Hawara*. London.

Petrie W.M.F. 1891. *Illahun, Kahun and Gurob*. London.

Petrie W.M.F. 1896. *Koptos*. London.

Petrie W.M.F. 1906. *Hyksos and Israelite Cities* (BSAE 12). London.

Petrie W.M.F. 1925. *Buttons and Design Scarabs* (BSAE 38). London.

Petrie W.M.F. 1930. *Beth Pelet* I: *Tell Fara* (BSAE 48). London.

Petrie W.M.F. 1933. *Ancient Gaza* III: *Tell el Ajjul* (BSAE 55). London.

Petrie W.M.F. 1934. *Ancient Gaza* IV: *Tell el Ajjul* (BSAE 56). London.

Petrie W.M.F. and Quibell J.E. 1896. *Naqada and Ballas*. London.

Petrie W.M.F., Mackay E. and Wainwright G. 1910. *Meydum and Memphis* III (BSAE 18). London.

Porada E. 1947. Seal Impressions of Nuzi (AASOR 24). New Haven.

Reisner G.A. 1923. *Excavations at Kerma Parts IV–V* (Harvard African Studies VI). Cambridge, Mass.

Reisner G.A. 1958. *Amulets* II (Catalogue général des antiquités égyptiennes du Musée du Caire Nos. 12528–13595). Cairo.

Rowe A. 1936. *A Catalogue of Egyptian Scarabs, Scaraboids, Seals and Amulets in the Palestine Archaeological Museum*. Cairo.

Salje B. 1990. *Der 'Common Style' der Mitanni-Glyptik und die Glyptik der Levante und Zyperns in der Späten Bronzezeit* (BaghF 11). Mainz.

Säve-Söderbergh T. and Troy L. 1991. *New Kingdom Pharaonic Sites. The Finds and the Sites* (The Scandinavian Joint Expedition to Sudanese Nubia 5:2 [Text]). Uppsala.

Schaeffer C.F.-A. 1948. *Stratigraphie comparée et chronologie de l'Asie occidentale (IIIe et IIe millénaires)*. Oxford.

Schaeffer-Forrer C.F.-A., Amiet P., Chenet G., Mallowan M., Kittel K. and Porada E. 1983. *Corpus des cylindres-sceaux de Ras Shamra- Ugarit et d'Enkomi-Alasia* I (Recherches sur les civilisations, "synthèse" 13). Paris.

Schiff Giorgini M. 1971. *Soleb* II: *les nécropoles*. Florence.

Śliwa J. 1985. *Egyptian Scarabs, Scaraboids and Plaques from the Cracow Collections* (Studia ad Archaeologiam Mediterraneam Pertinentia 8). Cracow.

Starkey J.L. and Harding G.L. 1932. Beth-Pelet Cemetery. In E. Macdonald, J.L. Starkey and G.L. Harding. *Beth-Pelet* II (BSAE 52). London. Pp. 22–35.

Tite M.S. and Bimson M. 1989. Glazed Steatite: An Investigation of the Methods of Glazing Used in Ancient Egypt. *World Archaeology* 21:87–100.

Tufnell O. 1958. Hieroglyphic and Ornamental Seals. In O. Tufnell. *Lachish* IV (*Tell ed Duweir): The Bronze Age*. London. Pp. 92–126.

Tufnell O. 1975. Seal Impressions from Kahûn Town and
Uronarti Fort: A Comparison. *JEA* 61:67–101.

Tufnell O. 1984. *Studies on Scarab Seals* II: *Scarab Seals
and Their Contribution to History in the Early Second
Millennium B.C.* Warminster.

Uehlinger C. 1990. Die Sammlung ägyptischer Siegelamulette
(Skarabäensammlung Fouad S. Matouk). In O. Keel, C.
Uehlinger, M. Gasser, C. Herrmann, H. Keel-Leu and
C. Müller-Winkler. *Altorientalische Miniaturkunst. Die
ältesten visuellen Massenkommunikationsmittel. Ein Blick
in die Sammlungen des Biblischen Instituts der Universität
Freiburg Schweiz.* Mainz. Pp. 58–86.

Ward W.A. 1978. *Studies on Scarab Seals* I: *Pre-12th Dynasty
Scarab Amulets.* Warminster.

Ward W.A. and Dever W.G. 1994. *Studies on Scarab Seals* 3:
*Scarab Typology and Archaeological Context. An Essay on
Middle Bronze Chronology.* Warminster.

Weinstein J.M. 1986. The Scarabs and a Ring with a
Cryptogram. In P.E. McGovern ed. *The Late Bronze and
Early Iron Ages of Central Transjordan: The Baq'ah Valley
Project, 1977–1981* (University Museum Monographs 65).
Philadelphia. Pp. 284–289.

Yurco F.J. 2001. Egypt and Nubia: Old, Middle, and New
Kingdom Eras. In E.M. Yamauchi ed. *Africa and Africans
in Antiquity.* East Lansing. Pp. 28–112.

CHAPTER 8

METALS AND METALLURGY

TRISTAN J. BARAKO, TAMARA STECH, ROBERT MADDIN AND JAMES D. MUHLY

METAL FINDS
Tristan J. Barako

Very few metal objects were available for study when the present author began working on the Tel Mor artifactual assemblages. Either these objects were badly corroded or altogether missing. One missing item is a bronze dagger (Fig. 8.1:1), discovered among the grave goods accompanying Burial 152 (see also Figs. 2.11, 2.12; M. Dothan 1960: Pl. 2:2). It is the only metal artifact that bears analysis. Also recovered were a few clay objects used in metal processing, including fragments of tuyères (Fig. 8.1:2–4) and a crucible (Fig. 8.1:5).

According to Shalev's typology, the dagger belongs to Type 7E of the 'Cast Hilt Daggers' (2004:46–48, Pl. 15:149; see also Yadin 1963: Fig. 187 [center]). The following features characterize this type: hilt with broadened tip and base (to improve grip); bone(?) inlay held in place by ridges along the hilt's border; graduated thickening at the juncture of hilt and blade; cast vein marked by engravings(?) at base of blade; and narrow and slightly rounded blade. Shalev provides the dimensions (in centimeters) of the item as follows: length 28.6; width 3.8 (hilt-tip), 3.7 (hilt-base), 3.2 (blade); and thickness 1.0 (hilt), 0.4 (blade). Of the other daggers assigned to this group, two were found in tombs ('Akko, Dan) and all four (including the dagger) date to LB IIA (for references and further discussion, see Shalev 2004).

Three tuyère fragments were retrieved from Installation 81 in Stratum VI (Fig. 8.1:2–4).[1] They are made of clay that was fired to a mottled light red color with a thick black core. Bronze residue adheres to Fig. 8.1:3, apparently the result of slagging. The average dimensions of the tuyères are as follows: preserved length 13 cm; outer diameter 8 cm; and air-hole diameter 2 cm. Two of the fragments (Fig. 8.1:2, 4) belong to the back end of the tuyères where the tube of the bellows was inserted. The third (Fig. 8:1:3) corresponds to the front end, or nozzle, that penetrated the furnace wall. Its air-hole shaft, which varies in width, is diverted at an angle of approximately 75° to the horizontal. Air was thus directed downward, probably into the bowl of the furnace or a pit containing a crucible (see below). *In situ* tuyères are visible in photographs of Furnace 81 (see Figs. 2.23, 2.24).

Tuyère fragments of the bent-axis type (similar to Fig. 8.1:3) have been found, for example, at Bet Shemesh, Tel Ḥarasim, Khirbet Raddana, Deir 'Alla, Tel Zeror, Ḥazor and, especially, Tel Dan (for references, see Ilan 1999:220–230). Excavations at Yoqne'am produced dozens of bent-axis tuyères in Stratum XVII (Yahalom-Mack and Shalev 2005). The angle of diversion on some of these nozzles varies from approximately 25° (Zeror; Tylecote 1992: Fig. 22) to 50° (Tel Dan; Biran 1989: Fig. 17), considerably less than that of Fig. 8.1:3.[2]

Figure 8.1:5 appears to be a handle belonging to a crucible in the shape of a ladle. It was found near or in the vicinity of either Furnace 81 or 97. The fabric is coarse, the vessel wall thick and the interior blackened. Aside from a deep finger impression, the underside of the crucible is clean and smooth. It appears that the heat source came from above, as is to be expected with a melting operation. Given its limited capacity, this crucible must have been used primarily for the production of small bronze objects. Most crucibles from this period are of the spouted bowl variety, known, for example, from Ḥazor in Stratum 1 of Area F (Yadin et al. 1960: Pl. 147:11) and Tel Dan in Stratum VI (Biran 1989: Fig. 3.1; see also Ilan 1999: Appendix 1).

Apparently a sherd with metal adhering to it, which probably belonged to a crucible, was also retrieved at Tel Mor in Stratum VI (Stech-Wheeler et al. 1981:259–260; see also Ilan 1999:222–223). The lower half of a beer jar bearing traces of bronze residue on the interior may also have been used as a crucible (see Fig. 4.11:17). Storage-jar bases from Area K at Megiddo may have functioned similarly (Y. Gadot, pers. comm.).

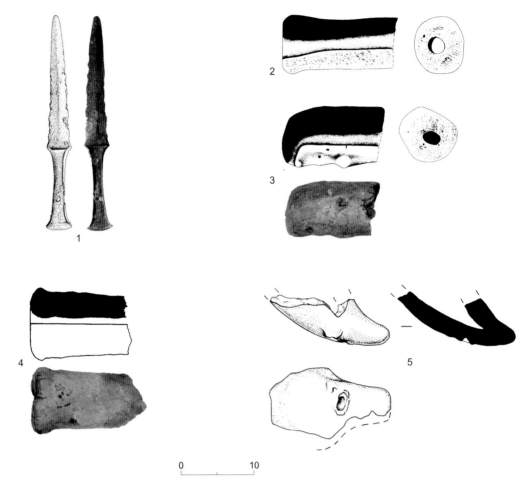

Fig. 8.1. Dagger and metal-processing items.

No.	Object	Reg. No.	Context (Stratum)	Elevation (m)	Description
1	Dagger	B250	Burial 152 (IX)	N/A	Bronze
2	Tuyère	A583/1	Furnace 81 (VI)	22.05	Surface; N/A
3	Tuyère	A612/1	Furnace 81 (VI)	21.90	Surface: 2.5YR 6/8 (light red); fabric: same; core: thick, black; inclusions: very many small voids
4	Tuyère	A611/1	Furnace 81 (VI)	21.90	Surface: 2.5YR 6/6 (light red); fabric: same; core: thick, dark gray; inclusions: many small to medium voids (straw), many fine to small white
5	Crucible	A592/1	Sq J18 (VI)	22.10	Surface (self-slip): 10YR 7/3 (very pale brown); fabric: 5YR 6/6 (reddish yellow); core: very thick, dark gray; inclusions: many fine to medium voids

In light of the emission spectroscopic and atomic absorption analyses carried out on two pieces of bronze spatter from Tel Mor (see below), it is interesting to note also the evidence for bronze recycling at other coastal Levantine sites toward the end of the Late Bronze Age. The courtyard of the LB IIB sanctuary

(Stratum G2) at Tel Nami produced ovens, crucibles, scrap metal and metalworking tools such as chisels and tongs (Artzy 1994:126–127, Figs. 5–8; 1995:23–25, Figs. 2.8–2.10). Installations, crucibles, a fragmentary tuyère, scrap metal, copper slag and a stone mold for casting jewelry were excavated in a transitional LB IIB/

early Iron Age level at Tel 'Akko in Area A/B (Dothan 1988:299; 1993:20–21).

The most complete assemblage of tools and raw material for bronze metalworking *c.* 1200 BCE, however, was recovered aboard the Cape Gelidonya shipwreck (Bass 1967). Its cargo included the following items: 34 copper oxhide ingots, 18 bronze ovoid 'slab' ingots, more than 20 complete and fragmentary bronze discoid 'bun' ingots, badly corroded tin ingots, scrap metal (including lead), casting waste, a bronze swage block, bronze chisels and a punch, a stone anvil, stone polishers and hammerheads, and a whetstone. Based on converging lines of evidence, especially the personal possessions of the crew, the excavator concluded that the ship's place of origin was coastal Canaan (more recently, see Bass 1997).

How might one explain this apparent increase in bronze recycling at sites along the Canaanite coast at the end of the Late Bronze Age? It may be that similar to the decrease (A. Mazar 1990:293, n. 26), or possibly even cessation (Gittlen 1981:51–52), of Cypriot ceramic imports into Canaan toward the end of the thirteenth century BCE, less copper arrived from the island as well. The shipwreck data, limited though it may be, bear out this trend of a dwindling copper supply in the eastern Mediterranean region. The cargo of the Ulu Burun shipwreck, which dates to *c.* 1300 BCE, included ten tons of Cypriot copper and one ton of tin in the form of ingots, but virtually no scrap metal (Pulak 1997). By contrast the Cape Gelidonya shipwreck, which sank approximately a century later, carried only about a ton of copper, bronze and tin in ingot form, along with over 100 pieces of mostly bronze scrap metal.

In addition to the metalworking tools (i.e., tuyères, crucible), a few pieces of bronze spatter were found in Stratum VI and, as mentioned above, analyzed. The results are described below.

ANALYSIS OF METAL PROCESSING DEBRIS
Tamara Stech, Robert Maddin and James D. Muhly

Three samples from metallurgical installations in Tel Mor Stratum VI (see Plan 2.5) were studied.[3] Those designated Mor-1 and Mor-2 are amorphous lumps of metal selected at random; Mor-3 is a corroded bit of metal adhering to a clay surface (furnace or crucible lining?). The samples were mounted in a thermosetting plastic at a temperature of 150°C with the application

of pressure. They were then ground and polished using standard metallographic methods.[4]

Mor-1, although extensively corroded along the grain boundaries, did have a surviving metallic matrix. The microstructure is shown in Fig. 8.2, a photograph at a magnification of ×200. The light areas constitute the metal matrix. The dark areas resulted from corrosion of the object before it was excavated. The lighter gray areas within the grain structure are particles of a second phase most likely of copper sulfide. Observations using the scanning electron microscope equipped with an energy dispersive x-ray spectrometer apparatus (EDAX)[5] show the matrix to consist of copper and tin; the presence of sulfur is also indicated (Figs. 8.3, 8.4). The shape and metallographic structure indicate that this is solidified spatter from a melting crucible or from a casting operation.

Mor-2 (Fig. 8.5) is in a somewhat better state of preservation, although also infested with corrosion. The dark sections in Fig. 8.5 are corroded areas; the light sections are the matrix and the network consisting of a second phase. Scanning electron microscopy indicated a matrix of copper showing the presence of sulfur. Elemental chemical analyses were obtained using emission spectroscopy and atomic absorption techniques. These results are shown in Tables 8.1 and 8.2.

Mor-3 was too corroded to be successfully analyzed metallographically, but semi-quantitative elemental analysis by optical emission spectrography (Table 8.2) shows that it contains only a small amount of tin. As compared with what the atomic absorption analyses indicates, it is clear that the tin percentages are not accurately conveyed by the emission spectrographs. It is likely that Mor-3 reflects a melting operation in which scrap was reprocessed, and perhaps in which extra copper was added, as does Mor-2.

The results from emission spectroscopy are semi-quantitative, while those from atomic absorption are quantitative. Although emission spectroscopy is more sensitive to the qualitative determination of elements, the results from atomic absorption give accurate quantitative determinations; however, the method is not so sensitive in detecting the presence of trace elements as is emission spectroscopy.

The difference in the amount of tin present in the three specimens and observations on other materials from the metallurgical installation (these observations were made in Jerusalem in 1976) suggest that a melting and reprocessing, rather than a smelting, operation

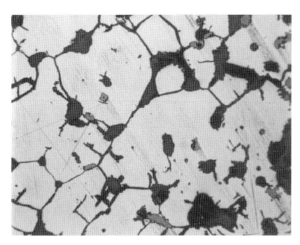

Fig. 8.2. Metallurgical microstructure (×200) of metal processing debris particle Mor-1, showing heavily corroded surface layers (dark foliated) and surviving metal core. The light area is the metallic matrix and the lighter gray area within the delineated grains is second phase material identified as copper sulfide.

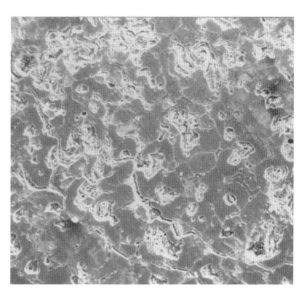

Fig. 8.3. Scanning electron microscope (SEM) photo micrograph of the metallurgical surface of Mor-1.

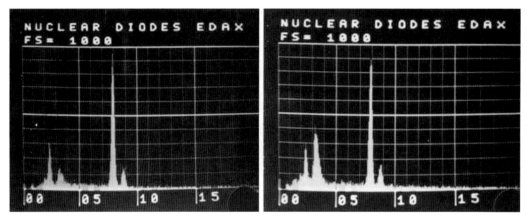

Fig. 8.4. The SEM is equipped with an energy dispersive x-ray spectrometer apparatus (EDAX), which permits qualitative elemental chemical analysis on any particle that can be seen with the SEM (see Fig. 8.3). The left figure shows the presence of sulfur, tin and copper for Mor-1; the right figure shows sulfur, tin and copper for another particle.

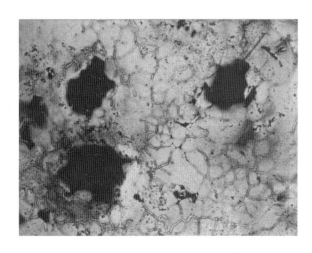

existed at Tel Mor. If a smelting operation had existed, large amounts of slag, as well as raw materials (copper ore and tin or tin rock) would have been found at the site. Further conclusions regarding metal processing at Tel Mor are as follows: (1) The tuyères (see Fig. 8.1:2, 3) were exposed to high heat, so they must have come into the fire from above. (2) The varying percentages of tin in the two metallic pieces (Mor-1 and -2) suggest

◄ Fig. 8.5. Metallurgical microstructure (×50) of Mor-2, showing a network characteristic of tin bronze. The black areas are corrosion.

Table 8.1. Results of Elemental Chemical Analysis of Examined Particles Using Atomic Absorption

Element	Mor-1	Mor-2
Cu	78.11	91.45
Zn	0.07	0.10
Ni	0.15	0.144
Au	0.07	0.03
Sb	0.46	0.24
Fe	0.13	1.28
Sn	11.42	1.19
Ca	nd	nd
Co	nd	nd
Cr	nd	nd
Pb	nd	nd
Mo	nd	nd
Mn	nd	nd
Mg	nd	nd
Pt	nd	nd
Pd	nd	nd
Na	nd	nd
Ag	nd	nd

Table 8.2. Results of Elemental Chemical Analysis of Examined Particles Using Emission Spectroscopy

Element	Mor-1	Mor-2	Mor-3
Fe	nd	nd	0.01
Cu	>95	>90	>90
Ag	nd	0.10	nd
Al	0.10	1–2	1–2
As	0.01	0.01	nd
Ca	0.10	1–2	1–2
Co	0.01	nd	nd
Mg	1–2	1–2	1–2
Mn	0.001	0.01	0.01
Mo	nd	nd	nd
Pb	0.01	0.01	0.01
Si	1–2	5–10	5–10
Sn	1–2	0.10	0.10
Ti	nd	0.01	nd
Ba	0.10	nd	nd
Ru	0.10	0.01	0.01

that bronze was not being made according to a definite formula, but rather with available materials. The evidence therefore indicates that Tel Mor was the site of a bronze recycling workshop.

NOTES

[1] There were "hundreds of pieces of slag and tuyères" associated with the Stratum VI furnaces, according to Waldbaum (1978:60; M. Dothan, pers. comm., 1966).

[2] A 70° angle was originally reported for nozzles found at Timna' (Rothenberg 1972:75), but this estimate was later lowered to between 25 and 50° (Rothenberg 1990:36–37, Figs. 55, 57, 58, 61).

[3] We wish to thank the University of Pennsylvania for use of the research facilities of the Laboratory of Research for the Structure of Matter (LRSM), Dr. Asha Varma for the elemental analyses, Robert White for his invaluable aid in the use of the SEM and Alex Vaskelis for photographic and metallographic assistance.

[4] The mounted specimens were polished using successively smaller grit and then further polished using a lapping technique and an ultimate grit size of 0.05 micron. The polished surfaces of the specimens were then chemically etched with a solution of ammonium hydroxide and hydrogen peroxide in equal proportions to disclose the grain structure.

[5] The scanning electron microscope is equipped with an EDAX that permits qualitative chemical analyses. These analyses can be obtained on any particles that can be seen in the scanning electron microscope.

REFERENCES

Artzy M. 1994. Incense, Camels and Collared Rim Jars: Desert Trade Routes and Maritime Outlets in the Second Millennium. *OJA* 13:121–147.

Artzy M. 1995. Nami: A Second Millennium International Maritime Trading Center in the Mediterranean. In S. Gitin ed. *Recent Excavations in Israel: A View to the West* (Archaeological Institute of America, Colloquia and Conference Papers 1). Dubuque. Pp. 17–40.

Bass G.F. 1967. *Cape Gelidonya: A Bronze Age Shipwreck* (Transactions of the American Philosophical Society 57.8). Philadelphia.

Bass G.F. 1997. Cape Gelidonya. In E.M. Meyers ed. *The Oxford Encyclopedia of Archaeology in the Near East* 1. New York. Pp. 414–416.

Biran A. 1989. The Evidence for Metal Industry at Dan. *Eretz Israel* 20:120–134 (Hebrew; English summary, p. 198).

Dothan M. 1960. The Ancient Harbour of Ashdod. *Christian News from Israel* 11:16–19.

Dothan M. 1988. The Significance of Some Artisans' Workshops along the Canaanite Coast. In M. Heltzer and E. Lipiński eds. *Society and Economy in the Eastern Mediterranean (c. 1500–1000 B.C.). Proceedings of the International Symposium Held at the University of Haifa from the 28th of April to the 2nd of May 1985* (Orientalia Lovaniensia Analecta 23). Leuven. Pp. 295–303.

Dothan M. 1993. Tel Acco. *NEAEHL* 1. Pp. 17–23.

Gittlen B.M. 1981. The Cultural and Chronological Implications of the Cypro-Palestinian Trade during the Late Bronze Age. *BASOR* 241:49–59.

Ilan D. 1999. *Northeastern Israel in the Iron Age I: Cultural, Socioeconomic and Political Perspectives.* Ph.D. diss. Tel Aviv University. Tel Aviv.

Mazar A. 1990. *Archaeology of the Land of the Bible 10,000–586 B.C.E.* New York.

Pulak C. 1997. The Uluburun Shipwreck. In S. Swiny, R.L. Hohlfelder and H.W. Swiny eds. *Res Maritimae: Cyprus and the Eastern Mediterranean from Prehistory to Late Antiquity. Proceedings of the Second International Symposium "Cities on the Sea," Nicosia, Cyprus, October 18–22, 1994* (ASOR Archaeological Reports 4 = CAARI Monograph Series 1). Atlanta. Pp. 233–262.

Rothenberg B. 1972. *Timna: Valley of the Biblical Copper Mines.* London.

Rothenberg B. 1990. Copper Smelting Furnaces, Tuyeres, Slags, Ingot-moulds and Ingots in the Arabah: The Archaeological Data. In B. Rothenberg ed. *The Ancient Metallurgy of Copper: Archaeology—Experiment—Theory* (Researches in the Arabah 1959–1984, 2). London. Pp. 1–74.

Shalev S. 2004. *Swords and Daggers in Late Bronze Age Canaan* (Prähistorische Bronzefunde, Abteilung IV, 13. Band). Stuttgart.

Stech-Wheeler T., Muhly J.D., Maxwell-Hyslop K.R. and Maddin R. 1981. Iron at Taanach and Early Iron Metallurgy in the Eastern Mediterranean. *AJA* 85:245–268.

Tylecote R.F. 1992. *A History of Metallurgy* (2nd ed.) (Institute of Materials 498). London.

Waldbaum J.C. 1978. *From Bronze to Iron: The Transition from the Bronze Age to the Iron Age in the Eastern Mediterranean* (SIMA 54). Göteborg.

Yadin Y. 1963. *The Art of Warfare in Biblical Lands in Light of Archaeological Study* I. New York.

Yadin Y., Aharoni Y., Amiran R., Dothan T., Dunayevsky I. and Perrot J. 1960. *Hazor* II: *An Account of the Second Season of Excavation, 1956.* Jerusalem.

Yahalom-Mack N. and Shalev S. 2005. Metal Production and Utilization. In A. Ben-Tor, A. Zarzecki-Peleg and S. Cohen-Anidjan eds. *Yoqne'am* II: *The Iron Age and the Persian Period Report of the Archaeological Excavations (1977–1988)* (Qedem Reports 6). Jerusalem. Pp. 367–376.

CHAPTER 9

LITHICS

JACOB VARDI AND STEVEN A. ROSEN

The lithic assemblage recovered from the excavations conducted by Moshe Dothan at Tel Mor[1] seems typical for the period of occupation (primarily Late Bronze and Iron Ages), the location of the site on the coastal plain, and the years the excavations were conducted, before the advent of more recent approaches to lithic collections of the historic periods (e.g., Rosen 1997:18–20). Although it contains no great surprises, the assemblage still constitutes another reference set in our data base for the period and provides conclusions concerning basic typologies of stone tools and agricultural practices of the period.

Only in the past twenty years have lithic assemblages from the Late Bronze and Iron Ages in the Levant been the focus of analytic study. Although as early as the 1930s they were recognized as common to these periods (e.g., Guy 1938:70), early reports concentrated on basic descriptive typologies. More recent studies of the lithic assemblages from these periods in particular, and from the early historic periods in general, have expanded the range of analysis to include such subjects as the organization of technology (e.g., Coqueugniot 1991; Chabot 1998), craft specialization and trade (Rosen 1997:103–116), chronology (e.g., Waechter 1958), agriculture (Marder, Braun and Milevski 1995) and other functions (e.g., Coqueugniot 1993; Rosen 1997:117–132). Of particular interest is the complex relationship between the development of metallurgy and the ultimate decline of lithic technology (Rosen 1997:151–66), with only secondary uses such as strike-a-lights (Runnels 1994) and threshing teeth (e.g., Bordaz 1965; Whallon 1978) continuing into recent times.

Tel Mor's location on the coastal plain in the Ashdod region is of importance in understanding the assemblage for various reasons. First, although flint is ubiquitous in the limestone areas of Israel, the coastal plain has no flint sources of good quality. It is not surprising, then, that most formal tools appear to have been manufactured from imported flint (cf. Hammond 1977). Second, the coastal plain has traditionally been home to populations producing a different material culture than that of the interior of the country, and this variability is of interest in examining the lithic assemblage. As it happens, no clear evidence for geographic distinctions can be seen in the stone tools.

It is also important to note that the excavations at Tel Mor were conducted before general recognition of the value of intensive collection of lithic materials (cf. Rosen 1997:35–38). As a result, the assemblage is lacking most elements of the debitage; thus there is a bias toward the more formal tool elements, which limits the range of questions that can be addressed.

The Tel Mor lithic collection consists of 135 flint artifacts and a single limestone exemplar. Of this collection, 119 are defined as tools, showing intentional retouch, and 17 as waste (debitage = 13, debris = 4). Broken artifacts number 71. General frequencies are summarized in Table 9.1. Raw material is heterogeneous, with a number of colors (Table 9.2) and textures distinguishable in the flint. There are several variants of brown flint (dark brown, light brown, gray

Table 9.1. Tools and Waste

Type		N
Sickle segments	Backed blade	13
	Simple blade	2
	Canaanean blade	2
	Large Geometric	83
Retouched blades	Backed blade	5
	Simple retouched	8
Composite tools		3
Various tools		3
Total Tools		119
Flakes		3
Primary flakes		1
Blades		4
Bladelets		1
CTE		2
Chunks		4
Various waste		2
Total Waste		17
Total		136

brown), as well as gray flint, black flint and purple flint, the latter apparently the result of burning. Six artifacts are of white flint. Categorization of texture is subjective, but two basic types can be distinguished: smooth and grainy. Most of the smooth brown flint, which dominates the assemblage numerically, was probably imported from farther inland since there are no appropriate sources in the Tel Mor vicinity.

TYPOLOGICAL DESCRIPTION

Sickle Segments

Sickle segments are classified as such either on the basis of the presence of sickle gloss (Anderson 1980; Semenov 1973; Rosen 1997:55–57) or morphological identity with other pieces showing gloss. This class is the largest tool class in the assemblage, constituting 84% of the tool assemblage. Although this high percentage may be partially the result of selective collection, it is also typical of Late Bronze and Iron Age assemblages.

Backed Sickle Blade Segments (n = 13)
These pieces are technologically blades (Fig. 9.1:1) and show abrupt retouch (backing) on one edge. Most were manufactured on light brown (n = 4) or dark brown (n = 5) flint. Three were manufactured on black flint and the remaining piece shows white patina. All are fine-grained. Although only one segment is unbroken, it is possible to determine that six were partially backed. Only a single segment retains a bulb of percussion, although another piece shows evidence of bulbar thinning.

Retouch is light on five segments (nibbling or irregular), regular and clear on seven pieces, and heavy—appearing on the ventral surface as well as the dorsal—on only one piece. Sickle gloss is present, but generally light, on all pieces. Two pieces show strong gloss and one exhibits very strong gloss, appearing on both the dorsal and ventral surfaces. Average dimensions are: width 2.76 ± 0.63 cm, and thickness 0.74 ± 0.198 cm. It was not possible to determine length dimensions due to breakage.

Simple Blade Sickle Segments (n = 2)
Both of the simple blade sickles are on light brown flint. One is unbroken, measuring 4.4 × 1.4 × 0.6 cm. Dimensions for the second are width 2.7 cm and thickness 0.7 cm. One retains cortex on the dorsal surface. Both show purple streaking and strong sickle gloss.

Table 9.2. Raw Material Frequencies by Color

Color	N	%
Light brown	63	46.3
Dark brown	38	27.9
Gray brown	4	2.9
Gray	10	7.4
Black	9	6.6
White	6	4.4
Purple	2	1.5
Light brown–white	1	0.7
Dark brown–white	2	1.5
Black–gray	1	0.7
Total	136	99.9

Table 9.3. Large Geometric Sickle-Segment Shape Frequencies

Shape	N	%
Parallelograms	34	41.0
Trapezoids	8	9.6
Triangles	5	6.0
Rectangles	2	2.4
Broken	34	41.0
Total	83	100.0

Canaanean Sickle Segments (n = 2)
Two pieces were classified as Canaanean sickle segments (Fig. 9.1:2), attributable to the Early Bronze Age (Rosen 1997:46–49). Both are white, but patination obscures the original color. One piece is broken and the second, measuring 6.7 cm in length, shows evidence of deliberate truncation. Neither retains the bulb of percussion. One piece has light retouch on one edge, perhaps the beginnings of backing or a second working edge, and heavy retouch on the working edge, which may have removed signs of sickle gloss (hence the classification as a sickle in spite of the absence of gloss). The second has light retouch and light gloss.

Large Geometric Sickle Segments (n = 83)
The Large Geometric sickle segments constitute the largest type class in the assemblage, comprising 61% of the total objects and 70% of the tools. The type can be divided into the following four primary shapes or subtypes based on the shape and direction of the truncations: parallelograms, trapezoids, triangles and rectangles. Only 34 of these artifacts are broken, a lower proportion than for the assemblage as a whole, indicating the general durability of the shape.

Fig. 9.1. Lithics.

Backing (44 artifacts) or partial backing (18 artifacts) is present on 75% of the artifacts in the general class. Sickle gloss (68 artifacts) is present on 82% of the pieces, the remainder apparently either incomplete or unused. The bulb of percussion is present on 11 pieces; there is evidence for thinning and deliberate removal on 13; the bulb of percussion is absent from the remainder. The general shape of the bulb of percussion on those pieces where it is preserved indicates soft hammer percussion (e.g., Pelegrin 2000:76–77; Rosen 1986:262).

The angled truncations, especially as evident on parallelograms and trapezoids, probably reflect technological adjustment to the crescent shape of the composite sickle. Earlier blade types may well have been crescent shaped, but Large Geometrics seem to reflect an improvement in the ability to provide a curved blade (e.g., Mozel 1983:182–184, Fig. 2; Gilead 1973:140, Fig. 5; Petrie 1932: Pl. 23; Rosen 1986:260, Pl. 1). Similarly, deliberate bulb removal and backing also probably served to facilitate hafting within wooden or bone handles.

Parallelograms are the most common shape or subtype in the assemblage, constituting 41% (34 artifacts) of the Large Geometric class (Figs. 9.1:3–6). Brown is the dominant color, both light (n = 16) or dark (n = 11); followed by four gray and gray-brown artifacts; and three on black flint, apparently burnt. Three pieces retain cortex, and one shows interior faults in the flint. One of the light brown pieces is on a relatively rare flint type, cream in color and showing purple streaks (Fig. 9.1:6). Most of the unbroken parallelograms are backed, either fully (n = 17) or partially (n = 8), and four show ventral backing. There is homogeneity in the alignment of the truncations such that if the working edge is aligned downwards, all but one of the parallelograms slant left. Only six pieces retain the bulb of percussion. Of the 28 lacking a bulb, 4 seem to reflect intentional thinning and removal. All pieces exhibit edge retouch of different degrees. Thus, 3 have minor edge damage, perhaps not intentional, and 33 are heavily (n = 13) or very heavily retouched (n = 19). Gloss is clearly present on 29 pieces, 16 of which have heavy gloss and 2 only light gloss. Five pieces lack obvious gloss. Average dimensions are length 2.08 ± 0.98 cm, width 1.77 ± 0.59 cm and thickness 0.63 ± 0.20 cm.

Trapezoids (n = 8) display angled truncations that give the artifact its shape. On six of these pieces the working edge is along the shorter rather than, what is more usual, the longer axis. One of these is asymmetric (as opposed to mirror image) in the angles of its truncations. Three pieces are fully backed and another three show partial backing. Three of the backed pieces are concave along the back. Only two pieces retain the bulb of percussion, and of the remainder, two show intentional bulbar thinning. Retouch intensity ranges from very heavy (n = 2), to heavy (n = 2), standard (n = 3) and light (n = 1). One piece is also notched. Only one trapezoid does not exhibit gloss. The remainder have very heavy gloss (n = 2), heavy gloss (n = 4) or light gloss (n = 1). Five pieces are on light brown flint, two on dark brown flint and one on gray flint with numerous flaws. One is burnt and also has ventral retouch. Only a single piece retains cortex. Average dimensions are length 4.84 ± 1.25 cm, width 3.2 ± 0.57 cm and thickness 0.78 ± 0.27 cm.

Triangles (n = 5) show only a single truncated edge, with the back edge meeting the working edge to form the triangle. One of the triangles has a borer point at one corner, reflecting recycling and reuse of the artifact after its use as a sickle (not included in the statistical summaries). Another artifact was recovered in three pieces and refitted. Four were made on dark brown and one on light brown flint. Four of the triangles have right angle truncations on the right side of the piece (with working edge down). Retouch is very heavy on three pieces and light on two. Three pieces show clear sickle gloss (two strong, one light) and two seem to lack gloss. All have backing retouch, although one is only partially backed. One also has a notch on the backed edge. None retain the bulb of percussion. Average dimensions are length 5.65 ± 1.52 cm, width 2.7 ± 0.68 cm and thickness 0.62 ± 0.13 cm. One piece is especially large, measuring 7.8 cm in length (Fig. 9.1:7).

Rectangles (n = 2) constitute the smallest subtype of Large Geometric sickle segments. Both are on light brown flint. Only one is backed and neither retains the bulb of percussion. Both show heavily retouched working edges and both have sickle gloss, one light and one heavy, on the ventral surface (Fig. 9.1:8).

Retouched Blades

Backed Blades (n = 5)
Two pieces are on dark brown flint, one on light brown, one on white and one gray, the latter a result of burning. All pieces in this group are broken and it is not possible to ascertain degrees of backing (partial or complete). Four pieces show light working edge retouch and the final, heavy retouch. Average dimensions: width 1.96 ± 0.38 cm and thickness 0.52 ± 0.11 cm.

Simple Retouched Blades (n = 8)
Four simple retouched blades are on light brown flint, one is on dark brown, one is on white flint and two are on gray. One of these is burnt, two retain cortex and only two pieces are unbroken (length average refers only to these two). Three show light edge retouch; two, strong working edge retouch; and two have heavy retouch, appearing on the ventral and dorsal faces. The bulb of percussion is absent from all pieces, although

one displays signs of deliberate bulbar thinning or removal. One piece seems to retain traces of plaster adhesive (Fig. 9.1:9). Average dimensions are: length 4.71 ± 1.22 cm, width 2.68 ± 0.68 cm and thickness 0.61 ± 0.22 cm.

Composite Pieces (Secondary Use)

One elliptical scraper with invasive retouch was manufactured on a Large Geometric sickle segment. The sickle gloss is cut by the scraper retouch, indicating conversion of the sickle to the scraper.

One drill, with steep retouch along two edges of a narrow elongated point, was also manufactured on a sickle segment. Strong sickle gloss is present on the dorsal face of the drill, clearly unconnected to the drill function.

One borer was manufactured on a sickle segment (Fig. 9.1:10). The original working edge of the sickle is intact, showing both heavy retouch and strong sickle gloss. The heavy retouch suggests that when the sickle was no longer useable, it was notched at a corner to create a piercing point.

Varia

This category includes one large, massively retouched chunk, one fragment of a polished limestone ax (Fig. 9.1:11) and one retouched flake showing signs of burning (purplish coloration along with heat spalling and a gray color).

Waste

Only three flakes were collected. In addition, one primary flake, four broken blades and one broken bladelet were gathered. The bladelet is probably intrusive. Two chunks and two wadi cobble fragments were also collected. It is clear that the scarcity of waste is due to selective collection.

SUMMARY AND CONCLUSIONS

The primary lithic class recovered from Tel Mor is the sickle segment, clearly related to the harvesting of cereal grasses (e.g., Semenov 1973:121–122; Anderson 1980; Rosen 1997:55–57). This dominance, along with the scarcity of other types, is both a reflection of the importance of farming in late second-millennium BCE society and of the declining use of flint in other realms of daily activity (Rosen 1997:151–166).

The importance of the flint sickle segments is also reflected in the fact that they seem to have been imported to the site. This is suggested first and foremost by the absence of appropriate raw material sources in the vicinity of Tel Mor. The nearest flint sources seem to be in the Shephelah and Judean Hills (e.g., Hammond 1977; Rosen 1997:32–34). Although collection bias appears to have been an issue at Tel Mor, the lack of corresponding debitage is also seen at contemporary sites where lithic collection was more systematic. In particular, such sites as Lakhish (Rosen 2004), Jericho (Payne 1983), Ashdod (Rosen 1993), Qiri (Rosen 1987) and others (Rosen 1997:11–12), contained numerous sickles, yet lacked cores for the manufacture of blanks. At Gezer, caches of blanks, again lacking cores, were discovered (Rosen 1986). Together these data suggest a picture of preliminary production at workshop sites and subsequent import to the centers of consumption/ use. This model fits the evidence from Tel Mor.

The dominance of the Large Geometric sickle segment type is typical of the second millennium BCE in the Levant and thus matches the chronological attributions of Tel Mor (see Chapter 2; Dothan 1993). Well-defined types, such as Canaanean segments, are either intrusive or were deliberately collected in antiquity. Other types, such as simple blade sickles, may reflect a spectrum of variation within specific categories. Difficulties in establishing provenience of most of the artifacts render further chrono-stratigraphic analysis impossible.

NOTE

[1] We are grateful to Tristan Barako for the opportunity to examine the lithic collection from Tel Mor. The artifacts were photographed by Alter Fogel of Ben-Gurion University of the Negev.

References

Anderson P.C. 1980. A Testimony of Prehistoric Tasks: Diagnostic Residues on Stone Tool Working Edges. *World Archaeology* 21:181–194.

Bordaz J. 1965. The Threshing Sledge—Ancient Turkish Grain Separating Method Still Proves Efficient. *Natural History* 74:216–229.

Chabot J. 1998. Analyse spatiale et stratigraphique des artefacts de pierre sur éclats de Tell 'Atij-Centre. In M. Fortin and O. Aurenche eds. *Natural Space, Inhabited Space in Northern Syria (10th–2nd Millennium B.C.)* (Canadian Society for Mesopotamian Studies, Bulletin 33, Travaux de la Maison de l'Orient 28). Québec–Lyons. Pp. 257–269.

Coqueugniot E. 1991. Outillage de pierre taillée du Bronze Récent. In M. Yon ed. *Ras Shamra-Ougarit* VI: *arts et industries de la pierre*. Paris. Pp. 127–204.

Coqueugniot E. 1993. Un atelier specialisé dans le palais de Mari. MARI 7:205–250.

Dothan M. 1993. Tel Mor. *NEAEHL* 3. Pp. 1073–1074.

Gilead D. 1973. Flint Industry of the Bronze Age from Har Yeruham and Tell Nagila. In Y. Aharoni ed. *Excavations and Studies. Essays in Honour of Professor Shemuel Yeivin*. Tel Aviv. Pp. 133–143 (Hebrew; English summary, p. xvii).

Guy P.L.O. 1938. *Megiddo Tombs* (OIP 33). Chicago.

Hammond W.M. 1977. *The Raw and the Chipped: An Analysis of Correlations between Raw Material and Tools of a Lithic Industry from Tell el Hesi, Israel*. Ph.D. diss. Columbia University. New York.

Marder O., Braun E. and Milevski I. 1995. The Flint Assemblage of Lower Ḥorvat 'Illin: Some Technical and Economic Considerations. *'Atiqot* 27:63–93.

Mozel I. 1983. A Reconstructed Sickle from Lachish. *Tel Aviv* 10:182–185.

Payne J.C. 1983. The Flint Implements of Jericho. In K.M. Kenyon and T.A. Holland eds. *Jericho* IV: *The Pottery Type Series and Other Finds*. London. Pp. 622–758.

Pelegrin J. 2000. Les techniques de débitage laminaire au tardiglaciaire: critères de diagnose et quelqes réflexions. In B. Valentin, P. Bodu and M. Christensen eds. *L'Europe centrale et septentrionale au tardiglaciere* (Mémoires du musée de préhistoire d'Ile-de-France 7). Nemours. Pp. 73–87.

Petrie W.M.F. 1932. *Ancient Gaza* II (*Tell el Ajjūl*) (BSAE 54). London.

Rosen S.A. 1986. The Gezer Flint Caches 1970–1. In W.G. Dever ed. *Gezer* IV: *The 1969–71 Seasons in Field VI, the "Acropolis"* (Annual of the Hebrew Union College/Nelson Glueck School of Biblical Archaeology 4). Jerusalem. Pp. 259–263.

Rosen S.A. 1987. The Lithic Assemblage of the Iron Age Strata. In A. Ben-Tor and Y. Portugali. *Tell Qiri, an Iron Age Village in the Jezreel Valley* (Qedem 24). Jerusalem. Pp. 246–248.

Rosen S.A. 1993. A Note on the Flint Assemblage (from Ashdod Area G). *'Atiqot* 23:117–121.

Rosen S.A. 1997. *Lithics after the Stone Age: A Handbook of Stone Tools from the Levant*. Walnut Creek.

Rosen S.A. 2004. The Chipped Stone Assemblages. In D. Ussishkin. *The Renewed Archaeological Excavations at Lachish* IV. Tel Aviv. Pp. 2197–2226.

Runnels C. 1994. Tinderflints and Firemaking in the Historical Period. *Lithic Technology* 19:7–16.

Semenov S.A. 1973. *Prehistoric Technology* (3rd ed.). Bath.

Waechter J. 1958. Flint Implements. In O. Tufnell. *Lachish* IV (*Tell ed-Duweir*): *The Bronze Age*. London. Pp. 325–327.

Whallon R. 1978. Threshing Sledge Flints: A Distinctive Pattern of Wear. *Paléorient* 4:319–324.

CHAPTER 10

GROUNDSTONE OBJECTS

JENNIE R. EBELING

A small assemblage of groundstone artifacts was excavated at Tel Mor and retained for analysis and publication (Fig. 10.1; Table 10.1). This assemblage includes examples of the typical stone bowls, processing equipment and other implements used in the southern Levant from the Middle Bronze Age through the Hellenistic period. Most of the raw stone material, which includes basalt, limestone, flint and beachrock, is available from relatively local sources; in addition, non-local igneous rock and, perhaps, limestone[1] were used to make several artifacts. This report considers the artifacts typologically and suggests some of the possible functions of the tools.

TYPOLOGY

Vessels and Mortars

Six stone vessel fragments, which are clearly identified by their remaining rims and/or legs, were unearthed at Tel Mor. Despite their morphological classification as vessels, which is based on wall thickness and other factors (Wright 1992:75), use-wear indicative of rotary grinding on the interiors of several of these objects attests to their use in processing activities. In addition, one roughly shaped mortar was found at the site.

Tripods (n = 3; Fig. 10.1:1–3)
Three fragments of tripod vessels, which are known in quantity from sites in the Levant from the Middle Bronze Age through the Iron Age (Elliott 1991:30; Hovers 1996:177 and published parallels listed therein), are among the assemblage. Figure 10.1:1 is unusual for its irregular form and shallow, uneven use-surface. Figure 10.1:2 is difficult to reconstruct due to its very fragmentary preservation. Figure 10.1:3 is a good example of this vessel type; its rough, highly vesicular texture, however, bears witness to its use in processing activities.

Other Vessels (n = 3; Fig. 10.1:4)
Three other fragments of vessels of unknown type were identified by their preserved rims. Reg. No. A422/7 (not drawn) is a fragmentary rim sherd of a limestone vessel or mortar with grinding wear on its interior and a very roughly finished exterior. Figure 10.1:4 has a very carefully made rim and smooth ground interior with a gradually thickening base. The third vessel is too fragmentary to reconstruct.

Mortar (n = 1)
One complete, roughly worked limestone mortar, oval in plan view, was retrieved. It features a small, oval-shaped central depression and is similar to a 'cup mark' boulder from the City of David in Jerusalem (Hovers 1996: Fig. 28:6). The size and shape of its central depression, coupled with use-wear indicative of pecking on its interior, suggests that it functioned as a mortar for grinding small quantities of various substances, perhaps nuts or seeds.

Grinding Slabs (n = 5; Fig. 10.1:5)

Grinding slabs comprise the lower, stationary component of the food processing toolkit in antiquity. These tools were used in conjunction with handstones or other mobile implements to process grain, other agricultural products and non-edible materials (Hovers 1996:176–177; Milevski 1998:62–64; Petit 1999:150–152). Although no complete grinding slabs survived at Tel Mor, five fragments could be identified as such with some degree of certainty (e.g., Fig. 10.1:5). Six fragments—five basalt and one beachrock—that could not be identified as grinding slabs with certainty are grouped under 'Miscellaneous Groundstone Fragments'.

Handstones

Eleven handstones of various shapes and sizes were found at Tel Mor. These tools were used primarily with grinding slabs to process grain and other products, although they may have been used in other processing activities as well. In addition to the eleven identifiable examples, the six fragments categorized under 'Miscellaneous Groundstone Fragments' may have been handstones.

Elongated Handstones (n = 6)
Six of the artifacts in the handstone assemblage represent an elongated type that was operated with both hands. Elongated handstones (also called 'upper grinding stones') are well known from Bronze and Iron Age sites in the southern Levant (Hovers 1996:178; Milevski 1998:64–65; Petit 1999:149 and published parallels listed therein).

Other Handstones (n = 5; Fig. 10.1:6, 7)
The remaining handstones in the assemblage vary in shape, size and material. Figure 10.1:6, which is not ground absolutely flat on its use-surface, has evidence of battering wear on its edges, perhaps indicating that this tool had multiple uses. Reg. No. A687/10 (not drawn) also has battering wear on one short end. Figure 10.1:7 is a loaf-shaped handstone with a convex use-surface; it is so thin from use that it is hard to grasp and is perhaps 'worn out'.

Hammerstones (n = 3; Fig. 10.1:8)

Three complete hammerstones, all roughly spherical in shape, were found at Tel Mor (e.g., Fig. 10.1:8). All feature clear evidence of battering wear on their surfaces, and they may have been used in any number of processing activities (Milevski 1998:71; Petit 1999:152). Reg. No. B10/6 (not drawn), which is made of basalt and features one smooth ground face, may have functioned as a grinding tool as well.

Polishers (n = 6; Fig. 10.1:9)

Six natural pebbles with distinctive wear on their polished surfaces and ground edges were probably used as polishers or abraders (Elliott 1991:23). Five are made of dense, non-local igneous rock (e.g., Fig. 10.1:9) and one is made of a possibly non-local limestone with shell inclusions. Reg. Nos. A236/11 and B94/14 and the polisher with no registration number (none drawn) are notable for the many non-random scratches on their faces.

Perforated Objects

Weights (n = 2; Fig. 10.1:10)
Two intentionally perforated limestone objects probably functioned as weights. The perforation in Fig. 10.1:10 was clearly drilled from both sides; wear marks indicate that it was probably a suspended weight. The original form of Reg. No. A743/1 (not drawn), which is poorly preserved, is impossible to reconstruct.

Fig. 10.1 ▶

No.	Object	Reg. No.	Context (Stratum)	Material	Notes/Use-Wear
1	Tripod	A137/1	Sq M19 (IV)	Dense basalt	Smooth ground interior
2	Tripod	B272/13?	Courtyard 118 (XII)	Dense basalt	Very smooth interior
3	Tripod	None	N/A	Vesicular basalt	Ground interior
4	Unidentified vessel/mortar	A563/7	Sqs G–H18	Dense basalt	Smooth ground interior
5	Grinding slab	A705/2	Area 26 (V)	Limestone	Fragmentary bifacial tool; ground use surfaces
6	Handstone	A568/1	Sqs G–H18	Dense basalt	Battering wear on edges
7	Handstone	A799/5	N/A	Vesicular basalt	Very smooth, convex use surface
8	Hammerstone	A301/31	Sq J18 (VI)	Flint	Battered surface
9	Polisher	A551/16	Room 71 (VI)	Igneous rock	Complete; ground edges, facets
10	Perforated weight	A360/1	M20 (V?)	Limestone	Drilled perforation
11	Socle	A726/2	N/A	Limestone	Rotary wear

Socle (n = 1; Fig. 10.1:11)

One perforated limestone object with clear rotary wear marks on its interior probably functioned as a socle stone (Fig. 10.1:11). The shape of this object and the intentional chipping along its outer edges suggest that it was cut to fit a specific space. The wear inside the perforation, which, like Fig. 10.1:10, was clearly drilled from both sides, does not suggest that it was used as a suspended weight.

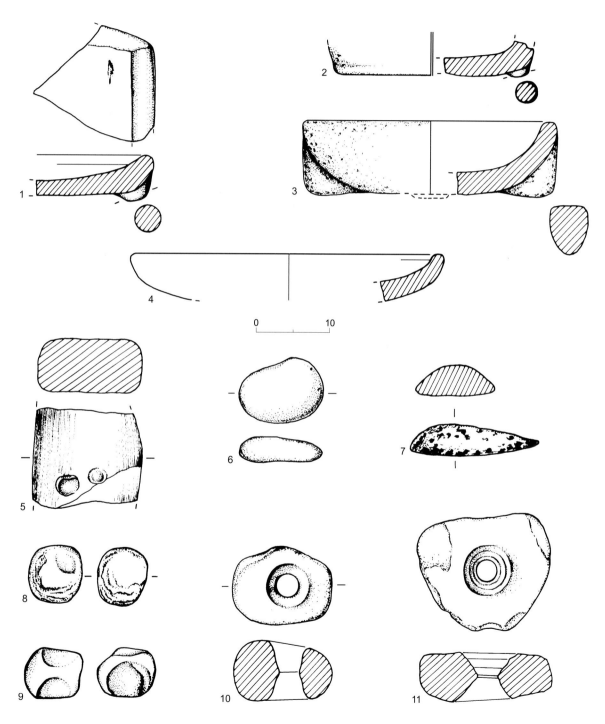

Fig. 10.1. Groundstone objects.

Table 10.1. Groundstone Objects (not illustrated)

Object	Reg. No.	Context (Stratum)	Material	Measurements (cm)	Notes/Use-Wear
Unidentified vessel/ mortar	A422/7	Sq H19	Limestone	Rim Th 2–2.5; Rim L 10.3	Smooth ground interior
Unidentified vessel/ mortar	None	N/A	Dense basalt	Rim Th 1.75	N/A
Mortar	None	N/A	Limestone	L 17.2; W 11.1; H 8.6; Depression 7.5 × 4.8 × 1.5	Pecking wear in depression
Grinding slab	A473/16	Sq M20	Dense basalt	L 18.3; W 15; Th 5.7	Fragmentary; smooth ground use surface
Grinding slab	A715/4	N/A	Dense basalt	L 14.4; W 12.3; Th 3.6	Fragmentary; ground to preserved edges
Grinding slab	A726/3	N/A	Dense basalt	L 22.8; W 14.6; Th 3.9	Fragmentary; very smooth ground to preserved edges
Grinding slab	N/A	N/A	Vesicular basalt	L 22.5 W 14.4; Th 4.5	Fragmentary bifacial tool; ground use surfaces
Elongated handstone	A436/10	Area 65 (V)	Vesicular basalt	L 15.5; W 10.7; Th 4.1	< half preserved
Elongated handstone	A626/11	Sq H18	Dense basalt	L 14.9; W 11.2; Th 3.7	< half preserved
Elongated handstone	N/A	N/A	Dense basalt	L 11.4; W 10.8; Th 3.4	< half preserved
Elongated handstone	N/A	N/A	Vesicular basalt	L 12.7; W 11.6; Th 4.7	< half preserved
Elongated handstone	N/A	N/A	Vesicular basalt	L 21.3; W 11.9; Th 5.4	> half preserved
Elongated handstone	N/A	N/A	Vesicular basalt	L 19.3; W 11.5 Th 4.7	> half preserved
Handstone	A5/21	N/A	Limestone	L 8.3; W 10.8; Th 4.5	< half preserved; flat use surface
Handstone	A28/29	Sq K19 (II?)	Beachrock	L 9; W 5; Th 4.3	Complete; convex use surface
Handstone	A687/10	Room 63? (VIII?)	Limestone	L 10.6; W 8.5; Th 8.1	Complete; flat use surface; battering wear on one short end
Hammerstone	B10/6	Sq M20 (II)	Dense basalt	Diam. 4.5–4.7	One ground face
Hammerstone	B78/10	Probe 117 (X)	Flint	Diam. 5–5.3	Battered surface
Polisher	A100/12	N/A	Igneous rock	L 7.2; W 5.3; Th 3.6	Complete; ground edges
Polisher	A236/11	Sq M19 (VI)	Limestone	L 7.5; W 5.7; Th 3.5	< half preserved; ground edges; scratches on both faces
Polisher	A458/5	N/A	Igneous rock	L 8.5; W 6.5: Th 4	Complete; ground and chipped edges
Polisher	B94/14	Subfloor fill for Room 108? (IX?)	Igneous rock	L 9.9; W 7.1; Th 3.9	Nearly complete; ground and chipped edges; scratches on both faces
Polisher	N/A	N/A	Igneous rock	L 10.1; W 9.3; Th 5.7	Complete; ground edges; battered one end; scratches on both faces
Perforated weight	A743/1?	N/A	Limestone	L 12.5; W 9.5; Th 14.2	< half preserved
Miscellaneous groundstone fragment	A363/13	Well 55 (I)	Vesicular basalt	10.7 × 9.8 × 2.7	Fragmentary
Miscellaneous groundstone fragment	A382/12	Well 55 (I)	Vesicular basalt	8 × 7.8 × 3.7	Fragmentary

Table 10.1 (cont.)

Object	Reg. No.	Context (Stratum)	Material	Measurements (cm)	Notes/Use-Wear
Miscellaneous groundstone fragment	A440/4	Sq J20 (VI)	Dense basalt	11.1 × 6.5 × 4.7	Fragmentary
Miscellaneous groundstone fragment	A576/15	Room 75 (VII)	Vesicular basalt	9.5 × 9.2 × 3.9	Fragmentary
Miscellaneous groundstone fragment	316?	N/A	Dense basalt	12.7 × 12.4 × 4	Fragmentary
Miscellaneous groundstone fragment	N/A	N/A	Beachrock	11.5 × 7.3 × 4.5	Fragmentary; shell inclusions
Unidentified	A260/7	Ṭabun 24 (V)	Limestone	L 9.5; W 6.5; Th 5.3	Evidence of flaking
Bowl?	A408/22	Sq M20 (VI)	Dense basalt	L 8.1; W 2.7; Th 3.1	No grinding evidence
Smoothed pebble?	A549/9	Room 75 (VIII–VII)	Limestone	L 7.1; W 6; Th 1.5	Fragmentary
Axe?	A717/11	Ṭabun 24 (V)	Igneous rock	L 11; W 9.5; Th 6	Intentionally chipped edges; hafting wear?

Miscellaneous Groundstone Fragments (n = 6)

Five fragments of basalt and one fragment of beachrock with some grinding evidence are also part of the assemblage; they may be fragments of grinding slabs, handstones or other implements.

Varia (n = 4)

This category includes four artifacts that are difficult to classify but were found in good contexts (none drawn). Reg. No. A260/7 is a chunk of intentionally flaked limestone; its function is not clear. Reg. No. A408/22 is a piece of basalt that looks like a rim sherd of a bowl, the edges of which were intentionally straightened. Reg. No. A549/9 appears to be the corner of a smooth limestone pebble. Reg. No. A717/11 might be the poorly preserved remains of an axe; it has intentionally chipped edges and possible hafting wear on one short side.

CONCLUSIONS

The size of the groundstone assemblage from Tel Mor does not permit far-reaching conclusions about stone-tool use at the site, but some general observations can be made. The presence of grinding equipment, including grinding slabs, handstones and other implements, indicates that 'domestic'-type food processing activities were practiced at Tel Mor. The presence of tripods and other vessels (also likely used in food processing activities) suggests that more specialized and costly equipment was desired by the site's inhabitants. Non-local raw materials that were apparently required to make certain specialized forms—specifically polishers and perhaps an axe—may have been brought to the site through maritime activities. More than anything, the artifacts in this assemblage reflect the diversity of processing activities practiced at Tel Mor during its long history of occupation, and the need for specific types of stone tools to accomplish these tasks.

NOTES

[1] Naomi Porat of the Geological Survey of Israel identified polisher A100/12 and hafted object A717/11 as non-local igneous stone, and polisher A236/11 as possibly non-local limestone (July 3, 2003).

REFERENCES

Elliott C. 1991. The Ground Stone Industry. In M. Yon ed. *Ras Shamra-Ougarit* VI: *arts et industries de la pierre.* Paris. Pp. 9–100.

Hovers E. 1996. The Groundstone Industry. In A. de Groot and D.T. Ariel eds. *Excavations at the City of David* IV, *1978–85, Directed by Y. Shiloh* (Qedem 35). Jerusalem. Pp. 171–192.

Milevski I. 1998. The Groundstone Tools. In G. Edelstein, I. Milevski and S. Aurant. *Villages, Terraces, and Stone Mounds: Excavations at Manahat, Jerusalem, 1987–1989* (IAA Reports 3). Jerusalem. Pp. 61–77.

Petit L.P. 1999. Grinding Implements and Material Found at Tall Dayr 'Alla, Jordan: Their Place and Role in Archaeological Research. *ADAJ* 43:145–167.

Wright K.I. 1992. A Classification System for Ground Stone Tools from the Prehistoric Levant. *Paléorient* 18:53–81.

CHAPTER 11

FAUNAL REMAINS

EDWARD F. MAHER

The nearly five decades that have elapsed since Moshe Dothan's fieldwork at Tel Mor was carried out (Dothan 1959; 1960a–c; 1973) has had a detrimental affect on the site's archaeofaunal assemblage and associated contexts.[1] Time lag between field excavation and analysis/publication represents a common problem often encountered during archaeological research. The original excavations undoubtedly recovered more fauna than the 49 bones that have survived to the present day (Table 11.1). Even some of those that have, cannot be assigned a specific provenience, further diminishing the number of bones that could provide additional zooarchaeological data. Of these, only 15 (31%) can be assigned to a particular stratum. Seven taxonomically identified bones are associated with the Late Bronze Age II and Iron I strata (IX–V).

Table 11.1. Fauna Species and Elements

Reg. No.	Element	Side	Species	Aging Data	Comments	Stratum
A706/12	Limb		Large mammal		Burned end	IX?
B325/56	Pubis		*Ovis/capra*			IX?
A607/1	Fovea capitis		Medium mammal		Spindle whorl?	VII?
A303/9	Unidentified		Unidentified		Bone fused to sherd	VII?
A250/7	Radius	L	Cervidae	Unfused proximal		VII
A272/22	Molar fragment		Equid		Burned	VII
A259/6	Rib		Large mammal		Cut marks	VII
A281/12	Molar fragment		*Bos*			VI?
A261/9	Limb		Medium mammal		Burned	VI
A300/13	Mandible	L	*Canis*		Unerupted M1	V?
A234/11	Thoracic vertebra		Large mammal			V?
A182/34	Rib		Medium mammal		Polished rounded end	V?
A240/15	Rib		Medium mammal		Burned	V?
A167/11	Upper 2nd molar		*Ovis/capra*	Juvenile		V?
A306/31	Second phalanx		*Ovis/capra*	Fused proximal		V
A294/10	Calcaneus	R	*Bos*	Unfused proximal	Cut marks	N/A
A294/10	Magnum		*Bos*			N/A
A294/10	Lunar		*Bos*		Cut marks	N/A
A294/10	Unciform		*Bos*		Cut marks	N/A
A294/10	Cuneiform		*Bos*		Cut marks	N/A
A369	Incisor		*Bos*			N/A
B127/10	Mandible	R	*Bos*			N/A
B127/10	Lower 3rd molar	R	*Bos*			N/A
B127/10	Upper 1st molar		*Bos*			N/A
B127/10	Upper 2nd molar		*Bos*			N/A
A369	Humerus	L	*Capra*	Fused distal		N/A
A294/10	Humerus	L	Cervidae	Unfused distal		N/A

Table 11.1 (cont.)

Reg. No.	Element	Side	Species	Aging Data	Comments	Stratum
A294/10	Humerus	R	Cervidae	Unfused distal		N/A
A269/1	Horn core		Gazelle			N/A
A369	Scapula		Large mammal			N/A
A369	Limb		Large mammal			N/A
A369	Femur		Large mammal	Unfused distal		N/A
A369	Humerus		Medium mammal			N/A
B132	Rib		Medium mammal			N/A
A369	Scapula	R	Ovis			N/A
A369	Metatarsal		Ovis	Fused distal	Cut marks	N/A
A369	Lower 3rd milk molar		Ovis			N/A
A369	Lower 3rd milk molar		Ovis			N/A
A369	Humerus	L	Ovis	Fused distal	Cut marks	N/A
A369	Mandible	R	Ovis			N/A
A369	3rd molar		Ovis			N/A
A369	Radius	L	Ovis/capra	Fused proximal	Cut marks	N/A
A369	Horn core		Ovis/capra	Juvenile		N/A
A369	Acetabulum		Ovis/capra			N/A
A369	Cervical vertebra		Ovis/capra			N/A
A369	Mandible		Ovis/capra	Juvenile		N/A
A369	Tooth fragment		Ovis/capra			N/A
A700/12	Tibia	L	Ovis/capra	Unfused proximal		N/A
A369	Unidentified		Unidentified	Juvenile		N/A

DESCRIPTION

Late Bronze Age (Strata XI–VII)

Seven animal bones are assigned to the Late Bronze Age, of which three were identified: a sheep/goat pubis, a burnt molar fragment from a small equid and the unfused proximal radius of a juvenile deer (Cervidae). An unidentified bone fused to a pottery sherd may relate to the settlement's conflagration at the end of the thirteenth century BCE, an event noted by Dothan (1960a; 1960c). Additional remains of other species assigned to Stratum IX were briefly studied by D. Reese (n.d.). He identified deer antlers, an equid molar, and miscellaneous bones of cattle, sheep/goat, and a large bird, all of which were excavated in Sqs M22 and N22.

Four bones from Stratum VII were found in a large building (Sqs M18–19). The proximal end of a femur from a medium-sized mammal was cut, polished and drilled through its middle. From Sq L19, this object was likely used as a spindle whorl (Fig. 11.1).

Moshe Dothan (e.g., 1959:271; 1960a:17) reported that the "horns" of a fallow deer (*Dama mesopotamica*) found on the floor of a Stratum XI sanctuary were surrounded by a number of pottery vessels (Fig. 11.2; see also Fig. 2.3). Unfortunately these deer remains were unavailable for study, but some comments can be offered. It should be noted that deer have antlers rather

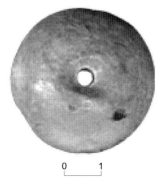

0   1

Fig. 11.1. Modified bone, possibly a spindle whorl, from Stratum VII (Reg. No. A607/1).

Fig. 11.2. Deer antlers (Dama mesopotamica)
from the area of the Stratum XI bāmāh.

than horns. Antlers are boney outgrowths extending from the cranium, and shed seasonally, whereas horns consist of a core sheathed by a layer of keratin, and are usually never shed. Even though antler tine configuration may be used for species identification (Hillson 1999:7–9), the method has limited utility in this case since the antler's fragmentary state obscures this thereby blurring its taxonomic identity. The antler's state of preservation seemed to be rather fragile even at the time of excavation, and it is not surprising that it has not survived to the present day. The mere presence of antlers is a sexually dimorphic trait that designates the animal as a male. With the exception of the reindeer (*Rangifer*), female deer do not posses antlers (Davis 1987:59). Based on Fig. 11.2 it is not possible to estimate the size of the antlers because a suitable scale was not included. However, a scale appearing in another field photo of the area in which the antlers were discovered indicates their preserved length was approximately 40 cm from base to tip. It is difficult to determine if the antlers were shed or still attached to a portion of the cranium. Since antlers are shed at specific times of year, they may indicate season of use; however, it should not be ruled out that shed antler may have continued in use beyond their original season of detachment. Deer remains associated with a cultic area

are also known from the early Iron Age occupation at Har 'Eval (Mount Ebal; Horwitz 1986/87).

Late Bronze/Iron Age Transition–Iron I (Strata VI–V)

Four of the eight bones associated with Strata VI–V were identified. Two came from Stratum VI: a cattle molar fragment in Sq J18 and the burnt limb of a medium-sized mammal in Sq L19. Reese (n.d.) also identified fish bones in this stratum. Six bones were assigned to Stratum V (Sqs K–L18, K19 and M18). Based on guidelines established by Silver (1969), two of the bones could be aged. A sheep/goat toe bone (second phalanx) belonged to an individual at least 13–16 months old, and an upper second molar without wear came from a juvenile. The mandible of a young dog was also found. Its unerupted lower first molar indicates an age of less than 4–5 months. The distal end of a rib from an unidentified medium-sized mammal was rounded from use, resulting in a polished surface. Iron Age animal remains previously excavated from an ancient water well at Tel Mor indicate that sheep, goats, and cattle were numerous in this period (Davidowitz, Tchernov and Horwitz 1986), indicating the importance of domestic stock.

Unstratified Remains

The majority of the faunal assemblage could not be assigned to a particular stratum. Out of 34 bones, 28 (82%) were taxonomically identified. Most of the remains are from domesticated species such as sheep and goats (15 bones) and cattle (10 bones). However, evidence for deer (2 bones) and gazelle (1 bone) indicate that wild animals were occasionally hunted.

CONCLUSIONS

The chronologically heterogeneous animal remains from Tel Mor represent a very small assemblage— for which any interpretation must be regarded as tentative—from an important site that may have been the harbor for ancient Ashdod. The subsistence base was primarily dependent on domesticates, though wild species were also hunted. Deer antlers lying on the surface of a Late Bronze Age sanctuary show the involvement of animals with cultic ceremonies. Perhaps the most striking detail demonstrated by the assemblage relates to its species diversity, as five different species were recognized out of the few bones that could be identified. Species range increases when considering the unstratified sample, which includes gazelle. Additional data from D. Reese's earlier study further expands the range of animals exploited to include fish and a species of large-bodied bird (possibly domestic fowl). Such diverse animal use that included wild and domestic stock, as well as terrestrial, avian, and aquatic species, could reflect Tel Mor's status as a bustling harbor town that may have been characterized by a population with varying interests, backgrounds, and culinary preferences.

NOTE

[1] I would like to thank Tristan Barako for inviting me to study the faunal assemblage from Tel Mor. I am grateful to David Reese for providing access to his unpublished manuscript prepared on September 29, 1980 on the fauna he studied from Tel Mor, and also to Liora Horwitz, whose comments greatly improved the manuscript. My colleagues at the Department of Evolution, Systematics, and Ecology at the Hebrew University of Jerusalem, Givat Ram, kindly granted me access to their excellent comparative faunal collection.

REFERENCES

Davidowitz G., Tchernov E. and Horwitz L.K. 1986. Faunal Remains from a Well at Tel Mor. In Y. Nir and I. Eldar eds. Ground Water Levels in Ancient Wells as an Indicator of Ancient Sea Levels and of Neo-Tectonic Changes in the Mediterranean Coast of Israel. *Geological Survey of Israel Report* 34. Jerusalem (Hebrew).

Davis S.J.M. 1987. *The Archaeology of Animals*. New Haven.

Dothan M. 1959. Tel Mor (Tell Kheidar). *IEJ* 9:271–272.

Dothan M. 1960a. The Ancient Harbour of Ashdod. *CNI* 11:16–19.

Dothan M. 1960b. Excavations at Tel Mor (1959 Season). *BIES* 24:120–132 (Hebrew).

Dothan M. 1960c. Tell Mor (Tell Kheidar). *IEJ* 10:123–125.

Dothan M. 1973. The Foundation of Tel Mor and of Ashdod. *IEJ* 23:1–17.

Hillson S. 1999. *Mammal Bones and Teeth: An Introductory Guide to Methods of Identification*. London.

Horwitz L.K. 1986–1987. Faunal Remains from the Early Iron Age Site on Mount Ebal. *Tel Aviv* 13–14:173–189.

Reese D.S. No date. Faunal Remains from Tel Mor, Israel.

Silver A. 1969. The Aging of Domestic Animals. In D. Brothwell and E.S. Higgs eds. *Science in Archaeology* (2nd ed.). London. Pp. 283–302.

CHAPTER 12

MARINE SHELLS

DAVID S. REESE

Shells were not systematically saved during the Tel Mor excavations of 1959–1960. Except for a large sample of *Murex brandaris* related to the Hellenistic purple-dye industry at the site, only about thirty marine shells are preserved for study, noted in Table 12.1.[1] Of the isolated shells, nineteen are from Late Bronze Age contexts, one is from Iron I, one is from the Hellenistic period and eight are undated. Most (sixteen) of the isolated shells are *M. brandaris*, followed by three *Ostrea edulis* (oyster), three *Murex trunculus*, three *Acanthocardia tuberculata* (cockle) and three *Glycymeris* (dog-cockle). Two *Acanthocardia* and two *Glycymeris* naturally holed at the umbo were probably used as ornaments. The one *Pinctada margaritifera* fragment is worthy of special note as this large bivalve occurs in the Red Sea, whereas all the other shells are from the Mediterranean. It may have been used as a source of mother-of-pearl for ornaments or inlays.

SHELL PURPLE-DYE PRODUCTION AT TEL MOR

A probable dyeing workshop was uncovered in 1959. It consists of a deep well (L153) full of thousands of *M. brandaris* (Fig. 12.1), and next to it a large rectangular plastered basin (L150) and a small semicircular plastered basin (L151; see Plan 2.7, Figs. 2.33, 2.34). The area was full of Hellenistic pottery (Stratum I, largely second century BCE; Dothan 1959:272, 1960:125; Milgrom 1983:64 [photo by Reese]; Stern 1994:195–198 [as found in late 1960s]). Horn dates it to the fourth–second centuries BCE (1968:21, Fig. 14). Crushed shells were also apparently recovered. A sample of 547 complete and fresh *M. brandaris* from the well were retained and studied by the author (largest: L 71 mm, W 49 mm; smallest: L 36 mm, W 23.5 mm).

EVIDENCE FOR PURPLE-DYE PRODUCTION AT COASTAL LEVANTINE SITES

I have elsewhere surveyed the evidence for Bronze Age shell purple-dye production in the Mediterranean basin (Reese 1987). This study is now somewhat out of date. More recently I have surveyed the Iron Age evidence from the Aegean (Reese 2000) and Italy (Reese 2005). This is not the place to discuss the details of this industry, which I and other researchers have presented elsewhere (Reese 1980, 1987; Jackson 1916; Thompson 1947:209–218; Forbes 1956:112–141; Jensen 1963; Bruin 1970; McGovern and Michel 1984, 1990; Michel and McGovern 1987; Reinhold 1970; Spanier, Karmon and Linder 1982; Spanier 1987; Ziderman 1987, 1990; Cooksey 1994; Edens 1999). Suffice it to say that enormous numbers of *M. brandaris*, *M. trunculus* or *Thais haemastoma* are required to produce the dye.

To place the Tel Mor Hellenistic evidence in its wider context, I survey here the shell evidence from elsewhere on the Levantine coast of the Persian period and later date.

Israel

Yavne-Yam
Many uncrushed *M. brandaris*, *M. trunculus* and *Thais* of Persian, Hellenistic and Roman date were found at Yavne-Yam (personal analysis).

Apollonia-Arsuf
Apollonia-Arsuf produced murex shells in the Persian and Hellenistic periods (Karmon 1999).

Tel Mevorakh
Numerous Iron Age shells (Stern 1978:25, 95, Pl. 45:2, 4), including *M. trunculus* and *Thais*, were found at Tel Mevorakh, as was as a fourth/third-century BCE dye vat (Stern 1978:24, Pl. 44:4), which may have produced shell purple-dye.

Table 12.1. Marine Shells Preserved for Study

Reg. No.	Species	Context (Stratum)	Measurements (mm)*	Comments
B212/63	M. brandaris	Sqs M–N22 (XI–IX)	L 56, W 43	Rather fresh, has slit hole on body (probably recent)
B283/4	M. brandaris	Area 135 (X–IX)	L 45, W 43	Worn, open apex
A664/14	M. brandaris	Sqs H–J21 (IX)	L 59, W 43	Rather fresh
B85/18	M. brandaris	N/A (IX?)	L 59, W 43	Fresh
B262/10	Ostrea	Sq L21 (IX)	L 80, W 52	Fresh
B270/21	Ostrea	Tabun 135 (IX)	L 63, W 60	Fresh
B197/2	M. trunculus	Sqs M–N22 (IX)	L 48, W 38	Worn
B327/27	Glycymeris	Room 111 (IX)	L (pres.) 22, W 37	Water-worn, lacks proximal third
B361/16	Acanthocardia	N/A (IX)	L 37, W 38, hole 7	Water-worn, holed umbo
A305	Cymatium parthenopium	Area 41 (VII)	L 86, W 47	Fresh
A533/9	M. brandaris	W66? (VIII–VII?)	L 68, W 44	Fresh
A533/10	M. brandaris	W66? (VIII–VII?)	L 49, W 37	Worn
A641/20	M. brandaris	Room 84 (VII)	L 42, W 37	Water-worn
N/A	M. brandaris	Sq M18? (VII?)	L 46, W 42	Fresh, broken distal
A281/13	M. brandaris	Sq J18 (VI?)	L 50, W 44	Rather fresh
A568/3	M. brandaris	Room 71 (VI?)	L 48, W 36	Rather fresh
A568/6	M. brandaris	Room 71 (VI?)	L 51, W 35	Worn
A633/9	M. brandaris	Sqs K–L19 (VI?)	L 43, W 36	Water-worn
N/A	Pinctada	Sq M18? (VI?)	c. 24 × c. 18	Hinge fragment
A241/30	Acanthocardia	Sqs K–L18 (V?)	L 43, W 42, hole 5	Water-worn, holed umbo
A306/32	Ostrea	Sqs K–L18 (V?)	L 82, W 70	Fresh, recent hole in center
A92/20	Acanthocardia?	Area 10 (III)	L 31, W (pres.) 25	Water-worn, burnt black
A79/2	Glycymeris	Area 10 (III)	L 28, W 25	Very water-worn, open umbo, burnt gray
A79/3	Glycymeris	Area 10 (III)	L 29, W 30	Water-worn, holed umbo, burnt black/tan
Various	M. brandaris	Well 153 (I)		547 fresh and complete shells
A375/4	M. brandaris	Pit 55 (I)	L 61, W 44	Rather fresh, irregular hole on upper body
A198/10	M. brandaris	Sq J19	L 48, W 43	Water-worn, lacks distal
A235/10	M. brandaris	Sq J19	L 46, W 42	Water-worn
A264/12	M. trunculus	Sq J19	L (pres.) 62, W 47	Water-worn, broken lip
A545/16	M. brandaris	Sq H19	L 45, W 37	Water-worn
A691/15	Thais	N/A	L 35, W 26	Fresh, small
B199/12	M. trunculus	Sq L20	L 50, W 32	Worn, broken lip

* L = length; W = width; pres. = preserved

Tel Dor

In the Area C workshop area of Tel Dor a thick fill layer of thousands of crushed, similarly sized *M. trunculus* was exposed between two Hellenistic (Stratum IV) floors. Some whole shells were also recovered (Karmon and Spanier 1987:155, Fig. 11; Stern 1994:198). In 1986 a Persian (mid-fifth century BCE) dump of murex shells, huge clay jars and lime was discovered next to clay-coated basins in Area G, the center of the town, thought

to be a dump from the dye industry (Stern and Sharon 1987:208, Pl. 27c; Stern 1994:198, 199, Fig. 132).

Also in 1986 a purple-dye manufacturing installation of the Persian/Hellenistic period was found in Area D1, at the extreme southwestern edge of the mound. It consisted of a deep pit filled to the top with crushed *M. trunculus* that was lined with stones at the upper edge of the pit. A small channel or canal 2 m long led from this pit to another. Near the second pit was a small,

Fig. 12.1. Murex brandaris shells from Well 153 in Stratum I (adapted from M. Dothan 1960c: Pl. 11:2).

nearly square, stone-lined and plastered basin, in turn next to a third pit. Along the channel, inside the basin, and in the second pit were remains of a purple material; moreover, the soil inside the pit was impregnated with the color (Stern and Sharon 1987:208, Pl. 26a; Stern 1994:199, Figs. 133, 134). The bottoms of other Iron Age vessels from the site also contained traces of purple coloration (Stern 1994:200). Finally, rock-cut installations along the coast here may have been used for raising murex or as part of a dyeing installation (Raban 1981:21; Stern 1994:198).

Tel Megadim
The 1967–1969 excavations directed by M. Broshi at the coastal site of Tel Megadim produced numerous *M. brandaris* and *M. trunculus* from Persian (fifth-century BCE) strata (personal analysis and pers. comm. from S. Wolff, March 5, 2002). The 1968 excavation in L58 produced 56 fresh *M. brandaris* (most large and five burnt gray) as well as two *M. trunculus* (one fresh, columella/part body, very large; one water-worn, open apex and body, medium/large). A second sample produced 54 fresh *M. brandaris* (most large and one fragment burnt gray), one water-worn *M. brandaris* (small/medium) and one fresh *M. trunculus* (distal/lip fragment, medium). A third sample yielded 22 fresh *M. brandaris* (most large, two burnt gray) and one fresh *M. trunculus* (broken body, medium).

Capernaum
In the summer of 1987 a cache of over 65 complete *M. trunculus* (mainly) and *M. brandaris* were uncovered

on the floor of a Byzantine house at Capernaum (J. Russell, pers. comm., November 17, 1987, and V. Tzaferis, pers. comm. February 29, 1988). The site is 40 km from the Mediterranean and it is unclear if this sample actually is related to shell purple-dye production.

Tel 'Akko
Area H at Tel 'Akko yielded a fairly large number of crushed, broken and intact shells (including *M. brandaris*, *M. trunculus* and *Thais*), dating to the Persian and Hellenistic periods (Karmon and Spanier 1987:153; 1988). Crushed murex from LB IIB were also found (Dothan 1981:111).

Tel Kabri
Tel Kabri produced two Iron II potsherds with a purple pigment on the interior, which chemical analysis showed was from *M. trunculus* (Koren 1994:40–43; 1995; 2003; Mienis 2003a:405; 2003b:28). The actual shells from the 1986–1993 excavations, however, indicate that the dye was not produced there. The dye-producing shells found include only twelve *M. trunculus*: one Late Neolithic, two EB II, eight MB II (seven deposits) and one undated; four *Thais*: one EB IA, one EB II and two MB II (two deposits); and one MB II *M. brandaris*. All are old shells collected dead on the beach (Mienis 2003a:402; 2003b:28, 30, 36).

Lebanon

Tyre
Most evidence for purple-dye production in Tyre is earlier than the Persian period. Murex shells were found in 1793, and in 1811 Lord Valentin found *M. trunculus*. W.R. Wilde discovered round pits cut into the sandstone along the coast that contained broken *M. trunculus* shells in breccia as well as heaps of murex-shell breccia (1839; 1844:148–151, 378–380, 468–488). Girardin was also an early writer on the purple-dye of Tyre (1877:91–103). Lenormant noted both *M. trunculus* and *M. brandaris* from here (1881:107). Tristram too mentioned large quantities of crushed and broken *M. brandaris* (1865:48). Broken *M. trunculus* are recorded from Tyre by Born (1937:112). Jensen suggested that the Tyre industry mainly used *M. brandaris*, and that middens around Tyre used *Janthina* (called here *Helix ianthina*; 1963:105, 111). Chehab noted a Roman deposit of crushed murex from within

the industrial quarter of the city beneath a Byzantine dye shop (1965:114). Jidejian mentioned the Tyre shells, noting that some of the evidence dates to the first century CE (1969:142–159, Pls. 136–144). And it is interesting to note the use of *M. brandaris* on the coins of Tyre from 112 CE and later (Jackson 1916:5, 6). There is textual evidence for the imperial manufacture of purple here during the reign of Diocletian (before 300 CE; Eusebius, *Hist. Eccles.* vii, 32), and in 383 CE the production became a state monopoly (*Codex Justinianus* iv, 40, 1).

Sarepta

The main deposit of crushed *M. trunculus* at Sarepta was found in 1972 in a pit measuring 0.5 × 1.0 m and cut to a depth of 0.2 m into the floor of the room containing Kiln G (Area X, II-C-9, Level 6). It dates to LB III or Iron I (*c.* 1350–1200 BCE). The quantity collected from the pit and the surface of the floor filled ten of the standard rubber buckets used in the excavation (Pritchard 1978:126–127, Figs. 121, 122). The sample saved includes 925 fragments and 31 complete shells (mainly small examples) from at least 150 individuals. An LB III to Iron I sample in Area Y (II-K-20, Level 26, Strata E–G1; *c.* 1300–1025 BCE) produced 625 crushed *M. trunculus* fragments from at least 68 individuals, with many fragments water-worn and at least 35 water-worn pottery sherds. Also present in this sample are 48 other small gastropods. I assume that the water-worn sherds and these water-worn shells came to the site when this largely *M. trunculus* sample was collected from a shell purple-dye production dump on the coast and brought to Area Y, probably to be used as fill. There is also a large murex pile in the embankment along the shore of the excavated site that appears to be Hellenistic or Roman in date, but was not excavated or dated (from the late W.P. Anderson, pers. comm. September 28, 1996).

Sidon

Thompson noted that the shell heaps of Sidon and Tyre were first seen by de Sales in 1793 (1947:209).

In early 1863 de Saulcy found a colossal mass of broken *M. trunculus* here, some of which were holed (1864; 1865:283–285). Nearby, in 1864, the French physician Gaillardot discovered remains of broken *M. trunculus* as well as unbroken *M. brandaris* and *Thais* (1865; 1873). An early article (Anonymous 1874:237, 238), apparently based on the de Saulcy and Gaillardot publications, incorrectly referred to separate middens of *M. brandaris* and *Thais*, thereby misleading subsequent writers, including Born (1937:111) and Ziderman (1987:27; 1990:99). Lortet recorded that great banks of broken *M. trunculus*, 100 m long and several meters thick, were found in the area of Sidon (1883:102). One bank of only broken *M. trunculus* is recorded as 120 m long and 7–8 m high (Forbes 1956:118). Cooke also visited these shell mounds (1909). Jensen suggested that the Sidon industry used mainly *M. trunculus* and notes large shell mounds by the old walls of the city, by the south gate, as well as south of the city (1963:105, 111). Dunand's 1964–1965 excavations here also yielded enormous numbers of shells (1967). Dalley recorded that Sidon produced heaps of '*Purpura trunculus*' (1991:124, misreading Ziderman 1987). It is quite clear that *M. trunculus* was used here in the shell purple-dye industry, but that *M. brandaris* and *Thais*, and probably numerous other marine shell forms, were also found along the coast.

Syria

Tell Rifa‘at

Tell Rifa‘at on the Orontes River, more than 100 km from the Mediterranean coast, produced a large bank of crushed *M. trunculus* more than 2.5 m thick outside a Hellenistic house (Seton-Williams 1967:71; Biggs 1967:77, 1970:424 [Biggs studied only a very small sample of this material, about 20 individuals]).

Palmyra

Textiles using shell purple-dye have been identified in third-century CE samples from Palmyra (Pfister 1934: Nos. T.1, T.4, T.18, T.21 and T.23; 1935:44).

NOTE

[1] Only Basket No. 197/2 and the sample of 547 *M. brandaris* from the well, L153, have been personally identified. All other identifications are based on digital photographs taken by T.J. Barako.

REFERENCES

Anonymous. 1874. Eine Purpurfabrik im alten Phoenicien. *Globus* 26:237–238.

Biggs H.E.J. 1967. Notes on Mollusca. In M.V. Seton-Williams. The Excavations at Tell Rifaʿat, 1964. Second Preliminary Report. *Les Annales Archéologiques Arabes Syriennes* 17:77–78.

Biggs H.E.J. 1970. Molluscs from Human Habitation Sites, and the Problem of Ethnological Interpretation. In D. Brothwell and E. Higgs eds. *Science in Archaeology: A Survey of Progress and Research*. New York. Pp. 423–427.

Born W. 1937. Purple in Classical Antiquity. *Ciba Review* 4:111–117.

Bruin F. 1970. Royal Purple and the Dye Industries of the Mycenaeans and Phoenicians. In M. Mollat ed. *Sociétés et Compagnies de Commerce en Orient et dans l'Océan Indien*. Paris. Pp. 73–90.

Chehab M. 1965. Chronique. *Bulletin du Musée de Beyrouth* 18:112–114.

Cooke A.H. 1909. On the Shell Mound at Sidon. *Proceedings of the Malacological Society of London* 8:341.

Cooksey C.J. 1994. Bibliography: Tyrian (Shellfish) Purple. *Dyes in History and Archaeology* 12:57–66. (Updated at http://www.chriscooksey.demon.co.uk/tyrian/cjcbiblio.html.)

Dalley S. 1991. Ancient Assyrian Textiles and the Origins of Carpet Design. *Iran* 29:117–135.

Dothan M. 1959. Tell Mor (Tell Kheidar). *IEJ* 9:271–272.

Dothan M. 1960. Tell Mor (Tell Kheidar). *IEJ* 10:123–125.

Dothan M. 1981. ʿAkko, 1980. *IEJ* 41:110–112.

Dunand M. 1967. Rapport préliminaire sur les fouilles de Sidonen 1964–1965. *Bulletin du Musée de Beyrouth* 20:27–44.

Edens C. 1999. Khor Ile-Sud, Qatar: The Archaeology of Late Bronze Age Purple-Dye Production in the Arabian Gulf. *Iran* 61:71–88.

Eusebius. E. Schwartz and T. Mommsen eds. *Ecclestical History. Die Griechischen Christlichen Schriftsteller der ersten jahrhunderte* II, 1–2, 1903, 1908. Leipzig. English translation: K. Lake transl. (Loeb Classical Library). London 1926.

Forbes R.J. 1956. *Studies in Ancient Technology* IV. Leiden.

Gaillardot C. 1865. Lettre au Dr. Mougeot. *Annales de la Société d'Emulation des Vosges* 9. Paris.

Gaillardot C. 1873. Les kjoekkenmoeddings et les debris de fabriques de pourpre. *Bulletins de la Société d'Anthropologie de Paris*, 2eme serie, 8:750–759.

Girardin J. 1877. Sur la pourpre de Tyre. *Bulletin de la Société Libre d'Emulation du Commerce et de l'Industrie de la Seine Inférieur* 1876–77:91–103.

Horn P. 1968. Textiles in Biblical Times. *Ciba Review* 1968:1–37.

Jackson J.W. 1916. The Geographical Distribution of the Shell-Purple Industry. *Memoirs of the Manchester Philosophical Society* 60:1–29.

Jensen L.B. 1963. Royal Purple of Tyre. *JNES* 22:104–118.

Jidejian N. 1969. *Tyre through the Ages*. Beirut.

Karmon N. 1999. Muricid Shells of the Persian and Hellenistic Periods. In I. Roll and O. Tal eds. *Apollonia-Arsuf, Final Report of the Excavations* I: *The Persian and Hellenistic Periods*. Tel Aviv. Pp. 269–280.

Karmon N. and Spanier E. 1987. Archaeological Evidence of the Purple Dye Industry from Israel. In E. Spanier ed. *The Royal Purple and the Biblical Blue, Argaman and Tekhelet. The Study of Chief Rabbi Dr. Isaac Herzog on the Dye Industries in Ancient Israel and Recent Scientific Contributions*. Jerusalem. Pp. 147–158.

Karmon N. and Spanier E. 1988. Remains of a Purple Dye Industry at Tel Shiqmona. *IEJ* 38:184–186.

Koren Z.C. 1994. The Purple Potsherd Pigment. In A. Kempinski and W.-D. Niemeier eds. *Excavations at Kabri: Preliminary Report of 1992–3, Seasons 7–8*. Tel Aviv. Pp. 40–43.

Koren Z.C. 1995. High-Performance Liquid Chromotographic Analysis of an Ancient Tyrian Purple Dyeing Vat from Israel. *Israel Journal of Chemistry* 35:117–124.

Koren Z.C. 2003. A Purple-Stained Potsherd. In A. Kempinski (N. Scheftelowitz and R. Orit eds.) *Tel Kabri: The 1986–1993 Excavations Seasons*. Tel Aviv. Pp. 446–448.

Lenormant F. 1881. *La Grande-Grece: Paysages et Histoire* 1. Paris.

Lortet L. 1883. *La Syrie d'aujourd'hui*. Paris.

McGovern P.E. and Michel R.H. 1984. Royal Purple and the Pre-Phoenician Dye Industry of Lebanon. *MASCA Journal* 3:66–70.

McGovern P.E. and Michel R.H. 1990. Royal Purple Dye: Its Identification by Complementary Physicochemical Techniques. In W.R. Biers and P.E. McGovern eds. *Organic Contents of Ancient Vessels: Material Analysis and Archaeological Investigation. MASCA Research Papers in Science and Archaeology* 7:69–76.

Michel R.H. and McGovern P.E. 1987. The Chemical Processing of Royal Purple Dye: Ancient Descriptions as Elucidated by Modern Science. *Archaeomaterials* 1:135–143.

Mienis H.K. 2003a. Molluscs. In A. Kempinski (N. Scheftelowitz and R. Orit eds.) *Tel Kabri: The 1986–1993 Excavations Seasons*. Tel Aviv. Pp. 402–408.

Mienis H.K. 2003b. Molluscs from the Excavation at Tel Kabri. *Triton* 7 (March):28–37.

Milgrom J. 1983. Of Hems and Tassels: Rank, Authority and Holiness Were Expressed in Antiquity by Fringes on Garments. *BAR* 9:61–65.

Pfister R. 1934. *Textiles de Palmyre*. Paris.

Pfister R. 1935. *Teinture et Alchimie dans l'Orient Hellénestique* (Seminarium Kondakovianum 7). Prague.

Pritchard J.B. 1978. *Recovering Sarepta, A Phoenician City*. Princeton.

Raban A. 1981. Some Archaeological Evidence for Ancient Maritime Activities at Dor. *Sefunim* 6:15–26.

Reese D.S. 1980. Industrial Exploitation of Murex Shells: Purple-Dye and Lime Production at Sidi Khrebish, Benghazi (Berenice). *Libyan Studies* 11:79–93.

Reese D.S. 1987. Palaikastro Shells and Bronze Age Purple-Dye Production in the Mediterranean Basin. *BSA* 82:201–206.

Reese D.S. 2000. Iron Age Shell Purple-Dye Production in the Aegean. In J.W. Shaw and M.C. Shaw eds. *Kommos IV: The Greek Sanctuary*. Princeton. Pp. 643–645.

Reese D.S. 2005. Whale Bones and Shell Purple-Dye at Motya (Western Sicily, Italy). *OJA* 24:107–114.

Reinhold M. 1970. *History of Purple as a Status Symbol in Antiquity* (Collection Latomus 116). Brussels.

de Saulcy F. 1864. Lettre sur la pourpre phénicienne. *Revue archéologique* 9:218–219.

de Saulcy F. 1865. *Voyage en Terre Sainte*. Paris.

Seton-Williams M.V. 1967. The Excavations at Tell Rifa'at, 1964. Second Preliminary Report. *Les Annales Archéologiques Arabes Syriennes* 17:69–84.

Spanier E. ed. 1987. *The Royal Purple and the Biblical Blue, Argaman and Tekhelet. The Study of Chief Rabbi Dr. Isaac Herzog on the Dye Industries in Ancient Israel and Recent Scientific Contributions*. Jerusalem.

Spanier E., Karmon N. and Linder E. 1982. Bibliography concerning Various Aspects of the Purple Dye. *Levantina* 37:437–447. (Updated at http://www.tekhelet.com/pdf/ta02.pdf.)

Stern E. 1978. *Excavations at Tel Mevorakh (1973–1976)* I: *From the Iron Age to the Roman Period* (Qedem 9). Jerusalem.

Stern E. 1994. *Dor, Ruler of the Seas*. Jerusalem.

Stern E. and Sharon I. 1987. Tel Dor, 1986: Preliminary Report. *IEJ* 37:201–211.

Thompson D.W. 1947. *A Glossary of Greek Fishes*. London.

Tristram H.B. 1865. *The Land of Israel*. London.

Wilde W.R. 1839. On the Purple Dye of Tyre. *Transactions of the Royal Irish Academy* I:293–295.

Wilde W.R. 1844. *Narrative of a Voyage to Madeira, Teneriffe, and along the Shores of the Mediterranean* II. Dublin.

Ziderman I.I. 1987. First Identification of Authentic *Tĕkelēt*. *BASOR* 265:25–33.

Ziderman I.I. 1990. Seashells and Ancient Purple Dyeing. *BA* 53:98–101.

CHAPTER 13

SUMMARY AND HISTORICAL CONCLUSIONS

STRATUM XII (MB IIC)

The initial settlement at Tel Mor was established during MB IIC (Stratum XII), no doubt on account of the site's prime geographic location. Situated near the coast along a navigable river, it was accessible by sea. In terms of overland travel, the *Via Maris* was nearby, with the entrances to Naḥal Soreq and Naḥal Ha-Ela not far beyond. Tel Mor's safe anchorage most likely drew the first inhabitants to the site, probably from the nearby city of Ashdod, which had been founded roughly a century prior. The limited exposure of Stratum XII

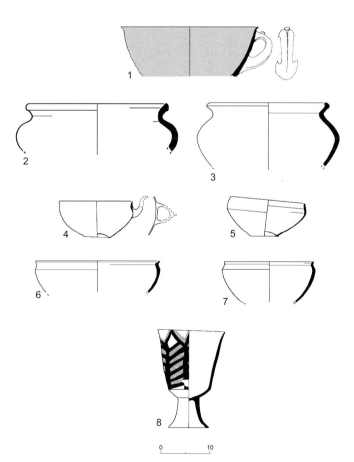

Fig. 13.1. Pottery from Pit 166 (Stratum XII).

produced pottery, including Cypriot imports, but no coherent architecture. The best stratified and earliest context (Pit 166) yielded pottery attesting to commercial contact with Cyprus from the outset (Fig. 13.1). The pit contained a red slip burnished deep bowl (Fig. 13.1:1) and cooking pots (Fig. 13.1:2, 3), all typical of the late MB II. It has been argued (see Chapter 5) that the Cypriot imports from this pit—Monochrome (Fig. 13.1:4, 5), Base Ring I (Fig. 13.1:6, 7) and Bichrome Ware (Fig. 13.1:8)—arrived at Tel Mor during MB IIC.

STRATA XI–X (LB IA)

Although Strata XI–X are poorly defined strati-graphically, the ceramic evidence indicates an LB I date for this period of settlement. The most stratigraphically secure context from Stratum XI is a scatter of pottery—much of it cultic in nature—in the area of Courtyard 118 referred to as the *bāmāh* (Fig. 13.2; see also Fig. 2.3). The six votive bowls (Fig. 13.2:1–6) and the chalice (Fig. 13.2:7), most of which are carinated, imitate MB IIC and LB I bowls. The well-developed, triangular-in-profile rim of the intact cooking pot (Fig. 13.2:8) is a feature of the Late Bronze Age; whereas the rare seven-spouted lamp (Fig. 13.2:9) has its closest parallels in MB II. A more precise date is not provided by the Egyptian-style slender ovoid jar (Fig. 13.2:10), which is a product primarily of the XVIIIth Dynasty.

Although the discovery of cultic vessels, as well as deer antlers (see Fig. 11.2), suggested to the excavators the presence of a *bāmāh* on the tell in Stratum XI, given the absence of architectural remains, it is better to propose more cautiously that only some kind of cultic activity took place at the site. It is possible that the Tel Mor of these early strata corresponds to *M<i>ḫš* mentioned in a topographical list of Tuthmosis III (see Chapter 1). If such is the case, then the only evidence for Egyptian contact at this time is the slender ovoid jar. There are no signs that any of the early strata ended in destruction.

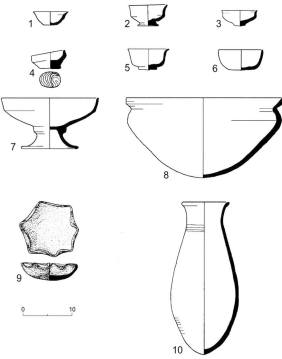

Fig. 13.2. Pottery from Courtyard 118 (Stratum XI).

STRATUM IX (LB IIA)

Stratum IX is the first stratum at Tel Mor that was excavated across a wide area and contained coherent architecture. Building A, located on the northern edge of the summit, was large in size with thick, well-preserved, mudbrick walls. Much of the pottery from Building A came from Room 111 (Fig. 13.3). Except for a few kraters (Fig. 13.3:11–13) and a cooking pot (Fig. 13.3:14), the assemblage from this room was composed of bowls (Fig. 13.3:1–10) and storage jars (Fig. 13.3:15–29). Even though most of the pottery was probably recovered from a destruction layer, there were no restorable vessels. Indeed, all but the storage-jar bases are small sherds and, as such, may be residual (e.g., Fig. 13.3:1, 2). Notwithstanding, most of the pottery from Room 111 is not out of place in LB II, and the best parallels for the storage-jar bases are from fourteenth-century strata (e.g., Tel Miqne-'Eqron IX, Tel Baṭash-Timna VII).

The significant quantity of fragmentary storage jars found in the destruction level of the rooms—especially

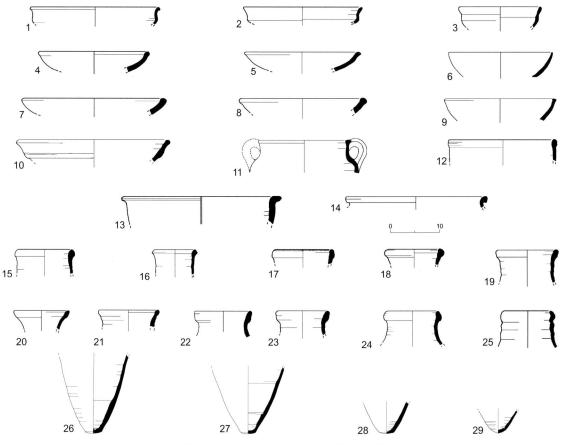

Fig. 13.3. Pottery from Room 111 (Stratum IX).

Room 111—suggests that Building A functioned as a warehouse. At the base of the eastern slope the excavators uncovered a cist grave that dates to the same period as Building A—namely, LB IIA/fourteenth century BCE. Cypriot imports (e.g., BR II) comprised half of the funerary assemblage (see Fig. 2.12). This burial was part of a larger cemetery, which included graves exposed by heavy winter rains subsequent to the excavation. There are only a few indications of an Egyptian influence on the overall ceramic assemblage from this period.

Tel Mor Stratum IX may correspond to the *Muḫḫazu* mentioned in the Amarna Letters, in which case there were ʿApiru present at the site in the mid-fourteenth century BCE (see Chapter 1). Stratum IX ended in destruction, perhaps as a result of Seti I's punitive campaign against the Shasu (M. Dothan 1993:1073). This event took place in Seti's first regnal year, which corresponds to 1290 or 1294 BCE according to the widely accepted Low Chronology (Kitchen 2000:43). Most of the hostilities, however, seem to have taken place south of Tel Mor along the 'Ways of Horus' (e.g., Murnane 1990:55–59). Whether the destructive agent was man-made or natural, the material culture of the succeeding strata (VIII–V) is distinctively Egyptian in character.

Strata VIII–VII (LB IIB)

Building B, a monumental structure with clear Egyptian architectural features, dominated the summit during Strata VIII and VII. Egyptianized pottery, mostly shallow bowls and beer jars, accounts for 7% of the registered sherds from this period (thirteenth century BCE); moreover, these strata yielded approximately half of the imported Egyptian pottery found at Tel Mor (see Chapter 4). Room 63 is the only room in Building B that produced restorable pottery (Fig. 13.4). The best preserved vessel is an intact beer jar (Fig. 13.4:1). It was found at least 1 m lower in elevation than the rest of the pottery from this room, which suggests that it belongs to the Stratum VIII phase of Building B. The jar's base diameter (*c.* 9 cm) indicates a XIXth Dynasty date. The imported neck-less storage-jar rim (Fig. 13.4:3), which probably belongs to Stratum VII, dates more broadly to the Ramesside period. The rare White Slip II Type IB bowl also fits comfortably in LB IIB (Fig. 13.4:4). The krater (Fig. 13.4:5) and beer-jar rims (Fig. 13.4:2) add no further chronological precision.

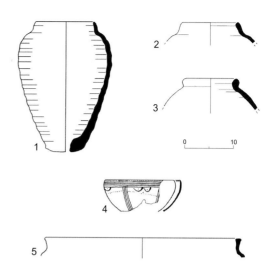

Fig. 13.4. Pottery from Room 63 (Strata VIII–VII).

Building B possessed many features commonly associated with Egyptian-style 'Administrative Buildings', such as mudbrick walls set in sand-lined trenches and measurements based on the Egyptian royal cubit. The buttressing on the exterior walls brings to mind the depiction of fortresses along the 'Ways of Horus' on a Karnak relief from the reign of Seti I. The combined ceramic, architectural and iconographic evidence strongly suggests that Tel Mor functioned as an Egyptian outpost or garrison during the XIXth Dynasty. This garrison may correspond to the *M'wḥ3d3* that appears in a topographical list dating to the reign of Ramesses II (see Chapter 1).

Given Tel Mor's small size, it is safe to assume that no more than 50 soldiers were garrisoned at the site. Although the Amarna texts date to an earlier period than Strata VIII–VII, they contain the most information about Egyptian garrison sizes in Late Bronze Age Canaan. The following letters are most illuminating on this point: Rib-Hadda requested that "20 men from Meluḫḫa and 20 men from Egypt" be sent to guard the city of Byblos (EA 108:67); Bayadi implored Pharaoh to dispatch a 50-man garrison (*ma-an-s.a-a[r-ta]*) to rescue his besieged city, probably located in Syria (EA 238:11); and Abdi-Heba, ruler of Jerusalem, asked that "the king send 50 men as a garrison (*ma-s.ar-ta*) to protect the land" (EA 289:42; Moran 1992). As opposed to the situation at Bet She'an (see Chapter 4), it is unlikely that Tel Mor was the seat of a high-ranking official. Instead, a petty officer probably commanded the garrison, which was periodically visited by a circuit official such as Ḥaya mentioned in the Afeq Letter (Owen 1981; Singer 1983).

As noted above, Tel Mor was geographically strategic both in terms of seaborne and overland travel. In the broader network of Egyptian outposts, Gaza (*c.* 40 km to the south) and Jaffa (*c.* 30 km to the north) could be reached by ship in less than half a day. To this coastal network, it is now possible to add Ashqelon, less than 25 km away (see Chapter 2, n. 7). On the other side of the sand dunes stretched the *Via Maris*, the well-trodden route of Egyptian armies since the XVIIIth Dynasty. Their itineraries reveal that the troops averaged between 11 (Tuthmosis III; Simons 1937:117; Aharoni 1979:48, 49) and 22 km/day along this stretch (Ramesses II; Breasted 1903:11, n. 40, 19, n. 67).[1] Thus, Jaffa and Gaza were probably no more than a two- or three-day march from Tel Mor. A useful model for understanding how the site functioned is perhaps as a smaller version of the Phoenician harbors frequently mentioned in the annals of Tuthmosis III (e.g., Breasted 1906: §§472, 492, 510, 519, 535). After being subjugated, these coastal cities served as depots for provisioning troops and as bases for Egyptian military operations farther inland.

A thick destruction layer, comprised mostly of fallen mudbricks, separated the Strata VIII and VII floors of Building B. The lack of evidence for burning led the excavators to conclude that the damage was caused by an earthquake. The layer that separated Strata VII and VI, on the other hand, contained a large amount of ash and burnt mudbrick. Dothan suggested either a punitive expedition by the pharaoh Merneptah or an incursion by Israelites as the possible authors of this destruction (1993:1073). According to the short poem at the end of the famous 'Israel Stela', Merneptah vanquished his enemies in Syria-Palestine, which included the nearby Canaanite cities of Ashqelon and Gezer, in the fifth year of his reign (1195 BCE; Kitchen 2003:15). In light of the significant quantity of Egyptianized pottery both before (Strata VII) and after the destruction (Stratum VI), however, it seems unlikely that the Egyptian army destroyed Tel Mor. It is more reasonable to suppose, instead, that attacks on Egyptian garrisons (such as Tel Mor) by rebellious Canaanites (e.g., Gezer) prompted Merneptah's campaign.

As for the Israelites, biblical notices (e.g., Josh 13:2–3; Judg 1:18 [LXX]) report that they did not capture Philistia, which presumably included Tel Mor. Moreover, few (i.e., collared-rim store jars) or none

(i.e., pillared houses) of the artifactual types usually associated with the Israelite settlement have been found at sites in the southern coastal plain (for a possible collared-rim store jar, see Fig. 3.23:9). If any group, then, is to claim responsibility for the destruction of Stratum VII, it should probably be the Canaanites.

STRATUM VI (LB IIB/IRON IA TRANSITION)

After a period of abandonment, a smaller, yet still massive, building was constructed on the summit of Tel Mor in Stratum VI (*c.* 1200 BCE). The external walls of Building F were 11 m long, 4 m thick, and preserved in places to a height of more than 2 m. The extraordinarily thick walls probably supported multiple stories, which led the excavators to describe this building as a *migdol*. Access to the second story (at least) was by means of a ramp, which was preserved along the northern and western sides. To the west of Building F were a number of open-air foundries that were used in the recycling of bronze, as analyses carried out on pieces of bronze spatter from this area indicate (see Chapter 8). Tuyère fragments and a crucible were among the associated finds.

Stratum VI ended in destruction. Numerous whole or almost complete vessels lay smashed on the floors of Building F. On top of these vessels were fallen mudbricks and then more broken pots, which, taken altogether, indicates a second-story collapse. More restorable pottery was recovered from Room 71 of Stratum VI than from any other well-defined stratigraphic context on the summit of the tell (Fig. 13.5). It is not possible to determine, however, whether most of this pottery came from the fill of a pit apparently dug from the room's floor or from the destruction layer on top of this floor. In terms of the Canaanite pottery, the semi-hemispherical bowls with incurving rim are such a basic type that they can be found throughout much of the Late Bronze Age (Fig. 13.5:1–3). All the following types, however, are characteristic of the transitional Late Bronze Age/early Iron Age: large, deep bowls with thick walls heavily tempered with straw and bearing rope impressions around the upper body (e.g., Fig. 13.5:4, 5); cooking pots with a slightly inverted rim and a carination that is high and more pronounced than their Late Bronze Age predecessors (e.g., Fig. 13.5:6, 7); jugs with a trefoil mouth (Fig. 13.5:8). Small lentoid (Fig. 13.5:9) and large globular (Fig. 13.5:10) pilgrim flasks; and lamps with a deeply

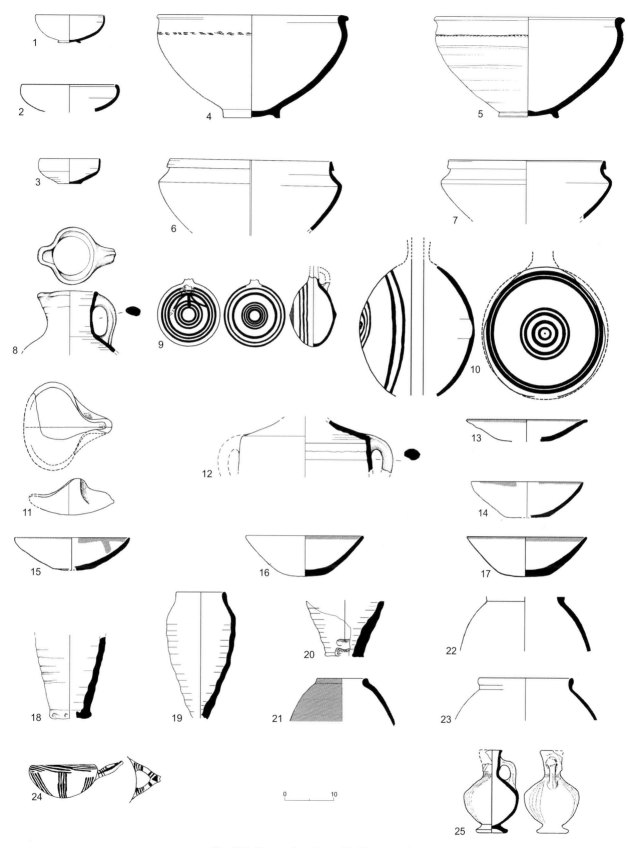

Fig. 13.5. Pottery from Room 71 (Stratum VI).

pinched spout and a well-developed flange (Fig. 13.5:11). The 'Canaanite jar' may be slightly residual (Fig. 13.5:12). A significant amount of locally produced Egyptianized pottery was also found in Room 71. Most common are simple bowls, often with a red band on the rim (e.g., Fig. 13.5:13–17), and beer jars (e.g., Fig. 13.5:18–20). Rolled rims from neck-less storage jars, both locally made (Fig. 13.5:21, 22) and imported (Fig. 13.5:23), were found in this locus as well. Regarding the chronological implications, suffice it to say here that the above types appear throughout the XIX and XXth Dynasties. Finally, the Cypriot imports include a couple of late White Slip II bowls (Type IDβ; e.g., Fig. 13.5:24) and a poor imitation of a Base Ring II jug (Fig. 13.5:25). Both types are commonly found at sites in Canaan in LB IIB contexts. The Stratum VI ceramic assemblage overall contained the highest percentage of Egyptianized pottery (15%); again, mostly shallow bowls and beer jars.

STRATUM V (IRON IA)

In Stratum V, Building F was rebuilt (but without the ramp), and a smaller building (H) was constructed to its north. Egyptianized pottery comprised about 12% of the registered sherds from this stratum. Noteworthy is Room 34 in Building H, which produced a few restorable vessels, both locally produced and imported (Fig. 13.6). The deep hemispherical bowls (Fig. 13.6:1, 2) and the large jug with a trefoil rim (Fig. 13.6:3) are typical of LB IIB. More useful for dating purposes is the globular cooking jar, probably imported from Egypt, a product of the XXth Dynasty (Fig. 13.6:4). The body of what appears to be an ovoid short-necked jar, either locally produced Egyptianized or imported Egyptian, was also came from this locus (Fig. 13.6:5). With the exception of small, probably residual sherds, neither Cypriot nor Mycenean imports were found in Stratum V. The ceramic evidence supports Dothan's original dating of Strata VI–V—namely, the end of the thirteenth and first half of the twelfth centuries BCE. It appears that Stratum V (including Building F) simply fell out of use, probably in the latter part of the twelfth century BCE.

The sequence of events at Tel Mor during this period can be correlated with the changing fortune of the Egyptian empire in Canaan. Egypt's hold on the region grew more tenuous toward the close of the XIXth Dynasty (e.g., Weinstein 1981:17). Possibly during

the reign of Merneptah or some later pharaoh, Egypt lost control of Tel Mor and the Stratum VII garrison was destroyed. During the reign of Ramesses III, the greatest pharaoh of the XXth Dynasty, Egypt succeeded in reasserting its hegemony over parts of Canaan, including Tel Mor. The Strata VI–V *migdol* corresponds to the Egyptian garrison reestablished at this time (in the first half of the twelfth century BCE). By the second quarter of this century, however, the Philistines had carved out a homeland immediately to the south of Tel Mor. In response to this hostile incursion, Egypt pursued a policy of containment by strengthening its outposts on the periphery of Philistia (Bietak 1991b; Stager 1995). Tel Mor was situated along the northern boundary of Philistia during this period of the initial Philistine settlement. It should come as no surprise, then, that the strata with the strongest ceramic evidence for an Egyptian presence date to the twelfth century BCE/XXth Dynasty (Strata VI–V).

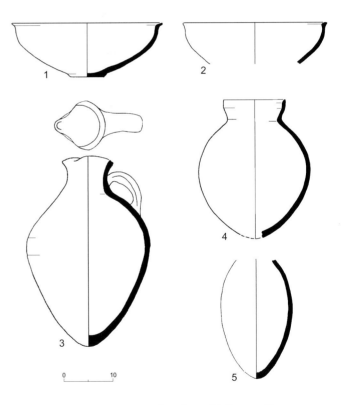

Fig. 13.6. Pottery from Room 34 (Stratum V).

STRATUM IV (EARLY IRON IB)

In the succeeding four strata, the character of the site changed considerably. A single massive structure no longer dominated the tell. Instead, the site was more open with relatively little architecture. Tel Mor no longer functioned as an Egyptian outpost and became instead a rural settlement inhabited primarily by the local population, which may have included at this point some Philistines. Stratum IV consisted only of a poorly preserved building, the walls of which roughly follow the outline of Building H from the preceding stratum. Two features distinguish the limited ceramic assemblage of this period: the virtual absence of Egyptianized pottery and the initial appearance of small amounts of Philistine pottery (see Fig. 3.32:4, 14, 15). At first glance the relatively small amount of Philistine pottery present at Tel Mor is surprising, especially given the proximity of Ashdod, which was a major production center for Myc. IIIC:1b, Philistine Bichrome and Ashdod Wares. This dearth is understandable, however, when considered against the backdrop of Tel Mor's settlement history during Iron I. Utilitarian pottery, and not luxury wares like Philistine Bichrome and Ashdod Wares, is to be expected at such a poor, relatively minor site.

The presence and absence of pottery types in these strata also has important chronological implications, particularly in light of recent attempts to lower the date of the Philistine settlement by approximately 50 years—that is, to *c.* 1130 BCE (e.g., Finkelstein 1995).[2] The basis for this 'Low Chronology' may be briefly described as follows: Because certain sites located near the Philistine pentapolis contain strata that are clearly datable to the reign of Ramesses III, but have not yielded Philistine pottery, this type of pottery found at sites elsewhere must have been produced for the first time after the destruction of these strata. For example, Tel Sera' Stratum IX produced an Egyptian inscription dating to Ramesses III (Goldwasser 1984), but no Philistine pottery. On the other hand, both Myc. IIIC:1b and Philistine Bichrome pottery were found in Strata B3–2 at nearby Tel Haror (Oren 1993:582, 583), once generally thought to be contemporaneous with Tel Sera' Stratum IX. According to the Low Chronology, then, Tel Haror Strata B3–2 (and the introduction of Myc. IIIC:1b) must postdate the destruction of Tel Sera' IX (i.e., 1130 BCE).

The underlying assumption of this argument is that cultural boundaries must be permeable for all types of material culture. A corollary holds that two neighboring sites that do not possess the same full range of material culture cannot be contemporaneous. To the various arguments that undermine this assumption, adduced

both from archaeology and ethnography, may be added the ceramic data from Strata VI–III at Tel Mor (for references and a fuller refutation of the Low Chronology, see Barako, in press a). The stratigraphy and associated pottery are tabulated in Table 13.1 (see also M. Dothan 1981: Table on p. 152).

Table 13.1. Tel Mor—Occurrence of Ceramic Types in Strata VI–III

Stratum	Philistine Pottery	Cypriot Imports	Egyptianized Pottery
VI	Absent	Present in small amount	15% of assemblage
V	Absent	Absent	12% of assemblage
IV	Present in small amount (Bichrome)	Absent	Absent
III	Present in small amount (Bichrome)	Absent	Absent

The critical strata at Tel Mor are Strata V and IV, wherein, respectively, Egyptianized pottery last appeared and Philistine pottery first appeared. Based on the initial appearance of Philistine Bichrome Ware, the stratigraphic sequences of Tel Mor and Ashdod match up as demonstrated in Table 13.2.

Table 13.2. Contemporaneity of First Appearance of Philistine Bichrome Ware at Ashdod and Tel Mor*

	Ashdod	Tel Mor
Stratum	XIII	V
Pottery	Philistine Monochrome	Egyptianized
Strata	XII–XI	IV–III
Pottery	Philistine Bichrome	Philistine Bichrome

* and see Table 3.1

Essential to the question of impermeability are Ashdod XIII and Tel Mor V, both dated by Moshe Dothan to the first half of the twelfth century BCE. Ashdod XIII produced significant amounts of Philistine Monochrome but no Egyptianized pottery, whereas the ceramic assemblage of Tel Mor Stratum V was comprised of approximately 12% Egyptianized pottery but no Philistine Monochrome. For some Syro-Palestinian archaeologists, this marked patterning of Egyptianized and Philistine material culture is best explained by chronological revision. The evidence from Tel Mor indicates, however, that two propinquitous sites can, indeed, be both contemporaneous *and* possess different material culture assemblages.

STRATUM III (LATE IRON IB)

Stratum III contained more Philistine pottery, mostly Bichrome but also 'Aegean-style' cooking jugs and a few fragments of Ashdod Ware. Again, no Philistine Monochrome pottery was found in this stratum. Its overall ceramic assemblage is very broad in terms of chronological range. Parallels from regional sites (e.g., Tell Qasile, Gezer, Ashdod, Tel Baṭash-Timna, Tel Miqne-'Eqron, Lakhish) span the latter part of the twelfth, eleventh and beginning of the tenth centuries BCE. The generally poor stratigraphic contexts at Tel Mor in Stratum III are doubtlessly to blame; however, the one relatively secure locus (Pit 17) yielded restorable vessels, particularly pilgrim flasks, datable primarily to the eleventh century BCE (Fig. 13.7). Altogether, nine small lentoid (Fig. 13.7:1–6) or large globular (Fig. 13.7:7–9) flasks were found in the pit fill. Both types are typical of Iron I. The triangular space below the rim of Fig. 13.7:4, however, is a feature of the Late Bronze Age. The best parallel for the rare amphoroid krater (Fig. 13.7:10) comes from Tell Qasile XI. The type represented by the three elongated storage jars (Fig. 13.7:11–13) appears at neighboring sites primarily in eleventh-century BCE strata. No good comparanda could be found for the squat jug (Fig. 13.7:14). Finally, the two Aegean-style cooking jugs (Fig. 13.7:15, 16) are very common at Philistine sites throughout Iron I.

There was even less architecture in this stratum. A series of post holes, but no walls, suggests a semi-enclosed space on the northern edge of the summit. A few pits, one of which contained the upper half of an enormous storage vessel, were dug nearby. A thick, ashy layer covered Stratum III, above which was a deposit of sand indicating that the summit was destroyed and then abandoned.

Dothan tentatively attributed this destruction to the military activity of either King David or Pharaoh Siamun (1993:1073). According to the Hebrew Bible, however, the Israelites penetrated no deeper into Philistia than Gezer (2 Sam 5:25 = 1 Chron 15:16), Gath (Tell es-Safi; 1 Chron 18:1; cf. 2 Sam 8:1) and Ekron (Tel Miqne-'Eqron; 1 Sam 17:52) under David's leadership. There is no indication that they subdued any of the Philistine pentapolis sites along the coast such as Ashdod. Some scholars reconstruct an Egyptian

campaign in Philistia during the reign of Siamun (978–959 BCE) based on tenuous evidence contained in the Hebrew Bible (1 Kgs 9:16) and a fragmentary relief from Tanis (e.g., Kitchen 1986: §§235, 236). Whether this campaign occurred or not, it is unlikely that the Egyptian army would have bothered with a site as insignificant as Tel Mor Stratum III.

STRATUM II (IRON IIA?)

All that remained of Stratum II were two large walls that stretched across the summit of the tell. No associated floors were found; therefore, the small amount of pottery retrieved must derive from fills. Dothan assigned this stratum to the eighth century BCE and proposed that the walls were part of King Uzziah's building activity in the territory of Ashdod (e.g., 1993:1074). According to 2 Chron 26:6, Uzziah "built cities in (the territory of) Ashdod" after having destroyed the region.[3] Of the small amount of pottery collected from Stratum II, however, none of it belongs to the eighth century BCE (see Chapter 3), the time of Uzziah's reign (783–742 BCE). Some pottery from the latter part of the Iron Age was found at Tel Mor (see Fig. 3.26:14–16), but in unstratified contexts. It is unlikely, then, that the army of Sargon II was responsible for the destruction of Stratum II. Regardless of the date, it is clear that Ashdod-Yam had replaced Tel Mor as the maritime outlet for the city-state of Ashdod by the second half of the eighth century BCE (Kaplan 1969). During the Persian period that distinction may have passed to a fortress just north of Ashdod or to Nebi Yunis, situated at the mouth of Naḥal Lakhish (Stern 2001:407–408).

STRATUM I (HELLENISTIC) TO MODERN TIMES

After a period of abandonment that lasted several centuries, Tel Mor was reinhabited during the Hellenistic period (Stratum I). The focus of the site at this time shifted from the summit, where only a small building stood (K), to the base of the eastern slope. Here the excavators discovered the remains of another building (J) and several installations, most of which appear to have been part of a single complex for the production of purple dye (אַרְגָּמָן). Thousands of *Murex brandaris* shells, the raw material for this precious dye, were found in the fill of an adjacent well (see Chapter 12). It is likely that the textiles dyed at Tel Mor were among the plunder reportedly taken by Judas Maccabeus' men

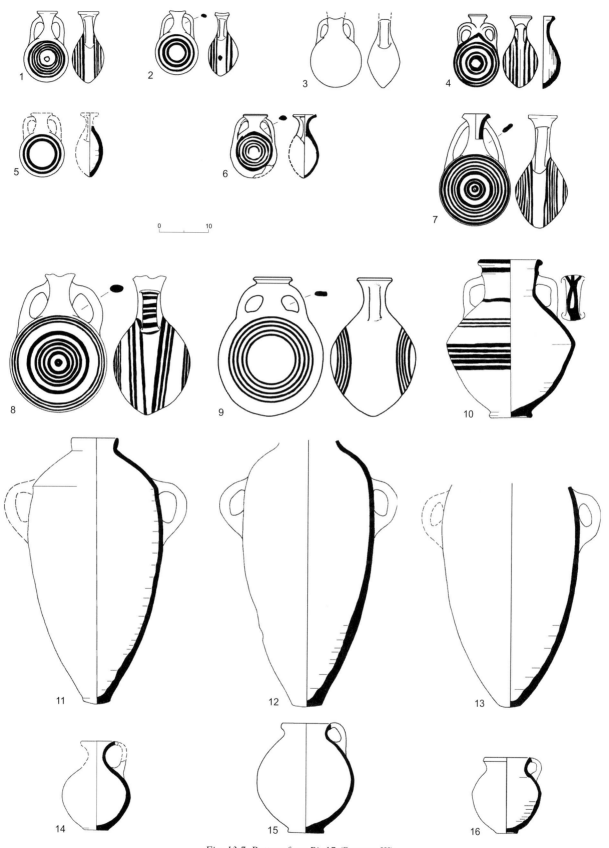

Fig. 13.7. Pottery from Pit 17 (Stratum III).

in the area of Azotus (Ashdod; 1 Macc 4:15, 23). It is not clear whether Stratum I was destroyed or simply was abandoned.

The main architectural feature from the Roman period is a well on the summit of the tell. After the shaft had filled with debris, probably sometime after the fourth century CE, Tel Mor was abandoned until the early modern period. At this time the summit was dominated by a *welî* surrounded by a children's cemetery. During World War I, the mound of Tel Mor was the scene of fighting between Australian and Turkish forces (see Chapter 1). Once secured as a beachhead, British Forces used Naḥal Lakhish as an anchorage to land supplies. It is likely that this same natural feature drew Egyptians to the site during the Late Bronze Age, when Tel Mor was at its height. It is possible to extend the comparison even further in that both imperial powers, as inevitably happens, were forced eventually to withdraw.

NOTES

[1] Note that *M<i>ḫš* (Tel Mor?) appears directly before Jaffa in Tuthmosis III's topographical list (see Chapter 1).

[2] Ussishkin was the first to propose this lower date based on his excavations at Lakhish (1985); however, Finkelstein has been, by far, the more vocal advocate for chronological revision.

[3] The *Biblia Hebraica Stuttgartensia* proposes instead that Uzziah "plundered the cities of Ashdod". Viewed within the context of the entire verse, which recounts Uzziah's conquest of northern Philistia, this reading is preferable.

REFERENCES

Aharoni Y. ed. 1973. *Beer-Sheba* I: *Excavations at Tel Beer-Sheba, 1969–1971 Seasons* (Publications of the Institute of Archaeology 2). Tel Aviv.

Aharoni Y. 1975. *Lachish* V: *Investigations at Lachish. The Sanctuary and the Residency* (Publications of the Institute of Archaeology 4). Tel Aviv.

Aharoni Y. 1979. *The Land of the Bible: A Historical Geography* (2nd rev. ed.). London.

Aḥituv S. 1984. *Canaanite Toponyms in Ancient Egyptian Documents*. Jerusalem.

Albright W.F. 1932. *The Excavation of Tell Beit Mirsim* I: *The Pottery of the First Three Campaigns* (AASOR 12). New Haven.

Albright W.F. 1933. The Excavation of Tell Beit Mirsim IA: The Bronze Age Pottery of the Fourth Campaign. *AASOR* 13:55–127.

Allen S.J. 1997. Spinning Bowls: Representation and Reality. In J. Phillips ed. *Ancient Egypt, the Aegean, and the Near East. Studies in Honour of Martha Rhoads Bell* I. San Antonio. Pp. 17–38.

Alt A. 1925. Das Institut im Jahre 1924. *Palästina-Jahrbuch* 21:5–58.

Amiran R. 1969. *Ancient Pottery of the Holy Land: From Its Beginnings in the Neolithic Period to the End of the Iron Age*. Jerusalem.

Anati E. 1959. Excavations at the Cemetery of Tell Abu Hawam. *'Atiqot* 2:80–92.

Anthes R. 1939. Foundation Deposits of Ramses IV. In U. Hölscher. *Excavations at Medinet Habu* II: *The Temples of the Eighteenth Dynasty*. Chicago. Pp. 116–117.

Arnold D. 1993. Techniques and Traditions of Manufacture in the Pottery of Ancient Egypt. In D. Arnold and J.D. Bourriau eds. *An Introduction to Ancient Egyptian Pottery*. Mainz. Pp. 1–141.

Artzy M. 1980. The Utilitarian "Persian" Storejar Handles. *BASOR* 238:69–73.

Artzy M. 1995. Nami: A Second Millennium International Maritime Trading Center in the Mediterranean. In S. Gitin ed. *Recent Excavations in Israel, a View to the West: Reports on Kabri, Nami, Miqne-Ekron, Dor, and Ashkelon* (Archaeological Institute of America, Colloquia and Conference Papers 1). Dubuque. Pp. 17–40.

Artzy M., Asaro F. and Perlman I. 1973. The Origin of the "Palestinian" Bichrome Ware. *JAOS* 93:446–461.

Ashkenazi T. 1938. *Tribus semi-nomades de la Palestine du nord*. Paris.

Aston B. 1994. *Ancient Eyptian Stone Vessels. Materials and Forms* (Studien zur Geschichte und Archäologie Altägyptens 5). Heidelberg.

Aston D.A. 1989. Ancient Egyptian "Fire Dogs"—A New Interpretation. *Mitteilungen des Deutschen Archäologischen Instituts Abteilung Kairo* 45:27–32.

Aston D.A. 1991. The Pottery. In M.J. Raven. *The Tomb of Jurudef, a Memphite Official in the Reign of Ramses II* (Egypt Exploration Society Excavation Memoir 57). London. Pp. 47–54.

Aston D.A. 1996. *Egyptian Pottery of the Late New Kingdom and Third Intermediate Period* (Studien zur Geschichte und Archäologie Altägyptens 13). Heidelberg.

Aston D.A. 1997. The Pottery. In G.T. Martin. *The Tomb of Tia and Tia at Saqqara: A Royal Monument of the Ramesside Period in the Memphite Necropolis* (Egypt Exploration Society Excavation Memoir 58). London. Pp. 83–103.

Aston D.A. 1998. *Die Keramik des Grabungsplatzes Q I* Teil I: *Corpus of Fabrics, Wares and Shapes, Forschungen in der Ramses-Stadt. Die Grabungen des Pelizqeus Museums Hildesheim in Pantir-Pi-Ramesse* I. Mainz.

Aston D.A. 1999. *Elephantine* XIX: *Pottery from the Late New Kingdom to the Early Ptolemaic Period* (Archäologische Veröffentlichungen 95). Mainz.

Aston D.A. 2001. The Pottery from H/VI Süd Strata a and b: Preliminary Report. *Ägypten und Levante* 11:167–196.

Aston D.A. and Pusch E.B. 1999. The Pottery from the Royal Horse Stud and Its Stratigraphy: The Pelizaeus Museum Excavation at Qantir/Per-Ramesses, Sector Q IV. *Ägypten und Levante* 9:39–75.

Aston D.A., Aston B. and Brock E.C. 1998. Pottery from the Valley of the Kings—Tombs of Merenptah, Ramesses III, Ramesses IV, Ramesses VI and Ramesses VII. *Ägypten und Levante* 8:137–214.

Aston D.A., Aston B. and Ryan D. 2000. Pottery from the Valley of the Kings. KV 21, 27, 28, 44, 45 and 60. *Cahiers de la céramique égyptienne* 6:11–38.

Astour M.C. 1970. Ma'Ûadu, the Harbour of Ugarit. *Journal of the Economic and Social History of the Orient* 13: 113–127.

Åström P. 1964. Red-on-Black Ware. *Opuscula Atheniensia* 5:59–88.

Åström P. 1972a. Foreign Relations. In L. Åström. *The Swedish Cyprus Expedition* IV, 1D: *The Late Cypriote Bronze Age, Other Arts and Crafts*. Lund. Pp. 706–754.

Åström P. 1972b. *The Swedish Cyprus Expedition* IV, 1C: *The Late Cypriote Bronze Age Architecture and Pottery*. Lund.

Badawy A. 1966. *A History of Egyptian Architecture: The First Intermediate Period, the Middle Kingdom, and the Second Intermediate Period.* Berkeley.

Bader B. 2001. *Typologie und Chronologie der Mergel C—Ton Keramik. Materialien zum Binnenhandel des Mittleren Reiches und der Zweiten Zwischenzeit* (Tell el-Dab'a 13 = Untersuchungen der Zweigstelle Kairo des Österreichischen Archäologischen Instituts 19). Vienna.

Bader B. 2002. A Concise Guide to Marl C-Pottery. *Ägypten und Levante* 12:29–54.

Bakler N. 1982. The Geology of Tel Ashdod. In M. Dothan and Y. Porath. *Ashdod* IV: *Excavation of Area M, the Fortifications of the Lower City* ('*Atiqot [ES]* 15). Jerusalem. Pp. 65–69.

Balensi J. 1980. *Les fouilles de R.W. Hamilton à Tell Abu Hawam, niveau IV et V: dossier sur l'histoire d'un port Méditerranéen durant les ages du bronze et du fer (?1600–950 av. J.C.).* Ph.D. diss. Université Strasbourg. Strasbourg.

Baly D. 1974. *The Geography of the Bible: A Study in Historical Geography* (New rev. ed.). New York.

Barako T.J. 2000. The Philistine Settlement as Mercantile Phenomenon? *AJA* 104:513–530.

Barako T.J. 2003. One If by Sea…Two If by Land: How Did the Philistines Get to Canaan? *BAR* 29:24–33, 64–65.

Barako T.J. In press a. Coexistence and Impermeability: Egyptians and Philistines in Southern Canaan during the Twelfth Century BCE. In M. Bietak ed. *Proceedings of the Second EuroConference of SCIEM 2000 at the Austrian Academy, Vienna, May 28 to June 1, 2003.* Vienna.

Barako T.J. In press b. Philistines and Egyptians in Southern Canaan during the Early Iron Age. In A.E. Killebrew, G. Lehman and M. Artzy eds. *The Philistines and Other "Sea Peoples" in Text and Archaeology.* Leiden.

Barta W. 1968. *Aufbau und Bedeutung der altägyptischen Opferformel* (Ägyptologische Forschungen 24). Glückstadt.

Beck P. and Kochavi M. 1985. A Dated Assemblage of the Late 13th Century B.C.E. from the Egyptian Residency at Aphek. *Tel Aviv* 12:29–42.

Beit-Arieh I. 1985. Further Burials from the Deir el-Balaḥ Cemetery. *Tel Aviv* 12:43–53.

Ben-Ami D. 2005. The Pottery of the Late Bronze Age. In A. Ben-Tor, D. Ben-Ami and A. Livneh. *Yoqne'am* III: *The Middle and Late Bronze Ages. Final Report of the Archaeological Excavations (1977–1988)* (Qedem Reports 7). Jerusalem. Pp. 165–240.

Ben-Ami D. and Livneh A. 2005. The Typological Analysis of the Pottery of the Middle and Late Bronze Ages. In Ben-Tor, Ben-Ami and Livneh. *Yoqne'am* III: *The Middle and Late Bronze Ages. Final Report of the Archaeological Excavations (1977–1988)* (Qedem Reports 7). Jerusalem. Pp. 247–347.

Ben-Arieh S. and Edelstein G. 1977. *Tombs near Akko* ('*Atiqot* 12). Jerusalem.

Bennett W.J., Jr. and Blakely J.A. 1989. *Tell el-Hesi: The Persian Period (Stratum V)* (The Joint Archaeological Expedition to Tell el-Hesi 3). Winona Lake.

Ben-Shlomo D. 2005. Material Culture. In Dothan M. and Ben-Shlomo D. 2005. *Ashdod VI: The Excavations of Areas H and K (1968–1969)* (IAA Reports 24). Jerusalem. Pp. 63–246.

Ben-Shlomo D., Shai I. and Maeir A. 2004. Late Philistine Decorated Ware ("Ashdod Ware"): Typology, Chronology, and Production Centers. *BASOR* 335:1–35.

Ben-Tor A., Bonfil R., Garfinkel Y., Greenberg R., Maeir A. and Mazar A. 1997. *Hazor V: An Account of the Fifth Season of Excavations 1968.* Jerusalem.

Bergoffen C.J. 1989. *A Comparative Study of the Regional Distribution of Cypriote Pottery in Canaan and Egypt in the Late Bronze Age.* Ph.D. diss. New York University. New York.

Bergoffen C.J. 2001a. The Base Ring Pottery from Tell el-'Ajjul. In P. Åström ed. *The Chronology of Base-Ring Ware and Bichrome Wheel-Made Ware. Proceedings of a Colloquium Held in the Royal Academy of Letters, History and Antiquities, Stockholm, May 18–19, 2000* (Konferenser 54). Stockholm. Pp. 31–50.

Bergoffen C.J. 2001b. The Proto White Slip and White Slip I Pottery from Tell el-'Ajjul. In V. Karageorghis ed. *The White Slip Ware of Late Bronze Age Cyprus. Proceedings of an International Conference Organized by the Anastasios G. Leventis Foundation, Nicosia in Honour of Walcom Wiener, Nicosia 29th–30th October 1998* (Österreichische Akademie der Wissenschaften, Denkschriften der Gesamtakademie XX = Contributions to the Chronology of the Eastern Mediterranean II). Vienna. Pp. 145–155.

Bergoffen C.J. 2002. Early Late Cypriote Ceramic Exports to Canaan: White Slip I. In E. Ehrenberg ed. *Leaving No Stones Unturned: Essays on the Ancient Near East and Egypt in Honor of Donald P. Hansen.* Winona Lake. Pp. 23–42.

Bergoffen C.J. 2004. *The Cypriot Bronze Age Pottery from Sir Leonard Woolley's Excavations at Alalakh (Tell Atchana).* Vienna.

Bietak M. 1991a. *Tell el-Dab'a V: Ein Friedhofsbezirk der Mittleren Bronzezeitkultur mit Totentempel und Siedlungsschichten 1* (Untersuchungen der Zweigstelle Kairo des Österreichischen Archäologischen Instituts IX). Vienna.

Bietak M. 1991b. Zur Landnahme Palästinas durch die Seevölker und zum Ende der ägyptischen Provinz Kana'an. *Mitteilungen des Deutschen Archäologischen Instituts Abteilung Kairo* 47 (Festschrift Werner Kaiser):35–50.

Bietak M. 1993. The Sea Peoples and the End of the Egyptian Administration in Canaan. In A. Biran and J. Aviram eds. *Biblical Archaeology Today: Proceedings of the Second International Congress on Biblical Archaeology.* Jerusalem. Pp. 292–306.

Bietak M. 2001. Towards a Chronology of Bichrome Ware? In P. Åström ed. *The Chronology of Base-Ring Ware and Bichrome Wheel-Made Ware. Proceedings of a Colloquium Held in the Royal Academy of Letters, History and Antiquities, Stockholm, May 18–19, 2000* (Konferenser 54). Stockholm. Pp. 175–201.

Biran A. and Negbi O. 1966. The Stratigraphical Sequence at Tel Ṣippor. *IEJ* 16:160–173.

Bourriau J.D. 1981. *Umm el-Ga'ab—Pottery from the Nile Valley before the Arab Conquest*. Cambridge.

Bourriau J.D. and Aston D.A. 1985. The Pottery. In G.T. Martin. *The Tomb Chapels of Paser and Raiʻa at Saqqara* (Egypt Exploration Society Excavation Memoir 52). London. Pp. 32–55.

Bourriau J.D. and Nicholson P.T. 1992. Marl Clay Pottery Fabrics of the New Kingdom from Memphis, Saqqara and Amarna. *JEA* 78:29–91.

Bourriau J.D., Aston D.A., Raven M.J. and van Walsem R. Forthcoming. *The Memphite Tomb of Horemheb* III. *The Pottery*.

Brandfon F.R. 1984. The Pottery. In Z. Herzog. *Beer-Sheba* II: *The Early Iron Age Settlements* (Publications of the Institute of Archaeology 4). Tel Aviv. Pp. 37–69.

Breasted J.H. 1903. *The Battle of Kadesh: A Study in the Earliest Known Military Strategy*. Chicago.

Breasted J.H. 1906. *Ancient Records of Egypt* II: *The Eighteenth Dynasty*. Chicago.

Brunton G. 1930. *Qau and Badari* III (BSAE 50). London.

Brunton G. and Engelbach R.E. 1927. *Gurob* (BSAE 41). London.

Busiri M. 1964. An Aramaic Ostracon from Mizpeh-Yonah (Nebi-Yunis). *HA* 11:4–5.

Busiri M. 1967. Inspection in the South. *HA* 21–22:26.

Cadogan G., Herscher E., Russell P. and Manning S. 2001. Maroni-Vournes: A Long White Slip Sequence and Its Chronology. In V. Karageorghis ed. *The White Slip Ware of Late Bronze Age Cyprus. Proceedings of an International Conference Organized by the Anastasios G. Leventis Foundation, Nicosia in Honour of Walcom Wiener, Nicosia 29th–30th October 1998* (Österreichische Akademie der Wissenschaften, Denkschriften der Gesamtakademie XX = Contributions to the Chronology of the Eastern Mediterranean II). Vienna. Pp. 75–88.

Canaan T. 1924. Mohammedan Saints and Sanctuaries in Palestine. *JPOS* 4:1–84.

Clamer C. 2004a. Additional Late Bronze Age Pottery Assemblages, Section A: The Pottery from Levels P-2 and P-1 in Area P. In D. Ussishkin. *The Renewed Archaeological Excavations at Lachish (1973–1994)* III: *The Pre-Bronze Age and Bronze Age Pottery and Artefacts* (Tel Aviv University, Sonia and Marco Nadler Institute of Archaeology, Monograph Series 22). Tel Aviv. Pp. 1155–1234.

Clamer C. 2004b. The Pottery and Artefacts from the Level VI Temple in Area P. In D. Ussishkin. *The Renewed Archaeological Excavations at Lachish (1973–1994)* III: *The Pre-Bronze Age and Bronze Age Pottery and Artefacts* (Tel Aviv University, Sonia and Marco Nadler Institute of Archaeology, Monograph Series 22). Tel Aviv. Pp. 1288–1368.

Cohen-Weinberger A. 1998. Petrographic Analysis of the Egyptian Forms from Stratum VI at Tel Beth-Shean. In S. Gitin, A. Mazar and E. Stern eds. *Mediterranean Peoples in Transition, Thirteenth to Early Tenth Centuries BCE*. Jerusalem. Pp. 406–412.

Cohen-Weinberger A. and Wolff S. 2001. Production Centers of Collared-Rim Pithoi from Sites in the Carmel Coast and Ramat Menashe Regions. In S. Wolff ed. *Studies in the Archaeology of Israel and Neighboring Lands in Memory of Douglas L. Esse* (SAOC 59/ASOR Books 5). Chicago–Atlanta Pp. 639–657.

Conder C.R. and Kitchener H.H. 1998. *The Survey of Western Palestine 1882–1888. Memoirs of the Topography, Orography, Hydrography, and Archaeology* I: *Galilee* (Archive Editions reprint of 1881 original). London.

Cross F.M. 1964. An Ostracon from Nebī Yūnis. *IEJ* 14:185–186.

Cross F.M. and Stager L.E. 2006. Cypro-Minoan Inscriptions Found at Ashkelon. *IEJ* 56:129–159.

Davies W.V. 1982. *Egypt's Golden Age: The Art of Living in the New Kingdom, 1558–1085 B.C.* Boston.

Del Olmo Lete G. and Sanmartín J. 2003. *A Dictionary of the Ugaritic Language in the Alphabetic Tradition,* Part Two: *[l–z]* (Handbook of Oriental Studies, Section 1: The Near and Middle East = Handbuch der Orientalistik 67). W.G.E. Watson. transl. Leiden.

Dever W.G. 1974. The MB IIC Stratification in the Northwest Gate Area at Shechem. *BASOR* 216:31–52.

Dever W.G. 1986. *Gezer* IV: *The 1969–71 Seasons in Field VI, the "Acropolis"* (Annual of the Hebrew Union College/Nelson Glueck School of Biblical Archaeology 4). Jerusalem.

Dever W.G., Lance H.D. and Wright G.E. 1970. *Gezer* I: *Preliminary Report of the 1964–66 Seasons* (Annual of the Hebrew Union College/Nelson Glueck School of Biblical Archaeology 1). Jerusalem.

Dever W.G., Lance H.D., Bullard R.G., Cole D.P. and Seger J.D. 1974. *Gezer* II: *Report of the 1967–70 Seasons in Fields I and II* (Annual of the Hebrew Union College/Nelson Glueck School of Biblical Archaeology 2). Jerusalem.

Dothan M. 1952. An Archaeological Survey of the Lower Rubin River. *IEJ* 2:104–117.

Dothan M. 1955. The Excavations at ʻAfula. *ʻAtiqot* 1:19–70.

Dothan M. 1956. The Excavations at Nahariya. Preliminary Report (Seasons 1954/55). *IEJ* 6:14–25.

Dothan M. 1959. Tell Mor (Tell Kheidar). *IEJ* 9:271–272.

Dothan M. 1960a. The Ancient Harbour of Ashdod. *CNI* 11:16–19.

Dothan M. 1960b. Découverte du port de l'ancien Achdod. *Nouvelles culturelles d'Israël* 5:30–31.

Dothan M. 1960c. Excavations at Tel Mor (1959 Season). *BIES* 24:120–132 (Hebrew).

Dothan M. 1960d. Tell Mor (Khaidar). *RB* 67:396–398.

Dothan M. 1960e. Tell Mor (Tell Kheidar). *IEJ* 10:123–125.

Dothan M. 1965. Tel Mor—Transition from the Bronze Age to the Iron Age on the Philistine Coast. In *Third World Congress of Jewish Studies*. Jerusalem. Pp. 295–297 (Hebrew).

Dothan M. 1971. *Ashdod* II–III: *The Second and Third Seasons of Excavations 1963, 1965, Soundings in 1967* (*'Atiqot [ES]* 9–10). Jerusalem.

Dothan M. 1972. Relations between Cyprus and the Philistine Coast in the Late Bronze Age (Tel Mor, Ashdod). *Praktika* 1:51–56.

Dothan M. 1973. The Foundation of Tel Mor and of Ashdod. *IEJ* 23:1–17.

Dothan M. 1981. The Beginning and End of Archaeological Periods at Adjacent Sites. *Eretz Israel* 15:151–153 (Hebrew; English summary, p. 198).

Dothan M. 1993. Tel Mor. *NEAEHL* 3. Pp. 1073–1074.

Dothan M. and Freedman D.N. 1967. *Ashdod* I: *The First Season of Excavations, 1962* (*'Atiqot [ES]* 7). Jerusalem.

Dothan M. and Porath Y. 1982. *Ashdod* IV: *Excavation of Area M, the Fortifications of the Lower City* (*'Atiqot [ES]* 15). Jerusalem.

Dothan M. and Porath Y. 1993. *Ashdod* V: *Excavation of Area G, the Fourth–Sixth Seasons of Excavations, 1968–1970* (*'Atiqot [ES]* 23). Jerusalem.

Dothan T. 1963. Spinning-Bowls. *IEJ* 13:97–112.

Dothan T. 1979. *Excavations at the Cemetery of Deir el-Balah* (Qedem 10). Jerusalem.

Dothan T. 1982. *The Philistines and Their Material Culture.* New Haven.

Dothan T. 1993. Deir el-Balah. *NEAEHL* 1. Pp. 343–347.

Dothan T. 1998. The Pottery. In S. Gitin ed. *Excavations 1995–1996—Field XNW, Areas 77, 78, 89, 90, 101, 102: Iron Age I* (Ekron Limited Edition Series 7). Jerusalem. Pp. 19–49.

Dothan T. 2000. Reflections on the Initial Phase of Philistine Settlement. In E.D. Oren ed. *The Sea Peoples and Their World: A Reassessment* (University Museum Monograph 108 = University Museum Symposium Series 11). Philadelphia. Pp. 145–158.

Dothan T. and Dothan M. 1992. *People of the Sea: The Search for the Philistines.* New York.

Dothan T. and Zukerman A. 2004. A Preliminary Study of the Mycenaean IIIC:1 Pottery Assemblages from Tel Miqne-Ekron and Ashdod. *BASOR* 333:1–54.

Dothan T., Gitin S. and Zukerman A. 2006. The Pottery: Canaanite and Philistine Traditions and Cypriote and Aegean Imports. In M. Meehl, T. Dothan and S. Gitin 2006. *Tel Miqne-Ekron Excavations: Field INE East Slope, Iron Age I (Early Philistine Period)* (Tel Miqne-Ekron Final Field Report Series 8). Jerusalem. Pp. 71–176.

Duncan J. 1930. *Corpus of Dated Palestinian Pottery* (BSAE 49). London.

Edelstein G. and Aurant S. 1992. The 'Philistine' Tomb at Tell 'Eitun. *'Atiqot* 21:23–41.

el-Maksoud M.A. 1987. Une nouvelle forteresse sur la route d'Horus, Tell Heboua 1986 (Nord Sinaï). *Cahiers de recherches de l'institut de papyrologie et d'égyptologie de Lille* 9:13–16.

Engelbach R.E. 1915. *Riqqeh and Memphis* VI (BSAE 26). London.

Engelbach R.E. 1923. *Harageh* (BSAE 28). London.

Epigraphic Survey. 1986. *Reliefs and Inscriptions at Karnak* IV: *The Battle Reliefs of King Sety I* (OIP 107). Chicago.

Epstein C. 1965. Bichrome Vessels in the Cross Line Style. *PEQ* 20:42–53.

Epstein C. 1966. *Palestinian Bichrome Ware* (Documenta et Monumenta Orientis Antiqui 12). Leiden.

Eriksson K.O. 1995. Egyptian Amphorae from Late Cypriote Contexts in Cyprus. In S. Bourke and J.P. Desoeudres eds. *Trade, Contact, and the Movement of Peoples in the Eastern Mediterranean.* Sydney. Pp. 199–205.

Erman A. 1900. Ein Unterstützungsgesuch. *Zeitschrift für Ägyptische Sprache und Altertumskunde* 38:151–152.

Finkelstein I. 1986. *'Izbet Ṣarṭah: An Early Iron Age Site near Rosh Ha'ayin, Israel* (BAR Int. S. 299). Oxford.

Finkelstein I. 1995. The Date of the Settlement of the Philistines in Canaan. *Tel Aviv* 22:213–239.

Finkelstein I. 1996. Stratigraphy and Chronology of Megiddo and Beth-Shan in the 12th–11th Centuries BCE. *Tel Aviv* 23:170–184.

Finkelstein I. and Singer-Avitz L. 2001. Ashdod Revisited. *Tel Aviv* 28:231–259.

Finkelstein I. and Zimhoni O. 2000. The Pottery from the Late Bronze Gate. In I. Finkelstein, D. Ussishkin and B. Halpern eds. *Megiddo* III: *The 1992–1996 Seasons* (Tel Aviv University, Sonia and Marco Nadler Institute of Archaeology, Monograph Series 18). Tel Aviv. Pp. 223–243.

Finkelstein I., Ussishkin D. and Halpern B. eds. 2000. *Megiddo* III: *The 1992–1996 Seasons* (Tel Aviv University, Sonia and Marco Nadler Institute of Archaeology, Monograph Series 18). Tel Aviv.

Finkelstein I., Zimhoni O. and Kafri A. 2000. The Iron Age Pottery Assemblages from Areas F, K and H and Their Stratigraphic and Chronological Implications. In I. Finkelstein, D. Ussishkin and B. Halpern eds. *Megiddo* III: *The 1992–1996 Seasons* (Tel Aviv University, Sonia and Marco Nadler Institute of Archaeology, Monograph Series 18). Tel Aviv. Pp. 244–324.

Fischer P.M. 2001. Cypriote Bichrome Wheel-Made Ware and Base-Ring Ware from the New Excavations at Tell el-'Ajjul: Synchronism and Dating. In P. Åström ed. *The Chronology of Base-Ring Ware and Bichrome Wheel-Made Ware. Proceedings of a Colloquium Held in the Royal Academy of Letters, History and Antiquities, Stockholm, May 18–19, 2000* (Konferenser 54). Stockholm. Pp. 223–230.

Fitzgerald G. 1930. *The Four Canaanite Temples of Beth-Shean* II: *The Pottery*. Philadelphia.

Forbes R.J. 1964. *Studies in Ancient Technology* IV (2nd rev. ed.). Leiden.

Frankfort H. and Pendlebury J.D.S. 1933. *The City of Akhenaten* II (Egypt Exploration Society 40). London.

Freedman D.N. 1963. The Second Season at Ancient Ashdod. *BA* 26:134–139.

Frisch B., Mansfeld G. and Thiele W. 1985. *Kamid el-Loz 6. Die Werkstätten der spätbronzezeitlichen Paläste* (Saarbrücker Beiträge zur Altertumskunde 33). Bonn.

Furumark A. 1941. *The Mycenaean Pottery Analysis and Classification.* Stockholm.

Gadot, Y., Yasur-Landau A. and Ilan D. 2006. The Middle Bronze III and Late Bronze I Pottery from Areas F and N. In I. Finkelstein, D. Ussishkin and B. Halpern eds. *Megiddo IV: The 1998–2002 Seasons* (Tel Aviv University, Sonia and Marco Nadler Institute of Archaeology, Monograph Series 24). Tel Aviv. Pp. 171–190.

Gal Z. 1989. Loom Weights or Jar Stoppers? *IEJ* 39:281–283.

Gardiner A.H. 1920. The Ancient Military Road between Egypt and Palestine. *JEA* 6:99–116.

Gardiner A.H. 1923. The Eloquent Peasant. *JEA* 9:5–25.

Garstang J. 1934. Jericho: City and Necropolis, Fourth Report. *Annals of Archaeology and Anthropology* 21:99–136.

Gilboa A. 2001a. The Significance of Iron Age "Wavy-Band" Pithoi along the Syro-Palestinian Littoral, with References to the Tel Dor Pithoi. In S.R. Wolff ed. *Studies on the Archaeology of Israel and Neighboring Lands in Memory of Douglas L. Esse* (SAOC 59/ASOR Books 5). Chicago–Atlanta. Pp. 639–657.

Gilboa A. 2001b. *Southern Phoenicia during Iron I–IIA in the Light of the Tel Dor Excavations: The Evidence of the Pottery.* Ph.D. diss. The Hebrew University. Jerusalem.

Gilboa A. and Sharon I. 2003. An Archaeological Contribution to the Early Iron Age Chronological Debate: Alternative Chronologies for Phoenicia and Their Effects on the Levant, Cyprus, and Greece. *BASOR* 332:7–80.

Gitin S. 1990. *Gezer* III: *A Ceramic Typology of the Late Iron II, Persian and Hellenistic Periods.* Jerusalem.

Gitin S. 1998. Philistia in Transition: The Tenth Century BCE and Beyond. In S. Gitin, A. Mazar and E. Stern eds. *Mediterranean Peoples in Transition, Thirteenth to Early Tenth Centuries BCE (in Honor of Professor Trude Dothan).* Jerusalem. Pp. 162–183.

Gittlen B.M. 1977. *Studies in the Late Cypriote Pottery Found in Palestine.* Ph.D. diss. University of Pennsylvania. Philadelphia.

Gittlen B.M. 1993. The Cypriote Pottery. In F.W. James and P.E. McGovern. *The Late Bronze Egyptian Garrison at Beth Shan: A Study of Levels VII and VIII* (University of Pennsylvania Museum Monographs 85). Philadelphia. Pp. 111–124.

Givon S. 1995. *The Fifth Season of Excavation at Tel Harassim (Nahal Barkai) 1994 (Preliminary Report 5).* Tel Aviv.

Givon S. 1996. *The Sixth Season of Excavation at Tel Harassim (Nahal Barkai) 1995 (Preliminary Report 6).* Tel Aviv.

Givon S. 1997. *The Seventh Season of Excavation at Tel Harassim (Nahal Barkai) 1996 (Preliminary Report 7).* Tel Aviv.

Givon S. 1998. *The Eighth Season of Excavation at Tel Harassim (Nahal Barkai) 1997 (Preliminary Report 8).* Tel Aviv.

Givon S. 1999. *The Ninth Season of Excavation at Tel Harassim (Nahal Barkai) 1998 (Preliminary Report 9).* Tel Aviv.

Goldwasser O. 1984. Hieratic Inscriptions from Tel Sera' in Southern Canaan. *Tel Aviv* 11:77–93.

Gonen R. 1992. *Burial Patterns and Cultural Diversity in Late Bronze Age Canaan* (ASOR Dissertation Series 7). Winona Lake.

Gophna R. and Meron D. 1970. An Iron Age Tomb between Ashdod and Ashkelon. *'Atiqot* 6:1–5 (Hebrew).

Gould B. Forthcoming. Egyptian Pottery. In T. Dothan and B. Brandl. *Excavations at the Cemetery and Settlement of Deir el-Balah* II: *The Finds* (Qedem). Jerusalem.

Goren Y. 2000. Technology, Provenience, and Interpretation of the Early Bronze Age Egyptian Ceramics. In I. Finkelstein, D. Ussishkin and B. Halpern eds. *Megiddo* III: *The 1992–1996 Seasons* (Tel Aviv University, Sonia and Marco Nadler Institute of Archaeology, Monograph Series 18). Tel Aviv. Pp. 496–501.

Grace V.R. 1956. The Canaanite Jar. In S.S. Weinberg ed. *The Aegean and the Near East.* Locust Valley. Pp. 80–109.

Grant E. 1929. *Beth Shemesh (Palestine): Progress of the Haverford Archaeological Expedition* (Biblical and Kindred Studies). Haverford.

Grant E. 1934. *Rumeileh, Being Ain Shems Excavations (Palestine)* III (Biblical and Kindred Studies 5). Haverford.

Grant E. and Wright G.E. 1938. *Ain Shems Excavations (Palestine)* IV *(Pottery)* (Biblical and Kindred Studies 7). Haverford.

Griffith F.L. 1890. *The Antiquities of Tell el-Jahudiyeh* (Egypt Exploration Fund Excavation Memoir 5). London.

Gullett H.S. 1923. *The Australian Imperial Force in Sinai and Palestine, 1914–1918.* Sydney.

Gunneweg J. and Yellin Y. 1991. The Origin of the Tel Batash-Timna Ceramics of the 7th Century BC in Light of Instrumental Neutron Activation Analysis. In M.J. Hughes, M.R. Cowell and D.R. Hook eds. *Neutron Activation and Plasma Emission Spectrometric Analysis in Archaeology* (British Museum Occasional Paper 82). London. Pp. 91–103.

Guy P.L.O. 1938. *Megiddo Tombs* (OIP 33). Chicago.

Hachmann R. 1996. *Kamid el-Loz* 16. *"Schatzhaus"—Studien* (Saarbrücker Beiträge zur Altertumskunde 59). Bonn.

Hamilton R.W. 1935. Excavations at Tell Abu Hawām. *QDAP* 4:1–69.

Helck W. 1971. *Das Bier im Alten Ägypten.* Berlin.

Helck W. 1975. Bier. In W. Helck and E. Otto eds. *Lexikon der Ägyptologie* I. Wiesbaden. Pp. 789–792.

Herr L. 2001. The History of the Collared Pithos at Tell el-'Umeiri, Jordan. In S.R. Wolff ed. *Studies on the Archaeology of Israel and Neighboring Lands in Memory of Douglas L. Esse* (SAOC 59/ASOR Books 5). Chicago–Atlanta. Pp. 237–250.

Higginbotham C.R. 2000. *Egyptianization and Elite Emulation in Ramesside Palestine: Governance and Accommodation on the Imperial Periphery* (Culture and History of the Ancient Near East 2). Leiden.

Holaubek J. 1992. Frau und Familie im Alten Ägypten. In E. Specht ed. *Nachrichten aus der Zeit. Ein Streifzug durch die Frauengeschichte des Altertums* (Frauenforschung 18). Vienna. Pp. 39–56.

Holthoer R. 1977. *New Kingdom Pharaonic Sites: The Pottery* (Scandinavian Joint Expedition to Sudanese Nubia 5:1). Lund.

Hope C.A. 1989. *Pottery of Ancient Egypt. Three Studies.* Burwood.

Hope C.A., Blauer H.M. and Riederer J. 1981. Recent Analysis of Eighteenth Dynasty Pottery. In D. Arnold ed. *Studien zur altägyptischen Keramik.* Mainz. Pp. 139–165.

Horn P. 1968. Textiles in Biblical Times. *Ciba Review* 2:1–37.

Huehnergard J. 1987. *Ugaritic Vocabulary in Syllabic Translation* (Harvard Semitic Studies 32). Atlanta.

Ilan D. 1999. *Northeastern Israel in the Iron Age I: Cultural, Socioeconomic and Political Perspectives.* Ph.D. diss. Tel Aviv University. Tel Aviv.

Ilan D., Hallote R.S. and Cline E.H. 2000. The Middle and Late Bronze Age Pottery from Area F. In I. Finkelstein, D. Ussishkin and B. Halpern eds. *Megiddo* III: *The 1992–1996 Seasons* (Tel Aviv University, Sonia and Marco Nadler Institute of Archaeology, Monograph Series 18). Tel Aviv. Pp. 186–222.

Issar A. 1961. The Plio-Pleistocene Geology of the Ashdod Area. *Bulletin of the Research Council of Israel* 10G:173–182.

James F.W. 1966. *The Iron Age at Beth Shan: A Study of Levels VI–IV* (University of Pennsylvania Museum Monographs). Philadelphia.

James F.W. and McGovern P.E. 1993. *The Late Bronze Egyptian Garrison at Beth Shan: A Study of Levels VII and VIII* (University of Pennsylvania Museum Monographs 85). Philadelphia.

Johnson P. 1982. The Middle Cypriote Pottery Found in Palestine. *Opuscula Atheniensia* 14:49–72.

Kaplan J. 1969. The Stronghold of Yamani at Ashdod-Yam. *IEJ* 19:137–149.

Kaplan J. 1972. The Archaeology and History of Tel Aviv-Jaffa. *BA* 35:66–95.

Kaplan J. 1993. Yavneh-Yam. *NEAEHL* 4. Pp. 1504–1506.

Karmon N. and Spanier E. 1987. Archaeological Evidence of the Purple Dye Industry from Israel. In E. Spanier ed. *The Royal Purple and the Biblical Blue (Argaman and Tekhelet): The Study of Chief Rabbi Dr. Isaac Herzog on the Dye Industries in Ancient Israel and Recent Scientific Contributions.* Jerusalem. Pp. 147–158.

Katz J.C. 2000. *The Archaeology of Cult in Middle Bronze Age Canaan: The Sacred Area of Tel Haror, Israel.* Ph.D. diss. University of Pennsylvania. Philadelphia.

Kelley A.L. 1976. *The Pottery of Ancient Egypt. Dynasty I to Roman Times.* Toronto.

Kelm G.L. and Mazar A. 1995. *Timnah: A Biblical City in the Sorek Valley.* Winona Lake.

Kenyon K.M. 1960. *Excavations at Jericho* I: *The Tombs Excavated in 1952–4.* London.

Killebrew A.E. 1996. *Tel Miqne-Ekron. Report of the 1985–1987 Excavations in Field INE: Areas 5, 6, 7. The Bronze and Iron Ages. Text and Data Base (Plates, Sections, Plans)* (Tel Miqne-Ekron Limited Edition Series). Jerusalem.

Killebrew A.E. 1998a. *Ceramic Craft and Technology during the Late Bronze and Early Iron Ages: The Relationship between Pottery Technology, Style, and Cultural Diversity.* Ph.D. diss. The Hebrew University. Jerusalem.

Killebrew A.E. 1998b. Ceramic Typology of Late Bronze II and Iron I Assemblages from Tel Miqne-Ekron: The Transition from Canaanite to Philistine Culture. In S. Gitin, A. Mazar and E. Stern eds. *Mediterranean Peoples in Transition, Thirteenth to Early Tenth Centuries BCE.* Jerusalem. Pp. 379–405.

Killebrew A.E. 2000. Aegean-Style Early Philistine Pottery in Canaan during the Iron I Age: A Stylistic Analysis of Mycenaean IIIC:1b Pottery and Its Associated Wares. In E.D. Oren ed. *The Sea Peoples and Their World: A Reassessment* (University Museum Monograph 108 = University Museum Symposium Series 11). Philadelphia. Pp. 233–253.

Killebrew A.E. 2001. The Collared Rim Pithos in Context: A Typological, Technological, and Functional Reassessment. In Wolff S.R. ed. 2001. *Studies in the Archaeology of Israel and Neighboring Lands in Memory of Douglas L. Esse* (SAOC 59/ASOR Books 5). Chicago–Atlanta. Pp. 377–398.

Killebrew A.E. 2005. *Biblical Peoples and Ethnicity. An Archaeological Study of Egyptians, Canaanites, Philistines, and Early Israel, 1300–1100 B.C.E.* Atlanta.

Killebrew A.E., Goldberg P. and Rosen A.M. 2006. Deir el-Balah: A Geological, Archaeological, and Historical Reassessment of an Egyptianizing 13th and 12th Century B.C.E. Center. *BASOR* 343:97–119.

King P.J. and Stager L.E. 2001. *Life in Biblical Israel.* London.

Kitchen K.A. 1986. *The Third Intermediate Period in Egypt (1100–650 B.C.)* (2nd ed. with supplement). Warminster.

Kitchen K.A. 1993. *Ramesside Inscriptions Translated & Annotated, Translations* I: *Ramesses I, Sethos I and Contemporaries.* Oxford.

Kitchen K.A. 1996. *Ramesside Inscriptions Translated & Annotated, Translations* II: *Ramesses II, Royal Inscriptions.* Oxford.

Kitchen K.A. 2000. Regnal and Genealogical Data of Ancient Egypt (Absolute Chronology I): The Historical Chronology of Ancient Egypt, a Current Assessment. In M. Bietak ed. *The Synchronisation of Civilisations in the Eastern Mediterranean in the Second Millennium B.C. Proceedings of an International Symposium at Schloß Haindorf, 15th–17th of November 1996 and at the Austrian Academy, Vienna, 11th–12th of May 1998* (Österreichischen Akademie der Wissenschaften, Denkschriften der Gesamtakademie XIX). Vienna. Pp. 39–52.

Kitchen K.A. 2003. *Ramesside Inscriptions Translated & Annotated, Translations* IV: *Merneptah and the Late Nineteenth Dynasty.* Oxford.

Kochavi M. 1990. *Aphek in Canaan: The Egyptian Governor's Residence and Its Finds* (Israel Museum Catalogue 312). Jerusalem.

Kochavi M., Gadot Y. and Yannai E. Forthcoming. *Aphek-Antipatris* II: *The Upper City of Aphek. Bronze and Iron Age Remains from Areas X, A and G.* Tel Aviv.

Kutscher E.Y. 1937. Lexical Questions: מחוז=נמל. *Lešonénu* 8:135–145 (Hebrew).

Kutscher E.Y. 1969–1970. Consistent with Ugaritica V. *Lešonénu* 34:6–19 (Hebrew).

Lamon R.S. and Shipton G.M. 1939. *Megiddo* I: *Seasons of 1925–34, Strata I–V* (OIP 42). Chicago.

Leclant J. 1971. Fouilles et travaux en Égypte et au Soudan, 1969–1970. *Orientalia* 40:224–266.

Leonard A., Jr. 1994. *An Index to the Late Bronze Age Aegean Pottery from Syria-Palestine* (SIMA 114). Jonsered.

Loat W.L.S. 1905. *Gurob* (BSAE 10). London.

Loud G. 1948. *Megiddo* II: *Seasons of 1935–39* (OIP 62). Chicago.

Lucas A. and Harris J.R. 1962. *Ancient Egyptian Materials and Industries.* London.

Lutz H.F. 1922. *Viniculture and Brewing in the Ancient Orient.* Leipzig.

Mackenzie R. ed. 1957. *The Differential Thermal Investigation of Clays.* London.

Martin M. 2004. Egyptian and Egyptianized Pottery in Late Bronze Age Canaan. *Egypt and the Levant* 14:265–284.

Martin M. 2005. *The Egyptian and Egyptian-Style Pottery. Aspects of the Egyptian Involvement in Late Bronze and Early Iron Age Canaan. A Case Study.* Ph.D. diss. University of Vienna. Vienna.

Martin M. 2006a. Cream Slipped Egyptian Imports in Late Bronze Age Canaan. In E. Czerny, I. Hein, H. Hunger, D. Melman and A. Schwab eds. *Timelines. Studies in Honour of Manfred Bietak* II (Orientalia Lovaniensa Analecta 146). Leuven. Pp. 197–212.

Martin M. 2006b. The Egyptianized Pottery Assemblage from Area Q. In A. Mazar. *Excavations at Tel Beth-Shean 1989–1996* I: *From the Late Bronze Age IIB to the Medieval Period* (Beth-Shean Valley Archaeological Project 1). Jerusalem. Pp. 140–157.

Martin M. Forthcoming a. The Egyptian and Egyptianized Pottery Assemblage from Tel Sera'. In E. Oren. *The Late Bronze Age Strata at Tel Sera'.* Be'er Sheva'.

Martin M. Forthcoming b. The Egyptian-Style Pottery from Areas S, N North and N South. In A. Mazar. *Excavations at Tel Beth-Shean 1989–1996* III. Jerusalem.

Martin M., Gadot Y. and Goren Y. Forthcoming. A Typological and Technological Study of the Imported Egyptian and Local Egyptian-Style Pottery from Late Bronze and Iron Age Strata. In M. Kochavi, Y. Gadot and E. Yadin eds. *Aphek-Antipatris* II: *Bronze and Iron Age Remains from the Acropolis of Aphek.* Tel Aviv.

Master D.M. 2003. Trade and Politics: Ashkelon's Balancing Act in the Seventh Century B.C.E. *BASOR* 330:47–64.

Mazar A. 1980. *Excavations at Tell Qasile,* Part One—*The Philistine Sanctuary: Architecture and Cult Objects* (Qedem 12). Jerusalem.

Mazar A. 1985. *Excavations at Tell Qasile,* Part Two—*The Philistine Sanctuary: Various Finds, the Pottery, Conclusions, Appendixes* (Qedem 20). Jerusalem.

Mazar A. 1988. Israeli Archaeologists. In J.F. Drinkard, Jr., G.L. Mattingly and J.M. Miller eds. *Benchmarks in Time and Culture: An Introduction to Palestinian Archaeology* (Archaeology and Biblical Studies 1). Atlanta. Pp. 109–128.

Mazar A. 1990. *Archaeology of the Land of the Bible 10,000–586 B.C.E.* New York.

Mazar A. 1993. Beth-Shean. *NEAEHL* 1. Pp. 214–223.

Mazar A. 1997. Beth-Shean. Four Thousand Years of History. *BA* 60:62–76.

Mazar A. 2006. *Excavations at Tel Beth-Shean 1989–1996* I: *From the Late Bronze Age IIB to the Medieval Period* (Beth-Shean Valley Archaeological Project 1). Jerusalem.

Mazar A. and Panitz-Cohen N. 2001. *Timnah (Tel Batash)* II: *The Finds from the First Millennium BCE* (Qedem 42). Jerusalem.

Mazar B. 1975. Dor and Rehov in an Egyptian List of Towns. In B. Mazar. *Cities and Districts in Eretz-Israel.* Jerusalem. Pp. 154–159 (Hebrew).

Mediterranean Pilot. 1988. Vol. V: *Coasts of Libya, Egypt, Israel, Lebanon and Syria, South Coasts of Greek Islands from Kríti to Ródhos and Turkey with the Island of Cyprus* (6th rev. ed.). Somerset.

Merrillees R.S. 1968. *The Cypriote Bronze Age Pottery Found in Egypt* (Studies in Mediterranean Archaeology 18). Lund.

Metzger M. 1993. *Kāmid el-Lōz* 8: *Die spätbronzezeitlichen Tempelanlagen. Die Kleinfunde. Tafeln* (Saarbrücker Beiträge zur Altertumskunde 40). Bonn.

Miron R. 1990. *Kāmid el-Lōz* 10: *Das 'Schatzhaus' im Palastbereich. Die Funde* (Saarbrücker Beiträge zur Altertumskunde 46). Bonn.

Mond R. and Myers O.H. 1940. *Temples of Armant: A Preliminary Survey.* London.

Moran W.L. 1992. *The Amarna Letters.* Baltimore.

Mountjoy P.A. 1986. *Mycenaean Decorated Pottery: A Guide to Identification* (SIMA 73). Göteborg.

Mountjoy P.A. 1999. *Regional Mycenaean Decorated Pottery.* Rahden–Westfalen.

Mullins R.A. 2006. A Corpus of Eighteenth Dynasty Egyptian-Style Pottery from Tel Beth Shan. In A.M. Maeir and P. de Miroschedji eds. *"I Will Speak the Riddles of Ancient Times": Archaeological and Historical Studies in Honor of Amihai Mazar on the Occasion of His Sixtieth Birthday.* Winona Lake. Pp. 247–262.

Munsell *Munsell Soil Color Charts* (rev. ed.). New Windsor 2000.

Murnane W.J. 1990. *The Road to Kadesh: A Historical Interpretation of the Battle Reliefs of King Sety I at Karnak* (SAOC 42) (2nd rev. ed.). Chicago.

Na'aman N. 1975. *The Political Disposition and Historical Development of Eretz-Israel According to the Amarna Letters.* Ph.D. diss. Tel Aviv University. Tel Aviv (Hebrew).

Nagel G. 1938. *La céramique du nouvel empire à Deir el Medineh* (Documents des fouilles de l'institut français d'archéologie orientale du Caire X). Cairo.

Negbi O. 1986. The Climax of Urban Development in the Bronze Age Cyprus. *RDAC*:97–121.

Negbi O. 1989. Bronze Age Pottery (Strata XVII–XV). In Z. Herzog, G. Rapp, Jr. and O. Negbi. *Excavations at Tel Michal, Israel* (Tel Aviv University Institute of Archaeology Publications 8). Minneapolis. Pp. 43–63.

Netzer E. 1973. A List of Selected Plans Drawn by I. Dunayevsky. *Eretz Israel* 11: xiii–xxiv (Hebrew).

Nicholson P.T. and Rose P.J. 1985. Pottery Fabrics and Ware Groups at el-Amarna. In B.J. Kemp. *Amarna Reports* II (Egypt Exploration Society 2). London. Pp. 133–174.

Nir J. and Eldar I. 1986. *Ground Water Level of Ancient Wells as an Indicator for Ancient Sea Levels and for Neo-Tectonic Changes in the Central Coastline of Israel*. Jerusalem (Hebrew).

Nordström H.A. 1986. Ton. In W. Helck and W. Westendorf eds. *Lexikon der Ägyptologie* VI. Wiesbaden. Pp. 629–634.

Nordström H.A. and Bourriau J.D. 1993. Ceramic Technology: Clay and Fabrics. In D. Arnold and J. Bourriau eds. *Introduction to Ancient Egyptian Pottery*. Mainz. Pp. 144–190.

Nougayrol J., Laroche E., Virolleaud C. and Schaeffer C.F.A. 1968. *Ugaritica* V: *nouveaux textes accadiens, hourrites et ugaritiques des archives et bibliothèques privées d'Ugarit* (Mission de Ras Shamra 16 = Bibliothèque archéologique et historique 80). Paris.

Nys K. 2001. Base-Ring Bull-Shaped Vases in Context. In P. Åström ed. *The Chronology of Base-Ring Ware and Bichrome Wheel-Made Ware. Proceedings of a Colloquium Held in the Royal Academy of Letters, History and Antiquities, Stockholm, May 18–19, 2000* (Konferenser 54). Stockholm. Pp. 95–122.

Oren E.D. 1969. Cypriot Imports in the Palestinian Late Bronze I Context. *Opuscula Atheniensa* 9:127–150.

Oren E.D. 1973. *The Northern Cemetery of Beth Shan*. Leiden.

Oren E.D. 1980. Egyptian New Kingdom Sites in North-Eastern Sinai. *Qadmoniot* 13:26–33 (Hebrew).

Oren E.D. 1984. "Governors' Residences" in Canaan under the New Kingdom: A Case Study of Egyptian Administration. *Journal of the Society for the Study of Egyptian Antiquities* 14:37–56.

Oren E.D. 1993. Tel Haror. *NEAEHL* 2. Pp. 580–584.

Oren E.D. and Shershevsky J. 1989. Military Architecture along the 'Ways of Horus'—Egyptian Reliefs and Archaeological Evidence. *Eretz Israel* (Yadin Volume) 20:8–22 (Hebrew; English summary, p. 193*).

Orni E. and Efrat E. 1971. *Geography of Israel* (3rd rev. ed.). Jerusalem.

Ortiz S.M. 2000. *The 11th/10th Century Transition in the Aijalon Valley Region: New Evidence from Tel Miqne-Ekron Stratum IV*. Ph.D. diss. University of Arizona. Tuscon.

Owen D.I. 1981. Akkadian Letter from Ugarit at Tel Aphek. *Tel Aviv* 8:1–17.

Palmer E.H. 1998. *The Survey of Western Palestine 1882–1888* VIII: *Arabic and English Name Lists* (Archive Editions reprint of 1881 original). London.

Panitz-Cohen N. and Maeir A.M. 2004. The Pottery Assemblage. In A.M. Maeir. *Bronze and Iron Age Tombs at Tel Gezer, Israel: Finds from the Excavations by Raymond-Charles Weill in 1914 and 1921* (BAR Int. S. 1206). Oxford. Pp. 9–41.

Panitz-Cohen N. and Mazar A. 2006. *Timnah (Tel Batash) III: The Finds from the Second Millennium BCE* (Qedem 45). Jerusalem.

Peet E. and Woolley C.L. 1923. *The City of Akhenaten* I. London.

Petersen A. 2001. *A Gazetteer of Buildings in Muslim Palestine* (Part 1) (British Academy Monographs in Archaeology 12). Oxford.

Petrie W.M.F. 1890. *Kahun, Gurob and Hawara*. London.

Petrie W.M.F. 1891. *Tell el Hesy (Lachish)*. London.

Petrie W.M.F. 1897. *Six Temples at Thebes*. London.

Petrie W.M.F. 1905. *Ehnasya*. London.

Petrie W.M.F. 1906. *Hyksos and Israelite Cities* (BSAE 12). London.

Petrie W.M.F. 1907. *Gizeh and Rifeh* (BSAE 13). London.

Petrie W.M.F. 1908. *Athribis* (BSAE 14). London.

Petrie W.M.F. 1909. *Qurneh* (BSAE 16). London.

Petrie W.M.F. 1930. *Beth-Pelet* I *(Tell Fara)* (BSAE 48). London.

Petrie W.M.F. 1931. *Ancient Gaza* I *(Tell el Ajjūl)* (BSAE 53). London.

Petrie W.M.F. 1932. *Ancient Gaza* II *(Tell el Ajjūl)* (BSAE 54). London.

Petrie W.M.F. 1933. *Ancient Gaza* III *(Tell el Ajjūl)* (BSAE 55). London.

Petrie W.M.F. 1934. *Ancient Gaza* IV *(Tell el Ajjūl)* (BSAE 56). London.

Petrie W.M.F and Brunton G. 1924. *Sedment* II (BSAE 35). London.

Petrie W.M.F, Mackay E. and Wainwright G.A. 1912. *The Labyrinth, Gerzeh and Mazghuneh*. London.

Pliny *NH*: *Natural History*. H. Rackham transl. (Loeb Classical Library). Cambridge 1938–1963.

Popham M.R. 1972. White Slip Ware. In P. Åström. *The Swedish Cyprus Expedition* IV, 1C: *The Late Cypriote Bronze Age Architecture and Pottery*. Lund. Pp. 431–471.

Preston R.M.P. 1921. *The Desert Mounted Corps: An Account of the Cavalry Operations in Palestine and Syria, 1917–1918*. Boston.

Pritchard J.B. 1980. *The Cemetery at Tell es-Sa'idiyeh, Jordan* (University Museum Monograph 41). Philadelphia.

Pulak C. 1997. The Uluburun Shipwreck. In S. Swiny, R.L. Hohlfelder and H.W. Swiny eds. *Res Maritimae: Cyprus and the Eastern Mediterranean from Prehistory to Late Antiquity. Proceedings of the Second International Symposium "Cities on the Sea," Nicosia, Cyprus, October 18–22, 1994* (ASOR Archaeological Reports 4 = CAARI Monograph Series 1). Atlanta. Pp. 233–262.

Raban A. 2001. Standardized Collared-Rim Pithoi and Short-Lived Settlements. In Wolff S.R. ed. 2001. *Studies in the Archaeology of Israel and Neighboring Lands in Memory of Douglas L. Esse* (SAOC 59/ASOR Books 5). Chicago–Atlanta. Pp. 493–518.

Rainey A.F. 1975. Two Cuneiform Fragments from Tel Aphek. *Tel Aviv* 2:125–129.

Rainey A.F. 1990. Administrative Inscriptions. In M. Kochavi. *Aphek in Canaan: The Egyptian Governor's Residence and Its Finds* (Israel Museum Catalogue 312). Jerusalem. P. xvi.

Redford D.B. 1990. *Egypt and Canaan in the New Kingdom* (Beer Sheva 4). Be'er Sheva'.

Reese D.S. 1980. Industrial Exploitation of Murex Shells: Purple-Dye and Lime Production at Sidi Khrebish, Benghazi (Berenice). *Libyan Studies* 11:79–93.

Reisner G.A. 1955. Clay Sealings of Dynasty XIII from Uronarti Fort. *Kush* 3:26–69.

Rose P.J. 1984. The Pottery Distribution Analysis. In B.J. Kemp. *Amarna Reports* I (Egypt Exploration Society, Occasional Publications 1). London. Pp. 133–153.

Rose P.J. 1987. The Pottery from Gate Street 8. In B.J. Kemp. *Amarna Reports* IV (Egypt Exploration Society, Occasional Publications 5). London.

Rowe A. 1929. The Palestine Expedition. Report of the 1928 Season. *The Museum Journal* 20:37–88.

Rowe A. 1930. *The Topography and History of Beth-Shan with Details of the Egyptian and Other Inscriptions Found on the Site.* Philadelphia.

Seger J.D. 1974. The Middle Bronze II C Date of the East Gate at Shechem. *Levant* 6:117–130.

Seger J.D. 1988. *Gezer* V: *The Field I Caves* (Annual of the Hebrew Union College/Nelson Glueck School of Biblical Archaeology 5). Jerusalem.

Simons J. 1937. *Handbook for the Study of Egyptian Topographical Lists Relating to Western Asia.* Leiden.

Singer I. 1983. Takuhlinu and Haya: Two Governors in the Ugarit Letter from Tel Aphek. *Tel Aviv* 10:3–25.

Singer-Avitz L. 1989. Iron Age Pottery (Strata XIV–XII). In Z. Herzog, G. Rapp, Jr. and O. Negbi. *Excavations at Tel Michal, Israel* (Tel Aviv University Institute of Archaeology Publications 8). Minneapolis. Pp. 76–87.

Singer-Avitz L. 2004a. The Middle Bronze Age Pottery from Areas D and P. In D. Ussishkin. *The Renewed Archaeological Excavations at Lachish (1973–1994)* III (Tel Aviv University, Sonia and Marco Nadler Institute of Archaeology, Monograph Series 22). Tel Aviv. Pp. 900–965.

Singer-Avitz L. 2004b. The Pottery of the Late Bronze I Phase. In D. Ussishkin. *The Renewed Archaeological Excavations at Lachish (1973–1994)* III (Tel Aviv University, Sonia and Marco Nadler Institute of Archaeology, Monograph Series 22). Tel Aviv. Pp. 1012–1031.

Singer-Avitz L. and Levi Y. 1992. Two Late Bronze Age Tombs at Palmaḥim. *'Atiqot* 21:15*–26* (Hebrew; English summary, pp. 174–175).

Sjöqvist E. 1940. *Problems of the Late Cypriote Bronze Age.* Stockholm.

Spalinger A. 1986. Baking during the Reign of Seti I. *Bulletin de l'institut francais d'archéologie orientale du Caire* 86:307–352.

Spencer A.J. 1979. *Brick Architecture in Ancient Egypt.* Warminster.

Stager L.E. 1995. The Impact of the Sea Peoples in Canaan (1185–1050 BCE). In T.E. Levy ed. *The Archaeology of Society in the Holy Land.* London. Pp. 332–348.

Starkey J. and Harding L. 1932. Beth-Pelet Cemetery. In E. MacDonald, J. Starkey and L. Harding. *Beth-Pelet* II. London. Pp. 22–35.

Stech-Wheeler T., Muhly J.D., Maxwell-Hyslop K.R. and Maddin R. 1981. Iron at Taanach and Early Iron Metallurgy in the Eastern Mediterranean. *AJA* 85:245–268.

Steindorff G. 1913. *Das Grab des Ti.* Leipzig.

Stern E. 1978. *Excavations at Tel Mevorakh (1973–1976).* Part One: *From the Iron Age to the Roman Period* (Qedem 9). Jerusalem.

Stern E. 1994. *Dor, Ruler of the Seas.* Jerusalem.

Stern E. 2001. *Archaeology of the Land of the Bible* II: *The Assyrian, Babylonian, and Persian Periods, 732–332 BCE.* New York.

Stieglitz R.R. 1974. Ugaritic Mûd—The Harbor of Yabne-Yam? *JAOS* 94:137–138.

Toombs L.E. 1985. *Tell el-Hesi: Modern Military Trenching and Muslim Cemetery in Field I, Strata I–II* (The Joint Archaeological Expedition to Tell el-Hesi II). Waterloo, Ontario.

Tubb J.N., Dorrell P.G. and Cobbing F.J. 1996. Interim Report on the Eighth (1995) Season of Excavations at Tell es-Sa'idiyeh. *PEQ* 128:16–36.

Tufnell O. 1953. *Lachish* III *(Tell ed-Duweir): The Iron Age.* London.

Tufnell O. 1958. *Lachish* IV *(Tell ed-Duweir): The Bronze Age.* London.

Tufnell O., Inge C.H. and Harding L. 1940. *Lachish* II *(Tell el-Duweir): The Fosse Temple.* London.

Ussishkin D. 1983. Excavations at Tel Lachish 1978–1983: Second Preliminary Report. *Tel Aviv* 10:97–175.

Ussishkin D. 1985. Levels VII and VI at Tel Lachish and the End of the Late Bronze Age in Canaan. In J.N. Tubb ed. *Palestine in the Bronze and Iron Ages, Papers in Honour of Olga Tufnell.* London. Pp. 213–228.

Vogelsang-Eastwood G.M. 1987–1988. A Note on the So-Called "Spinning Bowls." *Jaarbericht Ex Oriente Lux* 30:78–88.

Waldbaum J.C. 1978. *From Bronze to Iron: The Transition from the Bronze Age to the Iron Age in the Eastern Mediterranean* (SIMA 54). Göteborg.

Ward W.A. 1966. The Egyptian Inscriptions of Level VI. In F.W. James F.W. 1966. *The Iron Age at Beth Shan: A Study of Levels VI–IV* (University of Pennsylvania Museum Monographs). Philadelphia. Pp. 161–79.

Warren C. and Conder C.R. 1998. *The Survey of Western Palestine 1882–1888* I: *Galilee* (Archive Editions reprint of 1884 original). London.

Watrous L.V. 1992. *Kommos* III: *The Late Bronze Age Pottery.* Princeton.

Watterson B. 1991. *Women in Ancient Egypt.* New York.

Weinstein J.M. 1981. The Egyptian Empire in Palestine: A Reassessment. *BASOR* 241:1–28.

Wheeler N.F. 1967. Uronarti. In D. Dunham. *Second Cataract Forts* II: *Uronarti, Shalfak, Mirgissa (Excavated by George Andrew Reisner and Noel F. Wheeler).* Boston. Pp. 3–114.

Williams B.B. 1992. *New Kingdom Remains from Cemeteries R, V, S and W at Qustol and Cemetery K at Adindan.* Chicago.

Wolff S.R. ed. 2001. *Studies in the Archaeology of Israel and Neighboring Lands in Memory of Douglas L. Esse* (SAOC 59/ASOR Books 5). Chicago–Atlanta.

Wood B.G. 1987. Egyptian Amphorae of the New Kingdom and Ramesside Periods. *BA* 50:75–83.

Yadin Y. 1963. *The Art of Warfare in Biblical Lands in Light of Archaeological Study* I. New York.

Yadin Y. and Geva S. 1986. *Investigations at Beth Shean: The Early Iron Age Strata* (Qedem 23). Jerusalem.

Yadin Y., Aharoni Y., Amiran R., Ben-Tor A., Dothan M., Dothan T., Dunayevsky I., Geva S., and Stern E. 1989. *Hazor* III–IV: *An Account of the Third and Fourth Seasons of Excavation, 1957–1958. Text.* Jerusalem.

Yadin Y., Aharoni Y., Amiran R., Dothan T., Dothan M., Dunayevsky I. and Perrot J. 1961. *Hazor* III–IV: *An Account of the Third and Fourth Seasons of Excavation, 1957–1958. Plates.* Jerusalem.

Yadin Y., Aharoni Y., Amiran R., Dothan T., Dunayevsky I. and Perrot J. 1958. *Hazor* I: *An Account of the First Season of Excavations, 1953.* Jerusalem.

Yadin Y., Aharoni Y., Amiran R., Dothan T., Dunayevsky I. and Perrot J. 1960. *Hazor* II: *An Account of the Second Season of Excavation, 1956.* Jerusalem.

Yannai E. 1996. *Aspects of the Material Culture of Canaan during the Egyptian 20th Dynasty (1130–1200 BCE).* Ph.D. diss. Tel Aviv University. Tel Aviv (Hebrew).

Yannai E. 2004. The Late Bronze Age Pottery from Area S. In D. Ussishkin. *The Renewed Archaeological Excavations at Lachish (1973–1994)* III: *The Pre-Bronze Age and Bronze Age Pottery and Artefacts* (Tel Aviv University, Sonia and Marco Nadler Institute of Archaeology, Monograph Series 22). Tel Aviv. Pp. 1032–1146.

Yellin J., Dothan T. and Gould B. 1986. The Provenience of Beerbottles from Deir el-Balaḥ: A Study by Neutron Activation Analysis. *IEJ* 36:68–73.

Yellin J., Dothan, T. and Gould B. 1990. The Origin of Late Bronze White Burnished Slip Wares from Deir el-Balaḥ. *IEJ* 40:257–261.

Zarzecki-Peleg P., Cohen-Anidjar S. and Ben-Tor A. 2005. Pottery Analysis. In Ben-Tor, Zarzecki-Peleg and Cohen-Anidjan. *Yoqne'am* II: *The Iron Age and the Persian Period. Final Report of the Archaeological Excavations (1977–1988)* (Qedem Reports 6). Jerusalem. Pp. 235–344.

Zimhoni O. 1997. *Studies in the Iron Age Pottery of Israel: Typological, Archaeological, and Chronological Aspects* (Journal of the Institute of Archaeology of Tel Aviv University Occasional Publications 2). Tel Aviv.

APPENDIX 1

A STAMPED AMPHORA HANDLE AND A HERODIAN COIN
DONALD T. ARIEL

STAMPED AMPHORA HANDLE

In addition to the complete Rhodian amphora retrieved from the excavations at Tel Mor (Dothan 1960:129, Pl. 12:3), produced by Σωκράτης 2nd in the term of Ἱέρων 1st (*c.* 186 BCE; Finkielsztejn 2001:192), one classical period stamped amphora handle (IAA No. 1960-1248) was found (Fig. App. 1.1), in a poor stratigraphic context in Area B2. The handle is preserved from the point of its break with the amphora's neck, the inner surface of which may be seen. Enough is preserved of the rounded profile to note that it makes a 90° turn from the neck downward. The limited profile of the handle indicates that it belonged to a two-handled Hellenistic transport amphora; further classification is not possible. The color of its ware (light reddish brown [Munsell 5YR 6/4]) and the large quantity of small white, gray and brown inclusions are somewhat reminiscent of stamped amphorae known to have been produced in Cyprus, including the Kouriote group

(Grace 1979). In Israel, finds of Hellenistic amphora fragments of Cypriot provenance are rare but not unknown (Ariel and Finkielsztejn 2003:144). Based upon these finds, it is likely that the Tel Mor handle dates to the late fourth or third centuries BCE.

A rectangular stamp was impressed on the curve of the handle. The stamp's dimensions are 11 × 22 mm. It appears that because of the handle's curve, one corner of the stamp was poorly impressed. Nevertheless, two characters may be read, as well as a dot next to one of them. The characters look like wedges, forming a short herringbone pattern. Two unpublished handles from the region are known to have been impressed with the same die. One derives from excavations conducted by J.W. Crowfoot in Jerusalem in 1928, and the other comes from excavations of Moshe Dothan in Tel ‘Akko.[1]

Based on its size and the presence of only two (similar) characters, the stamp may possibly be associated with a group of small stamps bearing Semitic inscriptions. A significant number of such jar

0   0.5

0   1

Fig. App.1.1. Stamped amphora handle from the Hellenistic period.

handles have been found throughout the Mediterranean region. Their shape is either rectangular (measuring between 15 and 22 mm in length), with or without curved edges, or oval. The stamps generally contain letters and not words, occasionally in combination with a motif. The jar handles probably date to the Hellenistic period and the script appears to be Semitic, most likely Punic (Ariel 2005:187). Most commonly two letters appear, frequently the same letter, and often in retrograde fashion. The handles, which derive mainly from North Africa, Sicily and Spain, have been most comprehensively studied by Wolff (1986:81), who identified them as far to the east as 'Akko (i.e., the anepigraphic stamp depicting a Tanit symbol; see Dothan 1974; 1976:31).[2]

However, owing to the likely Cypriot ware of the Tel Mor, Jerusalem and Tel 'Akko handles, it is more likely to view them not as Punic, but rather as Cypriot. What, then, of the shape of the stamps and the duplication of the signs on the stamp—a characteristic of the plentiful material noted above, which may make up a separate Punic stamped amphora class? In fact, a stamped handle from Kition-Bamboula contains two letters thought to be Phoenician (Calvet 1982:47, 48, No. 129). Also, an unpublished Cypriot stamped amphora handle from excavations at Caesarea also contains letters which are apparently Punic (Finkielsztejn, forthcoming).[3]

In a personal communication Finkielsztejn has suggested that the two wedge-like characters are reminiscent of the letter 'o' of the Cypriot syllabic alphabet. That letter is composed of two superimposed wedges above a horizontal line (Masson 1961:58, Fig. 1). Nevertheless, Finkielsztejn and this author agree that the dot below the lower wedge is unlikely to take the place of the horizontal line, and that the identification of the stamp as a Cypriot letter is doubtful.

It is not impossible that the Tel Mor handle is Cypriot, and—despite the fact that the signs on its

stamp cannot be identified—it concurrently reflected a Punic stamping tradition. The Kition-Bamboula and Caesarea handles noted above may be other examples of such a phenomenon. It is becoming increasingly clear that numerous stamping traditions coexisted in the Levant during the Hellenistic and, possibly, late Persian periods. In addition to the Greek (Finkielsztejn 1998) and local traditions (Grace 1956; Ariel and Shoham 2000), there was, it seems, a more distant Punic tradition of stamping. For the time being, the question of the classification of the Tel Mor handle must remain open.

HERODIAN COIN

One intrusive Herodian coin was found in a poorly stratified early Iron Age context (Fig. App. 1.2).

Herod the Great (40–4 BCE)

Fig. App.1.2. Herodian coin.

Reg. No. 416/2. IAA 4780.
Herod, Jerusalem, 37–4 BCE.
Obv. ΒΑΣΙΛΕΩΣ ΗΡΩΔΟΥ Saltire within open diadem.
Rev. Table with three curved legs standing on a platform; upon it a flat vessel; on l. and r., two bent palm branches.
Æ, ↑, 2.87 gm, 18 mm.
TJC:221–222, No. 48.

NOTES

[1] The handle from Jerusalem is IAA No. P-3564, while the handle from Tel 'Akko is Reg. No. IV *ayin* G45/61. Both handles were examined by Gérald Finkielsztejn, and I thank him for this information along with many helpful comments regarding the Tel Mor handle's class and date. The Tel 'Akko handle is noted courtesy of Michal Artzy.

[2] Note also the figured parallels of Punic stamps on amphorae from Sicily collected by Signorello (1995: Pls. 2:5 [Erice], 4:5 [Lilebeo], 13:31–34 and 14:4 [Selinunte]).

[3] Deriving from excavations of Y. Porath, this handle is noted courtesy of Gérald Finkielsztejn and the excavator.

REFERENCES

Ariel D. T. 2005. Stamped Amphora Handles and Unstamped Fragments from Montmusard, Acre ('Akko). *'Atiqot* 50:181–193.

Ariel D. T. and Finkielsztejn G. 2003. Amphora Stamps and Imported Amphoras. In A. Kloner. *Maresha Excavations Final Report* I: *Subterranean Complexes 21, 44, 70* (IAA Reports 17). Jerusalem. Pp. 137–151.

Ariel D. T. and Shoham Y. 2000. The Locally Stamped Handles and Related Body Sherds. In D.T. Ariel ed. *Excavations in the City of David Directed by Yigal Shiloh 6. Inscriptions* (Qedem 41). Jerusalem.

Calvet Y. 1982. *Les timbres amphoriques. Kition-Bamboula* I. Paris.

Dothan M. 1960. Excavations at Tel Mor (1959 Season). *BIES* 24:120–132, (Hebrew; English summary, pp. ii–iii).

Dothan M. 1974. A Sign of Tanit in Tel 'Akko. *IEJ* 24:44–49.

Dothan M. 1976. Akko: Interim Excavation Report. First Season, 1973/4. *BASOR* 224:1–48.

Finkielsztejn G. 1998. Timbres amphoriques du Levant d'époque hellénistique. *Transeuphratène* 15:83–121.

Finkielsztejn G. 2001. *Chronologie détailée et révisée des éponymes amphoriques rhodiens de 270 à 108 av. J.-C. environ. Premier bilan* (BAR Int. S. 990). Oxford.

Finkielsztejn G. Forthcoming. Amphora Stamps from Herod's Circus at Caesarea. In Y. Porat. *The Israel Antiquities Authority Excavations at Caesarea Maritima* I: *King Herod's Circus and the Related Buildings* (IAA Reports). Jerusalem.

Grace V.R. 1956. The Canaanite Jar. In S.S. Weinberg ed. *The Aegean and the Near East. Studies Presented to Hetty Goldman*. Locust Valley. Pp. 90–109.

Grace V.R. 1979. Kouriaka. In V. Karageorghis, H.W. Catling, K. Nicolaou, A. Papageorghiou, M. Loulloupis, D. Christou and I. Nicolaou eds. *Studies Presented in Memory of P. Dikaios*. Nicosia. Pp. 178–188.

Masson O. 1961. *Les inscriptions chypriotes syllabiques. Recueil critique et commenté*. Paris.

Munsell *Munsell Soil Color Charts*. Evanston 1975.

Signorello M. L. 1995. *Le anfore puniche in Sicilia dal V a.c. al I a.c.* Trapani.

Wolff S.R. 1986. *Maritime Trade at Punic Carthage*. Ph.D. diss. University of Chicago. Chicago.

LIST OF LOCI AND WALLS*

Locus No.	Square(s)	Stratum	Elevation (m)	Description
1	N/A	None	N/A	Arab burial
2	N/A	None	N/A	Arab burial
3	N/A	None	N/A	Arab burial
4	M19	None	25.60	Arab burial
5	M19	None	25.60	Arab burial
6	M18	None	25.60	Arab burial
7	N/A	None	N/A	Arab burial
8	N/A	None	N/A	Arab burial
9	N/A	None	N/A	Arab burial
10	M19	III	24.55–24.30	Area
10A	M19	III	24.40	*Ṭabun*
11	M19	III	24.56	Combined with L10
12	N19	III	24.57	Pillar base
13	M18	III	24.70–24.35	Area
14	N/A	N/A	N/A	Wall
15	M19	III	24.58	Pillar base
16	N/A	N/A	N/A	Wall
17	M19	III	24.23–23.70	Pit
18	L18	III	24.38–23.95	Pit
19	L19	III	24.45–24.25	Area
20	M19	IV	24.00	Room
20	M19	V	24.10–23.85	Room
21	M19	IV	24.30–24.00	Wall
22	M19	IV	24.21–23.95	Wall
23	L19	III	24.30–23.90	Pit
24	L19	V	24.05–23.50	*Ṭabun*
25	M19	IV	24.30–23.95	Room
25	M19	V	23.60–23.50	Room
26	M18	V	24.05–23.50	Area
27	M18	V	24.05–23.65	Wall
28	M19	V	24.05–23.64	Area
29	M19	V	23.80–23.50	Area
29	N19	V	24.05–23.55	Wall

* The discrepancies in elevation between those in the figure tables and those in the list of loci and walls are a result of the excavators' errors in record-keeping.

Locus No.	Square(s)	Stratum	Elevation (m)	Description
30	L18–19	II	25.41–24.45	Wall
31	K18–19	II	25.28–24.69	Wall
32	L19	VI	23.56–23.40	Flat stone
33	L18	V	24.10–23.62	Wall
34	M19	V	23.70–23.50	Room
35	M18	VI	23.40–22.50	Pit
36	M18	VI	23.55–23.20	Area
37	M18	VI	23.73–23.07	Wall
38	M18	VI	23.53–23.07	Wall
39	H–K19–20	VI–V	23.95–22.30	Wall
40	L18	V	23.40–23.20	Area
41	M19	VII	21.30–21.05	Area
42	L19	VII	21.90–21.60	Area
43	M18	VII	21.50–21.15	Area
44	Cancelled			
45	L19	V	23.50–22.47	Pit
46	H21	I	20.29–20.00	Wall
47	H21	I	20.57–19.92	Wall
48	H21	I	20.35–20.02	Wall
49	H21	I	N/A	Room
50	M20	V	24.13–23.40	Wall
51	M19	V	24.00–23.58	Wall
52	M19	V	23.96–23.10	Wall
53	M19	V	23.70–23.23	Wall
54	L19–20	V	24.10–23.50	Wall
55	K20	I	24.35–10.60	Well
56	N/A	N/A	N/A	N/A
57	K18	V	23.21–21.95	Ṭabun
58	L20	V	23.70–23.40	Room
59	L18	VI	21.75–21.00	Area
60	Cancelled			
61	K18	VI	21.65	Area
62	L18	VII	21.40	N/A
63	J18	VIII–VII	22.15–21.20	Room
64	J20	VI	21.10	Room
	J20	V	N/A	Room
65	H18	V	23.00–22.33	Area
66	G–L19	VIII–VII	22.60–20.70	Wall
67	J20	VI–V	23.60–22.04	Wall
68	J20	VI–V	23.42–21.00	Wall
69	N/A	N/A	N/A	N/A

Locus No.	Square(s)	Stratum	Elevation (m)	Description
70	Cancelled			
71	J–K20	V	N/A	Room
	J–K20	VI	22.22	Room
72	J16	VI	22.20–21.93	Furnace
73	H18	VIII–VII	21.14–20.56	Wall
74	H18	VI	21.10–21.55	Furnace
75	K18–19	VII	21.75–21.05	Room
	K18–19	VIII	21.55–21.20	Room
	K18–19	IX	21.20–20.70	Subfloor fill?
76	J21	I	N/A	N/A
77	L–K15–18	VIII–VII	22.95 (E)–20.10 (W)	Wall
78	K18	VIII–VII	21.24–20.84	Wall
79	J21	V	N/A	Room
	J–K20–21	VI	22.10	Room
80	L18	VII	21.20–21.00	Area
81	J18	VI	N/A	Furnace
82	N/A	N/A	N/A	N/A
83	K17–18	VII	21.75–21.55	Room
	K17–18	VIII	21.40–21.18	Room
84	J–K18–19	VII	21.90–21.52	Room
	J–K18–19	VIII	c. 21.00	Room
85	H20	IX	20.90–20.15	Pit/Area
86	K18	IX	21.20–20.95	Probe
87	N/A	N/A	N/A	N/A
88	K–G18	VIII–VII	21.86–20.70	Wall
89	N/A	N/A	N/A	N/A
90	Cancelled			
91	N/A	N/A	N/A	N/A
92	G–H16–18	VIII–VII	N/A	Room
93	L19	V	24.00–23.31	Wall
94	H–K19	VI	23.20–21.30	Ramp
95	K–L19–L20	VI	24.13–23.32	Ramp
96	K16	VI	22.45–22.02	Wall
97	J18	VI	21.79–21.01	Furnace
98	J18	VI	21.91–21.21	Furnace
99	N18–19	VII	22.50–21.85	Wall?
100	L–M19–20	VII	23.03–21.80 (NE), 22.57–21.91 (SW)	Wall
101	N/A	None	N/A	Arab burial
102	M20	None	c. 25.00	Arab burial
103	M20	None	c. 24.50	Arab burial
104	N/A	None	N/A	Arab burial

Locus No.	Square(s)	Stratum	Elevation (m)	Description
105	N/A	None	N/A	Arab burial
106	N/A	None	N/A	Arab burial
107	M21?	None	*c.* 23.00	Arab burial
108	M20	VI	23.20–21.90	Room fill?
	M20	VII	21.80–21.32	Room
	M20	VIII	*c.* 21.70	Subfloor fill?
109	N/A	N/A	N/A	N/A
110	M20	VII	22.80–22.40	*Ṭabun*
111	L–M20	VII	*c.* 21.50	Room
	L–M20	VIII	21.55–21.00	Fill
	L20–21	IX	21.55–20.60	Room
112	N/A	None	N/A	Arab burial
113	N/A	N/A	N/A	Wall?
114	M20	VII	22.44–22.06 (NE), 23.00–22.04 (SW)	Wall
115	M20 21	IX	21.93 (top)	Wall
116	M21	XI	20.40–20.20	Probe
117	M21	X	20.15–19.65	Probe
118	M–N22	IX	20.75–20.00	Courtyard
	M–N22	X	20.50–20.30	Courtyard
	M–N22	XI	20.40–19.10	Courtyard
	M–N22	XII	19.10–17.90	Courtyard
119	M20	VIII	21.80–21.35	Pit
120	Cancelled			
121	N/A	N/A	N/A	N/A
122	M20	IX	21.24 (top)	Wall
123	L–N21	IX	21.02–19.60 (N), 22.04–20.40 (S)	Wall
124	N/A	N/A	N/A	N/A
125	N/A	N/A	N/A	Arab burial?
126	L20	III	24.60–24.05	Installation
127	L21	VI–V	N/A	Area
128	L21	VII	23.40–21.60	Area
	L21	VIII	23.40–21.60	Area
129	L20	VII	23.20–21.40	Area
	L20	VIII	21.80–21.60	Area
	K19–21	VI–V	24.34–21.50 (N), 23.94–21.04 (S)	Wall
130	L20–21	IX	21.97 (top)	Wall
131	L20	V	24.50–23.50	Area
	L20	VI	23.50–21.80	Area
132	L21	VII	*c.* 21.38	Area
	L21	VIII	21.60–21.30	Room
133	L20–21	VIII	21.53–21.13 (W), 21.96–21.58 (E)	Wall

Locus No.	Square(s)	Stratum	Elevation (m)	Description
134	L20–21	VII	23.04–22.04 (W), 23.04–22.23 (E)	Wall
135	L21	IX	20.95–20.38	*Ṭabun*
136	M20	IX	21.25–20.54	Room
137	M21	IX	21.00–20.60	Room
138	N20	IX	21.00–20.50	Room
139	N21	IX	*c.* 20.40	Room
140	N20	IX	20.70–20.40	Room
141	J21	VIII	21.96–21.03	Wall
142	H20	VIII	21.34–21.12	Wall
143	J18	VIII–VII	21.30 (top)	Wall
144	G19	VIII–VII	N/A	Wall
145	K15	VIII–VII	N/A	Wall
146	H–K16	VIII–VII	21.84 (N, top), 21.20 (S, top)	Wall
147	G19	VIII–VII	21.28 (NE)– 20.29 (SE)	Room
148	J–K17–18	VII	21.50	Room
	J–K17–18	VIII	21.00	Room
149	J17	VIII–VII	N/A	Room
150	M28–29	I	14.86 (W)–14.21 (E)	Basin
151	M29	I	14.01–13.40	Basin
152	M30	IX	12.25–11.55	Burial
153	M28–29	I	13.37–4.00	Well
154	L–M31–32	I	10.91–10.50 (W), 11.02–10.56 (E)	Basin
155	M31	I	10.50–9.87	Drain
156	L29	I	13.15 (W)–13.10 (E)	Room
157	M29	I	N/A	Room
158	M29	I	13.50–13.30	Room
159	Cancelled			
160	K16	VII	21.80	Room
	K16	VIII	20.88	Room
161	H–J21	VIII	21.29 (N)–21.37 (S)	Room
162	N17–21	IX	20.29–19.77 (W), 21.02–19.60 (E)	Wall
163	N20–21	IX	21.50 (W, top), 20.87 (E, top)	Wall
164	N19	IX	N/A	Wall
165	M21	IX	N/A	Wall
166	N22	XIIA	19.00–17.90	Pit
167	M21	X	N/A	Probe
	M21	XI	20.00	Probe
	M21	XII	19.00	Probe
168	M21–22	XI	20.40–19.95	Wall?
169	M–N20	IX	20.55	Room
170	N19	IX	N/A	Room
171	H17	VIII–VII	21.21 (W)–21.90 (E)	Wall

Locus No.	Square(s)	Stratum	Elevation (m)	Description
172	L20	VIII	22.00–21.45	Pit
173	K19	V	23.80–23.50	Wall
174	L–M29	I	13.30–13.08 (N), 13.62–13.08 (S)	Wall
175	L29	I	13.62–13.08 (W), 13.58 (E, top)	Wall
176	L29	I	13.21 (W, top), 13.10–12.82 (E)	Wall
177	L–M29	I	13.01–12.75	Wall
178	M29	I	13.42–13.08	Wall
179	L29	I	13.73–13.24	Basin
180	L29	I	13.57–13.23	Basin

IAA Reports

No. 1 G. Avni and Z. Greenhut, *The Akeldama Tombs: Three Burial Caves in the Kidron Valley, Jerusalem*, 1996, 129 pp.

No. 2 E. Braun, *Yiftaḥ'el: Salvage and Rescue Excavations at a Prehistoric Village in Lower Galilee, Israel,* 1997, 249 pp.

No. 3 G. Edelstein, I. Milevski and S. Aurant, *Villages, Terraces and Stone Mounds: Excavations at Manaḥat, Jerusalem, 1987–1989*, 1998, 149 pp.

No. 4 C. Epstein, *The Chalcolithic Culture of the Golan*, 1998, 352 pp. + plans. Hardcover.

No. 5 T. Schick, *The Cave of the Warrior: A Fourth Millennium Burial in the Judean Desert*, 1998, 137 pp.

No. 6 R. Cohen, *Ancient Settlement of the Central Negev: The Chalcolithic Period, the Early Bronze Age and the Middle Bronze Age* I (Hebrew, English Summary), 1999, 396 pp.

No. 7 R. Hachlili and A. Killebrew, *Jericho: The Jewish Cemetery of the Second Temple Period*, 1999, 202 pp.

No. 8 Z. Gal and Y. Alexandre, *Ḥorbat Rosh Zayit: An Iron Age Storage Fort and Village*, 2000, 247 pp.

No. 9 U. Dahari, *Monastic Settlements in South Sinai in the Byzantine Period: The Archaeological Remains*, 2000, 250 pp. + map.

No. 10 Z. Yeivin, *The Synagogue at Korazim: The 1962–1964, 1980–1987 Excavations* (Hebrew, English Summary), 2000, 216 pp.

No. 11 M. Hartal, *The al-Ṣubayba (Nimrod) Fortress: Towers 11 and 9*, 2001, 129 pp.

No. 12 R. Gonen, *Excavations at Efrata: A Burial Ground from the Intermediate and Middle Bronze Ages*, 2001, 153 pp.

No. 13 E. Eisenberg, A. Gopher and R. Greenberg, *Tel Te'o: A Neolithic, Chalcolithic and Early Bronze Age Site in the Ḥula Valley*, 2001, 227 pp.

No. 14 R. Frankel, N. Getzov, M. Aviam and A. Degani, *Settlement Dynamics and Regional Diversity in Ancient Upper Galilee: Archaeological Survey of Upper Galilee*, 2001, 175 pp. + color distribution maps and foldout map.

No. 15 M. Dayagi-Mendels, *The Akhziv Cemeteries: The Ben-Dor Excavations, 1941–1944*, 2002, 176 pp.

No. 16 Y. Goren and P. Fabian, *Kissufim Road: A Chalcolithic Mortuary Site*, 2002, 97 pp.

No. 17 A. Kloner, *Maresha Excavations Final Report* I: *Subterranean Complexes 21, 44, 70*, 2003, 183 pp.

No. 18 A. Golani, *Salvage Excavations at the Early Bronze Age Site of Qiryat 'Ata*, 2003, 261 pp.

No. 19 H. Khalaily and O. Marder, *The Neolithic Site of Abu Ghosh: The 1995 Excavations*, 2003, 146 pp.

No. 20 R. Cohen and R. Cohen-Amin, *Ancient Settlement of the Negev Highlands* II (Hebrew, English Summary), 2004, 258 pp.

No. 21 D. Stacey, *Exavations at Tiberias, 1973–1974: The Early Islamic Periods*, 2004, 259 pp.

No. 22 Y. Hirschfeld, *Excavations at Tiberias, 1989–1994*, 2004, 234 pp.

No. 23 S. Ben-Arieh, *Bronze and Iron Age Tombs at Tell Beit Mirsim*, 2004, 212 pp.

No. 24 M. Dothan and D. Ben-Shlomo, *Ashdod* VI: *The Excavations of Areas H and K (1968–1969)*, 2005, 320 pp.

No. 25 M. Avissar, *Tel Yoqne'am: Excavations on the Acropolis*, 2005, 142 pp.

No. 26 M. Avissar and E.J. Stern, *Pottery of the Crusader, Ayyubid, and Mamluk Periods in Israel*, 2005, 187 pp., 53 figs., 34 color plates.

No. 27 E.C.M. van den Brink and Ram Gophna, *Shoham (North), Late Chalcolithic Burial Caves in the Lod Valley, Israel,* 2005, 214 pp.

No. 28 N. Getzov, *The Tel Bet Yeraḥ Excavations, 1994–1995*, 2006, 204 pp.

No. 29 A.M. Berlin, *Gamla* I: *The Pottery of the Second Temple Period, the Shmarya Gutmann Excavations, 1976–1989*, 2006, 181 pp.

No. 30 R. Greenberg, E. Eisenberg, S. Paz and Y. Paz, *Bet Yeraḥ: The Early Bronze Age Mound* I: *Excavation Reports, 1933–1986,* 2006, 500 pp.

No. 31 E. Yannai, *'En Esur ('Ein Asawir)* I: *Excavations at a Protohistoric Site in the Coastal Plain of Israel*, 2006, 308 pp.

No. 32 T.J. Barako, *Tel Mor: The Moshe Dothan Excavations, 1959–1960*, 2007, 276 pp.

No. 33 G. Mazor and A. Najjar, *Bet She'an* I: *Nysa-Scythopolis:the Caesareum and the Odeum*, 2007.